At McGraw-Hill Higher-Education, we publish instructional materials targeted at the higher-education market. In an effort to expand the tools of higher learning, we publish texts, lab manuals, study guides, testing materials, software and multimedia products.

At Irwin/McGraw-Hill (a division of McGraw-Hill Higher Education), we realize that technology will continue to create new mediums for professors and students to manage resources and communicate information with one another. We strive to provide the most flexible and complete teaching and learning tools available and offer solutions to the changing world of teaching and learning.

**Irwin/McGraw-Hill is dedicated to providing the tools for today's instructors and students to successfully navigate the world of Information Technology.**

- **Seminar Series**—Irwin/McGraw-Hill's Technology Connection seminar series offered across the country ever year, demonstrate the latest technology products and encourage collaboration among teaching professionals.
- **Osborne/McGraw-Hill**—A division of The McGraw-Hill Companies known for its best selling Internet titles *Harley Hahn's Internet & Web Yellow Pages* and the *Internet Complete Reference*, that offers an additional resource for certification and has strategic publishing relationships with corporations such as Corel Corporation and America Online. For more information visit Osborne at www.osborne.com.
- **Digital Solutions**—Irwin/McGraw-Hill is committed to publishing Digital Solutions. Taking your course online doesn't have to be a solitary venture, nor does it have to be a difficult one. We offer several solutions, which will let you enjoy all the benefits of having course material online. For more information visit www.mhhe.com/solutions/index.mhtml.
- **Packaging Options**—For more information about our discount options, contact your local Irwin/McGraw-Hill Sales representative at 1-800-338-3987 or visit our Web site at www.mhhe.com/it.

Irwin
McGraw-Hill

# *Preface*
# *The Advantage Series*

## Goals/Philosophy

***The Advantage Series*** presents the **What, Why,** and **How** of computer application skills to today's students. Each lab manual is built upon an efficient learning model, which provides students and faculty with complete coverage of the most powerful software packages available today.

### Approach

***The Advantage Series*** builds upon an efficient learning model, which provides students and faculty with complete coverage and enhances critical thinking skills. This case-based, "problem-solving" approach teaches the What, Why, and How of computer application skills.

***The Advantage Series*** introduces the **"Feature-Method-Practice"** layered approach. The **Feature** describes the command and tells the importance of that command. The **Method** shows students how to perform the Feature. The **Practice** allows students to apply the feature in a keystroke exercise.

### About the Series

***The Advantage Series*** offers *three levels* of instruction. Each level builds upon the previous level. The following are the three levels of instructions:

***Brief:*** covers the basics of the application, contains two to four chapters, and is typically 120–190 pages long.

***Introductory:*** includes the material in the Brief Lab manual plus two to three additional chapters. The Introductory lab manuals are approximately 300 pages long and prepare students for the *Microsoft Office User Specialist Proficient Exam (MOUS Certification).*

***Complete:*** includes the Introductory lab manual plus an additional five chapters of advanced level content. The Complete lab manuals are approximately 600 pages in length and prepare students to take the *Microsoft Office User Specialist Expert Exam (MOUS Certification).*

### Approved Microsoft Courseware

APPROVED COURSEWARE

Use of the Microsoft Office User Specialist Approved Courseware Logo on this product signifies that it has been independently reviewed and approved in complying with the following standards: Acceptable coverage of all content related to the Microsoft Office Exam entitled *Microsoft PowerPoint 2000* and sufficient performance-based exercises that relate closely to all required content, based on sampling of text. For further information on Microsoft's MOUS certification program please visit Microsoft's Web site at http://www.microsoft.com/office/traincert/.

ADVANTAGE SERIES

MICROSOFT®

# POWERPOINT® 2000

## COMPLETE EDITION

Sarah E. Hutchinson

Glen J. Coulthard

Irwin McGraw-Hill

Boston Burr Ridge, IL Dubuque, IA Madison, WI New York San Francisco St. Louis
Bangkok Bogotá Caracas Lisbon London Madrid Mexico City
Milan New Delhi Seoul Singapore Sydney Taipei Toronto

ADVANTAGE

SERIES

MICROSOFT®

# POWERPOINT® 2000

## COMPLETE EDITION

**McGraw-Hill Higher Education**
A Division of The **McGraw-Hill** Companies

# MICROSOFT® POWERPOINT® 2000
# COMPLETE EDITION



This book is printed on acid-free paper.

1 2 3 4 5 6 7 8 9 0 WEB/WEB 0 9 8 2 1 0

ISBN 0-07-234809-7

Vice president/Editor in chief: *Michael W. Junior*

Publisher: *David Kendric Brake*

Senior sponsoring editor: *Jodi McPherson*

Sponsoring editor: *Trisha O'Shea*

Developmental editor: *Erin Riley*

Associate editors: *Steve Schuetz/Beth Cigler*

Senior marketing manager: *Jeff Parr*

Project manager: *Christina Thornton-Villagomez*

Production supervisor: *Debra Sylvester*

Freelance design coordinator: *Laurie J. Entringer*

Interior Designer: *AM Design*

Cover Image: *©Schlowsky/Workbook Co/Op Stock*

Senior supplement coordinator: *Carol Loreth*

Compositor: *GTS Graphics*

Typeface: *11/13 Stone Serif*

Printer: *Webcrafters, Inc.*

**Library of Congress Cataloging-in-Publication Data**

Hutchinson, Sarah E.
Microsoft PowerPoint 2000 / Sarah E. Hutchinson, Glen J. Coulthard. / Complete ed.
p. cm.
ISBN 0-07-234809-7 (alk. paper)
1. Microsoft PowerPoint (Computer file) 2. Computer graphics. I. Coulthard, Glen J. II. Title.
T385.H885 2000c
006.6'869 dc—21 99-054015

INTERNATIONAL EDITION ISBN 0-07-116818-4


http://www.mhhe.com

# About the Book

*Each lab manual features the following:*

- ***Learning Objectives:*** At the beginning of each chapter, a list of action-oriented objectives is presented detailing what is expected of the students.
- ***Chapters:*** Each lab manual is divided into chapters.
- ***Modules:*** Each chapter contains three to five independent modules, requiring approximately 30–45 minutes each to complete. Although we recommend you complete an entire chapter before proceeding, you may skip or rearrange the order of these modules to best suit your learning needs.

Case Study

- ***Case Studies:*** Each chapter begins with a Case Study. The student is introduced to a fictitious person or company and their immediate problem or opportunity. Throughout the chapter students obtain the knowledge and skills necessary to meet the challenges presented in the Case Study. At the end of each chapter, students are asked to solve problems directly related to the Case Study.
- ***Feature-Method-Practice:*** Each chapter highlights our unique **"Feature-Method-Practice"** layered approach. The ***Feature*** layer describes the command or technique and persuades you of its importance and relevance. The ***Method*** layer shows you how to perform the procedure, while the ***Practice*** layer lets you apply the feature in a hands-on step-by-step exercise.
- ***Instructions:*** The numbered step-by-step progression for all hands-on examples and exercises are clearly identified. Students will find it surprisingly easy to follow the logical sequence of keystrokes and mouse clicks, and no longer worry about missing a step.

In Addition

- ***In Addition Boxes:*** These content boxes are placed strategically throughout the chapter and provide information on advanced topics that are beyond the scope of the current discussion.
- ***Self-Check Boxes:*** At the end of each module, a brief self-check question appears for students to test their comprehension of the material. Answers to these questions appear in the Appendix.
- ***Chapter Review:*** The *Command Summary* and *Key Terms* provide an excellent review of the chapter content and prepare students for the short-answer, true-false and multiple-choice questions at the end of each chapter.

Easy
Moderate
Difficult

- ***Hands-On Projects:*** Each chapter concludes with six hands-on projects rated according to their difficulty level. The *easy* and *moderate* projects use a running-case approach, whereby the same person or company appears at the end of each chapter in a particular tutorial. The two *difficult* or *on your own* projects provide greater latitude in applying the software to a variety of creative problem-solving situations.
- ***Appendix: Microsoft Windows Quick Reference:*** Each lab manual contains a Microsoft Windows Quick Reference. This Quick reference teaches students the fundamentals of using a mouse and a keyboard, illustrates how to interact with a dialog box, and describes the fundamentals of how to use the Office 2000 Help System.

# Features of This Lab Manual

***Instructions:*** The numbered step-by-step progression for all hands-on examples and exercises are clearly identified. Students will find it surprisingly easy to follow the logical sequence of keystrokes and mouse clicks, and no longer worry about missing a step.

8. To return to a multicolumn list format:
CLICK: down arrow beside the Views button
CHOOSE: List

9. Let's open one of the documents in the list area:
DOUBLE-CLICK: WRD140
The dialog box disappears and the document is loaded into the application window. (*Note:* The "WRD140" filename reflects that this document is used in module 1.4 of the Word learning guide.)

10. Close the document before proceeding.

***In Addition Boxes:*** These content boxes are placed strategically throughout the chapter and provide information on topics that are beyond the scope of the current discussion.

**In Addition**
Storing and Retrieving Files on Web Servers

With the appropriate network connection, you can open and save Word documents on the Internet. In the Open or Save As dialog boxes, click the Web Folders button ( ) in the Places bar or select an FTP Internet site from the *Look in* drop-down list. This feature allows you to share and update Word documents with users from around the world.

***Self-Check Boxes:*** At the end of each module, a brief self-check question appears for students to test their comprehension of the material. Answers to these questions appear in the Appendix.

**1.4 Self Check** In the Open and Save As dialog boxes, how do the List and Details views differ?

## 1.5 Previewing and Printing

This module focuses on outputting your document creations. Most commonly, you will print a document for inclusion into a report or other such document.

### 1.5.1 Previewing a Document

***Feature-Method-Practice:*** Each chapter highlights our unique "**Feature-Method-Practice**" layered approach. The ***Feature*** layer describes the command or technique and persuades you of its importance and relevance. The ***Method*** layer shows you how to perform the procedure, while the ***Practice*** layer lets you apply the feature in a hands-on step-by-step exercise.

**FEATURE**
Before sending a document to the printer, you can preview it using a full-page display that closely resembles the printed version. In this Preview display mode, you can move through the document pages, and zoom in and out on desired areas.

**METHOD**
CLICK: Print Preview button ( ), or
CHOOSE: File, Print Preview

**PRACTICE**
You will now open a relatively large document and then preview it on the screen.

***Case Studies:*** Each chapter begins with a Case Study. Throughout the chapter students obtain the knowledge and skills necessary to meet the challenges presented in the Case Study. At the end of each chapter, students are asked to solve problems directly related to the Case Study.

Case Study

## 1-on-1 Tutoring Services

Dean Shearwater is helping to pay his university tuition by tutoring other university and high school students. Over the last two years, he has developed an excellent reputation for making complex topics simple and easy to remember. While he is an excellent tutor, last year he didn't earn as much as he had expected.

Dean thinks his lackluster earnings can be attributed to poor advertising and inadequate record keeping. This year, he has decided to operate his tutoring services more like a real business. His first priority is to learn how to use Microsoft Word so that he can prepare advertising materials, send faxes and memos, and organize his student notes.

In this chapter, you and Dean learn how to create simple documents from scratch, use built-in document templates, edit documents, and use the Undo command. You also learn how to preview and print your work.

***Chapters:*** Each lab manual is divided into chapters. Each chapter is composed of 2–5 ***Modules.*** Each module is composed of one or more ***Lessons.***

# 1.1 Getting Started with Word

Microsoft Word 2000 is a **word processing** program that enables you to create, edit, format, and print many types of documents including résumés and cover letters, reports and proposals, World Wide Web pages, and more. By the time you complete this learning guide, you will be skilled in creating all types of documents and in getting them to look the way you want. In this module, you load Microsoft Word and proceed through a guided tour of its primary components.

## 1.1.1 Loading and Exiting Word

***New Design:*** The ***new*** Advantage Series design offers a shaded area where the Feature-Method-Practice and numbered step-by-step instructions maintain the focus of the student.

**FEATURE**

You load Word from the Windows Start menu, accessed by clicking the Start button (Start) on the taskbar. Because Word requires a significant amount of memory, you should always exit the application when you are finished doing your work. Most Windows applications allow you to close their windows by clicking the Close button (×) appearing in the top right-hand corner.

# Teaching Resources

The following is a list of supplemental material, which can be used to teach this course.

## Skills Assessment

Irwin/McGraw-Hill offers two innovative systems that can be used with the Advantage Series, ATLAS and **SimNet,** which take skills assessment testing beyond the basics with pre- and post-assessment capability.

- **ATLAS—(Active Testing and Learning Assessment Software)**—Atlas is our **live** in the application skills assessment tool. ATLAS allows Students to perform tasks while working *live* within the office applications environment. ATLAS is web-enabled and customizable to meet the needs of your course. Atlas is available for Office 2000.
- **SimNet—(Simulated Network Assessment Product)**—SimNet permits you to test the actual software skills students learn about the Microsoft Office Applications in a **simulated** environment. SimNet is web-enabled and is available for Office 97 and Office 2000.

## Instructor's Resource Kits

The Instructor's Resource Kit provides professors with all of the ancillary material needed to teach a course. Irwin/McGraw-Hill is committed to providing instructors with the most effective instructional resources available. Many of these resources are available at our **Information Technology Supersite** at www.mhhe.com/it. Our Instructor's Resource Kits are available on CD-ROM and contain the following:

- **Diploma by Brownstone**—is the most flexible, powerful, and easy-to-use computerized testing system available in higher education. The diploma system allows professors to create an exam as a printed version, as a LAN-based Online version and as an Internet version. Diploma includes grade book features, which automate the entire testing process.
- **Instructor's Manual**—Includes:
  —Solutions to all lessons and end-of-chapter material
  —Teaching Tips
  —Teaching Strategies
  —Additional Exercises
- **Student Data Files**—To use the Advantage Series, students must have data files to complete practice and test lessons. The instructor and students using this text in classes are granted the right to post the student files on any network or stand-alone computer, or to distribute the files on individual diskettes. The student files may be downloaded from our IT Supersite at www.mhhe.com/it.
- **Series Web Site**—Available at www.mhhe.com/cit/apps/adv/.

## Digital Solutions

**PageOut Lite**—allows instructors to create their own basic Web sites hosted by McGraw-Hill. PageOut Lite includes three basic templates that automatically convert typed material into HTML Web Pages. Using PageOut Lite an instructor can set up a Home page, Web links, and a basic course syllabus and lecture notes.

**PageOut**—Irwin/McGraw-Hill's Course Webster Development Center. PageOut allows an instructor to create a more complex course Webster with an interactive syllabus and some course management features. Like PageOut Lite, PageOut converts typed material to HTML. For more information, please visit the PageOut Web site at www.mhla.net/pageout.

**OLC/Series Web Sites**—Online Learning Centers (OLCs)/Series Sites are accessible through our Supersite at www.mhhe.com/it. Our OLC/Series Sites provide pedagogical features and supplements for our titles online. Students can point and click their way to key terms, learning objectives, chapter overviews, PowerPoint slides, exercises, and Web links.

**The McGraw-Hill Learning Architecture (MHLA)**—is a complete course delivery system. MHLA gives professors ownership in the way digital content is presented to the class through online quizzing, student collaboration, course administration, and content management. For a walkthrough of MHLA, visit the MHLA Web site at www.mhla.net.

## Packaging Options

For more information about our discount options, contact your local Irwin/McGraw-Hill Sales representative at 1-800-338-3987 or visit our Web site at www.mhhe.com/it.

# Acknowledgments

This series of tutorials is the direct result of the teamwork and heart of many people. We sincerely thank the reviewers, instructors, and students who have shared their comments and suggestions with us over the past few years. We do read them! With their valuable feedback, our tutorials have evolved into the product you see before you.

Many thanks go to Trisha O'Shea and Carrie Berkshire from Irwin/McGraw-Hill whose management helped to get this book produced in a timely and efficient manner. Special recognition goes to all of the individuals mentioned in the credits at the beginning of this tutorial. And finally, to the many others who weren't directly involved in this project but who have stood by us the whole way, we appreciate your encouragement and support.

**The Advantage Team**

Special thanks go out to our contributing members on the Advantage team.

Verlaine Murphy
Walt Musekamp
Ingrid Neumann
Catherine Schuler

**Write to Us**

We welcome your response to this tutorial, for we are trying to make it as useful a learning tool as possible. Please contact us at

*Sarah E. Hutchinson*—sarah-hutchinson@home.com
*Glen J. Coulthard*—glen@coulthard.com

# Contents

## CREATING A PRESENTATION — CHAPTER 1



## DEVELOPING A PRESENTATION — CHAPTER 2

## CHAPTER 3 WORKING WITH TEXT



## CHAPTER 4 JAZZING UP YOUR PRESENTATIONS

## PREPARING TO DELIVER A PRESENTATION

CHAPTER 5



## CUSTOMIZING PRESENTATIONS

CHAPTER 6

## Chapter 7 DELIVERING PRESENTATIONS



## Chapter 8 DEVELOPING APPLICATIONS IN POWERPOINT

ADVANTAGE
SERIES

MICROSOFT®

# POWERPOINT® 2000

BRIEF EDITION

# Microsoft PowerPoint 2000

*Creating a Presentation*

## CHAPTER ONE

## Chapter Outline



## Learning Objectives

After reading this chapter, you will be able to:

- Describe the different components of the application window
- Select commands using the Menu bar and right-click menus
- Begin a new presentation using the AutoContent Wizard or a design template
- Insert text in Slide and Outline views
- Save, open, close, and print a presentation

Case Study

## Tristar Development

Tina Pusch is a public relations coordinator for Tristar Development, a large firm in New York. Earlier this morning Tina received a request from an important client to create a PowerPoint presentation summarizing the status of one of their projects. Then, during her coffee break, she received an e-mail message with a PowerPoint attachment from Kenyon, her sixth-grade nephew in Canada. Frustrated that she doesn't yet know how to use PowerPoint, Tina decides to roll up her sleeves and learn how to use this clearly popular tool.

In this chapter, you and Tina learn how to load Microsoft PowerPoint and open, close, and view existing presentations. You will create new presentations using the AutoContent Wizard and design templates, insert text, and insert and delete slides. You will also learn how to preview a presentation using grayscale tones and how to print.



# 1.1 Getting Started with PowerPoint

Microsoft PowerPoint 2000 is a presentation graphics program that enables you to create on-screen presentations, Web presentations, overhead transparencies, and 35mm slides. Even if you don't consider yourself a speechwriter or graphics designer, you can still create informative and attractive presentations using PowerPoint. In this module, you load Microsoft PowerPoint and proceed through a guided tour of its primary components.

## 1.1.1 Loading PowerPoint

**FEATURE**

You load PowerPoint from the Windows Start menu, accessed by clicking the Start button (Start) on the taskbar. Because PowerPoint requires a significant amount of memory, you should always exit the application when you are finished doing your work. Most Windows applications allow you to close their windows by clicking the Close button (☒) appearing in the top right-hand corner.

**METHOD**

- To load PowerPoint:
  CLICK: Start button (Start)
  CHOOSE: Programs, Microsoft PowerPoint
- To exit PowerPoint:
  CHOOSE: File, Exit from PowerPoint's Menu bar

**PRACTICE**

You will now load Microsoft PowerPoint using the Windows Start menu.

*Setup:* Ensure that you have turned on your computer and that the Windows desktop appears. If necessary, refer to the Preface for additional instructions.

1. Position the mouse pointer over the top of the Start button (Start) and then click the left mouse button once. The Start pop-up menu appears.

2. Point to the Programs cascading command using the mouse. Note that you do not need to click the left mouse button to display the list of programs in the fly-out or cascading menu.

3. Move the mouse pointer horizontally to the right until it highlights an option in the Programs menu. You can now move the mouse pointer vertically within the menu to select an option.

4. Point to the Microsoft PowerPoint menu item and then click the left mouse button once to execute the command. After a few seconds, the Microsoft PowerPoint screen appears.

5. An Office Assistant character, like "Clippit" (shown at the right), may now appear. You learn how to hide this character in lesson 1.1.2.

6. Unless the feature has been disabled, a startup dialog box similar to the one shown in Figure 1.1 appears. This dialog box is used to determine how you want to proceed when PowerPoint is first loaded. If the dialog box appears on your screen, do the following:
CLICK: Cancel command button

**Figure 1.1**
PowerPoint startup dialog box

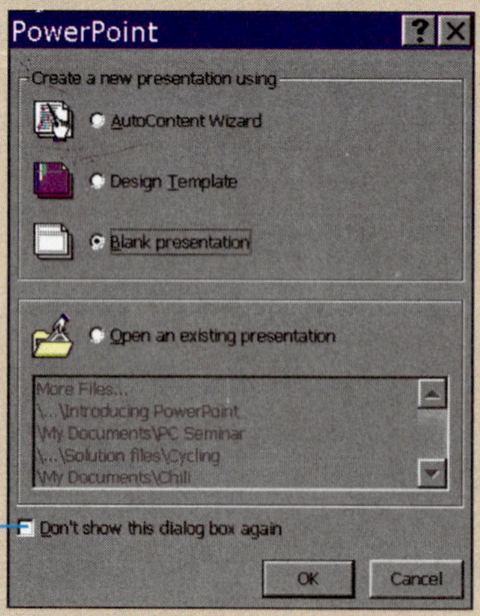


Select this check box if you don't want the startup dialog box to display the next time you load PowerPoint.

**In Addition**
**Switching Among Applications**

Each application that you are currently working with is represented by a button on the taskbar. Switching between open applications on your desktop is as easy as clicking the appropriate taskbar button, like switching channels on a television set.

## 1.1.2 Touring PowerPoint

**FEATURE**

The PowerPoint **application window** acts as a container for your presentation. It also contains the primary interface components for working in PowerPoint, including the *Windows icons, Menu bar, Toolbars,* and *Status bar*. Figure 1.2 identifies several of these components.

**PRACTICE**

In a guided tour, you will now explore the features of the PowerPoint application window.

*Setup:* Ensure that you've loaded PowerPoint and that the application window is empty.

1 PowerPoint's application window is best kept maximized to fill the entire screen, as shown in Figure 1.2. As with most Windows applications, you use the Title bar icons—Minimize (▁), Maximize (□), Restore (⧉), and Close (☒)—to control the display of a window using the mouse. Familiarize yourself with the components labeled in Figure 1.2.

**Figure 1.2**
PowerPoint's application window

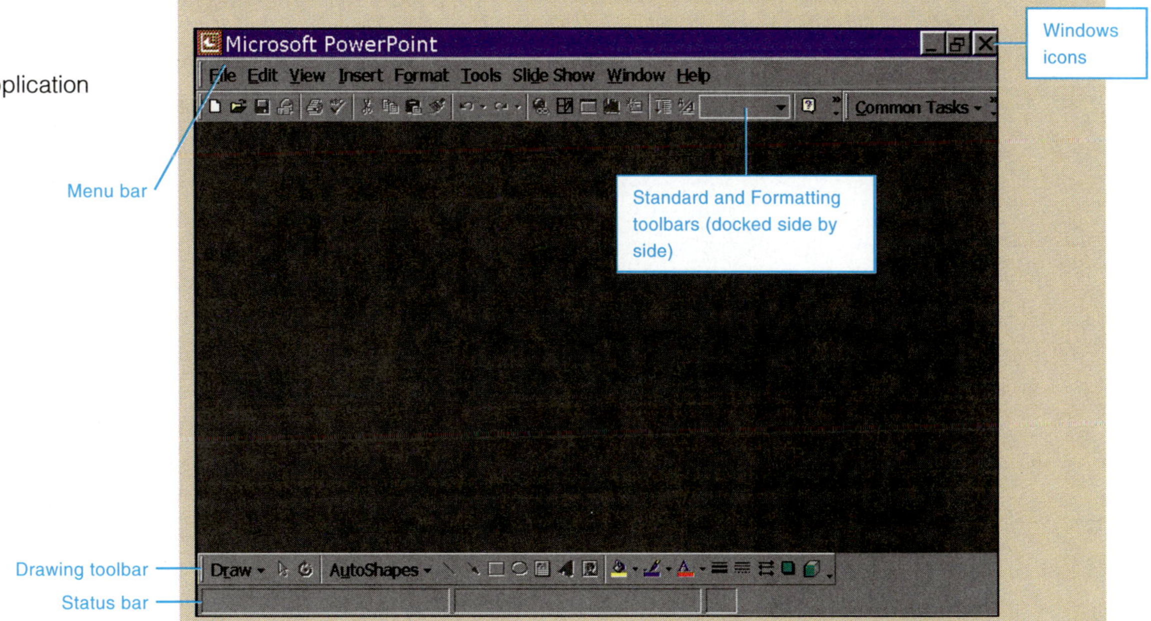

2 The Menu bar contains the PowerPoint menu commands. To execute a command, you click once on the desired Menu bar option and then click again on the command. Commands that appear dimmed are not available for selection. Commands that are followed by an ellipsis (...) will display a dialog box.

To practice working with the PowerPoint Menu bar:
CHOOSE: Help
This instruction tells you to click the left mouse button once on the Help option appearing in the Menu bar.

3 To display other pull-down menus, move the mouse to the left over other options in the Menu bar. As each option is highlighted, a pull-down menu appears with its associated commands.

4 To leave the Menu bar without making a command selection:
CLICK: in a blank area of the Title bar

5 PowerPoint provides context-sensitive *right-click menus* for quick access to menu commands. Rather than searching for the appropriate command in the Menu bar, you can position the mouse pointer on any object, such as a graphic or toolbar button, and right-click the mouse to display a list of commonly selected commands.

If an Office Assistant character currently appears on your screen, do the following to hide it from view:
RIGHT-CLICK: *the character*
CHOOSE: Hide from the right-click menu

## 1.1.3 Customizing Menus and Toolbars

**FEATURE**
Some people argue that software becomes more difficult to learn and use with the addition of each new command or feature. In response to this sentiment, Microsoft developed **adaptive menus** that display only the most commonly used commands. By default, Office 2000 ships with the adaptive menus feature enabled. However, you may find this dynamic feature confusing and choose to turn off the adaptive menus. Likewise, the Standard and Formatting toolbars are positioned side-by-side in a single row by default. Again, you may find it easier to locate buttons when these toolbars are positioned on separate rows.

**METHOD**

To disable the adaptive menus feature:

1. CHOOSE: Tools, Customize
2. CLICK: *Options* tab
3. SELECT: *Menus show recently used commands first* check box, so that no "✔" appears
4. CLICK: Close command button

To display the Standard and Formatting toolbars on separate rows:

1. CHOOSE: Tools, Customize
2. CLICK: *Options* tab
3. SELECT: *Standard and Formatting toolbars share one row* check box, so that no "✔" appears.
4. CLICK: Close command button

**PRACTICE**

After a brief tour of PowerPoint's adaptive menus, you will disable the adaptive menus feature. At the same time, you will display the Standard and Formatting toolbars on separate rows.

*Setup:* Ensure that you've completed the previous lesson.

1 Let's display the Tools menu.
CHOOSE: Tools
The Tools menu (shown on the right) should now appear. When a desired command does not appear on a menu, you can extend the menu to view all of the commands either by waiting for a short period or by clicking the downward pointing arrows (also called *chevrons*) at the bottom of a pull-down menu. You can also double-click a menu option to display the entire list of commands immediately.

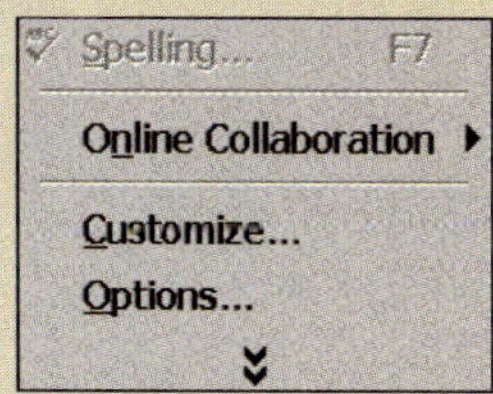


2 Let's display the entire list of commands in the Tools menu by double-clicking:
DOUBLE-CLICK: Tools in the Menu bar
The menu should now contain a complete list of options.

3 Let's turn off the adaptive menus feature and ensure that the Standard and Formatting toolbars appear on separate rows. Do the following:
CHOOSE: Customize from the Tools pull-down menu
CLICK: *Options* tab
The Customize dialog box should now appear similar to Figure 1.3.

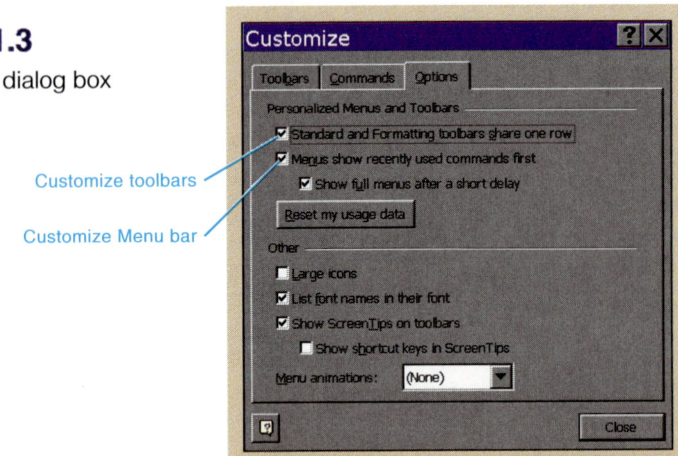


**Figure 1.3**
Customize dialog box

4. SELECT: *Menus show recently used commands first* check box, so that no "✔" appears

5. SELECT: *Standard and Formatting toolbars share one row* check box, so that no "✔" appears

6. To proceed:
CLICK: Close command button
Your screen should now appear similar to Figure 1.4.

*IMPORTANT: For the remainder of this learning guide, we assume that the adaptive menus feature has been disabled and that the Standard and Formatting toolbars are positioned on separate rows.*

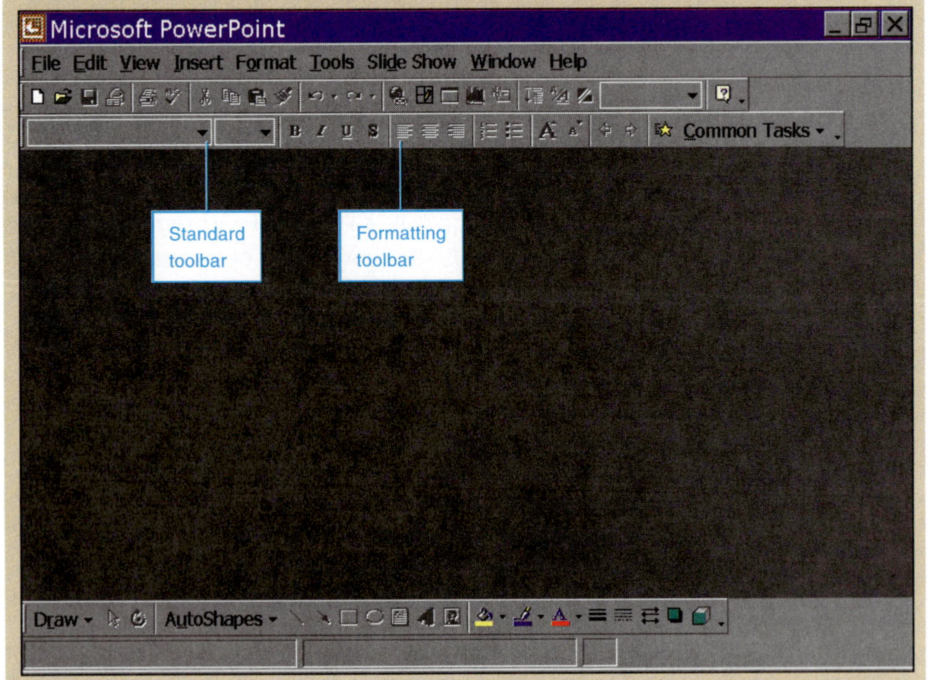


**Figure 1.4**
The Standard and Formatting toolbars are now positioned on separate rows

7. To display additional toolbars, you select the desired options from a right-click menu. For example:
RIGHT-CLICK: *any button* on the Standard toolbar
Notice that the Standard, Formatting, and Drawing options are currently selected, as illustrated by the check marks in the pop-up menu.

8. To display the Picture toolbar:
CHOOSE: Picture from the pop-up menu
You should see another toolbar appear in the application window.

9. To remove or hide the Picture toolbar:
RIGHT-CLICK: *any button on any toolbar*
CHOOSE: Picture
The toolbar disappears from the application window.

**1.1 Self Check** What is an adaptive menu?

# 1.2 Creating a New Presentation

The **AutoContent Wizard** provides the quickest and easiest method for beginning a new presentation by providing content and design suggestions. AutoContent presentations, consisting of 5 to 10 slides each, are available on a range of topics. Once created, you simply edit the text of the presentation to meet your needs.

If you want suggestions on the design of your presentation, but not on its content, consider beginning a new presentation from a design template. A **design template** determines the look of your presentation by defining its color scheme, background, and use of fonts. If neither the AutoContent Wizard nor a design template sounds tempting, you can always start a presentation from scratch by clicking the New button (▢).

## 1.2.1 Creating a Presentation Using the AutoContent Wizard

**FEATURE**

If you're finding it difficult to organize and write down your thoughts, consider letting the AutoContent Wizard be your guide. After progressing through the Wizard's dialog boxes, you'll have a skeletal framework for building a complete presentation.

**METHOD**

1. To launch the AutoContent Wizard:
   CHOOSE: File, New
   CLICK: *General* tab
   DOUBLE-CLICK: AutoContent Wizard
2. To proceed through the AutoContent Wizard, responding to its questions:
   CLICK: Next command button
3. To complete the Wizard:
   CLICK: Finish command button

**PRACTICE**

You will now practice launching the AutoContent Wizard from the New dialog box.

*Setup:* Ensure that PowerPoint is loaded. If the PowerPoint startup dialog box is displayed, click its Cancel command button.

1 CHOOSE: File, New from the Menu bar
CLICK: *General* tab
DOUBLE-CLICK: AutoContent Wizard icon

2 The AutoContent Wizard is launched and presents the initial AutoContent Wizard screen. The left side of the dialog box shows the steps the wizard will go through in order to format the final presentation. To proceed to the next step, do the following:
CLICK: Next command button

3 In this step, you select the type of presentation you're going to give (Figure 1.5). When you click a category option button, a list of related presentations appears in the list box to the right.

**Figure 1.5**
Selecting a presentation type

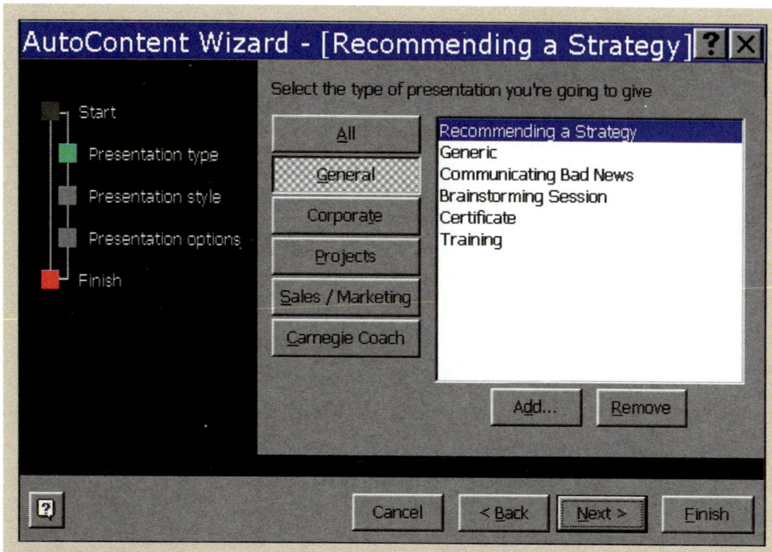


Do the following:
CLICK: Corporate button
SELECT: Company Meeting in the list box
CLICK: Next command button

4 You must now select an output option for the presentation:
SELECT: *On-screen presentation* option
CLICK: Next command button
Your screen should now appear similar to Figure 1.6.

**Figure 1.6**
Defining the opening slide

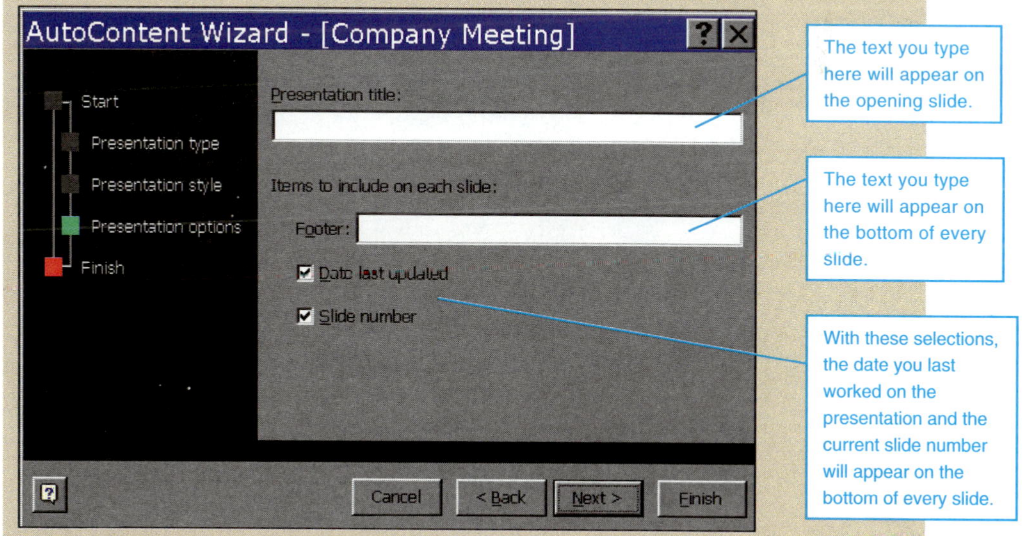


5 In this step, you enter the information you want to appear on the opening slide of your presentation.
CLICK: in the *Presentation title* text box
TYPE: **Effective Communication Skills**

**6** If you wish, you can review your selections by clicking the Back command button. Otherwise, do the following to proceed:
CLICK: Next command button
CLICK: Finish command button
At this point, as shown in Figure 1.7, the presentation is compiled with some content suggestions that you can edit to meet your needs. This view of your presentation is called **Normal view** and provides one place for building the different parts of your presentation. The **Outline pane** is used for typing text and rearranging your presentation. The **Slide pane** is used for seeing how your slide will look and for editing slides directly. The **Notes pane** provides a location for typing reminder notes and additional information that you want to share with your audience. We discuss switching views in lesson 1.2.5.

**Figure 1.7**
An AutoContent presentation

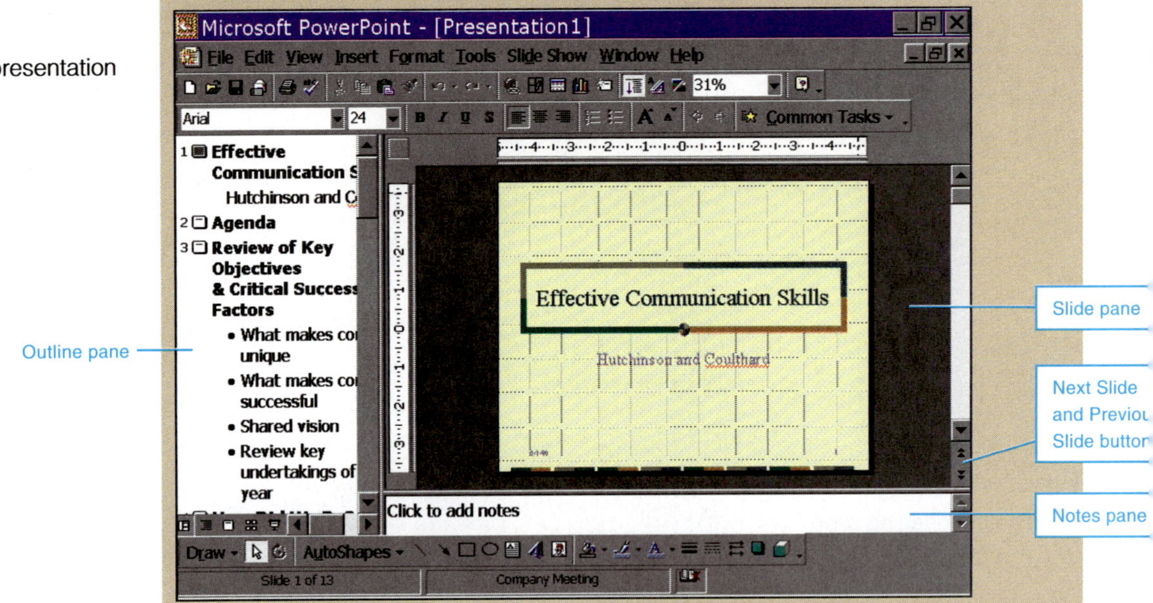


**7** The Next Slide (▼) and Previous Slide (▲) buttons on the vertical scroll bar enable you to navigate through your presentation. To illustrate:
CLICK: Next Slide button (▼) to view the second slide
CLICK: Previous Slide button (▲) to view the first slide

**8** Advance through the entire presentation using the Next Slide button (▼).

**9** To close the presentation, without saving:
CHOOSE: File, Close
CLICK: No when asked whether you want to save the presentation

## 1.2.2 Creating a Presentation from a Design Template

**FEATURE**
One of the problems with the advent of presentation software programs like PowerPoint is that the presentation author has been hurled into the role of graphic designer. Many people who are skilled writers and content researchers find it difficult to take on these additional responsibilities. Fortunately, PowerPoint provides a selection of design templates that you can use to start new presentations.

**METHOD**
To start a new presentation from a design template:
1. CHOOSE: File, New
2. CLICK: *Design Templates* tab
3. DOUBLE-CLICK: a design template

**PRACTICE**
You will now practice applying design templates.

*Setup:* Ensure that PowerPoint is loaded and that no presentations are open.

1 Your first step is to display the New Presentation dialog box:
CHOOSE: File, New

2 To select a design template:
CLICK: *Design Templates* tab
The New Presentation dialog box should now appear.

3 To view the design templates in a list:
CLICK: List button (▤) in the dialog box

4 To display a preview of a design template, you click once on the template name.
CLICK: Citrus template
Your screen should now appear similar to Figure 1.8. (*Note:* On your computer, different design templates may appear in the list box.)

**Figure 1.8**
New Presentation dialog box: *Design Templates* tab

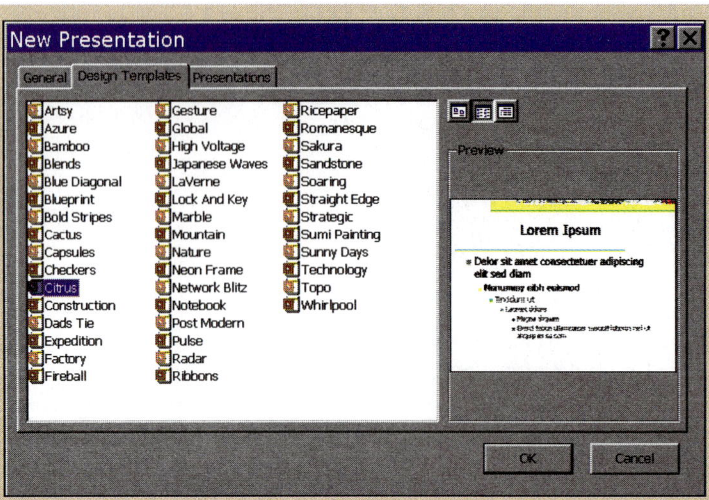


5. Let's open the "Citrus" design template:
DOUBLE-CLICK: Citrus
The New Slide dialog box should now appear (Figure 1.9). When you add a new slide to a presentation, you will always be prompted to select a slide type, called an **AutoLayout,** in the New Slide dialog box. PowerPoint provides 24 AutoLayouts from which you can choose.

**Figure 1.9**
New Slide dialog box

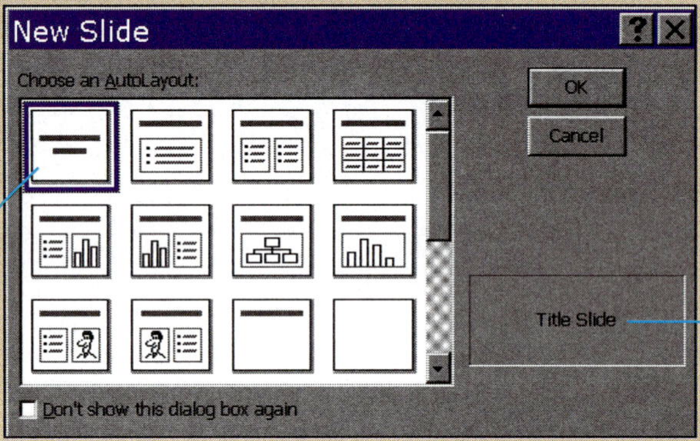


6. Let's create a title slide. Since the Title Slide AutoLayout is already selected:
CLICK: OK command button
A new slide appears, complete with a background design (Citrus) and areas, called *placeholders*, for entering a title and a subtitle. **Placeholders** mark the location of slide objects and provide instructions for editing them. Your screen should now appear similar to Figure 1.10.

**Figure 1.10**

Citrus design template

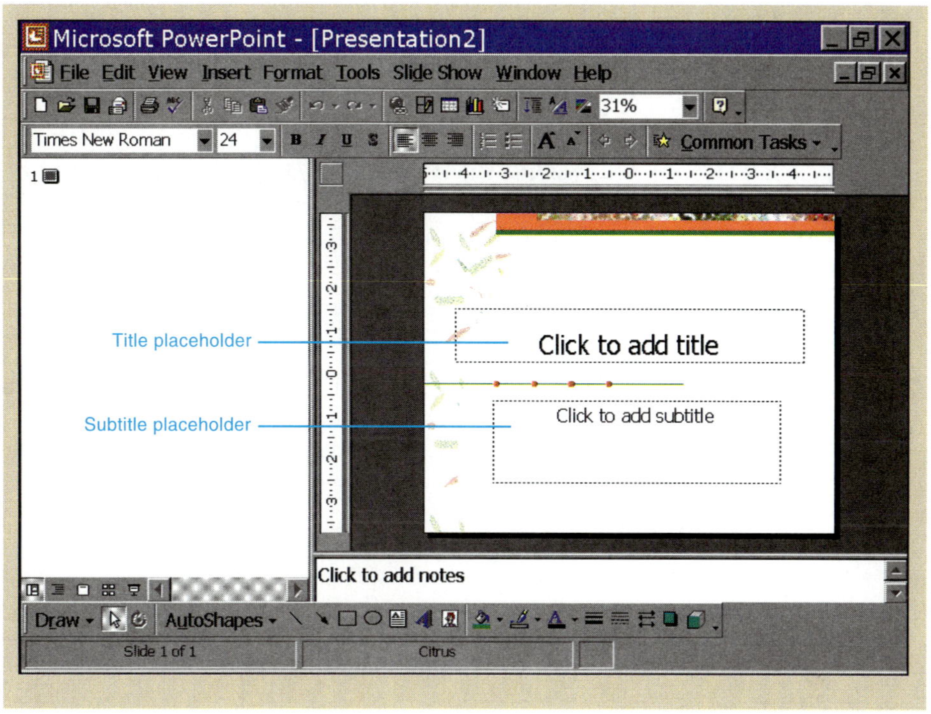


## 1.2.3 Adding Text

**FEATURE**

In most cases, the easiest way to add text to slides is to type it directly into a text placeholder in the Slide pane. If you type more text than can fit in the placeholder, PowerPoint's **AutoFit feature** will automatically resize the placeholder to accommodate the text. You can also insert text by typing in the Outline pane.

**METHOD**

To add text in the Slide pane:
CLICK: in a text placeholder and then begin typing

To add text in the Outline pane:

- CLICK: to the right of the slide number and icon to type title text
- PRESS: ENTER to insert a new slide or continue typing at the same heading level
- PRESS: TAB to begin typing at a demoted (lower) outline level
- PRESS: SHIFT + TAB to begin typing at a promoted (higher) outline level

**PRACTICE**

You will now practice adding text using the Slide and Outline panes.

*Setup:* Ensure that you've completed the previous lessons in this module and that a presentation based on the Citrus design template is open in the application window.

1 Let's practice using the Slide pane. To type text into the title placeholder:
CLICK: in the title placeholder, marked by the text "Click to add title"
The insertion point should be blinking in the title placeholder.

2 TYPE: `Getting Started with PowerPoint`
Notice that the title text appears in the Outline pane also.

3 To type text into the subtitle placeholder:
CLICK: in the subtitle placeholder, marked by "Click to add subtitle"

4 TYPE: *`By your name`*
Note that the subtitle text also appears in the Outline pane. Your screen should now appear similar to Figure 1.11.

**Figure 1.11**
Adding text

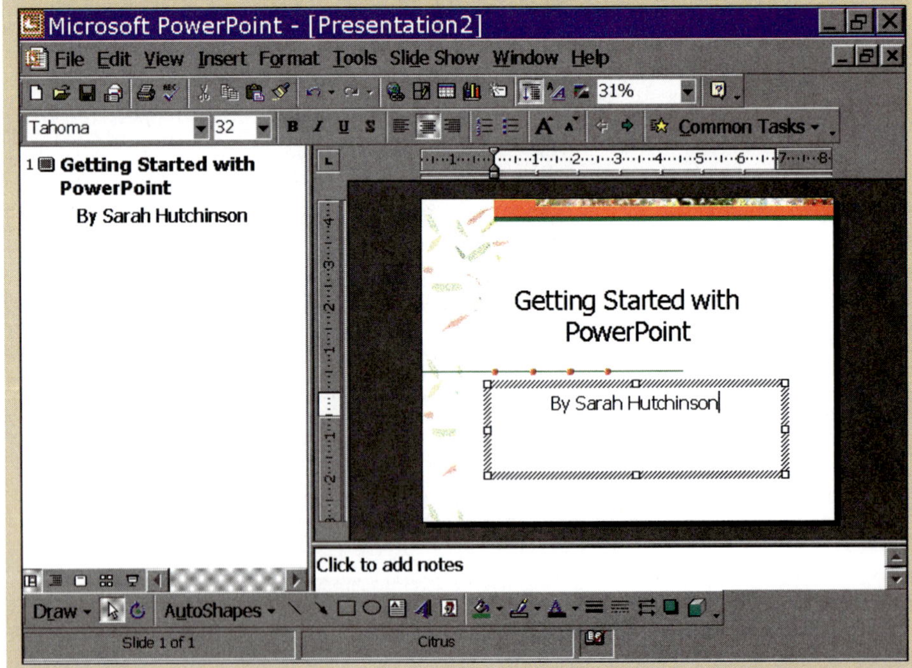

5 Now let's practice using the Outline pane. Let's edit the title text. In the Outline pane:
SELECT: the text "Getting Started with" by dragging with the mouse over the text
The selected text should be highlighted in reverse video.

6 TYPE: **Introducing**
The title should now read "Introducing PowerPoint" in both the Outline pane and the Slide pane.

7 CLICK: to the right of the subtitle text in the Outline pane

8 Let's see what happens when we press ENTER.
PRESS: ENTER
In the Outline pane, the insertion point moved down to the next line in the subtitle.

9 TYPE: ***your school or business name***
The subtitle now contains two lines of text.

10 PRESS: ENTER
In the Outline pane, the insertion point is now blinking on the third line of the subtitle.

11 To type at a promoted level:
PRESS: SHIFT + TAB
Since you're promoting the outline to the highest level, PowerPoint added another slide and is waiting for you to insert a title. PowerPoint automatically inserted a slide that uses the Bulleted List AutoLayout.

12 Note that the insertion point is blinking to the right of the slide number and icon in the Outline pane.
TYPE: **PowerPoint lets you create:**
PRESS: ENTER
Note that PowerPoint inserted another slide.

13 In this step, you demote the outline level so that you can type a bulleted list on slide 2.
PRESS: TAB to demote the current outline level
TYPE: **On-screen presentations**
PRESS: ENTER
TYPE: **Web presentations**
PRESS: ENTER
TYPE: **Overhead transparencies**
PRESS: ENTER
TYPE: **35mm slides**
Your screen should now appear similar to Figure 1.12.

POWERPOINT

**Figure 1.12**
Typing a bulleted list in the Outline pane

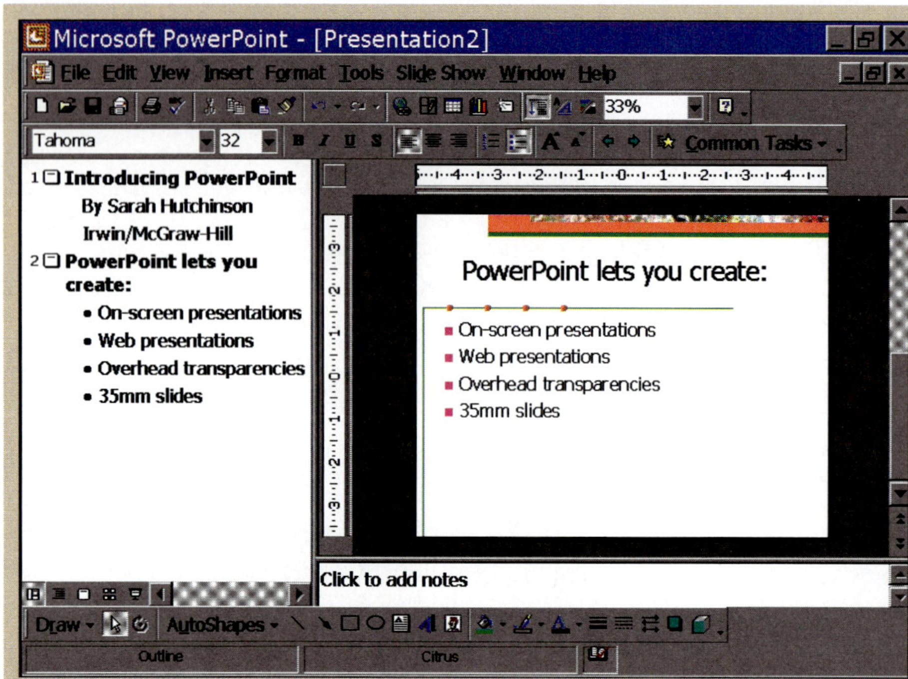


14 As one final step, let's use the Slide pane to add an additional item to the bulleted list.
CLICK: to the right of the last bulleted item in the Slide pane
PRESS: ENTER
TYPE: `Audience handouts`
As you can see, the Outline pane and the Slide pane can be used interchangeably for entering and editing text.

## 1.2.4 Inserting and Deleting Slides

**FEATURE**
The most common method for inserting new slides involves clicking the New Slide button (▣) on the Standard toolbar, however you can also insert slides while working in the Outline pane. New slides are inserted after the current, or displayed, slide. You can delete slides using the Menu bar or by selecting the slide in the Outline pane and pressing DELETE.

## METHOD

- To insert a new slide:
  CLICK: New Slide button ( ) on the Standard toolbar
  SELECT: an AutoLayout format
  PRESS: ENTER
- To delete an existing slide:
  CHOOSE: Edit, Delete Slide, or
  SELECT: the slide in the Outline panel and then press DELETE

## PRACTICE

You will now practice inserting and deleting slides.

*Setup:* Ensure that you've completed the previous lessons in this module and that the "PowerPoint lets you create" slide is displaying in the Slide pane.

1 To insert a new slide after the current slide:
CLICK: New Slide button ( ) on the Standard toolbar
SELECT: Text & Clip Art layout (located in the third row)
CLICK: OK command button
Your screen should appear similar to Figure 1.13. The presentation now includes three slides. Note that the Outline pane also includes three slide icons.

**Figure 1.13**
Inserting a new slide

To display an alternate slide in the Slide pane, click its icon in the Outline pane.

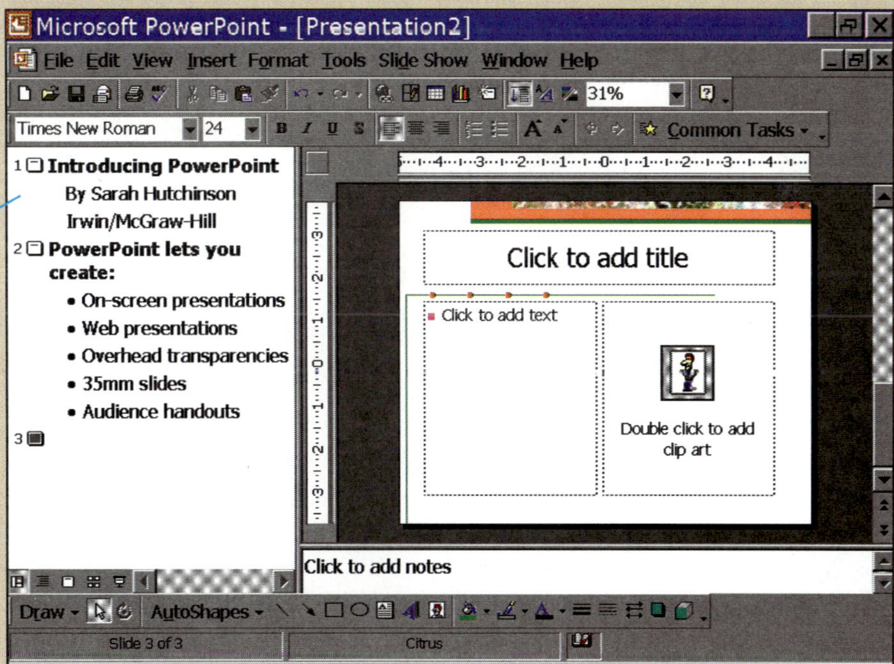

2 To delete the newly inserted third slide:
CHOOSE: Edit, Delete Slide
(*Note:* You could have also clicked the slide 3 icon in the Outline pane and then pressed DELETE.)

## 1.2.5 Switching PowerPoint Views

**FEATURE**

PowerPoint provides several ways to view a presentation to suit your preferred way of working. You switch views using the View command on the Menu bar or by clicking the View buttons located near the bottom-left corner of the application window. The active view of your presentation before being saved or closed becomes the default view when it is subsequently opened.

**METHOD**

- To switch views using the Menu bar:
  CHOOSE: View from the Menu bar
  CHOOSE: Normal, Slide Sorter, or Slide Show from the drop-down menu
- To switch views using the View buttons, located near the bottom-left corner of the application window:
  CLICK: Normal (), Outline (), Slide (), Slide Sorter (), or Slide Show () button

**PRACTICE**

You will now practice switching views.

*Setup:* Ensure that you've completed the previous lessons in this module and that a two-slide presentation is displaying in the application window.

1 In Normal view, as we described in lesson 1.2.1, you see the Outline pane, Slide pane, and Notes pane for the convenient editing of several parts of your presentation at once. You've been using Normal view until now in this chapter. To enlarge the Outline pane and reduce the size of the Slide and Notes pane:
CLICK: Outline View button () in the bottom-left corner of the application window
**Outline view,** which displays the titles and main text of your presentation, is ideal for typing the text of your presentation and rearranging bulleted lists, paragraphs, and slides.

**2** To enlarge the Slide pane, reduce the Outline pane, and remove the Notes pane:
CLICK: Slide View button ( ) in the bottom-left of the application window
**Slide view** enlarges the Slide pane for easier viewing of the object placeholders. This mode is ideal for building a presentation by editing placeholders directly or fine-tuning the position of graphics.

**3** To display the presentation in Slide Sorter view:
CHOOSE: View, Slide Sorter
Your screen should now appear similar to Figure 1.14. In **Slide Sorter view,** you view multiple slides at once using small thumbnail representations. Slide Sorter view gives you an immediate feeling for the continuity or flow of a presentation.



**Figure 1.14**
Slide Sorter view

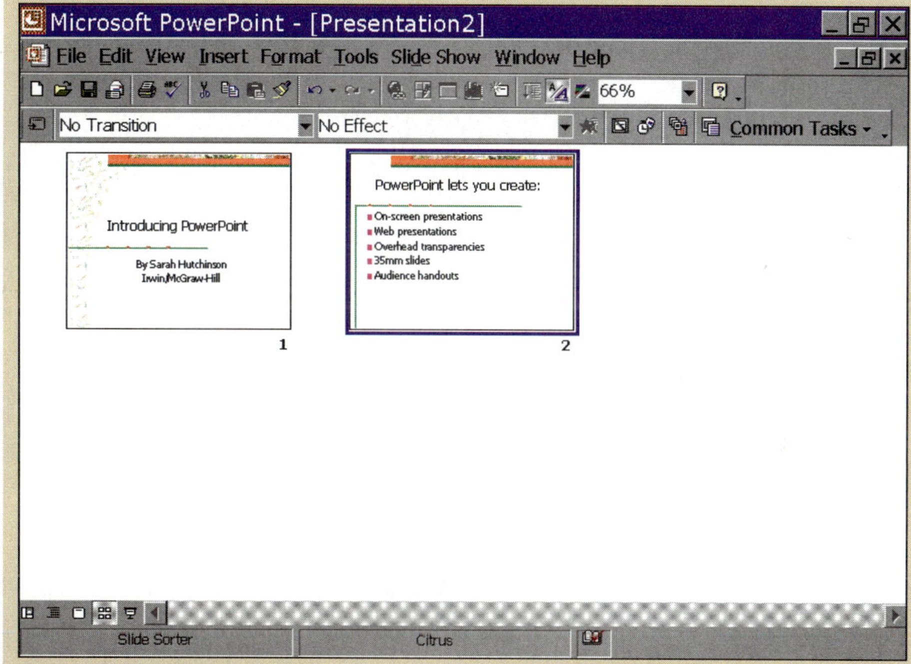


**4** To view the presentation in Slide Show view:
CHOOSE: View, Slide Show
In **Slide Show view,** the presentation is displayed as an on-screen slide show, complete with transitions and special effects.

**5** To proceed to the next slide in the presentation:
CLICK: left mouse button once
Your screen should now appear similar to Figure 1.15.

**Figure 1.15**
Slide Show view

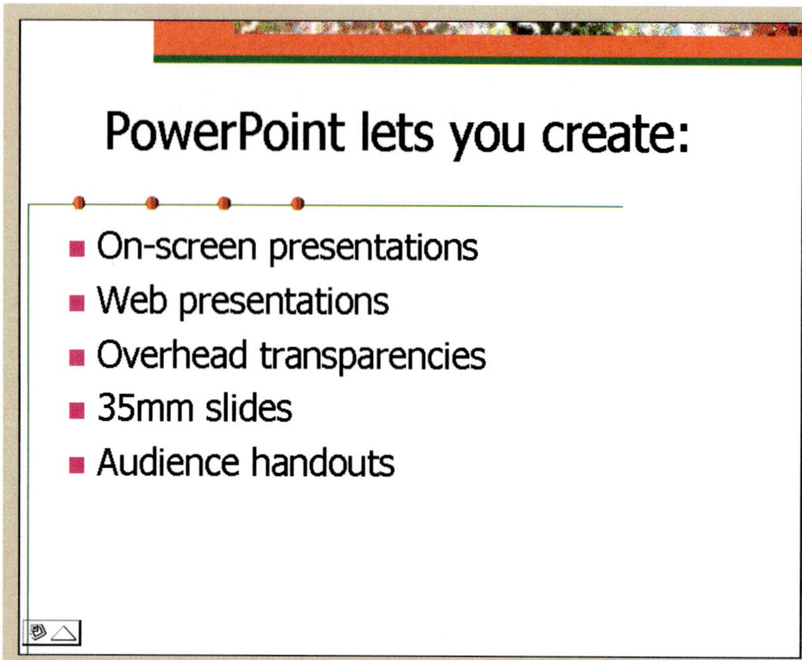


6 The most common methods for controlling a presentation's display while in Slide Show view appear in Table 1.1. You can also use the right-click menu to display similar options for navigating through a presentation.

**Table 1.1**
Controlling a Slide Show Presentation

| *Task Description* | *Keyboard and Mouse Methods* |
|---|---|
| Go to the next slide | CLICK: left mouse button, or PRESS: PgDn, →, ↓, ENTER, or Spacebar |
| Go to the previous slide | PRESS: PgUp, ←, or ↑ |
| Go to a specific slide | TYPE: **desired slide number,** and then PRESS: ENTER |
| Go to the first slide | PRESS: HOME |
| Go to the last slide | PRESS: END |
| Blank the screen to black | PRESS: **b** to blank screen to black<br>PRESS: **b** again to unblank screen |

| | |
|---|---|
| Blank the screen to white | PRESS: w to blank screen to white<br>PRESS: w again to unblank screen |
| Exit the slide show | PRESS: ESC |

To proceed to the next slide in the presentation:
CLICK: left mouse button once

7 To return to the previous slide using the keyboard:
PRESS: ⇧

8 To display the next slide using the keyboard:
PRESS: Spacebar

9 To exit Slide Show view:
PRESS: ESC

10 To return to Normal view:
CHOOSE: View, Normal

11 To close the presentation, without saving:
CHOOSE: File, Close
CLICK: No when asked whether you want to save the presentation

**1.2 Self Check** What is the difference between Slide Sorter and Slide Show view?

# 1.3 Managing Files

Managing the presentations that you create is an important skill. When you are creating a presentation, it exists only in the computer's RAM (random access memory), which is highly volatile. In other words, if the power to your computer goes off, your presentation is lost. For safety and security, you need to save your presentation permanently to the local hard disk, a network drive, or a floppy diskette.

Saving your work to a named file on a disk is similar to placing it into a filing cabinet. For important presentations (ones that you cannot risk losing), you should save your work at least every 15 minutes, or whenever you're interrupted, to protect against an unexpected power outage or other catastrophe. When naming your presentation files, you can use up to 255 characters, including spaces, but it's wise to keep the length under 20 characters. Furthermore, you cannot use the following characters in naming your presentations:

\ / : ; * ? " < > |

In the following lessons, you practice several file management procedures, including saving and closing presentations, and opening existing presentations.

***Important:*** *In this guide, we refer to the files that have been created for you as the* ***student data files.*** *Depending on your computer or lab setup, these files may be located on a floppy diskette, in a folder on your hard disk, or on a network server. If necessary, ask your instructor or lab assistant where to find these data files. To download the Advantage Series' student data files from the Internet, visit McGraw-Hill's Information Technology Web site at:*

**http://www.mhhe.com/it**

*You will also need to identify a personal storage location for the files that you create, modify, and save.*

## 1.3.1 Saving and Closing

**FEATURE**

You can save the currently displayed presentation by updating an existing file on the disk, by creating a new file, or by selecting a new storage location. The File, Save command and the Save button ( ) on the toolbar allow you to overwrite a disk file with the latest version of a presentation. The File, Save As command enables you to save a presentation to a new filename or storage location. When you are finished working with a presentation, ensure that you close the file to free up valuable RAM.

**METHOD**

- To save a presentation:
  CLICK: Save button ( ), or
  CHOOSE: File, Save, or
  CHOOSE: File, Save As
- To close a presentation:
  CLICK: its Close button ( ), or
  CHOOSE: File, Close

**PRACTICE**

You will now practice saving and closing a presentation.

*Setup:* Ensure that PowerPoint is loaded. If the PowerPoint startup dialog box is displayed, click its Cancel command button. You will also need to identify a storage location for your personal document files. If you want to use a diskette, place it into the diskette drive now.

1. So that we have a presentation to save, let's create a quick Auto-Content presentation.
CHOOSE: File, New
CLICK: *General* tab
DOUBLE-CLICK: AutoContent Wizard
CLICK: Finish button
A presentation should now appear in the application window.

2. When you are working in a new presentation that has not yet been saved, PowerPoint displays the Save As dialog box (Figure 1.16), regardless of the method you choose to save the file. To demonstrate:
CLICK: Save button (💾)
(*Note*: The filenames and directories that appear in your Save As dialog box may differ from those shown in Figure 1.16.) The **Places bar,** located along the left border of the dialog box, provides convenient access to commonly used storage locations.

**Figure 1.16**
Save As dialog box

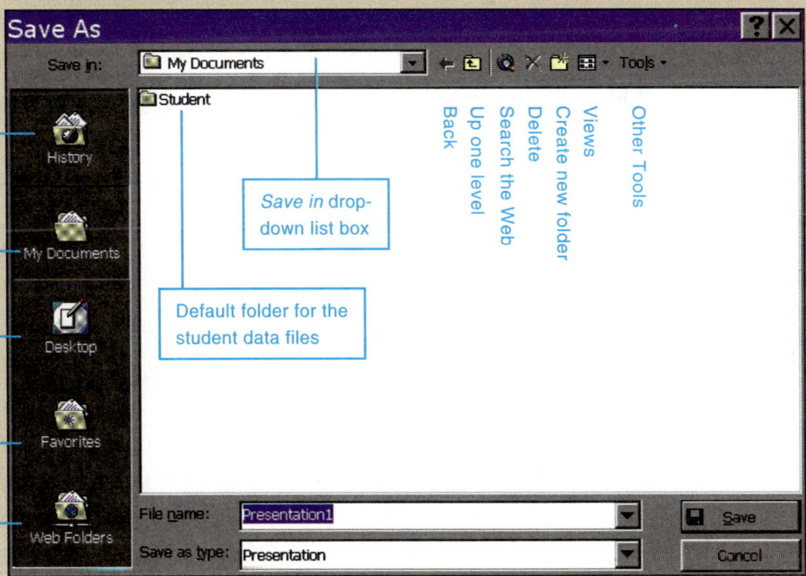

3. In the next few steps, you practice navigating your computer's disks. To begin, let's view a list of the files that you've worked with recently:
CLICK: History button () in the Places bar

4. To browse the files in your "My Documents" folder:
CLICK: My Documents button ()

5. Let's browse the local hard disk:
CLICK: down arrow attached to the *Save in* drop-down list box
SELECT: Hard Disk C: ()
(*Note:* Your hard drive may have a different name.) The list area displays the folders and files stored in the root directory of your local hard disk.

6. To drill down into one of the folders:
DOUBLE-CLICK: Program Files folder
(*Note:* If the Program Files folder isn't located on your local hard disk, select an alternate folder to open.) This folder contains the program files for several applications.

7. Let's drill down one step further:
DOUBLE-CLICK: Microsoft Office folder
This folder contains the Microsoft Office program files.

8. To return to the previous display:
CLICK: Back button () in the dialog box
(*Note:* The button is renamed "Program Files," since that is where you will end up once the button is clicked.)

9. To return to the "My Documents" display:
CLICK: Back button () twice
(*Hint*: You could have also clicked the My Documents button in the Places bar.)

10. Now, using either the Places bar or the *Save In* drop-down list box:
SELECT: *a storage location for your personal files*
(*Note*: In this guide, we save files to the My Documents folder.)

11. Next, you need to give the presentation file a unique name. Let's replace the existing name with one that is more descriptive. Do the following:
DOUBLE-CLICK: the *presentation name* appearing in the *File name* text box to select it
TYPE: Practice Presentation

12 To save your work:
CLICK: Save command button
Note that the presentation's name now appears in the Title bar.

13 In this step, let's insert a title on the first slide.
CLICK: the title placeholder
TYPE: **Increasing Business Revenues**

14 To save the revised presentation:
CLICK: Save button (💾)
There are times when you may want to save an existing presentation under a different filename. For example, you may want to keep different versions of the same presentation on your disk. Or, you may want to use one presentation as a template for future presentations that are similar in style and format. To do this, you can retrieve the original presentation file, edit the information, and then save it again under a different name using the File, Save As command.

15 Let's close the presentation:
CHOOSE: File, Close



## 1.3.2 Opening an Existing Presentation

**FEATURE**
You use the Open dialog box to search for and retrieve existing presentations that are stored on your local hard disk, a floppy diskette, a network server, or on the Web. If you want to load PowerPoint and an existing presentation at the same time, you can use the Open Office Document command on the Start menu. Or, if you have recently used the presentation, you can try the Start, Documents command, which lists the 15 most recently used files.

**METHOD**
To open an existing presentation:

- CLICK: Open button (📂), or
- CHOOSE: File, Open

**PRACTICE**
You will now open an existing file that addresses the topic of buying a personal computer.

*Setup:* Ensure that you've completed the previous lesson and that no presentations are displaying. Also, you should know the storage location for the student data files.

1. To display the Open dialog box:
CLICK: Open button ( )

2. Using the Places bar and the *Look in* drop-down list box, locate the folder containing the student data files. (*Note:* In this guide, we retrieve the student data files from a folder named "Student.")

3. To view additional information about each file:
CLICK: down arrow beside the Views button
CHOOSE: Details
Each presentation is presented on a single line with additional file information, such as its size, type, and date it was last modified, as shown in Figure 1.17.

**Figure 1.17**
Open dialog box in Details view

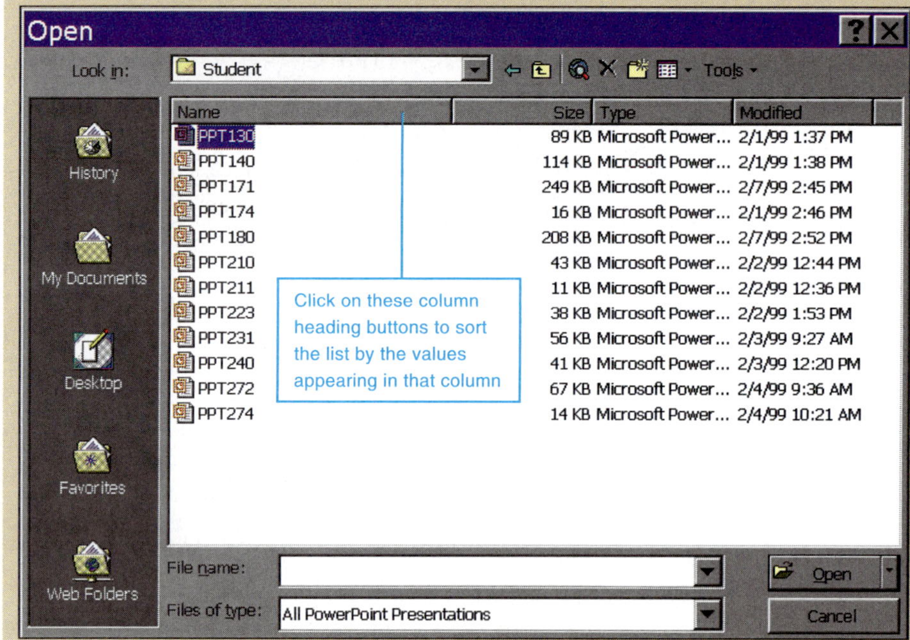


4. To alphabetically sort the list of files displayed in the Open dialog box:
CLICK: Name button in the column heading area

5. To sort the list by file size:
CLICK: Size button in the column heading area

6. To sort the list by when the file was last modified:
CLICK: Modified button

7. To return to a multicolumn list format:
CLICK: down arrow beside the Views button
CHOOSE: List

8. Let's open one of the presentations in the list area:
DOUBLE-CLICK: PPT130
The dialog box disappears and the presentation is loaded into the application window. (*Note:* The "PPT130" filename reflects that this presentation is used in module 1.3 of the PowerPoint learning guide.)

9. Close the presentation before proceeding.

**In Addition**
**Storing and Retrieving Files on Web Servers**

With the appropriate network connection, you can open and save PowerPoint presentations on the Internet. In the Open or Save As dialog boxes, click the Web Folders button () in the Places bar or select an FTP Internet site from the *Look in* drop-down list. This feature allows you to share and update PowerPoint presentations with users from around the world.

**1.3 Self Check** In the Save As dialog box, what is the Places bar used for?

# 1.4 Previewing and Printing

When you're satisfied with your presentation's appearance, you can send it to the printer. Most commonly, you will print a presentation for inclusion in a report or audience handout.

## 1.4.1 Previewing a Presentation in Black and White

**FEATURE**
Before printing to a noncolor printer, you may want to preview how your presentation's colors will convert to black, white, and shades of gray.

**METHOD**
CLICK: Grayscale Preview button () on the Standard toolbar

**PRACTICE**
You will now open a four-slide presentation and then preview it in black, white, and shades of gray.

*Setup:* Ensure that no presentations are open in the application window.

1. Open the PPT140 data file.

2. Before continuing, let's save the file using a new filename:
   CHOOSE: File, Save As
   TYPE: `Chili`

3. Using the *Save in* drop-down list box or the Places bar:
   SELECT: *your storage location*
   CLICK: Save command button

4. On your own, view the entire presentation using Slide Show view.

5. Let's preview the presentation using the Grayscale Preview button ().
   CLICK: Grayscale Preview button () on the Standard toolbar
   Figure 1.18 shows the first slide of your presentation using a selection of grayscales.

**Figure 1.18**
Grayscale preview

6. To redisplay the presentation in color:
   CLICK: Grayscale Preview button ()

## 1.4.2 Printing a Presentation

**FEATURE**
Whereas clicking the Print button () sends your presentation directly to the printer, choosing File, Print displays the Print dialog box for customizing one or more print options. For example, you can select what to print (audience handouts, notes pages, or your presentation's outline), whether you want to print your presentation using shades of gray or black and white, and how many copies to print.

**METHOD**
- To send a presentation directly to the printer:
  CLICK: Print button ()
- To customize one or more print settings:
  CHOOSE: File, Print

**PRACTICE**
You will now send a presentation to the printer.

*Setup:* Ensure that you've completed the previous lesson and that the "Chili" presentation is open in the application window.

1 Let's send the "Chili" presentation to the printer. Do the following:
CHOOSE: File, Print
The dialog box displayed in Figure 1.19 appears. (*Note:* The quickest method for sending the current presentation to the printer is to click the Print button () on the Standard toolbar.)

**Figure 1.19**
Print dialog box

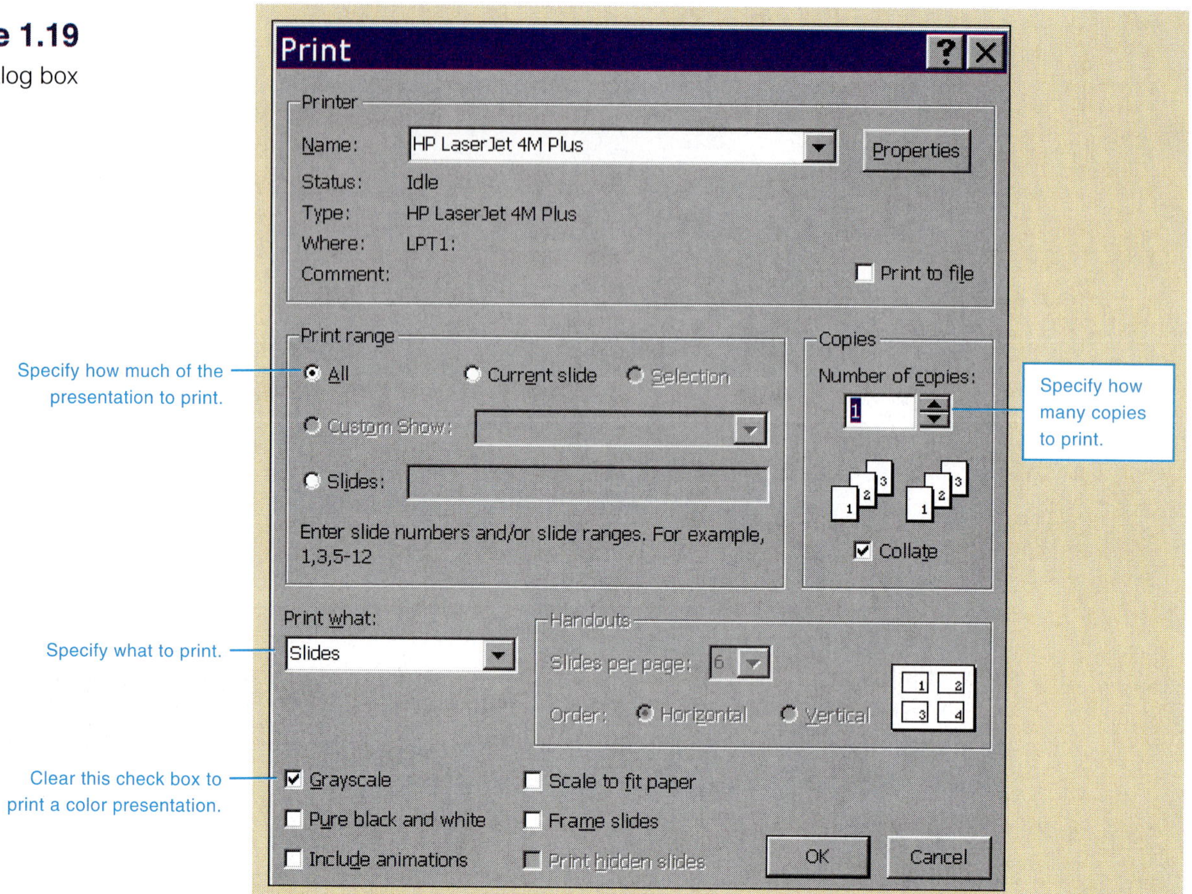


2. Note that "Slides" is the current selection in the *Print what* drop-down list. Let's see what the other options are:
CLICK: *Print what* drop-down arrow
Note the additional options of Handouts, Notes Pages, and Outline View.

3. To remove the drop-down list:
PRESS: ESC

4. If you do not have access to a printer, click the Cancel button. If you have a printer connected to your computer and want to print the presentation, do the following:
CLICK: OK command button
After a few moments, the presentation will appear at the printer.

5. Close the "Chili" presentation without saving the changes.

6. To exit Microsoft PowerPoint:
CHOOSE: File, Exit

# 1.5 Chapter Review

You have several options when starting a new presentation. For content and design suggestions, consider starting a presentation using the AutoContent Wizard. For design (and no content) suggestions, consider starting a presentation from a design template. You can also choose to begin a blank presentation, in which you ignore PowerPoint's content and design suggestions altogether.

To assist you in the way you work, PowerPoint lets you customize how you view a presentation. By default, a presentation appears in Normal view, which displays the Outline pane, Slide pane, and Notes pane. Other view modes include Outline, Slide, Slide Sorter, and Slide Show view.

After inserting a new slide, you can add text to it by clicking a text placeholder or by typing in the Outline pane. Besides creating presentations, it is important to know how to execute common file management procedures including saving, opening, and closing presentations. This chapter concluded with instructions on how to preview a presentation in black and white and how to print.



## 1.5.1 Command Summary

Many of the commands and procedures appearing in this chapter are summarized in the following table.

| Skill Set | To Perform This Task . . . | Do the Following . . . |
|---|---|---|
| **Creating a presentation** | Launch the AutoContent Wizard | CHOOSE: File, New<br>CLICK: *General* tab<br>DOUBLE-CLICK: AutoContent Wizard |
| | Choose a design template | CHOOSE: File, New<br>CLICK: *Design Templates* tab<br>DOUBLE-CLICK: a design template |
| | Begin a blank presentation | CLICK: New button (🗋) |
| | Insert slides | CLICK: New Slide button (▤)<br>DOUBLE-CLICK: an AutoLayout format |

*Continued*

| Skill Set | To Perform This Task . . . | Do the Following . . . |
|---|---|---|
| **Creating a presentation (*cont.*)** | Delete a selected slide | CHOOSE: Edit, Delete Slide |
| | Switch to Normal view | CHOOSE: View, Normal, or<br>CLICK: Normal View button () |
| | Switch to Slide Sorter view | CHOOSE: View, Slide Sorter, or<br>CLICK: Slide Sorter View button () |
| | Switch to Slide Show view | CHOOSE: View, Slide Show, or<br>CLICK: Slide Show View button () |
| | Switch to Outline view | CLICK: Outline View button () |
| | Switch to Slide view | CLICK: Slide View button () |
| **Working with Text** | Add text in Slide view | CLICK: in a text placeholder |
| | Add text in Outline view | CLICK: to the right of a slide icon in the Outline pane to type title text<br>PRESS: ENTER to insert a new slide or continue typing at the same level<br>PRESS: TAB to begin typing at a demoted (lower) level<br>PRESS: SHIFT + TAB to begin typing at a promoted (higher) level |
| **Managing Files** | Save a presentation | CLICK: Save button () |
| | Save as a new presentation | CHOOSE: File, Save As |
| | Close a presentation | CLICK: Close button (), or<br>CHOOSE: File, Close |
| | Open an existing presentation | CLICK: Open button (), or<br>CHOOSE: File, Open |

*Continued*

| Skill Set | To Perform This Task . . . | Do the Following . . . |
|---|---|---|
| **Creating Output** | Print a presentation | CLICK: Print button (), or CHOOSE: File, Print |
| | Print a color presentation | CHOOSE: File, Print and then make sure that the *Grayscale* and *Black and White* check boxes aren't selected |
| | Print slides in a variety of formats | CHOOSE: File, Print SELECT: an option from the *Print what* drop-down list |
| | Preview a presentation using grayscale colors | CLICK: Grayscale Preview button () |



## 1.5.2 Key Terms

This section specifies page references for the key terms identified in this chapter. For a complete list of definitions, refer to the Glossary provided immediately after the Appendix in this learning guide.

# 1.6 Review Questions

## 1.6.1 Short Answer

1. In Slide Show view, how do you proceed to the next slide?
2. Describe the procedure for inserting a new slide in a presentation.
3. How does starting a presentation from a design template differ from starting a presentation using the AutoContent Wizard?
4. How would you go about deleting the current slide?
5. What are the characteristics of Normal view?
6. What is an AutoLayout?
7. When opening a file, what is the History button used for?
8. What is the difference between choosing File, Print and clicking the Print button ( )?
9. What is the purpose of the PowerPoint's startup dialog box?
10. What happens when you click the New button ( )?

## 1.6.2 True/False

1. ____ In Normal view, the Outline pane is larger than the Slide pane.
2. ____ Placeholders are inserted on slides when you choose a slide layout.
3. ____ Clicking the New button ( ) starts a presentation from a design template.
4. ____ In Slide Sorter view, thumbnail representations of your presentation appear.
5. ____ To create a blank presentation, choose File, New.
6. ____ It is possible to change the layout of a slide.
7. ____ You can delete the current slide using the Menu bar or the Outline pane.
8. ____ PowerPoint's AutoFit feature automatically resizes placeholders to accommodate typed text.
9. ____ You can add text in both the Outline and Slide panes.
10. ____ To close a presentation, choose File, Exit from the Menu bar.

## 1.6.3 Multiple Choice

1. Which of the following provides the best environment for creating a presentation?
   a. Normal view
   b. Slide Sorter view
   c. Slide Show view
   d. Outline view

2. Which of the following enables you to exit Slide Show view?
   a. View, Exit
   b. File, Close
   c. File, Exit
   d. ESC

3. In Slide Show view, which of the following displays the previous slide?
   a. PgUp
   b. ←
   c. ↑
   d. All of the above

4. Which of the following provides design and content suggestions?
   a. design template
   b. AutoContent Wizard
   c. blank presentation
   d. Slide Show view

5. The New Slide dialog box provides:
   a. design suggestions
   b. AutoLayout options
   c. content suggestions
   d. All of the above

6. Which of the following marks the location of slide objects?
   a. HTML
   b. placeholders
   c. hyperlinks
   d. fonts

7. Which of the following must you choose when you insert a new slide?
   a. AutoContent Wizard
   b. AutoLayout option
   c. AutoFormat option
   d. None of the above

8. In Normal view, which of the following panes would you use to type in reminder notes?
   a. Slide pane
   b. Outline pane
   c. Notes pane
   d. None of the above

9. The Places bar is useful when ____________.
   a. saving and opening
   b. formatting text
   c. inserting slides
   d. All of the above

10. In ____________, your presentation displays with transitions and special effects.
    a. Slide view
    b. Outline view
    c. Normal view
    d. Slide Show view

# 1.7 Hands-On Projects

## 1.7.1 Outdoor Adventure Tours: Company Profile

This exercise practices opening an existing presentation and saving it to a new location, viewing the presentation using the Menu bar and View buttons, editing text, and deleting a slide.

1. Open the PPT171 presentation.
2. Save the presentation as "Outdoor" to your personal storage location. (*Hint:* Choose File, Save As.)
3. To view the presentation in Slide Sorter view:
   CHOOSE: View, Slide Sorter
4. To view the presentation in Slide Show view:
   CHOOSE: View, Slide Show
   CLICK: the left mouse button to advance through the entire presentation
5. To view the presentation in Normal view:
   CLICK: Normal View button (▣) located near the bottom-left corner of the application window

6. CLICK: Previous Slide button (▲) on the vertical scroll bar until slide 1 appears in the Slide pane
7. Using the Outline pane, let's change the text from "Go Wild!" to "Join us on the Wild Side!"
   SELECT: the text "Go Wild!" on the first slide
   TYPE: **Join us on the Wild Side!**
8. Using the Slide pane, let's edit the text on the second slide.
   CLICK: Next Slide button (▼) to display slide 2
   SELECT: the word "adventure" in the first bulleted point
   TYPE: **outdoor**
   The item should now read "Specialists in outdoor vacations."
9. Let's delete the slide entitled "Special Group Rates."
   CLICK: Next Slide button (▼) on the vertical scroll bar until the fifth slide appears
   CHOOSE: Edit, Delete Slide
10. Save the revised presentation and then print the presentation.
11. Close the "Outdoor" presentation.



## 1.7.2 Monashee Community College: Open House

In this exercise, you create a new presentation from a design template and add new slides.

1. To start a new presentation based on the "Artsy" design template, do the following:
   CHOOSE: File, New command
   CLICK: *Design Templates* tab
   DOUBLE-CLICK: Artsy template
   (*Note:* Select another suitable design template if "Artsy" isn't available).
2. Select the Title Slide layout for the first slide.
3. Let's add text to the slide.
   TYPE: **Computer Open House** in the title placeholder
   TYPE: **Monashee Community College** in the subtitle placeholder
4. To insert a new slide with a Bulleted List layout:
   CLICK: New Slide button (▣) on the Standard toolbar
   SELECT: Bulleted List in the New Slide dialog box
   CLICK: OK command button
5. To insert a title on the second slide:
   TYPE: **When?** in the title placeholder

6. Type the following text in the bulleted list:
   **8:00 am – 6:00 pm**
   **Saturday, September 18, 1999**
7. Insert another new slide with a Bulleted List layout and then type **Where?** in the title placeholder.
8. Type the following text in the bulleted list:
   **Monashee Community College**
   **100 College Way**
   **Spokane, Washington**
9. Insert another new slide with a Bulleted List layout and then type **Why?** in the title placeholder.
10. Type the following text in the bulleted list:
    **Visit our new Computer Labs**
    **Hourly information sessions**
    **Computer course registration**
    **Free refreshments**
11. Save the presentation as "Monashee Open House" to your personal storage location.

## 1.7.3 Coldstream Corporation: Marketing Overview

In this exercise, you create a new presentation using the AutoContent Wizard, edit existing text, insert and delete slides, and switch views.

1. Launch the AutoContent Wizard using the File, New command.
2. Select the "Selecting a Product or Service" presentation from the "Sales/Marketing" category.
3. Select "On-screen presentation" as the output option.
4. Type **Coldstream Corporation** in the *Presentation title* text box.
5. Insert **Arena Proposal** in the *Footer* text box and then click the Finish command button to compile the presentation.
6. Edit the subtitle placeholder on the first slide to include the text **Prepared by:** followed by ***your name***.
7. Delete slides 4 and 6.
8. Insert a slide that uses the Bulleted List layout after slide 2. (*Hint:* Display slide 2 in the Slide pane before inserting the slide.)

9. Edit the new slide by typing **New Ways to Promote Business** in the Title placeholder and **Web-based services**, **Local advertising**, and **Door-to-door sales** as bulleted items in the bulleted list placeholder.
10. Display the presentation in Slide Sorter view.
11. Save the presentation as "Coldstream Marketing" to your personal storage location.
12. Close the presentation.

## 1.7.4 Spiderman Web Marketing: Promotion

You will now open a previously created presentation and then edit, preview, and print the presentation.

1. Open the PPT174 presentation.
2. Save the presentation as "Spiderman" to your personal storage location.
3. Insert the text **Selling Your Product on the World Wide Web** in the subtitle placeholder of the first slide.
4. Insert a new slide that uses the Bulleted List layout after the first slide. Type **Who Uses the WWW?** in the title placeholder and the following text in the bulleted list:
   **Gender**
   **Age**
   **Education**
   **Nationality**
5. After the third slide, add a new slide with a bulleted list layout. Enter **Further Benefits** in the title placeholder. Type the following text in the bulleted list:
   **Easily updated**
   **Customer interaction**
   **Text, color, movement, sounds and music**
   **Online transactions**
6. Preview the presentation in shades of gray and then redisplay the presentation in color.
7. Save the revised presentation.
8. Print and then close the presentation.

POWERPOINT

### 1.7.5 On Your Own: Hobby

Using one of PowerPoint's design templates, create a new PowerPoint presentation on a topic or hobby that interests you. Your presentation should consist of one Title Slide followed by three Bulleted List Slides. The first slide should include the name of your hobby and your name. Suggestions for the following slides are (a) Why do I like my hobby?, (b) How to do my hobby, and (c) What does my hobby involve? Save your presentation as "Hobby" to your personal storage location.

### 1.7.6 On Your Own: Vacation

Create a presentation that tries to convince your audience (a relative, business associate, or other individual) why you need a vacation. Use your experience with PowerPoint to make the most compelling case possible. When you're finished, save the presentation as "Vacation" to your personal storage location and then print the presentation.

## 1.8 Case Problems: Tristar Development

After completing Chapter 1, Tina is eager to view her nephew's presentation and provide him with some feedback. Then she will edit the presentation and add several new slides. Finally, she will create a new presentation for her client, *Union Pipeline Limited.*

In the following case problems, assume the role of Tina and perform the same steps that she identifies. You may want to re-read the chapter opening before proceeding.

1. Tina opens her nephew's PowerPoint presentation entitled PPT180. She saves the presentation as "Budgies" to her personal storage location. Tina first uses the Slide Sorter view to preview Kenyon's presentation. Amazed at her quick progress in PowerPoint, she practices using the Normal, Outline, and Slide views. Tina chuckles at the animations while using the Slide Show view. After closing the presentation, she is ready to respond to Kenyon's e-mail by answering the questions in his "Budgie Test." Tina closes the presentation and sends Kenyon the following e-mail:
   *Dear Kenyon, I love your presentation! I learned a lot about budgies and here are my answers for your "Budgie Test".*

2. Tina decides to use Kenyon's presentation for practice with adding and modifying slides. She first saves a copy of Kenyon's presentation as "Kenyon" to her personal storage location. After the first slide, Tina adds a new slide with a Title Slide layout. She enters **Approved by Tina Pusch** in the title placeholder, **Public Relations Coordinator** on the first line of the subtitle placeholder, and **Tristar Development** on the second line. Tina then saves the revised presentation.

3. Tina continues working on the "Kenyon" presentation, changing the appearance of text and bullets. She adds a new slide before the final slide of the presentation. Using the Bulleted List layout, she types **Keep your Budgie away from:** in the title placeholder. In the bulleted list placeholder she types the following text:

   - **Hungry cats**
   - **Open windows**
   - **Hot stoves**
   - **Curious alligators!**

   Tina saves the revised presentation as "Kenyon Update" to her personal storage location and then prints and closes the presentation.

4. With an afternoon deadline quickly approaching, Tina begins working on a PowerPoint presentation for her client, *Union Pipeline Limited*. Using the AutoContent Wizard, she selects "Reporting Progress or Status" from the "Projects" category. She adds **Union Pipeline Limited** to the title placeholder. She then selects any existing text in the subtitle placeholder and types **Jonathon C. Union President and CEO**.

As Tina previews the Union Pipeline presentation in Normal and Slide Show views, she receives an important telephone call from Mr. Jonathon Union, the president of the company. He requests that she print an outline of the presentation and then fax it to him. Tina assures Mr. Union that she can immediately complete his request. After hanging up the telephone, Tina chooses File, Print and then selects Outline View from the *Print what* drop-down list. Relieved that she has completed her required tasks, she saves the presentation as "Union Status" before exiting PowerPoint.

# Notes

# Notes

# Notes

# Notes

MICROSOFT POWERPOINT 2000

*Developing a Presentation*

# CHAPTER TWO

## Chapter Outline



## Learning Objectives

After reading this chapter, you will be able to:

- Insert slides from other presentations and change slide order
- Apply different slide layouts and design templates
- Insert clip art, pictures, graphs, and organization charts
- Start and run slide shows

Case Study

## Snowmelt Hydrology Research

Natasha Newman is a graduate student who is preparing to defend her master's thesis. Her topic, Snowmelt Hydrology Research, involves data that she has collected from the Arctic region. Natasha has experience creating text-based presentations, but would like to present her data in a more interesting format using graphs, organization charts, and photographs.

In this chapter, you and Natasha learn how to change a presentation to meet your needs, embellish a presentation with graphs, organization charts, and pictures, and deliver online presentations.

# 2.1 Managing Existing Slides



Instead of reinventing the wheel each time you need to create a presentation, PowerPoint makes it easy to reuse slides that you've created previously. Although you can copy and paste slides in Slide Sorter view, the more efficient method involves using the Slide Finder tool. In the following lessons, we describe how to use the Slide Finder tool and how to reorder slides.

## 2.1.1 Inserting Slides from Other Presentations

**FEATURE**

The **Slide Finder** tool shows the contents of presentations using slide snapshots. You then select the slides you want to insert in your presentation.

**METHOD**

1. CHOOSE: Insert, Slides From Files
2. CLICK: Browse button and then locate the presentation you want to insert slides from
3. DOUBLE-CLICK: the presentation you located in the previous step
   CLICK: Display
4. SELECT: one or more slides by clicking them
5. CLICK: Insert to insert a selection of slides, or
   CLICK: Insert All to insert all of a presentation's slides

**PRACTICE**

You will now open an existing presentation and then add slides to it from another presentation.

*Setup:* Ensure that no presentations are open in the application window.

1. Open the PPT210 presentation.

2. Before continuing, save the presentation as "Wireless" to your personal storage location. This presentation contains two slides.

3. In the next few steps, you're going to insert slides from another presentation in the "Wireless" presentation. New slides are inserted after the current slide. Let's add a new slide after the second slide in the presentation. To view the second slide:
   CLICK: Next Slide ( ) on the vertical scroll bar
   The inserted slides will now be inserted after the second slide.

4. To insert slides from the PPT211 presentation in the current presentation:
   CHOOSE: Insert, Slides From Files
   The Slide Finder dialog box should now appear, as shown in Figure 2.1.

**Figure 2.1**
Slide Finder dialog box

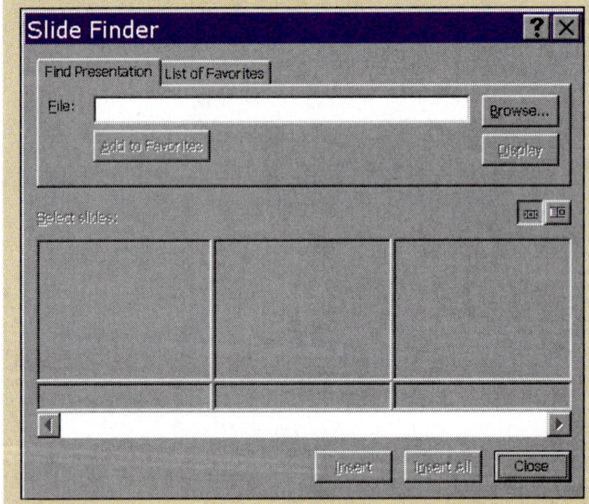


5. To locate the PPT211 student file:
   CLICK: Browse command button

6. Use the *Look in* drop-down list or the Places bar to locate the PPT211 file.

7 DOUBLE-CLICK: PPT211 file
CLICK: Display command button to reveal the slides in the Slide Finder dialog box
Your screen should now appear similar to Figure 2.2.

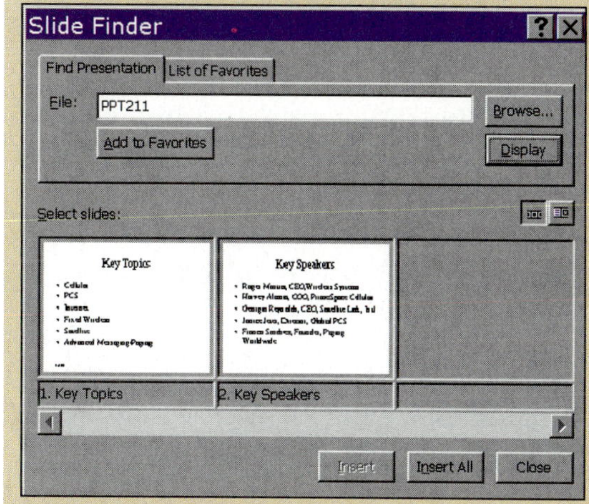


**Figure 2.2**
Displaying slides in the Slide Finder dialog box

8 To insert the entire PPT211 presentation:
CLICK: Insert All command button

9 To close the Slide Finder dialog box:
CLICK: Close command button
The presentation now contains four slides. Note that the inserted slides adopted the same design as the first two slides.

10 Save the revised presentation.

## 2.1.2 Changing Slide Order

**FEATURE**
Once inserted in a presentation, it's easy to reorder slides in both the Outline pane and in Slide Sorter view. At the heart of the operation is a simple drag and drop.

**METHOD**
- To reorder slides in the Outline pane:
  DRAG: slide icon up or down to a new location
- To reorder slides in Slide Sorter view:
  DRAG: a slide to a new location

**PRACTICE**
You will now practice reordering slides.

*Setup:* Ensure that you've completed the previous lesson and that the "Wireless" presentation is displaying in Normal view.

1. Using the Outline pane, let's move slide 4 so that it is positioned before slide 3. To begin, locate the slide 4 icon in the Outline pane.

2. Let's see what happens when we click the slide 4 icon.
CLICK: slide 4 icon
Note that the slide's title and bulleted items are selected.

3. Your current objective is to drag the slide 4 icon upward in the Outline pane so that it is positioned above slide 3. As you drag the icon, the slide's title and bulleted items will move with it. A narrow horizontal bar will mark where the slide will be inserted when you release the mouse button.
DRAG: the slide 4 icon upward until the horizontal bar is one line above the slide 3 icon and title (Key Topics)
Your screen should now appear similar to Figure 2.3.

**Figure 2.3**

Reordering slides in the Outline pane

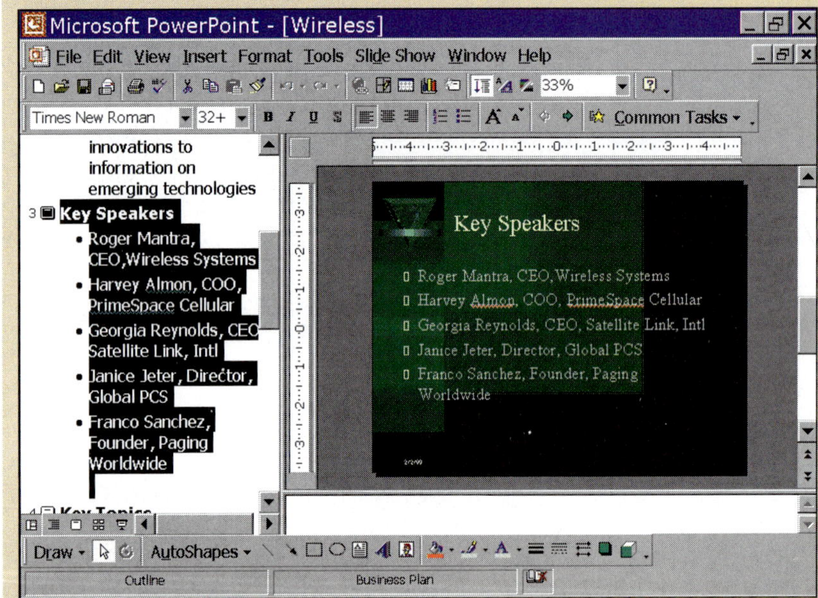


4. Now, let's practice changing slide order in Slide Sorter view. To begin:
CHOOSE: View, Slide Sorter

5 As you drag a slide in Slide Sorter view, a narrow vertical bar will mark where the slide will be inserted when you release the mouse button.
DRAG: the slide 3 thumbnail to the right of slide 4
The presentation has now been returned to its original order.

6 Save and then close the "Wireless" presentation.

**2.1 Self Check** What is the the Slide Finder tool used for?

# 2.2 Changing Slide Layout and Design



The look of your presentation is determined by several factors including the current design template and slide layouts. In this module, we explore procedures for changing the layout and design of your presentations to suit your specific requirements and preferences.

## 2.2.1 Applying a Different Layout

**FEATURE**
You may find that an existing slide layout doesn't meet your needs. For example, in addition to your bulleted list placeholder, you may decide that you need a graph placeholder. In this case, you will want to change the existing slide layout to meet your new requirements.

**METHOD**
1. CHOOSE: Format, Slide Layout
2. DOUBLE-CLICK: an AutoLayout format

**PRACTICE**
You will now begin a presentation for a class project on current trends in technology. In the process you will practice changing slide layouts.

*Setup:* Ensure that no presentations are open in the application window.

1 To create a new presentation:
CHOOSE: File, New

2 To select a design template:
CLICK: *Design Templates* tab
DOUBLE-CLICK: Technology

3. In the New Slide dialog box, the Title Slide layout is already selected. To accept this selection:
CLICK: OK command button

4. To insert text in the title placeholder:
CLICK: the title placeholder
TYPE: **CURRENT TRENDS**

5. To insert text in the subtitle placeholder:
CLICK: the subtitle placeholder
TYPE: **By**
PRESS: ENTER
TYPE: ***Your Name***
Your screen should now appear similar to Figure 2.4.

**Figure 2.4**
This slide uses the Title Slide layout

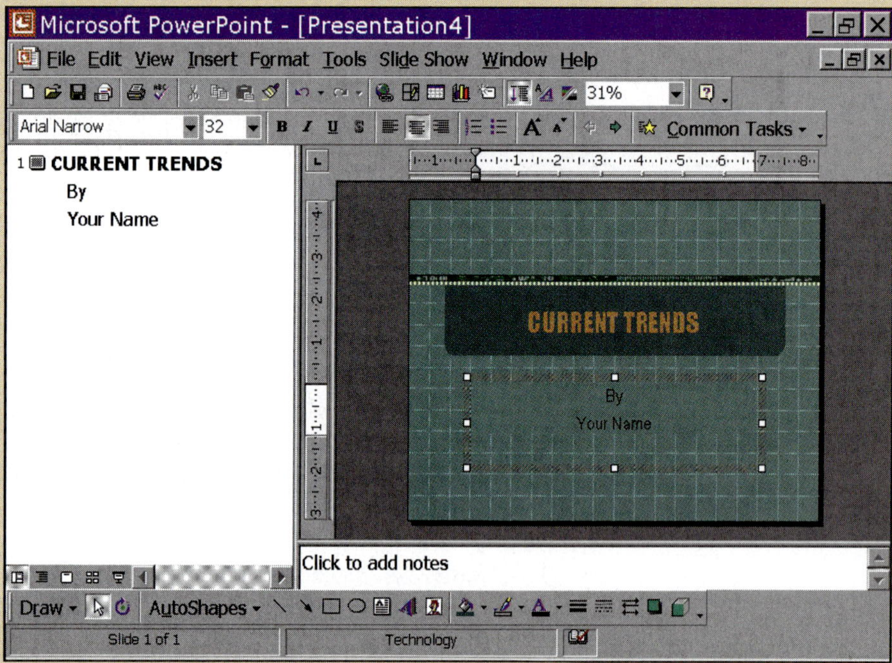


6. Let's add a second slide to the presentation.
CLICK: New Slide button ( ) on the Standard toolbar

7. SELECT: Text & Chart (located in the second row, first column)
CLICK: OK command button
The inserted slide now includes placeholders for a title, bulleted list, and graph.

8. To add a title to the slide:
CLICK: title placeholder
TYPE: **The Leading Trends**

9. To add content to the slide:
CLICK: bulleted list placeholder (located on the left side of the slide)
TYPE: **Connectivity**
PRESS: ENTER
TYPE: **Interactivity**
PRESS: ENTER
TYPE: **Online Access**
Your screen should now appear similar to Figure 2.5.

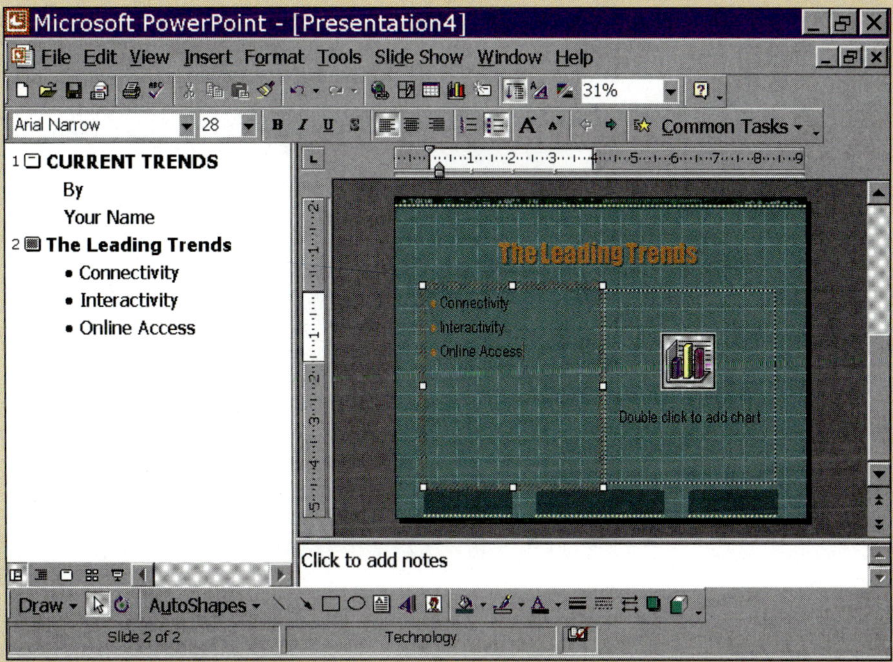


**Figure 2.5**
This slide uses the Text & Chart layout

10. To change the layout of the second slide from the "Text & Chart" layout to the Bulleted List layout:
CHOOSE: Format, Slide Layout
CLICK: Bulleted List layout (located in the first row, second column)
CLICK: Apply command button
The slide was changed to conform to the Bulleted List layout. The text in the bulleted list appears larger and the graph placeholder no longer appears.

11. Save the presentation as "Current Trends" to your personal storage location.

## 2.2.2 Modifying an Existing Layout

**FEATURE**

Just about anything you place on a slide, such as text, a table, clip art, a graph, or a movie, is an *object*. As described in Chapter 1, *placeholders* mark the location of slide objects and provide instructions for editing them. When you choose a layout for a new or existing slide, PowerPoint inserts an arranged group of placeholders on the slide. You can move, resize, and delete object placeholders to suit your needs.

**METHOD**

- Select an object by positioning the mouse pointer over the object's placeholder until a four-headed arrow (✥) appears and then click.
- Move a selected object by dragging.
- Resize a selected object by dragging its sizing handles.
- Delete a selected object by pressing DELETE.

**PRACTICE**

You will now practice editing slide objects.

*Setup:* Ensure that you've completed the previous lesson in this module and that slide 2 in the "Current Trends" presentation is displaying in the application window.

1. Visually, the bulleted items are positioned too close to the left edge of the slide. Let's practice resizing the bulleted list placeholder and moving it to the right. To select the placeholder:
CLICK: in the bulleted list placeholder, near one of the bulleted items
The object should be surrounded with **sizing handles** (tiny boxes surrounding the object).

2. When you position the mouse pointer over a sizing handle, the pointer will change to a double-headed arrow. To resize the placeholder:
DRAG: the sizing handle in the bottom-right corner inward about two inches
(*Hint:* Use the slide ruler as your guide.)

3. To move the placeholder to the right, position the mouse pointer over one of the placeholder borders until a four-headed arrow (✥) appears.

4. DRAG: the placeholder to the right about 1.5 inches
Your screen should now appear similar to Figure 2.6.

**Figure 2.6**
The bulleted list placeholder was resized and moved

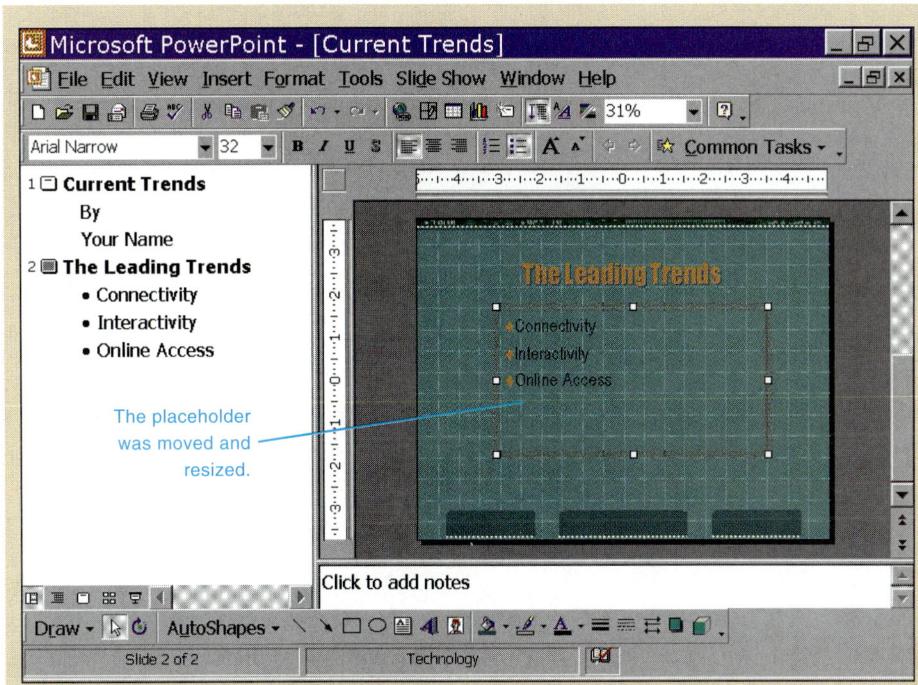


5 The placeholder should still be selected. To practice deleting the placeholder:
PRESS: DELETE
The contents of the placeholder are now deleted. To delete the placeholder itself:
PRESS: DELETE again

6 To undo the two previous deletions:
PRESS: the curved part of the Undo button (↶) twice

7 Save the revised presentation.

## 2.2.3 Changing an Existing Design Template

**FEATURE**
You learned how to create a new presentation from a design template in Chapter 1. Design templates determine what colors and text fonts are used in a presentation and the position of placeholders and other objects. By applying a design template to your presentation, you help give your presentation's slides a consistent look. You can apply one of PowerPoint's preset design templates or apply a design template from an existing presentation.

**METHOD**

- To apply one of PowerPoint's preset design templates:
  CHOOSE: Format, Apply Design Template
  DOUBLE-CLICK: a design template
- To apply a design template from an existing presentation:
  CHOOSE: Format, Apply Design Template
  CHOOSE: Presentations and Shows from the *Files of type* drop-down list
  DOUBLE-CLICK: a presentation file

**PRACTICE**

You will now practice applying design templates.

*Setup:* Ensure that you've completed the previous lessons in this module and that the "Current Trends" presentation is open.

1. Let's apply a design template to this presentation from a presentation named PPT223. To begin:
   CHOOSE: Format, Apply Design Template
   The contents of the Presentation Designs folder on your hard disk should appear, listing the design templates provided by PowerPoint.

2. To select a presentation file, rather than one of PowerPoint's template files:
   CHOOSE: Presentations and Shows from the *Files of type* drop-down list

3. Using the *Look in* drop-down list or the Places bar, navigate to where your student files are stored.

4. DOUBLE-CLICK: PPT223
   The design template used in the PPT223 presentation has now been applied to the current presentation. Your screen should now appear similar to Figure 2.7.

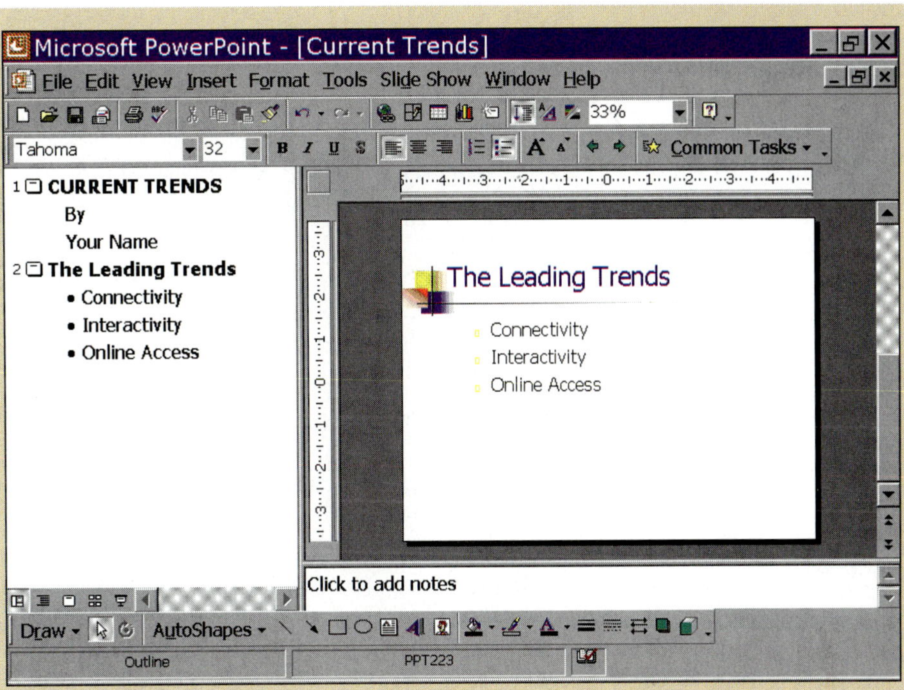


**Figure 2.7**
This design template was applied from the PPT223 presentation

5. Now, let's apply one of PowerPoint's design templates to the presentation.
   CHOOSE: Format, Apply Design Template

6. The templates in the Presentation Designs folder should be listed in the dialog box.
   DOUBLE-CLICK: Factory
   PowerPoint's "Factory" design template was applied to the presentation.

7. Save and then close the presentation.

**2.2 Self Check** What is the procedure for moving and resizing object placeholders?

# 2.3 Inserting Graphics Objects

A picture is worth a thousand words! Although this phrase is overused, its truth is undeniable. Graphics add personality to your presentations and often convey information more efficiently than text alone. In this module, you learn how to embellish your presentations with clip art and pictures, graphs, and organization charts.

## 2.3.1 Inserting Clip Art

**FEATURE**

The **Microsoft Clip Gallery** provides access to numerous images for inclusion in your presentations. **Clip art images** are computer graphics or pictures that you can insert into your documents, usually without having to pay royalties or licensing fees to the artist or designer. To make it easier for you to find that perfect image for conveying your message, clips are organized by category and you can search for clips based on typed keywords.

**METHOD**

Several methods exist for opening the Clip Gallery:

- DOUBLE-CLICK: a clip art placeholder, or
- CLICK: Insert Clip Art button (🖼) on the Drawing toolbar, or
- CHOOSE: Insert, Picture, Clip Art, or
- CHOOSE: Insert, Object and then double-click Microsoft Clip Gallery

To insert a clip:

1. CLICK: the clip you want to insert
2. CLICK: Insert clip button (🖼) on the shortcut menu

**PRACTICE**

You will now open a short presentation that currently contains three slides. Your objective is to locate clips for slides 1 and 3 of the presentation.

*Setup:* Ensure that no presentations are open in the application window.

1 Open the PPT231 data file.

2 Save the presentation as "PC Seminar" to your personal storage location.

3 In the remainder of this module, you won't be using the Outline pane. Therefore, to increase the size of the slide for more convenient editing, do the following:
CLICK: Slide view button (▭) at the bottom of the Outline pane
Your screen should now appear similar to Figure 2.8. A computer-related graphic would greatly enhance this first slide. Let's use the Clip Gallery to locate an image.

**Figure 2.8**
"PC Seminar" presentation

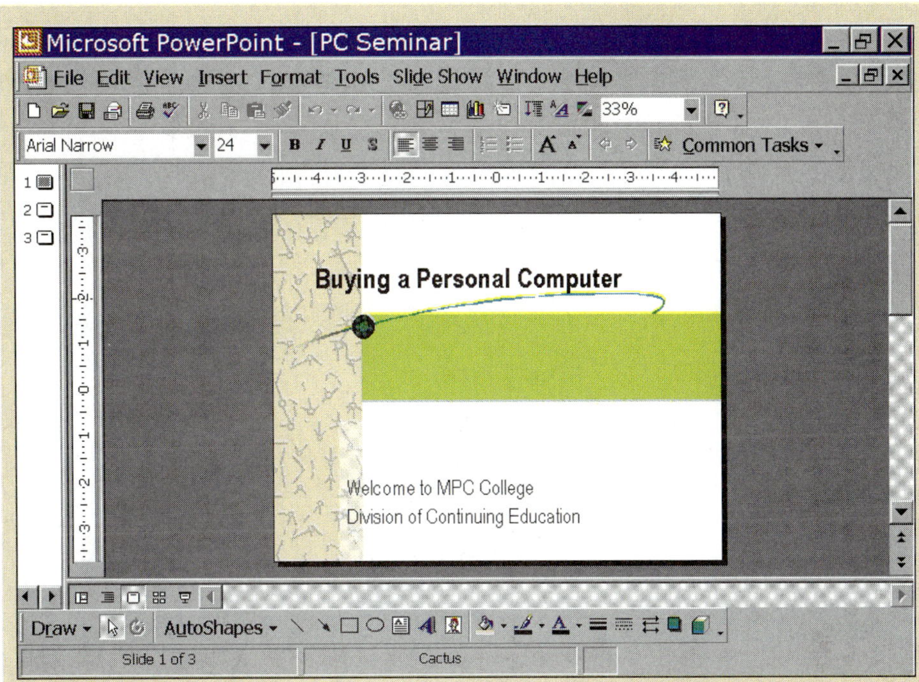


4 To locate an image clip for the first slide:
CHOOSE: Insert, Picture, Clip Art
The Insert ClipArt window should now appear.

5 To maximize the Insert ClipArt window
CLICK: the window's Maximize button (□)
Your screen should now appear similar to Figure 2.9.

**Figure 2.9**
Maximized Insert ClipArt window

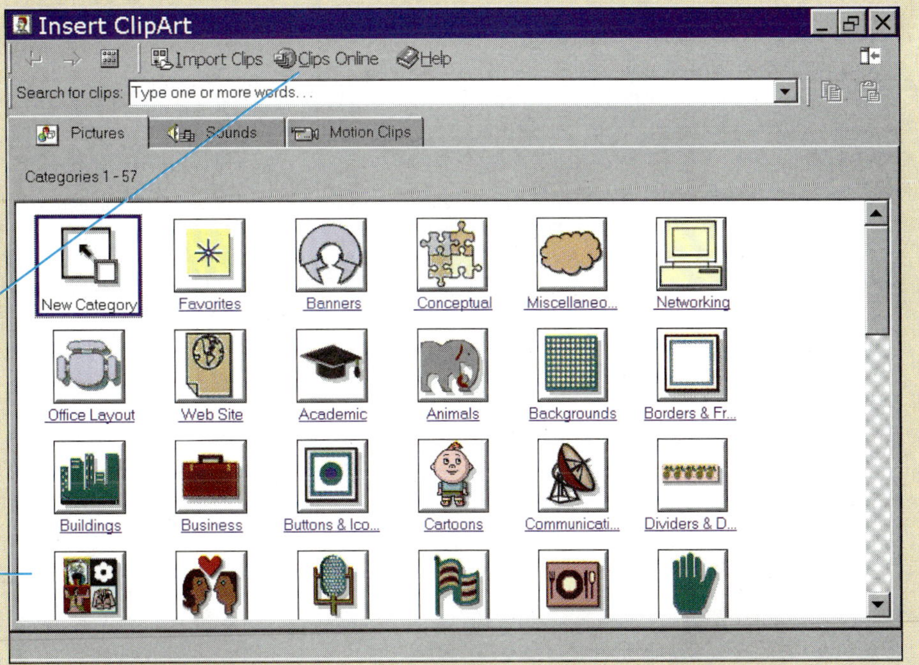

6 All the underlined words and phrases represent clip art categories. To display the contents of a category, you simply click the category name. To illustrate:
CLICK: Animals category
Your screen should now appear similar to Figure 2.10. (*Note:* Alternate clips may be available on your computer.)

**Figure 2.10**
Animals ClipArt category

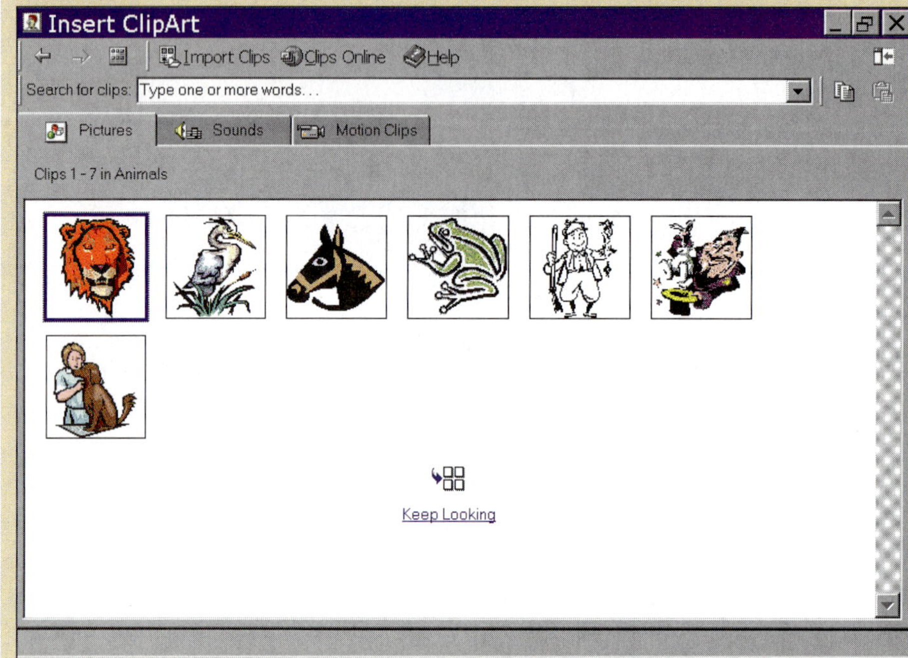


7 To return to the previous list of categories:
CLICK: Back button ( ) on the toolbar

8 Let's locate a computer-related image based on a typed keyword.
CLICK: in the *Search for clips* text box
The existing text should be selected.
TYPE: **computer**
PRESS: ENTER
Your screen should now appear similar to Figure 2.11.

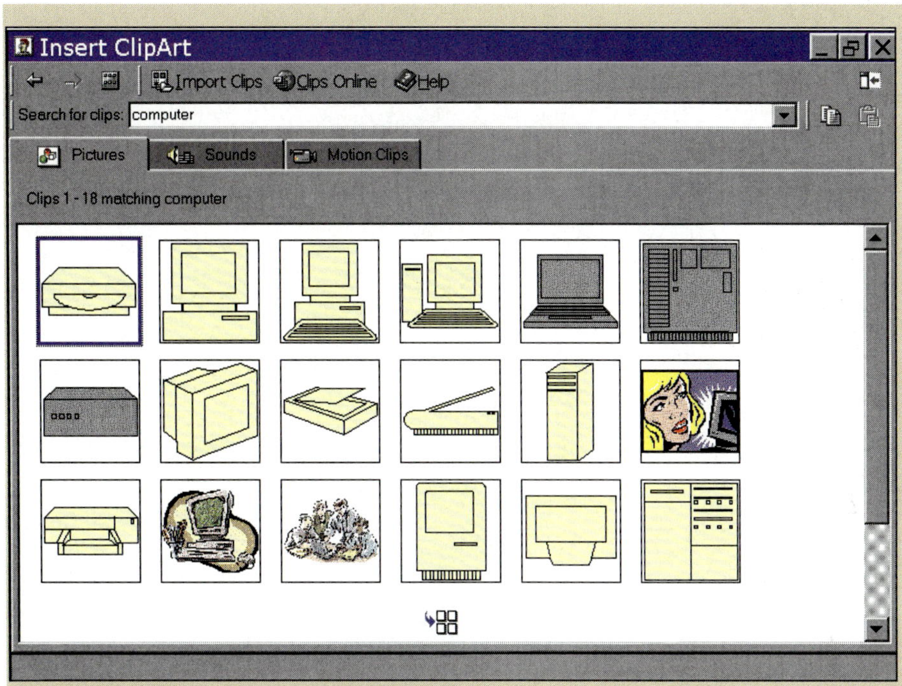


**Figure 2.11**
Search results for computer-related image clips

9 Practice pointing with the mouse at the different clips in the Clip Gallery window. Note that for each clip a yellow pop-up description appears detailing the name, dimension, and file type of the image.

10 When you click an image, a pop-up menu will appear. To illustrate:
CLICK: "computers" graphic (shown below)
The clip art image and associated pop-up menu appear below:

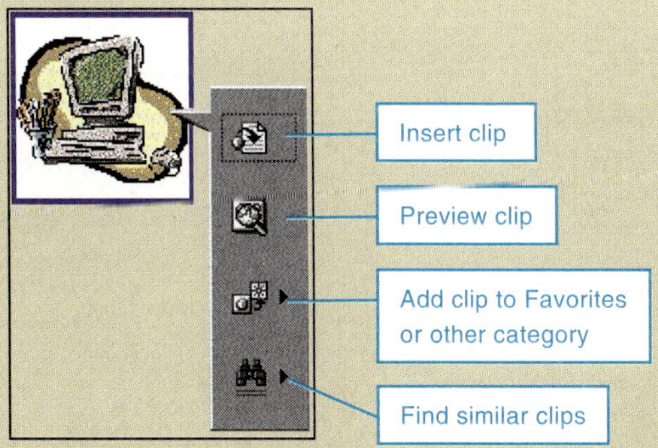


11 To insert the clip:
CLICK: Insert clip button ()
Although the clip was inserted in your presentation, you won't be able to see it until you minimize or close the Insert ClipArt dialog box.

12 To close the dialog box:
CLICK: the window's Close button (☒)
Your screen should now appear similar to Figure 2.12. Notice that the Picture toolbar appears for changing the characteristics of the selected image.

**Figure 2.12**
Inserting a clip art image

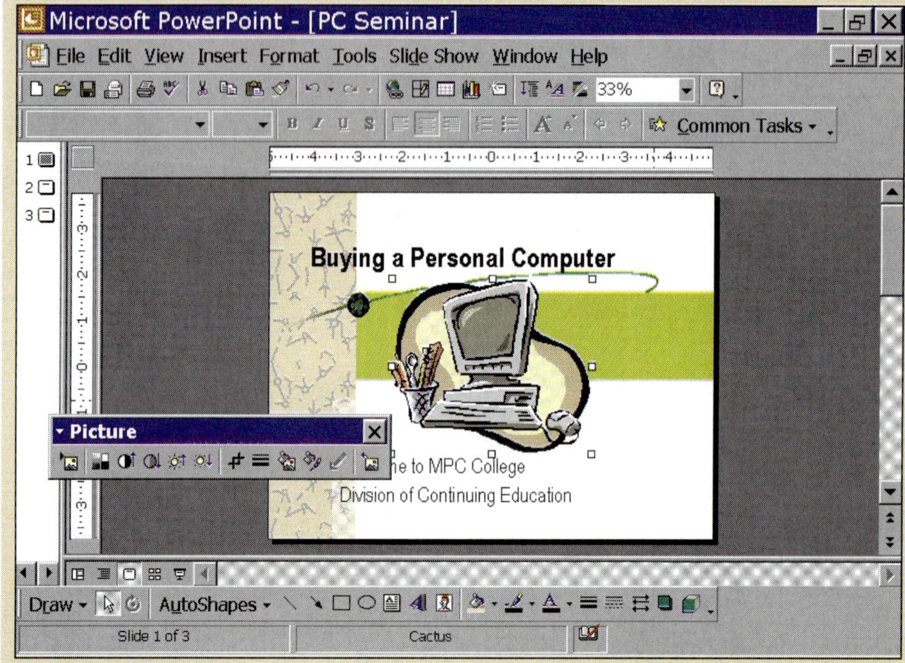


13 Since we're not going to use the Picture toolbar in this module, let's close it.
CLICK: the Picture toolbar's Close button (☒)
After you insert clip art and other graphics objects, you will often need to move, resize, or otherwise format them to fit the specific needs of your document. The methods for moving and resizing graphics objects are the same as for manipulating placeholders, a topic we discussed earlier in lesson 2.2.2. Since the graphic is somewhat large, you resize the image in the next step.

14 Resize and move the image so that your screen appears similar to Figure 2.13.

**Figure 2.13**

Moving and resizing a clip art image

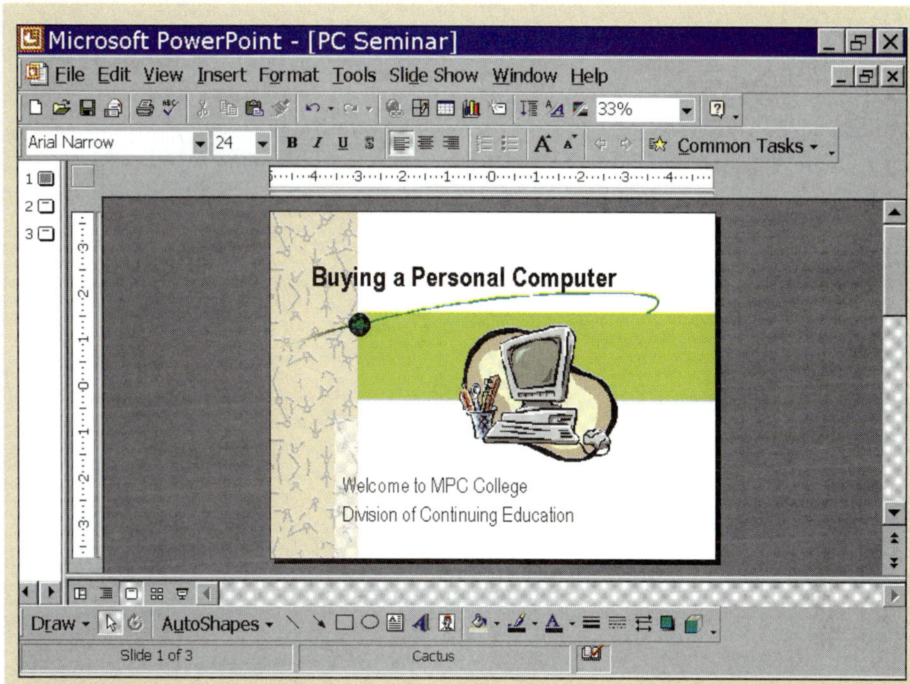


**15** Let's insert another image on slide 3 of this presentation, but this time let's use the clip art placeholder. To display slide 3:
PRESS: Next Slide button (▾) twice

**16** To insert an image on this slide:
DOUBLE-CLICK: clip art placeholder

**17** On your own, search for the clip pictured in Figure 2.14 and then insert it on the slide. (*Note:* If the clip pictured in Figure 2.14 isn't available, search for an alternate clip.) Move and resize the image as necessary.

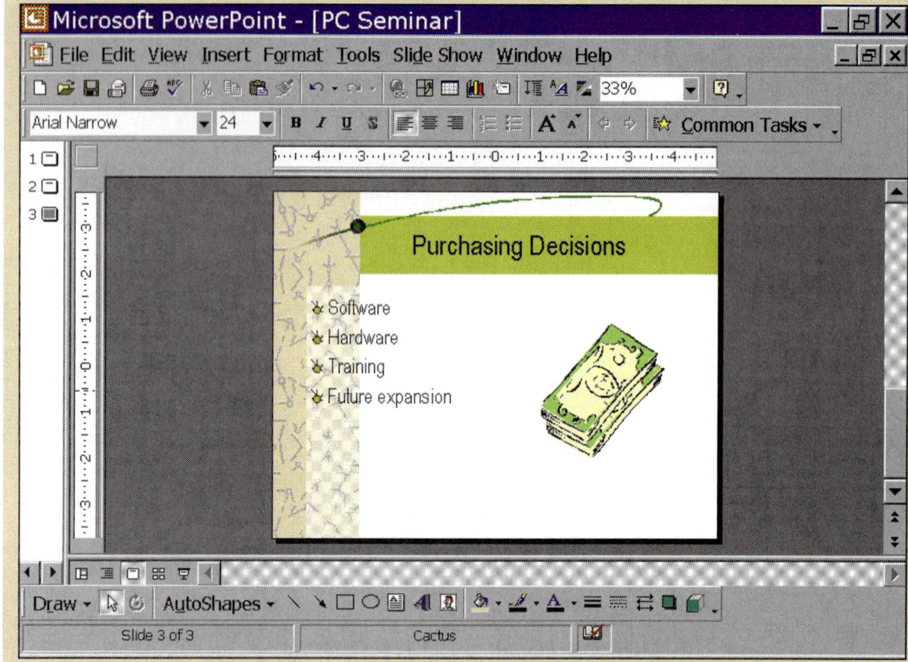


**Figure 2.14**
Using the clip art placeholder

18 To select an alternate clip image for the current slide, do the following:
SELECT: the clip image
PRESS: DELETE
DOUBLE-CLICK: the clip art placeholder

19 On your own, search for an alternate clip for the current slide. Move and resize the image as necessary.

20 Save and then close the revised presentation.

## 2.3.2 Inserting Pictures

**FEATURE**

In PowerPoint, you can embellish your presentations with images from a variety of sources. To insert a picture from a file, choose Insert, Picture, From File from the menu and then double-click the file you want to insert.

**METHOD**

1. CHOOSE: Insert, Picture, From File
2. SELECT: the desired disk drive and filename
   CLICK: OK command button

**PRACTICE**
You will now practice inserting a picture object from a file.

*Setup:* Ensure that no presentations are open in the application window.

1 To begin a blank presentation:
CLICK: New button (□)
The New Slide dialog box appears.

2 DOUBLE-CLICK: Title Only layout (located in the third row, third column)

3 To increase the size of the slide for convenient editing:
CLICK: Slide view button (□) at the bottom of the Outline pane

4 CLICK: the title placeholder
TYPE: **Two Boys**

5 To insert a photograph named PPT232 from the student files location:
CHOOSE: Insert, Picture, From File
SELECT: *the location of your student files*
SELECT: PPT232 from the list box
CLICK: Insert command button
The picture is inserted on the slide and appears selected. Also, the Picture toolbar appears.

6 Move and resize the picture so that the slide appears similar to Figure 2.15. (*Note:* If the Picture toolbar is displaying, click its Close button (☒).)

**Figure 2.15**

Inserting a picture from a file

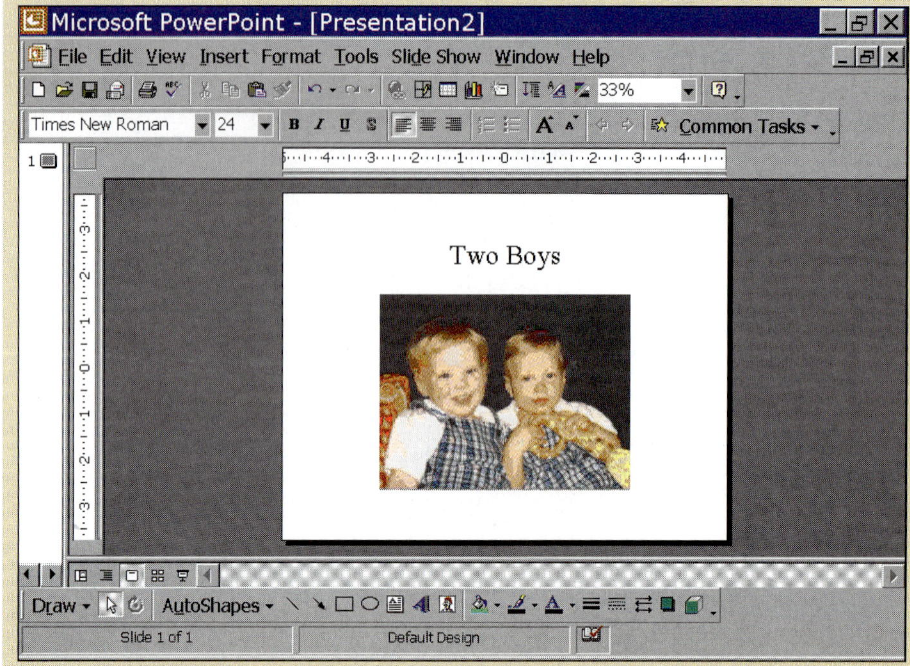


7. Save the presentation as "Two Boys" to your personal storage location.

8. Close the presentation.

## 2.3.3 Inserting Graphs

**FEATURE**

The **Microsoft Graph** mini-app helps you produce great-looking charts and graphs right from within PowerPoint! Graph does not replace a full-featured spreadsheet application like Microsoft Excel, but it does provide a more convenient tool for embedding simple charts into presentations.

**METHOD**

The following methods can be used to launch Microsoft Graph:

- CLICK: Insert Chart button ( ) on the Standard toolbar, or
- DOUBLE-CLICK: graph placeholder, or
- CHOOSE: Insert, Chart from the menu, or
- CHOOSE: Insert, Object and then select Microsoft Graph

To edit an inserted graph:
DOUBLE-CLICK: the graph object

**PRACTICE**

You will now insert a graph on a slide by editing a graph placeholder.

*Setup:* Ensure that no presentations are open in the application window.

1 To begin a blank presentation:
CLICK: New button ( )
The New Slide dialog box appears.

2 DOUBLE-CLICK: Chart layout (located in the second row, fourth column)

3 To increase the size of the slide for easy editing:
CLICK: Slide view button ( ) at the bottom of the Outline panel

4 CLICK: the title placeholder
TYPE: **Grading Formula**

5 To insert a graph:
DOUBLE-CLICK: the chart placeholder
The Graph datasheet appears in a separate window with sample information. Similar to using an electronic spreadsheet, you add and edit data in the datasheet that you want to plot on a graph. Figure 2.16 shows the datasheet as it first appears and how it will look after you edit it.

**Figure 2.16**
Editing the datasheet

Before

Presentation2 - Datasheet

| | | A | B | C | D |
|---|---|---|---|---|---|
| | | 1st Qtr | 2nd Qtr | 3rd Qtr | 4th Qtr |
| 1 | East | 20.4 | 27.4 | 90 | 20.4 |
| 2 | West | 30.6 | 38.6 | 34.6 | 31.6 |
| 3 | North | 45.9 | 46.9 | 45 | 43.9 |
| 4 | | | | | |

After

Presentation2 - Datasheet

| | | A | B | C | D |
|---|---|---|---|---|---|
| | | | | | |
| 1 | Word | 25 | | | |
| 2 | Excel | 25 | | | |
| 3 | Access | 20 | | | |
| 4 | PowerPoint | 15 | | | |
| 5 | Integrating | 15 | | | |

6. In this step, you delete all the data that currently appears in the datasheet. To do this, you first select the entire datasheet by clicking the upper-left corner of the datasheet, directly below the Title bar. You then press the DELETE key.
CLICK: the upper-left corner of the datasheet (refer to Figure 2.17)
PRESS: DELETE

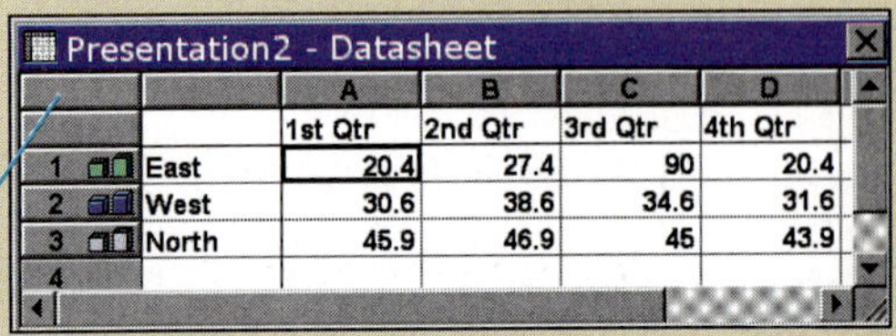


**Figure 2.17**
Deleting the contents of the datasheet

7. To enter data into the datasheet, you click the cross-hair mouse pointer on the appropriate *cell* (the intersection of a row and a column) in the datasheet. In this step, you enter the titles.
CLICK: in the cell to the right of the number 1
TYPE: **Word**
PRESS: ENTER
The insertion point automatically moved to the cell below.
TYPE: **Excel**
PRESS: ENTER
TYPE: **Access**
PRESS: ENTER
TYPE: **PowerPoint**
PRESS: ENTER
TYPE: **Integrating**
PRESS: ENTER

8. Now you prepare to enter the data.
PRESS: CTRL + HOME
The insertion point automatically moved to where you will type in the first value (25).

9. To enter the data:
TYPE: **25**
PRESS: ENTER
TYPE: **25**
PRESS: ENTER
TYPE: **20**
PRESS: ENTER
TYPE: **15**
PRESS: ENTER
TYPE: **15**
PRESS: ENTER

10 If you drag the bottom border of the datasheet window downward and then press CTRL + HOME, the datasheet should appear similar to the completed datasheet in Figure 2.16. (*Note:* You may have to use the scroll bar in the datasheet to view the headings.)

11 Let's display the graph on the slide:
CLICK: anywhere in the background of the presentation window
The graph is inserted automatically into your presentation. Your screen should now appear similar to Figure 2.18.

**Figure 2.18**
Inserting a graph

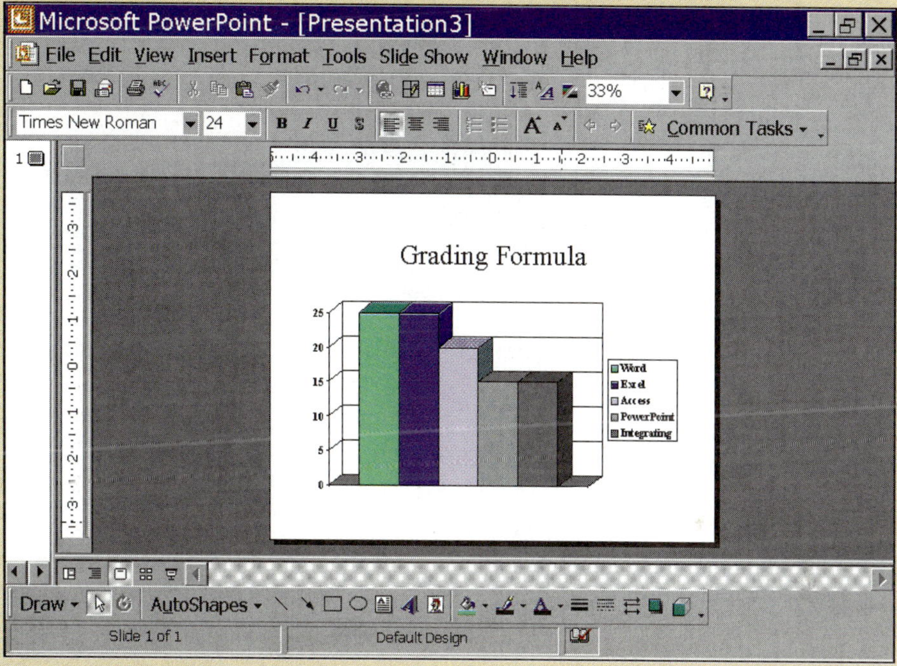


12 Once you've inserted a graph on a slide, you can edit it at any time by double-clicking the graph object to load Microsoft Graph. To illustrate, let's create a different type of chart:
DOUBLE-CLICK: the graph object
CHOOSE: Chart, Chart Type from the Menu bar
SELECT: Bar in the *Chart type* list box
CLICK: OK command button

13 To return to PowerPoint:
CLICK: anywhere in the background of the presentation window
Your screen should now appear similar to Figure 2.19.

**Figure 2.19**
A bar chart is inserted on the slide

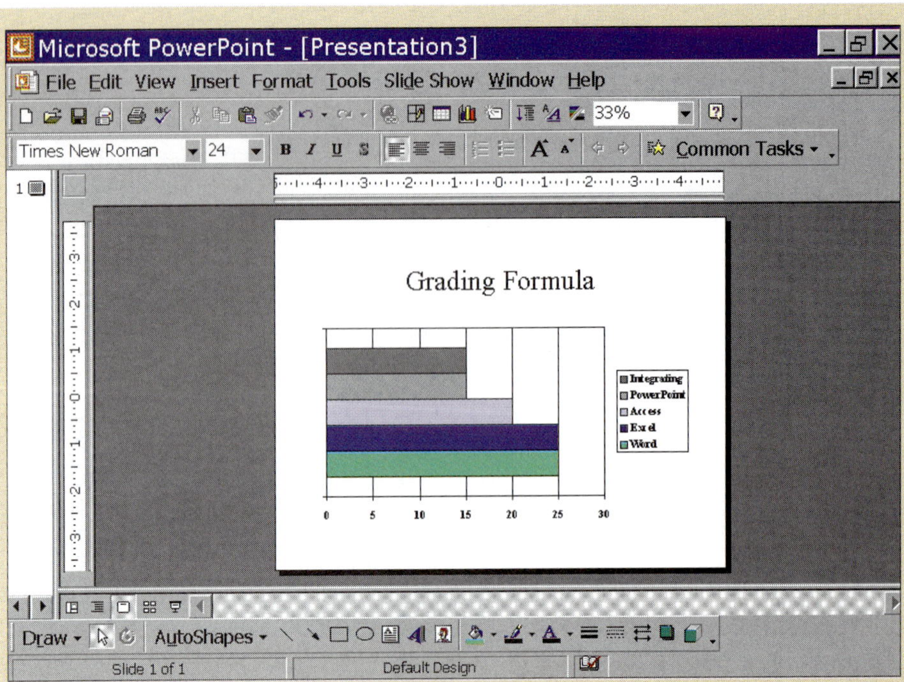


**14** Close the presentation, without saving.

## 2.3.4 Inserting Organization Charts

**FEATURE**

An **organization chart** is a schematic drawing showing a hierarchy of formal relationships, such as the relationships among an organization's employees. **Microsoft Organization Chart** allows you to create organization charts and other hierarchical diagrams. PowerPoint provides several methods for inserting organization charts in your presentations.

**METHOD**

Several methods exist for launching Microsoft Organization Chart including:

- DOUBLE-CLICK: organization chart placeholder, or
- CHOOSE: Insert, Picture, Organization Chart from the menu, or
- CHOOSE: Insert, Object and then select MS Organization Chart

To edit an existing organization chart:
DOUBLE-CLICK: organization chart object

**PRACTICE**
You will now insert an organization chart on a slide by editing an organization chart placeholder.

*Setup:* Ensure that no presentations are open in the application window.

1. To begin a blank presentation:
CLICK: New button (□)
The New Slide dialog box appears.

2. DOUBLE-CLICK: Organization Chart layout (located in the second row, third column)

3. To increase the size of the slide for convenient editing, do the following:
CLICK: Slide view button (□) at the bottom of the Outline pane

4. CLICK: the title placeholder
TYPE: **Practice Chart**

5. To insert an organization chart:
DOUBLE-CLICK: the organization chart placeholder
Microsoft Organization Chart appears in a separate window.
(*Note:* If this application isn't stored on your computer, proceed to the next module.)

6. To maximize the Organization Chart window:
CLICK: Maximize button (□)
Your screen should now appear similar to Figure 2.20. You should see four boxes in the chart area. The topmost box should already be selected.

**Figure 2.20**
Microsoft Organization Chart application window

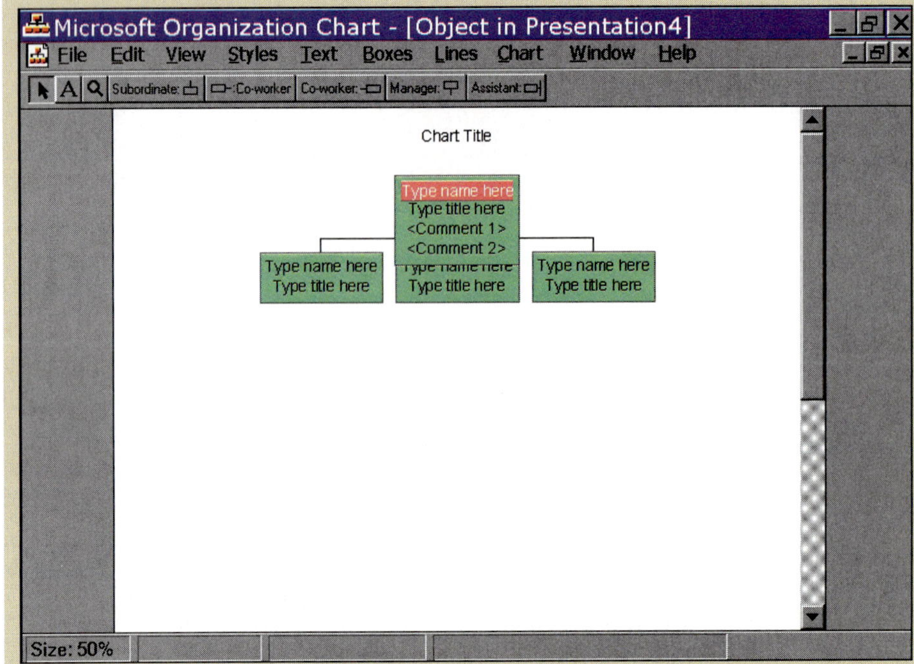


7 To edit the content of the organization chart boxes:
TYPE: ***Your Name***
PRESS: ENTER
TYPE: **Lead Instructor**

8 CLICK: the far left box, located in the second row of the chart
TYPE: **Feliberto Reyes**
PRESS: ENTER
TYPE: **Assistant Instructor**

9 CLICK: the box in the center of the second row
TYPE: **Frank Rogers**
PRESS: ENTER
TYPE: **Lab Assistant**

10 CLICK: the box on the right of the second row
TYPE: **Maritza James**
PRESS: ENTER
TYPE: **Lab Assistant**

11 To embed the organization chart on the current slide:
CHOOSE: File, Exit and Return to Presentation
CLICK: Yes command button to update the presentation
The organization chart should now appear on the slide, as shown in Figure 2.21.

**Figure 2.21**
Embedded organization chart

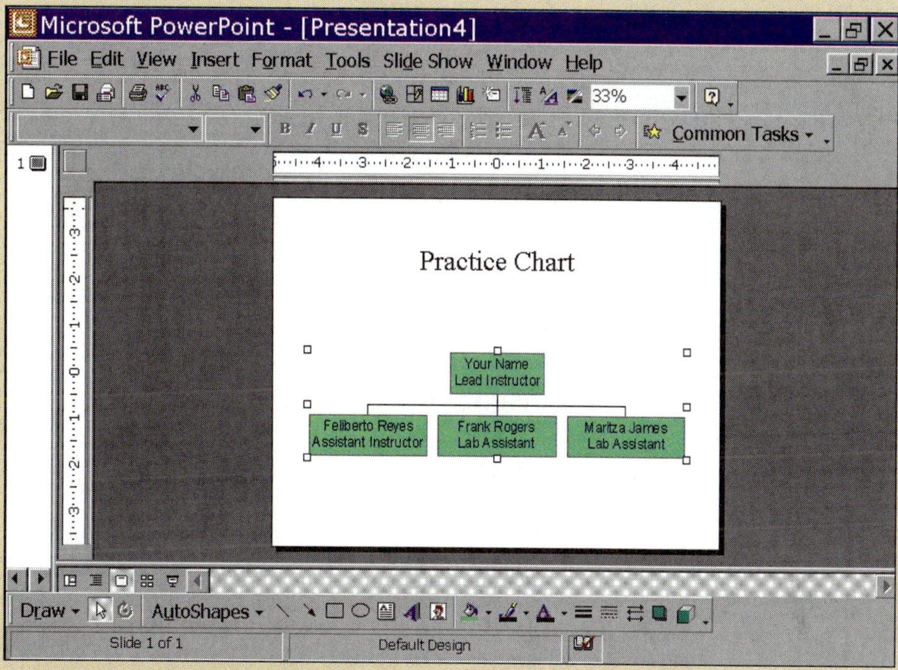


12 Let's edit the organization chart to include a new box on the second level.
DOUBLE-CLICK: organization chart object

13 To add a new box to the chart:
CLICK: Subordinate button on the toolbar
CLICK: the box that contains your name
A new box appears on the second level.

14 Because the new box is already selected, do the following:
TYPE: **Roxanna Adams**
PRESS: ENTER
TYPE: **Network Manager**

15 To embed the revised chart on the current slide:
CHOOSE: File, Exit and Return to Presentation
CLICK: Yes command button to update the presentation

16 Close the presentation, without saving.

**2.3 Self Check** What are organization charts used for?

**In Addition**
**Inserting Pictures from a Scanner**

To insert a scanned picture on a slide, your computer must first be connected to a scanner. Choose Insert, Picture, From Scanner or Camera and then follow the instructions of your scanner.

# 2.4 Delivering Online Presentations

It's showtime! PowerPoint provides several ways to deliver a presentation. Whereas handouts, overhead transparencies, and 35mm slides constitute static delivery approaches, online presentations are more dynamic, often incorporating special multimedia effects that help maintain an audience's attention. In this module, we focus on delivering online presentations.

## 2.4.1 Starting and Running Slide Shows

**FEATURE**

PowerPoint provides several tools for assisting your delivery of online presentations. You access these tools by right-clicking a slide in Slide Show view. Among the available commands on the right-click menu are options for navigating the slide show, changing the characteristics of the mouse pointer, and ending the slide show. Keep in mind that when you switch to Slide Show view, your presentation will start with the current slide.

**METHOD**

- To start a slide show:
  SELECT: the slide you want to start on
  CHOOSE: View, Slide Show (or click [Slide Show button])
- To access several tools for controlling running slide shows:
  RIGHT-CLICK: with the mouse in Slide Show view

**PRACTICE**

You will now open an existing presentation and then switch to Slide Show view. You will then practice using the right-click menu to control the running slide show.

*Setup:* Ensure that no presentations are open in the application window.

1. Open the PPT240 data file.

2. Save this four-slide presentation as "Getting to Know" to your personal storage location.

3 At this point, slide 1 is the current slide.
CHOOSE: View, Slide Show
The first slide should be displaying in Slide Show view.

4 To illustrate that you can start a presentation on any slide, let's exit Slide Show view, display slide 2, and then switch back to Slide Show view.
PRESS: ESC to exit Slide Show view
CLICK: Next Slide button ( ) on the vertical scroll bar to display slide 2
CHOOSE: View, Slide Show
The second slide should be displaying in Slide Show view.

5 In Chapter 1, you learned several methods for navigating a presentation using the mouse and keyboard. For example, pressing the Space Bar will display the next slide and pressing the PgUp key displays the previous slide. In this lesson, we would like to explore some additional options that become available when you right-click a slide.
RIGHT-CLICK: anywhere on the current slide
The right-click menu shown to the right should now appear.

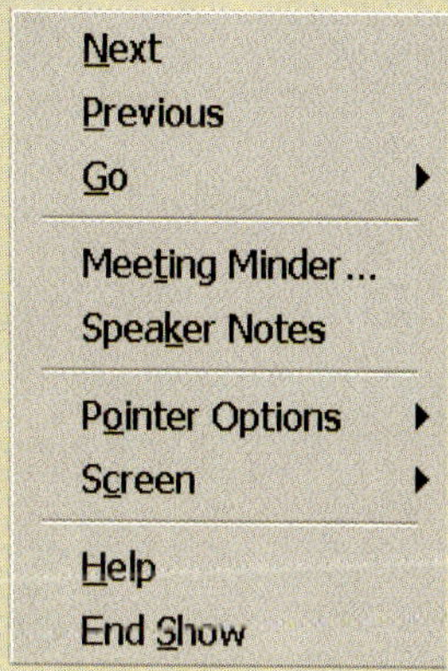


6 To move to the previous slide using the right-click menu:
CHOOSE: Previous
Slide 1 should now appear.

7 To see a listing of the slides in your presentation and then move to a specific slide:
RIGHT-CLICK: anywhere on the current slide
CHOOSE: Go, Slide Navigator
The Slide Navigator dialog box should now appear, as shown in Figure 2.22.

**Figure 2.22**
Slide Navigator dialog box

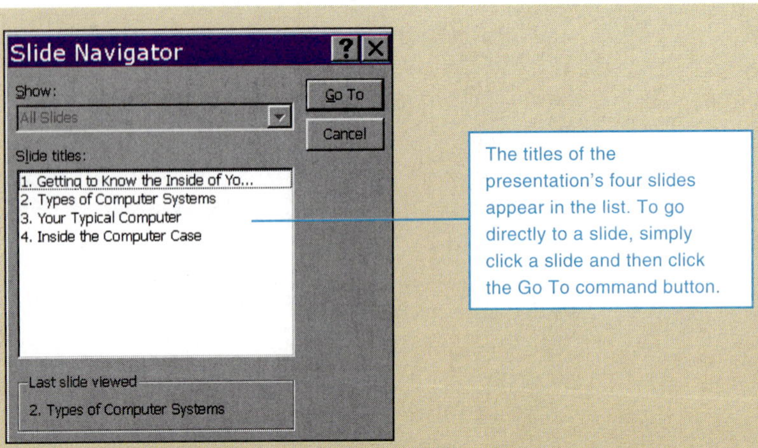


8. To display the third slide:
CLICK: "Your Typical Computer" title in the list box
CLICK: Go To command button
Slide 3 should now appear in Slide Show view.

9. To return to the previously viewed slide:
RIGHT-CLICK: anywhere on the current slide
CHOOSE: Go, Previously Viewed
Slide 1 should reappear in the window.

10. To change the pointer to a pen that you can write with on the screen:
RIGHT-CLICK: anywhere on the current slide
CHOOSE: Pointer Options
CHOOSE: Pen
The pen mouse pointer is now activated. You can draw on the screen by dragging the pen mouse pointer.

11. Let's emphasize the company name on the first slide by drawing a line under it with the pen mouse pointer.
DRAG: with the mouse under "Computers, Intl."
Your screen may now appear similar, but not identical, to Figure 2.23. (*Note:* You can change the pen color by choosing Pointer Options, Pen Color from the right-click menu.)

**Figure 2.23**
A line was drawn on this slide with the pen mouse pointer

12 To erase the inserted line:
RIGHT-CLICK: anywhere on the screen
CHOOSE: Screen, Erase Pen

13 In some presentations, an arrow will appear in the bottom-left corner of the screen. If you click this, the right-click menu will appear.
CLICK: arrow in the bottom-left corner of the window

14 To hide the arrow:
CHOOSE: Pointer Options, Hidden
The arrow should no longer appear in the left-hand corner.

15 To end the slide show using the right-click menu:
RIGHT-CLICK: anywhere on the screen
CHOOSE: End Show

16 Close the presentation.

**2.4 Self Check** How can you go to a specific slide in Slide Show view?

# 2.5 Chapter Review

Once created, slides can be manipulated with ease. The Slide Finder tool enables you to use your favorite slides in other presentations and the Outline pane and Slide Sorter view provide convenient environments for reordering slides. You can apply alternate layouts to slides and modify existing layouts by manipulating the slide's placeholders. You can also modify the entire look of your slides by applying an alternate design template.

Besides text, several objects are commonly inserted on slides, including clip art, pictures, graphs, and organization charts. These objects are often more effective at conveying information than text by itself, and help keep your audience's attention. The chapter concluded with practice delivering online presentations using PowerPoint's right-click menu that you can access in Slide Show view.

## 2.5.1 Command Summary

Many of the commands and procedures appearing in this chapter are summarized in the following table.

| Skill Set | To Perform This Task . . . | Do the Following . . . |
|---|---|---|
| **Creating a Presentation** | Insert slides from other presentations | CHOOSE: Insert, Slides From Files |
| **Modifying a Presentation** | Change slide order in the Outline pane | DRAG: the selected slide up or down |
| | Change slide order in Slide Sorter view | DRAG: the selected slide to a new location |
| | Apply a different layout | CHOOSE: Format, Slide Layout<br>DOUBLE-CLICK: an AutoLayout |
| **Customizing a Presentation** | Apply one of PowerPoint's design templates | CHOOSE: Format, Apply Design Template<br>DOUBLE-CLICK: a template |
| | Apply a template from another presentation | CHOOSE: Format, Apply Design Template<br>CHOOSE: Presentations and Shows from the *Files of type* drop-down list<br>DOUBLE-CLICK: a presentation file |

*Continued*

| Skill Set | To Perform This Task . . . | Do the Following . . . |
|---|---|---|
| **Working with Visual Elements** | Display the Clip Gallery | • DOUBLE-CLICK: a clip art placeholder, or<br>• CLICK: Insert Clip Art button ( ) on the Drawing toolbar, or<br>• CHOOSE: Insert, Picture, Clip Art, or<br>• CHOOSE: Insert, Object and then double-click Microsoft Clip Gallery |
| | Add clip art | CLICK: a clip in the Clip Gallery<br>CLICK: Insert clip button ( ) on the shortcut menu |
| | Insert a picture | CHOOSE: Insert, Picture, From File |
| | Insert a graph | • CLICK: Insert Chart button ( ), or<br>• DOUBLE-CLICK: graph placeholder, or<br>• CHOOSE: Insert, Chart, or<br>• CHOOSE: Insert, Object and then select Microsoft Graph |
| | Modify a graph | DOUBLE-CLICK: graph object |
| | Insert an organization chart | • DOUBLE-CLICK: organization chart placeholder, or<br>• CHOOSE: Insert, Picture, Organization Chart, or<br>• CHOOSE: Insert, Object and then select MS Organization Chart |
| | Modify an organization chart | DOUBLE-CLICK: organization chart object |
| **Delivering a Presentation** | Use on-screen navigation tools | RIGHT-CLICK: a slide in Slide Show view |

### 2.5.2 Key Terms

This section specifies page references for the key terms identified in this session. For a complete list of definitions, refer to the Glossary provided immediately after the Appendix in this learning guide.

clip art image, *p. 64*

organization chart, *p. 76*

Microsoft Clip Gallery, *p. 64*

Microsoft Graph, *p. 72*

Microsoft Organization Chart, *p. 76*

sizing handles, *p. 60*

Slide Finder, *p. 53*

## 2.6 Review Questions

### 2.6.1 Short Answer

1. In the Clip Gallery, what information displays in a pop-up window when you click an image?
2. What is the Slide Finder tool used for?
3. What is Microsoft Graph used for?
4. Describe the process of inserting a picture from a file into your presentation.
5. What mouse action enables you to modify an existing organization chart?
6. In Slide Show view, what is the Slide Navigator tool used for?
7. How would you go about starting a slide show on the fourth slide in a presentation?
8. What is the procedure for reordering slides in the Outline pane?
9. Describe two methods for inserting an organization chart on a slide.
10. How would you go about applying a different layout to the current slide?

## 2.6.2 True/False

1. ____ In the Clip Gallery, clips are organized by date.
2. ____ Design templates can be applied from existing presentations.
3. ____ You edit a graph placeholder by double-clicking.
4. ____ Organization charts are often used to represent spreadsheet data.
5. ____ You resize objects by dragging their sizing handles.
6. ____ Before using the Slide Finder, you must display open presentations in Slide Sorter view.
7. ____ To apply one of PowerPoint's design templates, choose Format, Apply Design Template from the Menu bar.
8. ____ It's possible to change a slide's layout in Slide Show view.
9. ____ Changing an existing slide layout may involve moving and resizing object placeholders.
10. ____ In PowerPoint, you can apply a design template from an existing presentation.



## 2.6.3 Multiple Choice

1. Which of the following reveals a presentation using slide snapshots?
   a. design template
   b. Slide Finder
   c. Title Master
   d. Slide Master

2. To insert a picture file in your presentation:
   a. CHOOSE: Insert, Picture, From File
   b. CLICK: Insert Picture button
   c. CHOOSE: File, Insert
   d. All of the above

3. To insert slides from another presentation, use the:
   a. Slide Finder
   b. Slide Master
   c. Title Master
   d. All of the above

4. You can reorder slides in ____________ .
   a. Slide view
   b. Outline pane
   c. Slide Sorter view
   d. Both b and c

5. To edit an organization chart on an AutoLayout slide, ______________ the placeholder.
   a. click
   b. double-click
   c. drag
   d. None of the above

6. Which of the following tools could you use to map a hierarchy of relationships?
   a. Picture toolbar
   b. Microsoft Graph
   c. Microsoft Organization Chart
   d. All of the above

7. Once you've inserted a graph on a slide, you can edit it in the future by ______________ .
   a. dragging
   b. clicking
   c. double-clicking
   d. None of the above

8. Which of the following should you use to create a bar chart?
   a. Microsoft Organization Chart
   b. Microsoft Graph
   c. Microsoft ClipArt Gallery
   d. None of the above

9. To change the overall look of a presentation, you should apply an alternate ______________ .
   a. AutoLayout
   b. placeholder
   c. design template
   d. All of the above

10. To delete an existing clip art image:
   a. double-click the image
   b. select the image and press DELETE
   c. drag the image to outside the Slide pane
   d. All of the above

# 2.7 Hands-On Projects

## 2.7.1 Outdoor Adventure Tours: Skiing Tours

This exercise practices inserting a clip art object on a slide.

1. Begin a blank presentation using the New button ( ).
2. In the New Slide dialog box:
   DOUBLE-CLICK: Title Only layout

3. Type **Total Skiing Tours** in the title placeholder.
4. To launch Microsoft Clip Gallery so that you can insert a clip art image on the slide:
   CHOOSE: Insert, Picture, Clip Art
5. To search for an image that relates to skiing:
   CLICK: in the *Search for clips* text box
   TYPE: **skiing** in the *Search for clips* text box
   PRESS: ENTER
   An appropriate image should now appear in the window, such as the one shown to the right. (*Note:* If no image appears, then search for an alternate image.)

6. To select the image:
   CLICK: the image
   CLICK: Insert clip button ( ) from the pop-up menu
7. Close the Insert ClipArt window by clicking its Close ( ) button.
8. If necessary, move and resize the image.
9. Save the presentation as "Outdoor Skiing Tours" to your personal storage location.
10. Close the presentation.



## 2.7.2 Monashee Community College: Animation

In this exercise, you will reorder slides, change slide layouts, insert clip art, and apply an alternate design template.

1. Open the PPT272 data file.
2. Save the presentation as "Monashee Animation" to your personal storage location.
3. In the Outline pane, drag the slide 5 icon upward so that it is positioned before slide 4.
4. Let's change the layout of slide 4 from the bulleted list layout to the "Text & Clip Art" layout. First, ensure that slide 4 is displaying in the Slide pane.
5. CHOOSE: Format, Slide Layout
   DOUBLE-CLICK: Text & Clip Art layout (located in the third row, first column)
6. To insert a clip art image on the slide:
   DOUBLE-CLICK: clip art placeholder
7. To search for the word "information":
   CLICK: in the *Search for clips* text box
   TYPE: **information**
   PRESS: ENTER
8. SELECT: the clip shown to the right
   CLICK: Insert clip button ( )
   (*Note:* If this clip isn't available on your computer, insert an alternate clip on the slide.)

9. Resize the image so that it is about half its original size. Also, move the image so that it lines up opposite the bulleted list.

10. To apply an alternate design template to the presentation:
    CHOOSE: Format, Apply Design Template
    DOUBLE-CLICK: "Blends" template in the list box
11. Display slide 1 in the Slide pane. The title might look better if it's positioned higher on the slide.
12. DRAG: the title placeholder upward about one-half inch so that the entire title is above the horizontal line
13. Save and then close the revised presentation.

### 2.7.3 Coldstream Corporation: Executive Committee

In this exercise, you create a new presentation and then insert and edit an organization chart.

1. Start a new presentation and select the Title Slide layout.
2. Save the new presentation as "Coldstream Executive" to your personal storage location.
3. Type **Coldstream Corporation** for the title and **Executive Committee** for the subtitle.
4. Insert another new slide that includes a title placeholder and an organization chart layout.
5. Type **Executive Committee Members** in the title placeholder.
6. Create the following organization chart:

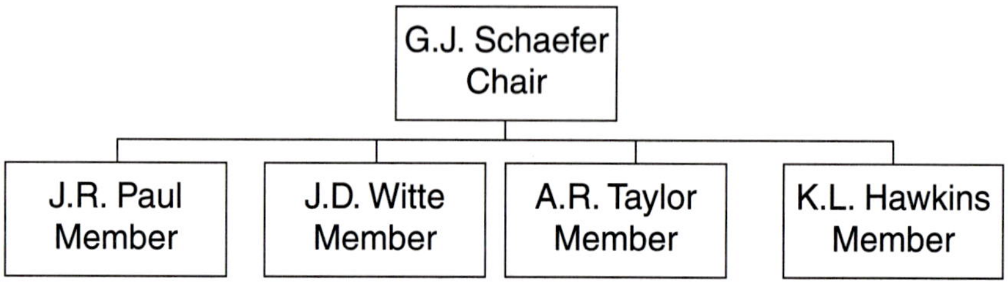


7. Display the organization chart on the slide.
8. Edit the organization chart to include two subordinates under "J.D. Witte": **D.E. Reid Secretary**; and **A.J. Epp Treasurer** as shown on nexgt page:

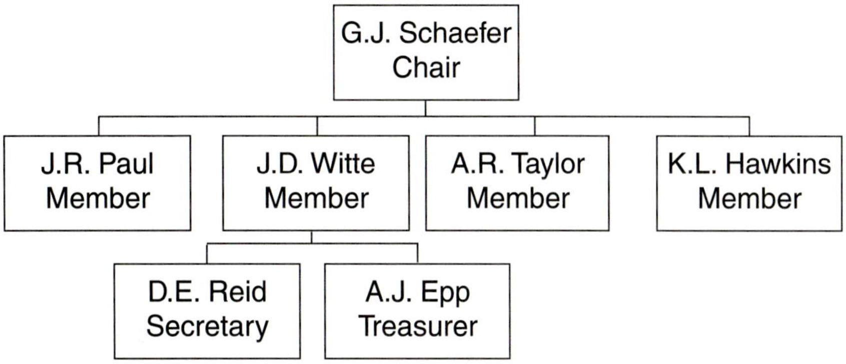


9. Adjust the size and position of the chart so that it is larger and centered beneath the title.
10. Apply the "Global" design template to the presentation.
11. Save your changes and close your presentation.



## 2.7.4 Spiderman Web Marketing: Technology

You will now add a photograph and a graph to an existing presentation.

1. Open the PPT274 presentation.
2. Save the presentation as "Spiderman Technology" to your personal storage location.
3. On the first slide, insert a photograph named PPT274a. (*Note:* If necessary, close the Picture toolbar.)
4. Move and resize the photo so that it fits in the large triangular white area beneath the title.
5. Insert a new slide that includes a title and a chart placeholder.
6. Type **Current Sales Breakdown** in the title placeholder and then double-click the chart placeholder to create the chart.
7. Edit the chart's datasheet to look like the following:

Solution-Spiderman Photo - Datasheet

| | | A | B | C | D |
|---|---|---|---|---|---|
| | | 1998 | 1999 | | |
| 1 | Web-Based | 2000 | 5500 | | |
| 2 | Mail Order | 2200 | 1850 | | |
| 3 | | | | | |
| 4 | | | | | |

8. Display the bar chart on the slide.
9. Move and resize the chart so that it fits in the black area of the slide.
10. Save and then print the revised presentation.

### 2.7.5 On Your Own: Wally's Widgets

Create a slide show that describes a fictitious company called "Wally's Widgets." The presentation should include five slides containing the information listed below:

- Wally's Widgets
  Address, phone number
  A photograph (stored in the PPT275 data file)
- Description of the product (features and benefits)
- Projected Sales (include a graph)
- Personnel (include an organization chart)
- Summary slide

Apply an appropriate design template to the presentation. Save your presentation as "Wally's Widgets" to your personal storage location.

### 2.7.6 On Your Own: Life as a Student

Create a true or fictitious presentation that describes your life as a student. Your presentation should include your course timetable in the form of a bulleted list. Your course grades should be presented in a graph, and the members of one of your study groups should be displayed in an organization chart. Insert the photograph named PPT276 or a scanned photograph of yourself. Save your presentation as "Student" to your personal storage location.

## 2.8 Case Problem: Snowmelt Hydrology Research

Now that Natasha has completed Chapter 2, she is ready to insert several objects into her PowerPoint presentation. After creating a title slide, Natasha will insert a graph, an organization chart, and a photograph.

In the following case problems, assume the role of Natasha and perform the same steps that she identifies. You may want to reread the chapter opening before proceeding.

1. Natasha creates a new presentation entitled "Thesis" and saves it to her personal storage location. On the first slide, she types **Spatial Variability in the Arctic Snowmelt Landscape** as the title and **presented by Natasha Newman** as the subtitle.

   Natasha decides to create a graph on the second slide that will visually compare her data. She inserts a second slide with the Chart layout. She types **Variability of Snow Distribution, Trail Valley Basin** in the title placeholder and then double-clicks the chart placeholder. Next, she edits the chart datasheet to include the following information:

| | May 23 | May 24 |
|---|---|---|
| Snow Covered Area | 93 | 66 |
| Total # of Patches | 54 | 75 |
| Patch Fractal Dimension | 34 | 36 |

   She experiments with several different chart types including Bar, Line, and Area charts. She prefers the 'Cone Chart' and the 'Column with a conical shape' sub-type (located in the first row, first column). She saves her changes.

2. In her thesis defense, Natasha would like to tell something about the different members in her research group. Using an organization chart on the third slide, she types **Snowmelt Research Group** in the title placeholder and creates the following organization chart:

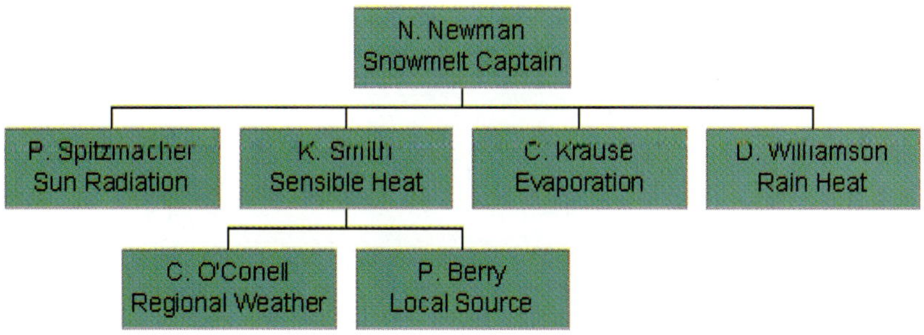


   She then saves the revised presentation.

3. Natasha has chosen the perfect photograph to include on her summary slide. She creates a final slide with the title **Field Measurement Difficulties** and inserts the photograph entitled PPT283. She moves and resizes the picture to fit nicely in the area beneath the horizontal border, and then saves her changes.

4. After experimenting with PowerPoint's selection of design templates, Natasha decides to apply the "Sunny Days" design template. She then reviews each slide in the presentation and moves and resizes placeholders to achieve the best visual result.

   After reviewing the presentation in Slide Show view, she decides to move slide 4 to before slide 3. She practices delivering her slide show, incorporating the use of the pen pointer and other options on the right-click menu. She saves her changes and is ready to defend her thesis!

# Notes

# Notes

# Microsoft PowerPoint 2000
## *Working with Text*

**CHAPTER THREE**

## Chapter Outline



## Learning Objectives

After reading this chapter, you will be able to:

- Change the appearance of text using varied fonts and point sizes, bulleted and numbered lists, and alignment commands
- Create and format tables for organizing tabular data
- Use the Spell Checker and Find and Replace utilities

Case Study

## Belton Bank

Richard Belton, president and CEO of Belton Bank, is preparing a presentation for the upcoming Shareholders' Meeting. Richard has already prepared an outline in Word and would like to use the same information in his PowerPoint presentation. He would also like to add a simple table to the presentation. Since the presentation includes a lot of text, he would like to format the text to add more visual interest. Finally, he wants to ensure that his presentation contains no spelling errors.

In this chapter, you and Richard will add visual interest to a presentation by formatting text, adding and customizing bulleted and numbered lists, and changing paragraph alignment. You will also create and format a table on a slide and use PowerPoint's proofing tools to check for spelling accuracy and to find and replace items.



# 3.1 Formatting Text

Formatting text in PowerPoint involves selecting typefaces, font sizes, and attributes for text. You can apply character formatting commands as you type or after you have selected text. Some of the attributes available in PowerPoint include bold, italic, underline, shadow, emboss, superscript, and subscript. You can also change the color of text.

PowerPoint's character formatting commands are accessed through the Font dialog box (Figure 3.1), the Formatting toolbar, or by using shortcut keyboard combinations. Since many of the features are accessible from the Formatting toolbar and shortcut keys, you may never need to use the Format, Font menu command except to select a special character attribute in the dialog box.

**Figure 3.1**
Font dialog box

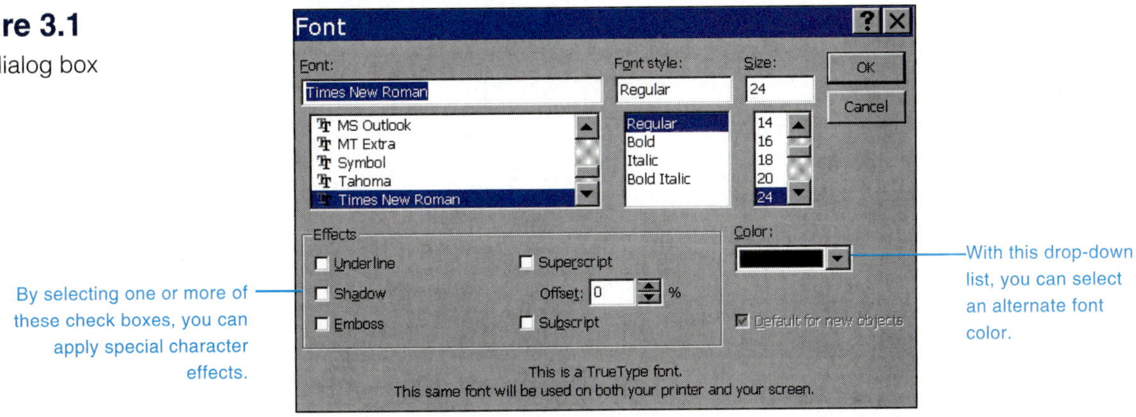

## 3.1.1 Bolding, Italicizing, and Underlining

**FEATURE**
The bold, italic, and underline attributes help to emphasize important text. You can apply these attributes using buttons on the Formatting toolbar.

**METHOD**
- To make text bold, click the Bold button (B)
- To italicize text, click the Italic button (I)
- To underline text, click the Underline button (U)

**PRACTICE**
You will now begin a blank presentation for practice with inserting text and applying the boldface, italic, and underline attributes.

*Setup:* Ensure that PowerPoint is loaded. If the PowerPoint startup dialog box is displayed, click its Cancel command button.

1. To create a blank presentation:
CLICK: New button ( )
The New Slide dialog box should now appear.

2. To insert a title slide:
SELECT: Title Slide layout
CLICK: OK command button
Your screen should now appear similar to Figure 3.2.

**Figure 3.2**
A blank slide

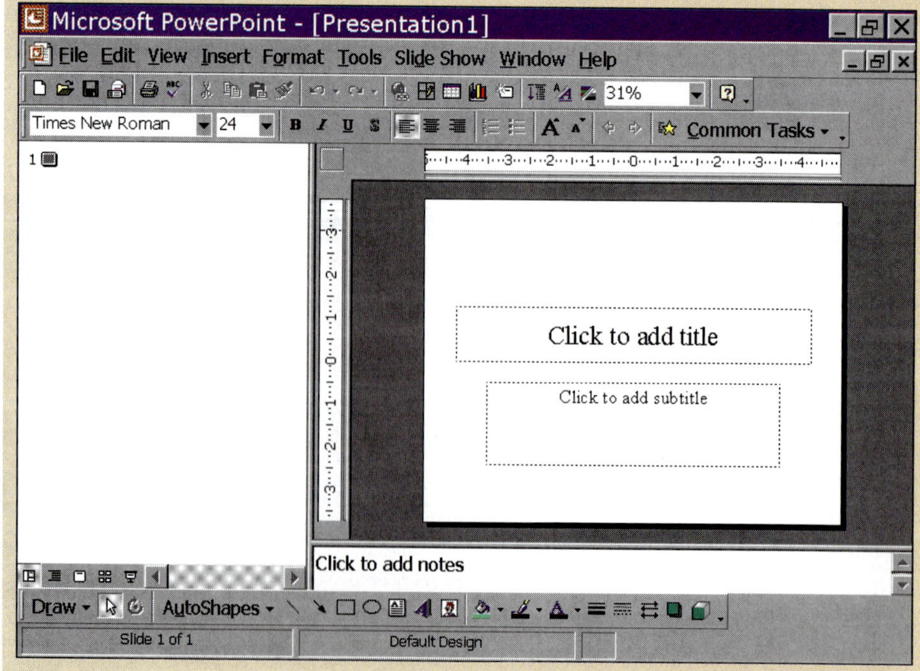

3 As you learned in Chapter 1, you can edit the text of the title slide by typing in the Outline pane or by clicking the title placeholder on the slide itself. Let's edit the slide directly.
CLICK: the title placeholder (appearing as "Click to add title")

4 TYPE: **The Future of Software**
The text is currently formatted using a Times New Roman, 44-point font size. The title's placeholder should appear similar to the following:

5 To apply the bold and underline attributes to the title:
SELECT: the title by dragging over the text with the mouse
CLICK: Bold button (B)
CLICK: Underline button (U)

6 To insert an italicized subtitle on the slide:
CLICK: the subtitle placeholder (appearing as "Click to add subtitle")
CLICK: Italic button (I) on the Formatting toolbar
TYPE: **By Bill Gates**

7 To stop typing in italic:
CLICK: Italic button (I)

8 Save the presentation as "Formatting Practice" to your personal storage location and keep it open for the next lesson.

## 3.1.2 Changing Fonts and Font Sizes

**FEATURE**
A **font** is defined as all the symbols and characters of a particular style of print. Font size is measured in *points*. By selecting fonts and font sizes, you provide your presentation with the right tone for your message.

**METHOD**
- To select a typeface:
  CLICK: down arrow beside the Font drop-down list (Times Roman)
  SELECT: the desired font
- To change the font size:
  CLICK: down arrow beside the Font Size drop-down list (10)
  SELECT: the desired point size

**PRACTICE**
You will now practice changing fonts and point sizes.

*Setup:* Ensure that you've completed the previous lesson and that the "Formatting Practice" presentation is displaying.

1. SELECT: the text in the title placeholder
2. To display a list of the available fonts:
   CLICK: down arrow beside the Font drop-down list (Times New Roman)
3. Scroll through the font choices by clicking the up and down arrows on the drop-down list's scroll bar or by dragging the scroll box.
4. SELECT: Arial (or a font that is available on your computer)
5. To display the range of available font sizes:
   CLICK: down arrow beside the Font Size drop-down list (10)
6. SELECT: 54-point font size
   CLICK: outside the placeholder to deselect the text
7. Save the revised presentation and keep it open for the next lesson.

## 3.1.3 Creating Bulleted and Numbered Lists

**FEATURE**
Bulleted and numbered lists provide an excellent means for organizing information for your audience. When you choose the Bulleted List AutoLayout, PowerPoint automatically creates a bulleted list placeholder on the slide. To insert bullets manually, use the Bullets button ( ). Similarly, to insert numbers on a slide, click the Numbering button ( ). To customize how bullets and numbers appear, use the Bullets and Numbering dialog box.

**METHOD**
- To create a bulleted list, click the Bullets button ( )
- To create a numbered list, click the Numbering button ( )
- To modify the bullet symbols or numbering scheme:
  CHOOSE: Format, Bullets and Numbering

**PRACTICE**
You will now practice creating and customizing bulleted and numbered lists.

*Setup:* Ensure that you've completed the previous lessons in this module and that the "Formatting Practice" presentation is displaying.

1 To insert a new slide:
CLICK: New Slide button ( )
SELECT: Bulleted List layout
CLICK: OK command button

2 To insert a title on the slide:
CLICK: in the title placeholder
TYPE: **Software Categories**

3 To create the bulleted list:
CLICK: in the bulleted list placeholder
TYPE: **Entertainment software**
PRESS: ENTER
TYPE: **Education and reference software**
PRESS: ENTER
TYPE: **Business and specialized software**

4 To change the appearance of the bullet symbol:
SELECT: the bulleted text
CHOOSE: Format, Bullets and Numbering
The Bullets and Numbering dialog box should now appear, as shown in Figure 3.3.

**Figure 3.3**
Bullets and Numbering dialog box

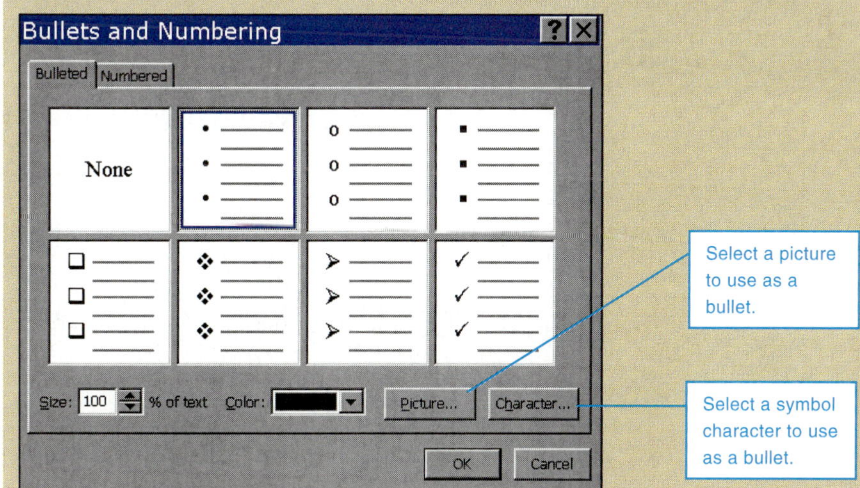


5 To change the bullet symbol from a circle (●) to a solid box (■):
CLICK: the solid box graphic

6 To change the color of the bullets to blue:
CHOOSE: royal blue from the *Color* drop-down list

POWERPOINT

7. To proceed:
CLICK: OK command button
The bullets should now be blue.

8. Let's try formatting the list using graphical bullets. To begin, ensure that the bulleted text is selected. Then:
CHOOSE: Format, Bullets and Numbering
CLICK: Picture command button
The Picture Bullet dialog box should now appear (Figure 3.4).

**Figure 3.4**
Picture Bullet dialog box

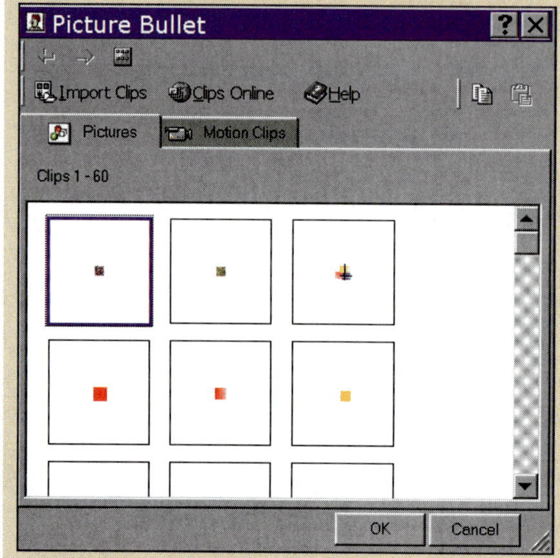


9. CLICK: the picture located in the first row, third column ()
CLICK: Insert Clip button () from the pop-up menu
The bullets should now be displaying with the chosen picture bullet.

10. To change the bullets to a numbered list:
SELECT: the bulleted text, if it isn't selected already
CLICK: Numbering button ()
The list should now appear numbered.

11. To use letters rather than numbers for the list:
CHOOSE: Format, Bullets and Numbering
CLICK: the option that shows a), b), and c)
CLICK: OK command button

12. To add an item to the list between items b) and c), position the I-beam pointer at the end of "Education and reference software" and press ENTER.

13 TYPE: **Basic productivity software**
Note that PowerPoint automatically renumbers, or in this case re-letters, the list for you when you insert new entries.

14 Save the revised presentation and keep it open for the next lesson.

## 3.1.4 Changing Paragraph Alignment

**FEATURE**
In PowerPoint, **justification** refers to how text is aligned within its placeholder. *Left justification* aligns text on the left side of its placeholder. *Center justification* centers text in its placeholder. *Right justification* positions text flush against the right side of its placeholder. *Full justification* positions text so that it is lined up on both sides of its placeholder.

**METHOD**
- CLICK: Align Left button (≡) on the Formatting toolbar
- CLICK: Center button (≡) on the Formatting toolbar
- CLICK: Align Right button (≡) on the Formatting toolbar
- CHOOSE: Format, Alignment, Justify to apply full justification

**PRACTICE**
You will now practice changing justification.

*Setup:* Ensure that you've completed the previous lessons in this module and that the "Formatting Practice" document is displaying.

1 CLICK: in title placeholder
The title "Software Categories" is currently centered in its placeholder.

2 CLICK: Align Left button (≡) on the Formatting toolbar
The title is now positioned on the left side of the placeholder.

3 CLICK: Align Right button (≡) on the Formatting toolbar
The title is positioned on the right side of the placeholder.

4 To move the paragraph back to its original position:
CLICK: Center button (≡) on the Formatting toolbar

5 Save the revised presentation and keep it open for the next lesson.

## 3.1.5 Copying Formatting Attributes

**FEATURE**

The Format Painter enables you to copy the formatting styles and attributes from one area in your presentation to another. Not only does this feature speed formatting operations, it ensures consistent formatting throughout your presentation.

**METHOD**

To copy formatting to another area in your presentation:

1. SELECT: the text with the desired formatting characteristics
2. CLICK: Format Painter button () on the Standard toolbar
3. SELECT: the slide and text that you want to format

To copy formatting to several areas in your presentation:

1. SELECT: the text with the desired formatting characteristics
2. DOUBLE-CLICK: Format Painter button ()
3. SELECT: the slide and text that you want to format
4. Repeat step 3, as desired.
5. CLICK: Format Painter button () to deselect it

**PRACTICE**

In this lesson, you practice using the Format Painter.

*Setup:* Ensure that you've completed the previous lessons in this module and that slide 2 of the "Formatting Practice" presentation is displaying.

1 SELECT: the text "Entertainment software"

2 To format the selected text:
CLICK: Bold button (B)
SELECT: Arial font from the Font drop-down list (Times New Roman)
SELECT: 28-point size from the Font Size drop-down list (10)
(*Note:* If you don't have the Arial font on your computer, select an alternate font.)

3 To copy the formatting characteristics of the selected text "Entertainment software:"
CLICK: Format Painter button () on the Standard toolbar

4 Move the mouse pointer into the slide area. Note that it becomes an I-beam attached to a paintbrush.

5 To copy the formatting to the second bulleted item:
DRAG: mouse pointer over the text "Education and reference software"
When you release the mouse button, the second bulleted item is formatted with the same characteristics as the first bulleted item.

6 To copy the formatting of the selected text to the remaining bulleted items:
DOUBLE-CLICK: Format Painter button

7 Using the I-beam paintbrush mouse pointer, select the remaining two bullets.

8 To copy the formatting to the subtitle on the first slide:
CLICK: Previous Slide button
SELECT: "By Bill Gates" in the subtitle placeholder

9 To finish using the paintbrush mouse pointer:
CLICK: Format Painter button

10 Save and then close the revised document.

**3.1 Self Check** How would you go about changing a bulleted list to a numbered list?

# 3.2 Inserting and Formatting a Table

Tables are extremely useful for organizing tabular data. Tables are composed of columns and rows, and the intersection of a column and row is called a **cell**. In this module, you create the slide pictured in Figure 3.5. Before inserting a table on a slide, first consider how many *columns* your table will require. If you insert and delete columns later on after you've added data, you disrupt the established format of the table, and getting it to fit within the slide boundaries can be time-consuming. You really don't need to worry about the length of your table because you can easily add rows as you go without changing the structure of the table.

**Figure 3.5**
A Word table

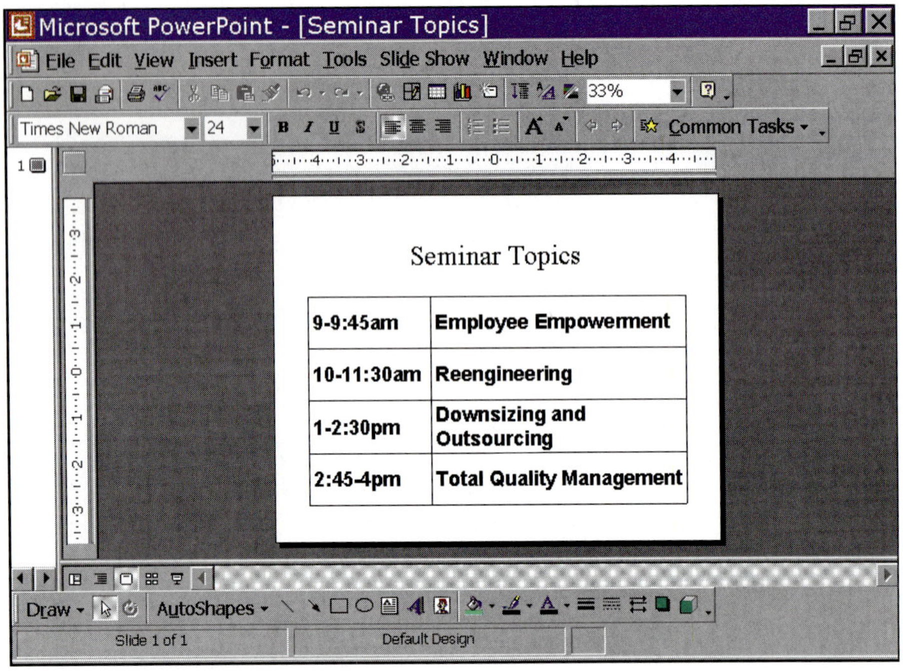


## 3.2.1 Creating the Table Structure

**FEATURE**

If you already know how to insert tables in Microsoft Word, you'll have no problem inserting them in PowerPoint. To create a table in PowerPoint, you use the Insert Table button (▦) on the Standard toolbar and then drag to select the number of columns and rows. Or, you can simply choose the Table layout when inserting a new slide, which places a table placeholder on the slide.

**METHOD**

To insert a table using the Insert Table button (▦):

1. Position the insertion point in the document where you want to insert the table.
2. CLICK: Insert Table button (▦) and hold it down
3. DRAG: the grid pattern to the desired number of rows and columns
4. Release the mouse button.

To insert a table using the Table layout:

1. DOUBLE-CLICK: Table layout in the New Slide or Slide Layout dialog box
2. DOUBLE-CLICK: the table placeholder to edit the object
3. Define the number of columns and rows in the Insert Table dialog box.
4. CLICK: OK command button

**PRACTICE**
You will now insert a table on a slide by editing a table placeholder.

*Setup:* Ensure that no presentations are open in the application window.

1 To begin a blank presentation:
CLICK: New button (▢)
The New Slide dialog box appears.

2 DOUBLE-CLICK: Table layout (located in the first row, fourth column)

3 In the remainder of this module, you won't be using the Outline pane. Therefore, to increase the size of the slide for convenient editing, do the following:
CLICK: Slide view button (▢) at the bottom of the Outline pane

4 To define the title:
CLICK: the title placeholder
TYPE: **Seminar Topics**

5 To edit the table placeholder:
DOUBLE-CLICK: the table placeholder
The Insert Table dialog box should now appear, as shown below:

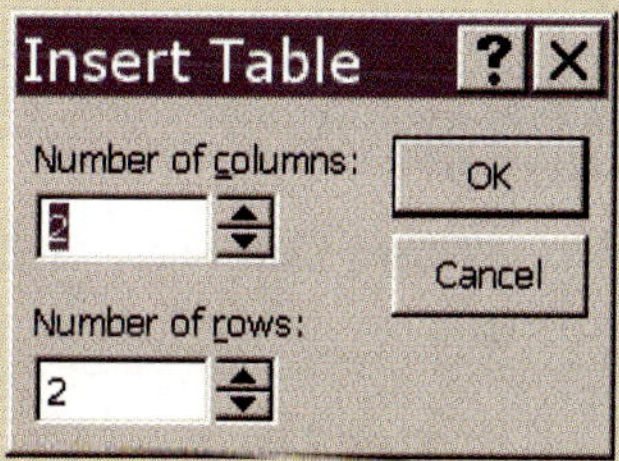


6 Let's create a table that contains two columns and four rows. To increase the number of rows:
PRESS: TAB to select the number in the *Number of rows* spin box
TYPE: **4**
CLICK: OK command button
PowerPoint places a table with four rows and two columns in the table placeholder. The Tables and Borders toolbar should also appear. This toolbar provides a number of convenient shortcuts for formatting tables. In addition, the Draw Table tool, which looks like a pencil, is now activated. You would use this tool if you were going to draw the table one cell at a time.

7 DRAG: the Tables and Borders toolbar to beneath the Formatting toolbar
Your screen should now appear similar to Figure 3.6.

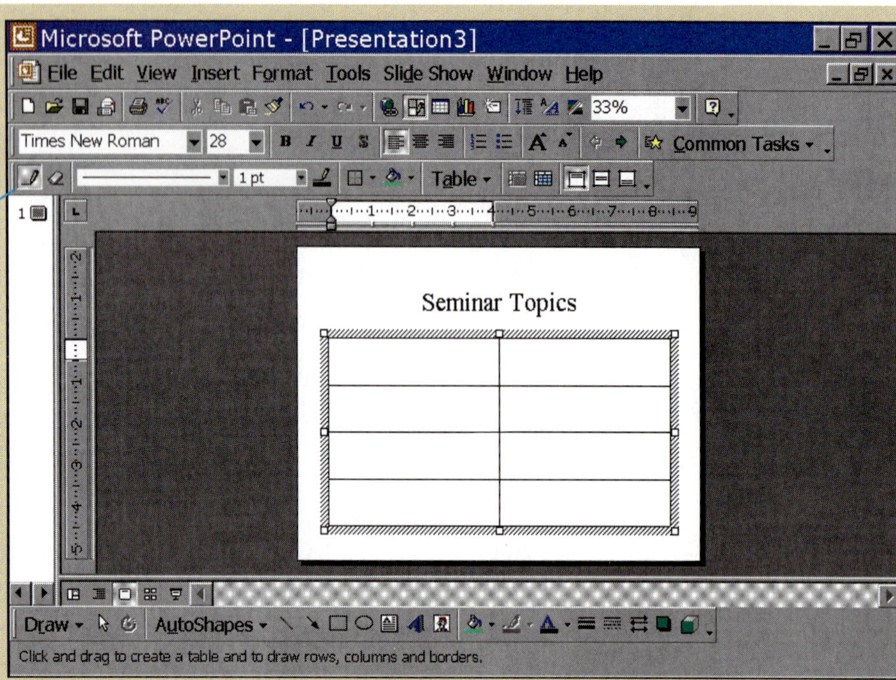


**Figure 3.6**
Inserting a table

Tables and Borders toolbar

8 To deselect the Draw Table tool:
CLICK: Draw Table button () on the Tables and Borders toolbar
It is important that you know how to select table cells, rows, and columns before you perform most procedures involving tables. The procedures for selecting items in a table are summarized in Table 3.1.

**Table 3.1**
Table selection methods

| To select this . . . | Do this . . . |
|---|---|
| The contents of the cell in the next column | PRESS: TAB |
| The contents of the cell in the previous column | PRESS: SHIFT + TAB |
| A row | CLICK: in the desired row<br>CLICK: Table on the Tables and Borders toolbar<br>CHOOSE: Select Row |
| A column | CLICK: in the desired column<br>CLICK: Table on the Tables and Borders toolbar<br>CHOOSE: Select Column |

**Table 3.1**
Table selection methods
*Continued*

| To select this . . . | Do this . . . |
|---|---|
| A range of cells, rows, or columns | Drag the mouse over the cells, rows, or columns. |
| An entire table | CLICK: in the table<br>CLICK: Table on the Tables and Borders toolbar<br>CHOOSE: Select Table |

9 Save the presentation as "Seminar Topics" to your personal storage location and keep it open for the next lesson.

## 3.2.2 Navigating a Table and Entering Data

**FEATURE**
Each cell can contain more than one paragraph and be formatted with its own unique character and paragraph formatting commands. In fact, you can think of a table cell as a mini document page.

**METHOD**

- PRESS: TAB to move to the cell on the right (if the insertion point is in the last table cell, pressing TAB inserts a new row)
- PRESS: CTRL + TAB to move the insertion point to the next tab stop
- PRESS: ↑, ↓, ←, or → to move around a table

**PRACTICE**
You will now enter some information into the table.

*Setup:* Ensure that you've completed the previous lesson and that the "Seminar Topics" presentation is displaying.

1 Position the insertion point in the first cell of the first column, if it is not already there.

2 Let's enter some information into the table:
TYPE: **9-9:45am**
PRESS: TAB
TYPE: **Employee Empowerment**
PRESS: TAB
Notice that the last TAB takes you to the first column of the next row.

3. In the same manner as above, enter the following two items.
   **10-11:30am Reengineering**
   **1-2:30pm Downsizing and Outsourcing**

4. Position the insertion point in the first cell of the fourth row, if it is not there already.

5. TYPE: **2:45-4pm**
   PRESS: TAB
   TYPE: **Total Quality Management**
   Your screen should now appear similar to Figure 3.7. (*Note:* If you accidentally pressed TAB after typing in the last cell and inserted a new row, choose Edit, Undo from the menu.)

**Figure 3.7**
Table with inserted text

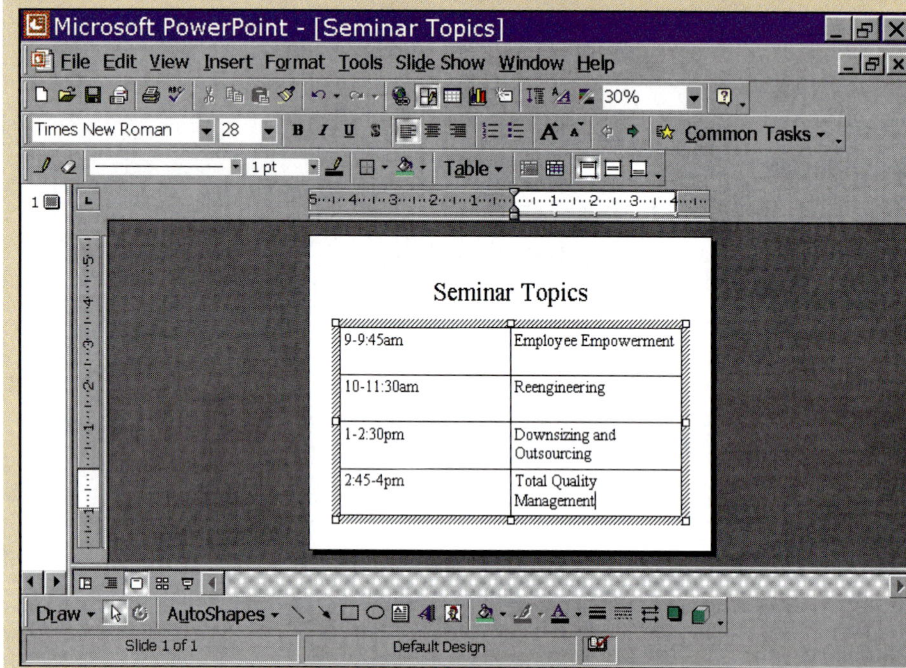


6. Save the revised presentation and keep it open for the next lesson.

**In Addition**
**Merging and Splitting Cells**

The ability to merge and split cells is extremely useful when customizing a table to your exact specifications. Once cells have been merged, or combined, into a single cell, the action of undoing this action is called *splitting.* To merge and split cells, select the cells you want to merge or split before clicking the Table button on the Tables and Borders toolbar. Then choose Merge Cells or Split Cells from the drop-down menu.

## 3.2.3 Formatting Table Cells

**FEATURE**

Character and paragraph formatting commands, like those you used in the last module, help make your tables more attractive and easier to read. When formatting tables, you can choose to format an entire table, a selection of rows or columns, or a selection of cells.

**METHOD**

- Apply character and paragraph formatting commands to tables the same way you apply them to normal text.
- Use the Tables and Borders toolbar to apply special table attributes affecting cells.
- Drag the column and row borders to adjust their width or height.

**PRACTICE**

You will now practice several table formatting procedures.

*Setup:* Ensure that you've completed the previous lessons in this module and that the "Seminar Topics" presentation is displaying. The insertion point should be positioned in the table.

1 To prepare for formatting the table, let's begin by selecting the entire table.
CLICK: Table on the Tables and Borders toolbar
CHOOSE: Select Table

2 Perform the following steps to format the table text:
CHOOSE: Arial from the Font drop-down list (Times New Roman)
CHOOSE: 32 from the Font Size drop-down list (10)
CLICK: Bold button (B)

3 To narrow the first column, position the mouse pointer over the border that separates the first and second column until a double-headed arrow appears.

4 DRAG: the middle border to the left 1.5 inches
(*Hint:* Use the Ruler as your guide.)

5 If you look closely, you'll notice that the text in each of the cells is aligned with the top border rather than the middle of each cell. To vertically center all the data in the table:
CLICK: Center Vertically button () on the Tables and Borders toolbar
Your screen should now appear similar to Figure 3.8.

**Figure 3.8**
Formatting the table

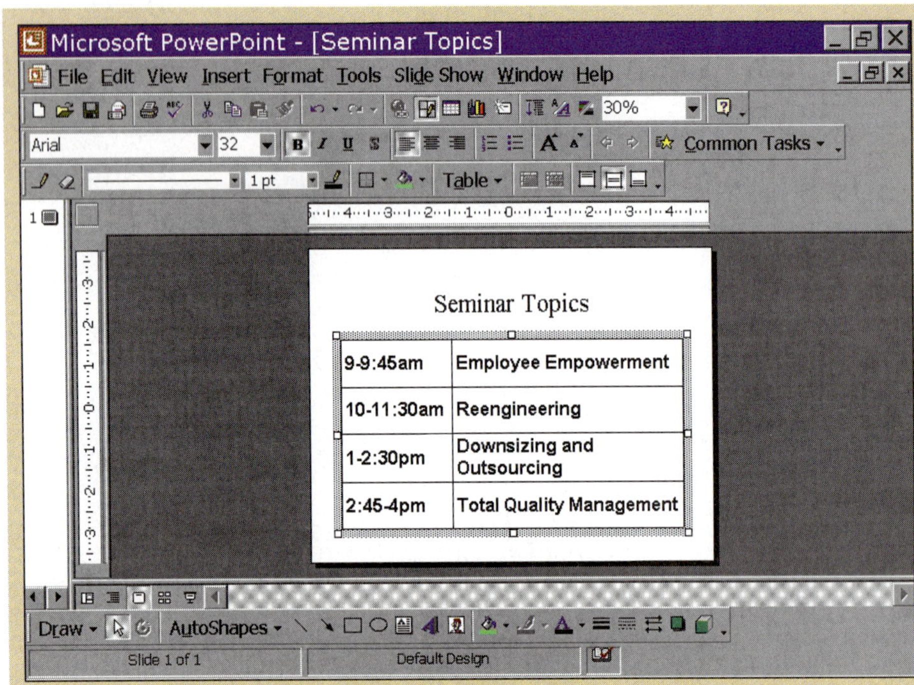


6 Save and then close the revised presentation.

**In Addition**
**Inserting and Deleting Columns and Rows**

When you insert columns and rows, the inserted column or row takes on the formatting of the previous column or row. For example, if the current row has a height of 18 points, the inserted row will be set at a height of 18 points. Inserted columns appear to the left of the selected column, and inserted rows appear above the selected row. To insert and delete columns, use the options on the Table menu, accessed from the Tables and Borders toolbar.

**3.2 Self Check** What is the procedure for changing the width of a table column?

# 3.3 Proofing a Presentation

As part of the process of finalizing a presentation, you should proof it for spelling errors. Although there's no substitute for reviewing a presentation carefully, PowerPoint's Spell Checker can help you locate some of the more obvious errors quickly. When PowerPoint performs a spelling check, it begins by comparing each word to entries in PowerPoint's main dictionary, which contains well over 100,000 words. If a word cannot be found, the Spell Checker attempts to find a match in a custom dictionary that you may have created. Custom dictionaries usually contain proper names, abbreviations, and technical terms.

There may be times when you'll need to use the Find and Replace utility, rather than the Spell Checker, to correct spelling errors. Imagine that you have just completed a 30-slide presentation supporting the importation of llamas as household pets in North America. As you are printing the final slides, a colleague points out that you spelled *llama* with one *l* throughout the presentation. The Spell Checker didn't catch the error since both *llama*, the animal, and *lama*, the Tibetan monk, appear in PowerPoint's dictionary. In this case, you should use the Find and Replace utility to correct your mistake.

In the following lessons, you import text from Word into a PowerPoint presentation and then proof the presentation using PowerPoint's Spell Checker and the Find and Replace utility.



## 3.3.1 Inserting a Word Outline in PowerPoint

**FEATURE**

The basis for a PowerPoint presentation is often a report created in Word. If your Word document has been formatted using Word's heading styles, it's a snap to build a presentation from your Word document.

**METHOD**

1. CHOOSE: Insert, Slides from Outline
2. Locate the Word document in the Insert Outline dialog box.
3. DOUBLE-CLICK: the Word file

**PRACTICE**

You will now start a blank presentation and then insert slides from an outline created in a Word document.

*Setup:* Ensure that no presentations are open in the application window.

1 CLICK: New button (□)
The New Slide dialog box should now appear.

2 To leave the New Slide dialog box without making a selection:
CLICK: Cancel command button

3. To add slides to this presentation from a Word outline:
CHOOSE: Insert, Slides from Outline

4. Using the *Look in* drop-down list or the Places bar, locate the PPT330 student file.

5. DOUBLE-CLICK: PPT330 student file
The Word outline was inserted in the PowerPoint presentation. (*Note:* An alternative method for bringing an outline into PowerPoint is to click the Open button () in PowerPoint and then choose All Outlines from the *Files of type* drop-down list.)

6. Save the presentation as "Delivering Presentations" to your personal storage location. Your screen should now appear similar to Figure 3.9.

**Figure 3.9**
Inserting a Word outline in PowerPoint

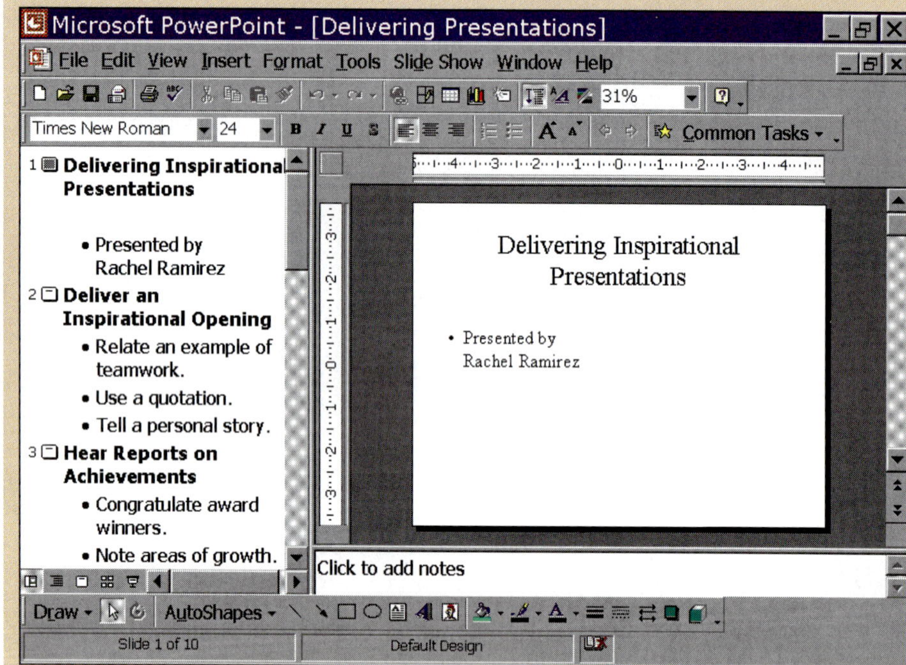


7. Before continuing, let's apply a design template to the presentation.
CHOOSE: Format, Apply Design Template
DOUBLE-CLICK: Blends template in the list box

8. To apply the Title Slide layout to the first slide, ensure that you're displaying the first slide, and then:
CHOOSE: Format, Slide Layout
CLICK: Title Slide layout
CLICK: Apply command button

9 Switch to Slide Show view and then view the presentation's five slides.

10 Save the revised presentation and keep it open for the next lesson.

## 3.3.2 Spell Checking As You Go

**FEATURE**
By default, PowerPoint checks your presentations for spelling errors as you type, marking spelling errors with a red wavy underline. You have the choice of accepting or ignoring PowerPoint's suggestions.

**METHOD**
1. Point to a word with a wavy red underline and then right-click with the mouse.
2. From the right-click menu, choose one of PowerPoint's spelling suggestions. Choose Ignore All if no error has been made, choose Add to add the word to a custom dictionary, or click on the slide and edit the error yourself.

**PRACTICE**
You will now create a spelling error in the "Delivering Presentations" presentation and then correct it using the right-click menu.

*Setup:* Ensure that you've completed the previous lesson and that slide 1 of the "Delivering Presentations" presentation is displaying.

1 CLICK: Next Slide button (▾) to display slide 2

2 Let's insert an additional bulleted item on this slide.
CLICK: to the right of the third bulleted item (Tell a personal story.)
PRESS: ENTER
Another bullet is inserted on the slide.

3 Now, let's force an intentional spelling error.
TYPE: **Read a testimoneal.**
Note that a red wavy underline appears beneath the misspelled word "testimoneal."

4 To correct the word, point to the word and then right-click using the mouse. Your screen should now appear similar to Figure 3.10.

**Figure 3.10**

The Spelling right-click menu

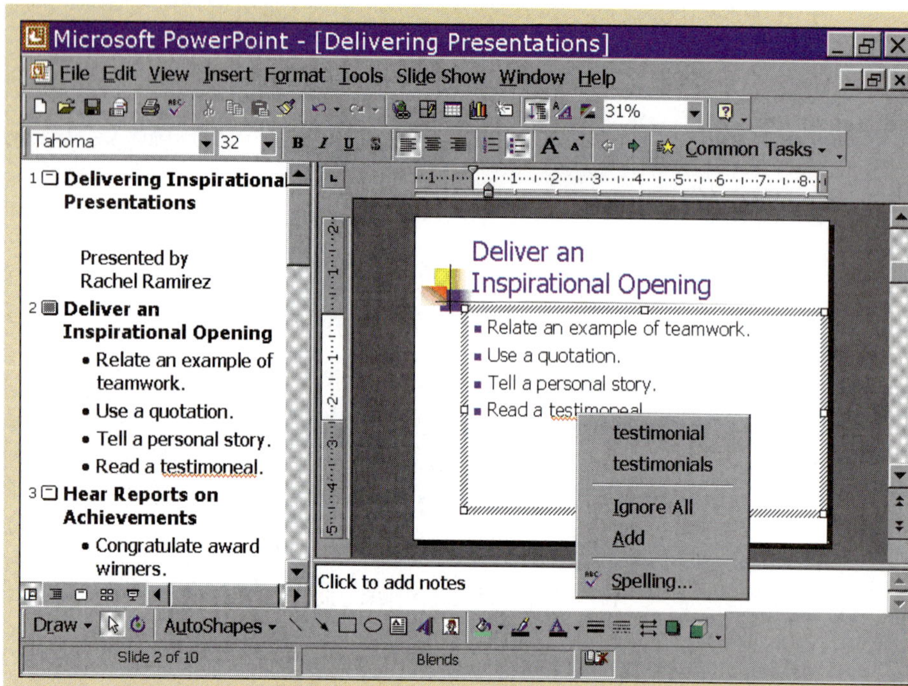


5. Using the mouse, choose the word "testimonial" from the menu. The word "testimonial" should have replaced "testimoneal" on the slide.

6. Save the revised presentation and keep it open for use in the next lesson.

## 3.3.3 Spell Checking All At Once

**FEATURE**

The Spelling command analyzes your presentation all at once for spelling errors and reports the results. It is good idea to use this command as a final check before delivering a presentation to others.

**METHOD**

1. CHOOSE: Tools, Spelling
2. When a misspelled word is found, you can accept PowerPoint's suggestion, change the entry, ignore the word and the suggested alternatives provided by PowerPoint, or add the term to the AutoCorrect feature or custom dictionary.

**PRACTICE**

You will now use the Spelling command to check an entire presentation for spelling errors.

*Setup:* Ensure that you have completed the previous lessons in this module and that the "Delivering Presentations" presentation is displaying.

1. Display slide 1.

2. To start the spelling check:
CHOOSE: Tools, Spelling
When PowerPoint finds the first misspelled word, it displays a dialog box (Figure 3.11) and waits for further instructions.

**Figure 3.11**
Spelling dialog box

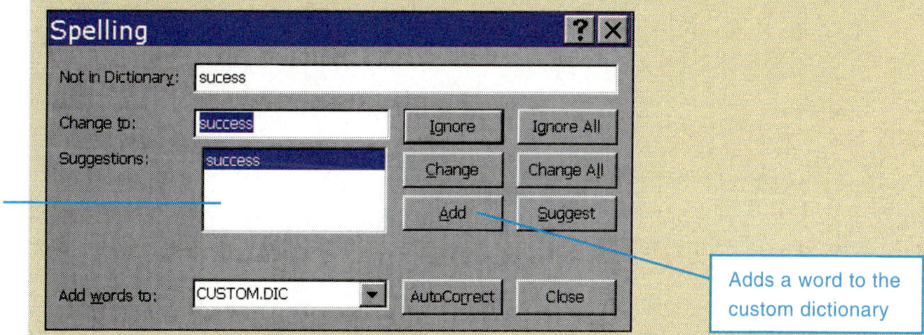


3. To correct the misspelled word "sucess," ensure that the correct spelling of the word is selected in the *Suggestions* list box and then:
CLICK: Change command button

4. The Spell command stops at the next misspelled word, "posible." The correct word, "possible," should be selected in the list box.
CLICK: Change command button

5. On your own, continue the spelling check for the rest of the presentation, changing "sollutions" to "solutions," "sollution" to "solution," "goles" to "goals," and "Acheive" to "Achieve."
Upon completion of the spell check, the following dialog box will appear:

6. To clear the dialog box:
CLICK: OK command button

7. Save the revised presentation and keep it open for use in the next lesson.

POWERPOINT

## 3.3.4 Using Find and Replace

**FEATURE**

The Find command enables you to search for text, nonprinting characters like the Paragraph Symbol (¶), and formatting characteristics. This command is useful for quickly locating a particular place in a presentation. The Replace command, which includes the capabilities of the Find command, also lets you make replacements. This command is extremely useful when you want to make the same change repeatedly throughout a presentation.

**METHOD**

To initiate the Find command:

1. CHOOSE: Edit, Find
2. TYPE: *the text you're looking for* in the *Find what* text box
3. Optionally, refine your search using the *Match case* and/or *Find whole words only* check boxes.
4. SELECT: Find Next

To initiate the Replace command:

1. CHOOSE: Edit, Replace
2. TYPE: *the text you're looking for* in the *Find what* text box
3. TYPE: *the replacement text* in the *Replace with* text box
4. Optionally, refine your search using the *Match case* and/or *Find whole words only* check boxes.
5. SELECT: Replace, Replace All, or Find Next

**PRACTICE**

You will begin by searching for the word "goal" in the presentation. You will then replace the word "goal" with "objective" throughout the presentation.

*Setup:* Ensure that you have completed the previous lessons in this module and that the "Delivering Presentations" presentation is displaying.

1 Display slide 1.

2 To begin a search for a word or phrase:
CHOOSE: Edit, Find
The Find dialog box should now appear (Figure 3.12).

**Figure 3.12**
Find dialog box

3. With the insertion point in the *Find what* text box:
TYPE: **goal**

4. To tell PowerPoint to begin the search:
CLICK: Find Next
Notice that the word "goal" is selected, but that it is part of the larger word "goals." (*Note:* You may have to drag the dialog box downward to see the selection.) To search for whole words, you must select the *Find whole words only* check box. For now, we'll leave this check box blank.

5. To continue the search:
CLICK: Find Next command button

6. On your own, search for the remaining occurrences of the word "goal." A dialog box will display indicating that you're finished with the search.
CLICK: OK command button

7. To close the Find dialog box:
CLICK: Close command button

8. Now, let's replace the word "goal" with the word "objective" throughout the presentation.
CHOOSE: Edit, Replace
Note that the word "goal" already appears in the *Find what* text box.

9. To enter the replacement text, first click the I-beam mouse pointer in the *Replace with* text box to position the insertion point.

10. TYPE: **objective**

11. So that the word "objective" replaces all occurrences of the word "goal" (lowercase) and not "Goal:"
SELECT: *Match case* check box
The Replace dialog box should now appear similar to Figure 3.13.

**Figure 3.13**
Replace dialog box

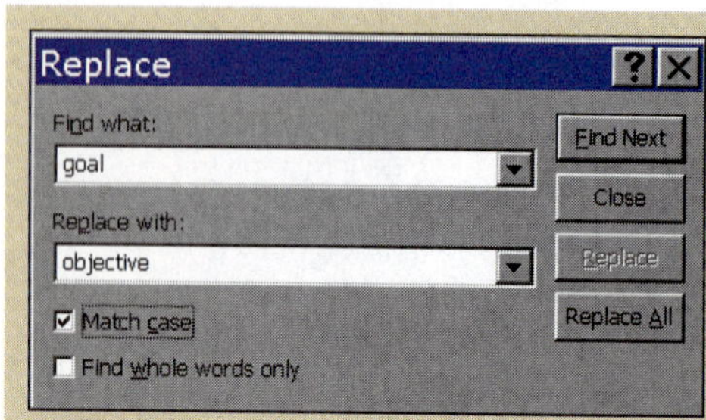


12 To execute the replacement throughout the presentation:
CLICK: Replace All command button
A dialog box will display informing you that three replacements were made in the presentation.

13 To close the dialog boxes:
CLICK: OK command button
CLICK: Close command button

14 Save and then close the presentation.

**3.3 Self Check** What is the procedure for correcting spelling errors using the right-click menu?

# 3.4 Chapter Review

In this chapter, you learned that you can change the appearance of text objects using familiar word processing commands. For example, you can apply the bold, italic, and underline attributes, change fonts and font sizes, create bulleted and numbered lists, and change paragraph alignment. You can organize tabular information using tables.

You can have great-looking slides and be a gifted communicator, but if your slides contain spelling errors, your persuasiveness will be greatly undermined. Not only should you carefully review your presentations before delivery, you should also use the Spell Checker to ensure that your presentation is free of spelling errors. The Find and Replace utilities are useful for moving to a particular location in a lengthy presentation and for making multiple changes at once.

## 3.4.1 Command Summary

Many of the commands and procedures appearing in this lesson are summarized in the following table.

| Skill Set | To Perform This Task . . . | Do the Following . . . |
|---|---|---|
| **Working with Text** | Bold, italicize, and underline text | CLICK: Bold (B), Italic (I), or Underline (U) buttons |
| | Change the current font | CLICK: down arrow beside the Font drop-down list (Times Roman) |
| | Change font size | CLICK: down arrow beside the Font Size drop-down list (10) |
| | Create a bulleted list | CLICK: Bullets button |
| | Create a numbered list | CLICK: Numbering button |
| | Customize bulleted and numbered lists | CHOOSE: Format, Bullets and Numbering |
| | Change paragraph alignment | • CLICK: Align Left button<br>• CLICK: Center button<br>• CLICK: Align Right button<br>• CHOOSE: Format, Alignment, Justify to apply full justification |
| | Copy formatting options to another area | CLICK: Format Painter button |
| | Copy formatting options to several areas | DOUBLE-CLICK: Format Painter button |
| | Import text from Word | CHOOSE: Insert, Slides from Outline |
| | Check a presentation for spelling errors | CHOOSE: Tools, Spelling |
| | Find text | CHOOSE: Edit, Find |
| | Replace text | CHOOSE: Edit, Replace |
| **Working with Visual Elements** | Insert a table | CLICK: Insert Table button, or DOUBLE-CLICK: a table placeholder |

### 3.4.2 Key Terms

This section specifies page references for the key terms identified in this lesson. For a complete list of definitions, refer to the Glossary provided immediately after the Appendix in this learning guide.

cell, *p. 107*

font, *p. 101*

justification, *p. 105*

## 3.5 Review Questions

### 3.5.1 Short Answer

1. What is the procedure for customizing a bulleted or numbered list?
2. Describe the procedure for changing a text selection from 10 points to 16 points.
3. How would you go about changing the font formatting of an individual table cell?
4. Describe two methods for inserting a table on a slide.
5. What is the Tables and Borders toolbar used for?
6. When navigating a table, how is the TAB key used?
7. What is the Format Painter used for?
8. What menu command enables you to replace text in a presentation?
9. What is the procedure for creating graphical bullets?
10. How would you go about copying formatting attributes to several areas in a presentation?

### 3.5.2 True/False

1. ____ Character formatting involves selecting typefaces, font sizes, and attributes for text.
2. ____ When you choose the Bulleted List AutoLayout, a bulleted list placeholder is inserted on the slide.
3. ____ To adjust row heights in a table, simply drag them up or down.
4. ____ The intersection of a column and row in a table is called a *cell.*
5. ____ To move to the next tab stop in a cell, press CTRL + TAB.
6. ____ When replacing text in PowerPoint, you can instruct Word to find whole words.

7. ____ Double-clicking the Format Painter button enables you to copy formatting attributes to multiple locations.
8. ____ When creating a table, you really don't have to worry about its length because you can easily add rows as you go.
9. ____ Before importing Microsoft Word text into PowerPoint, you must load Microsoft Word.
10. ____ The disadvantage to importing text from Word into a PowerPoint presentation is that you can't apply a design template to the imported text.

## 3.5.3 Multiple Choice

1. Text that you realign is repositioned within the current ____________.
   a. slide
   b. presentation
   c. placeholder
   d. None of the above

2. Which of the following can be used to insert a new row at the bottom of a table?
   a. ALT + TAB
   b. CTRL + TAB
   c. SHIFT + TAB
   d. TAB

3. When formatting tables, you can choose to format ____________.
   a. an entire table
   b. a selection of rows or columns
   c. a selection of cells
   d. All of the above

4. Which of the following would you use to draw a table one cell at a time?
   a. Draw Table tool ()
   b. Border button
   c. Line Weight drop-down list
   d. All of the above

5. To adjust column widths in a table, simply ____________ the column border.
   a. click
   b. CTRL + →
   c. drag
   d. None of the above

6. Which of the following simplifies the process of formatting text if the same formatting is required in more than one location?
   a. AutoText
   b. Format Painter
   c. Font dialog box
   d. None of the above

7. Which of the following enables you to make multiple changes in a presentation at once?
   a. Find command
   b. Replace command
   c. drag and drop
   d. Copy command

8. Which of the following commands should you always use before delivering a presentation to others?
   a. Find
   b. Replace
   c. Spell Checker
   d. All of the above

9. Which of the following keys can you use to navigate a table?
   a. ↑
   b. ↓
   c. →
   d. All of the above

10. To correct a misspelled word, ______________ the word.
    a. click
    b. double-click
    c. right-click
    d. None of the above

# 3.6 Hands-On Projects

## 3.6.1 Outdoor Adventure Tours: Winter Blues

This exercise practices applying the boldface, italic, and underline attributes; changing the font and point size; and creating and customizing a bulleted and numbered list.

1. Open the PPT361 presentation and save it as "Winter Blues" to your personal storage location.

2. To apply the bold and underline attributes to the title "Cure those Winter Blues:"
   SELECT: the title by dragging over the text with the mouse
   CLICK: Bold button (B) on Formatting toolbar
   CLICK: Underline button (U) on Formatting toolbar
3. Let's add italicized text to the subtitle placeholder:
   CLICK: the subtitle placeholder (appearing as "Click to add subtitle")
   CLICK: Italic button (I) on the Formatting toolbar
   TYPE: **Outdoor Adventure Tours.**
4. Now let's change the title font:
   SELECT: the text in the title placeholder. Note the title text is currently formatted using an Arial, 44-point font size.
   CLICK: down arrow beside the Font drop-down list (Times New Roman) to display a list of the available fonts
   SELECT: Times New Roman (or a font that is available on your computer)
5. Let's increase the title font size:
   CLICK: down arrow beside the Font Size drop-down list (10) to display the range of available font sizes
   SELECT: 54-point font size
   CLICK: outside the placeholder to deselect the text
6. We're ready to create and customize a bulleted list on a new slide:
   CLICK: New Slide button ( ) on Standard toolbar to insert a new slide
   SELECT: Bulleted List layout
   CLICK: OK command button
7. To insert a title on the slide:
   CLICK: in the title placeholder
   TYPE: **Winter Adventure Possibilities**
8. To create the bulleted list:
   CLICK: in the bulleted list placeholder
   TYPE: **Ice Fishing**
   PRESS: ENTER
   TYPE: **Skating**
   PRESS: ENTER
   TYPE: **Heli-skiing**

9. To change the appearance of the bullet symbol to an arrowhead (➢):
   SELECT: the bulleted text
   CHOOSE: Format, Bullets and Numbering
   CLICK: the arrowhead graphic (➢)
   CLICK: OK command button
10. To change the bullets to a numbered list:
    SELECT: the bulleted text, if it isn't selected already
    CLICK: Numbering button (▤) on Formatting toolbar
    The list should now appear numbered.
11. To add an item to the list between items 2) and 3), position the I-beam pointer at the end of "Skating" and press ENTER.
    TYPE: **Cross-country skiing**
    Note how PowerPoint automatically renumbered the list.
12. Save, print, and close the "Winter Blues" presentation.

## 3.6.2 Monashee Community College: Staff Meeting

In this exercise, you open an existing presentation, change paragraph alignment, and then copy formatting attributes.

1. Open the PPT362 presentation and save it as "Staff Meeting" to your personal storage location.
2. Let's change the paragraph alignment of the title:
   CLICK: in title placeholder
   CLICK: Align Right button (▤) on the Formatting toolbar
   The title is now positioned on the right side of the placeholder.
3. To align the title to the left side of the placeholder:
   CLICK: Align Left button (▤) on the Formatting toolbar
4. To change the paragraph alignment of the subtitle:
   CLICK: in subtitle placeholder
   CLICK: Align Right button (▤) on the Formatting toolbar to position the subtitle on the right side of the placeholder
5. Now let's change the formatting of the subtitle:
   SELECT: the text "Monashee Community College"
   CLICK: Bold button (B) on the Formatting toolbar
   CLICK: Italic button (I) on the Formatting toolbar
   SELECT: Arial font from the Font drop-down list (Times New Roman ▾)
   SELECT: 36-point size from the Font Size drop-down list (10 ▾)
   (*Note:* If your computer does not have Arial font, select an alternate font.)

6. To copy the subtitle formatting attributes using the Format Painter, ensure the subtitle "Monashee Community College" is still selected and then:
   CLICK: Format Painter button () on the Standard toolbar
7. To copy the formatting to the text "Year End" of the title:
   DRAG: mouse pointer over the title text "Year End"
   When you release the mouse button, the text "Year End" is formatted with the same characteristics as the subtitle.
8. To copy the formatting to more than one item, ensure that "Year End" is still selected and then:
   DOUBLE-CLICK: Format Painter button ()
9. Using the I-beam paintbrush mouse pointer:
   SELECT: the rest of the title text "Staff Meeting"
   CLICK: Next Slide button () to move to the second slide
   SELECT: "Agenda" in the title placeholder
10. To finish using the paintbrush mouse pointer:
    CLICK: Format Painter button ()
11. On your own, change the first bullet item of the second slide to include the underline attribute and an Arial, 40-point font. Use the Format Painter to copy this formatting to the remaining bullet items.
12. Save, print, and then close the revised presentation.



## 3.6.3 Coldstream Corporation: Employees

In this exercise, you create a new presentation with a Table layout and then enter and edit the text and the table.

1. Start a new presentation and select the Table layout (located in the first row, fourth column).
2. Save the new presentation as "Coldstream Employees" to your personal storage location.
3. Type **Coldstream Employees** in the title placeholder.
4. Double-click the table placeholder and create a table with two columns and five rows.
5. Type the following text and numbers in your table:

| Department | Employees |
|---|---|
| Finance | 156 |
| Marketing | 138 |
| Communications | 237 |
| Real Estate | 369 |

6. Select the entire table and change the text to Arial, 32-point font. Change the text "Department" and "Employees" to 36-point font with boldface attribute.

7. To narrow the second column, drag the middle border to the right one inch.
8. Vertically center all the data in the table using the Center Vertically button (▤) on the Tables and Borders toolbar.
9. Save, print, and then close the "Coldstream Employees" presentation.

## 3.6.4 Spiderman Web Marketing: Internet Business

You will now start a blank presentation and insert a Word outline in PowerPoint. You will then proof the presentation using the Spelling command and the Find and Replace command.

1. Begin a new presentation and cancel from the New Slide dialog box without making a selection.
2. Insert the Word document entitled PPT364 using the Insert, Slides from Outline menu command.
3. Apply an appropriate design template to the presentation.
4. Change the first slide to a Title Slide layout.
5. Switch to Slide Show view and then view the presentation's six slides.
6. Return to the first slide and use the Spelling command to check the entire presentation for spelling errors. Replace "comunication" with "communication," "possibel" with "possible," "Retalers" with "Retailers," and delete the extra "to."
7. Return to the first slide. Using the Find and Replace command, replace all the occurrences of the phrase "World Wide Web" with "WWW."
8. Save your presentation as "Web Marketing" to your personal storage location.
9. Print and then close the presentation.

## 3.6.5 On Your Own: Bernice's Belly Dancing Lessons

Create an interesting presentation announcing the opening of your new business that offers belly dancing lessons. Vary the formatting of the text within your presentation using different fonts, sizes, and formatting attributes. Create a slide listing the benefits of belly dancing and customize the bullets within the list using graphical bullets. Also change the paragraph alignment throughout the presentation. Save your presentation as "Belly Dancing" and print a copy.

### 3.6.6 On Your Own: Birdhouse Construction

The local Naturalist club has asked you to create a presentation for their upcoming Information Night. Begin the presentation with a title page titled "Birdhouse Construction." The second slide should include the title "Birdhouse Dimensions" and the following table:

| Species | Box Hight | Entrence Diameter |
|---|---|---|
| Bluebird | 8–12 feet | 1.5 feet |
| Chickadee | 8–10 feet | 1.2 feet |
| Purpel Martin | 6 feet | 2.25 feet |

Format the table cells to distinguish the headings from the data underneath. Replace all the occurrences of the word "feet" with "inches." Vertically center the text within the table. Proof the presentation for spelling errors. Save your presentation as "Birdhouse" and print a copy.



## 3.7 Case Problems: Belton Bank

Now that Richard has learned some techniques for working with text, he is ready to tackle his upcoming Shareholders Meeting presentation. Since the text for his presentation has already been created in a Word document, he will first insert the Word outline into PowerPoint. He will then add a simple table and then embellish his presentation by formatting the text, customizing a list, and changing paragraph alignment. Finally, he will proof his presentation for spelling errors.

In the following case problems, assume the role of Richard and perform the same steps that he identifies. You may want to re-read the chapter opening before proceeding.

1. Richard begins a new presentation and leaves the New Slide dialog box without making a selection. He inserts the Word document entitled PPT371 using the Insert, Slides from Outline menu command. He applies the Bold Stripes design template and changes the first slide to a Title Slide layout.

   On the first slide, he types **Presented by Richard Belton, President and CEO** in the subtitle placeholder. He saves the presentation as "Shareholders" to his personal storage location.

2. Richard adds a fifth slide to the presentation with a Table layout. He inserts the misspelled title "Fund Comparaison" and then creates the following table:

| | 1998 | 1997 |
|---|---|---|
| Growth Fund | 3300 | 1756 |
| Income Fund | 2488 | 2000 |
| Security Fund | 250 | 1574 |

He changes the typeface of the entire table to Arial. Richard adds bold attributes to the headings "1998" and "1997," and italic attributes to the funds listed in the first column. To the data in the remaining cells, he changes their paragraph alignment to align right. Richard saves the revised "Shareholders" presentation.

3. Richard would like to customize the bulleted lists of his presentation. He moves to the second slide. Using the Bullets and Numbering dialog box, he selects an appropriate picture bullet using the Picture command button. On the third slide, he changes the list to a numbered list. For the fourth slide, Richard changes the list bullets to a), b), and c).

   To ensure accuracy and save time, Richard uses the Format Painter to change the titles on each of the slides to bold, Arial, 48-point font. To be consistent with the first slide, he realigns all the slide titles to the right. Richard saves the revised "Shareholders" presentation.

4. Richard uses the Find and Replace command to change each occurrence of the word "Fund" to "Funds." Finally, he uses the Spelling command to ensure that no spelling errors exist. Richard saves the revised "Shareholders" presentation and prints a copy. Looking over the printed copy, Richard is ready for show time!

# Notes

# Notes

# Notes

# Notes

# Microsoft PowerPoint 2000

## *Jazzing Up Your Presentations*

## Chapter Four

# Chapter Outline



# Learning Objectives

After reading this chapter, you will be able to:

- Create and modify objects using the Drawing toolbar
- Label AutoShapes and other parts of a slide
- Change the formatting and layout of every slide in a presentation

Case Study

## Walters Import Cars

Karl Walters recently purchased *Lucky Lou's Car Dealership*. After gaining ownership, Karl changed the name of his new business to *Walters Import Cars* and immediately built a new showroom to display the latest models of import cars.

Karl is eager to promote his new business using PowerPoint at an upcoming Car Show. Karl has discovered one of Lucky Lou's previously created PowerPoint presentations; however, he would like to add some original graphics to the presentation. He also thinks Lou's presentation requires a more consistent look.

In this chapter, you and Karl learn how to create, manipulate, and format graphics using the Drawing toolbar. You also learn how to change the order of several graphic objects, group them, insert and manipulate text in graphic objects, and insert text outside of placeholders. Finally, you will achieve a consistent look throughout your presentation using the Slide Master.



# 4.1 Working with Draw Objects

Think of a slide as a single piece of paper comprised of two layers. On the first layer, called the *slide layer*, you enter, edit, and format the text of your presentation. The second layer, known as the **draw layer,** exists as an invisible surface floating above (and mostly independent of) the slide layer. This transparent layer holds *objects*, such as lines, arrows, and text boxes. You can size, move, and delete objects on the draw layer without affecting the data stored on the underlying slide.

In this module, you learn how to insert and manipulate a variety of graphic objects on a presentation's draw layer.

## 4.1.1 Inserting Objects on the Draw Layer

**FEATURE**
You place lines, arrows, rectangles, ovals, and other shapes (collectively known as **AutoShapes**) on a slide's draw layer. AutoShapes can serve to draw the viewer's attention to specific areas or simply enhance a worksheet's visual appearance.

**METHOD**

1. CLICK: an object button on the Drawing toolbar
2. CLICK: on a slide to insert the object
3. DRAG: the object's sizing handles to size the object
4. DRAG: the center of the object to move it

**PRACTICE**

You now insert and manipulate AutoShape objects on the slide's draw layer.

*Setup:* Ensure that no documents are open in the application window.

1. Open the PPT410 data file.

2. Save the document as "Metro" to your personal storage location. In the next few steps, you're going to embellish this presentation with a few AutoShapes.

3. To add graphics to the draw layer, you must use the Drawing toolbar. By default, this toolbar is positioned along the bottom of the application window. (*Note:* If this toolbar isn't displaying, right-click an existing toolbar and then choose Drawing.) Let's insert the Sun AutoShape in the area between the main title and the subtitle. To begin:
   CLICK: AutoShapes button (AutoShapes ▾) on the Drawing toolbar
   CHOOSE: Basic Shapes

4. On the Basic Shapes submenu:
   CHOOSE: Sun (☼)
   The pop-up menu disappears and your mouse pointer changes to a small cross-hair as you move it over the slide area.

5. There are two methods for placing an object on the draw layer. For most objects, you simply click the cross-hair mouse pointer anywhere on the slide to create a default-sized graphic. For more precision, you drag the mouse pointer and size the object as you place it. Let's insert a default-sized Sun graphic object:
   CLICK: beneath the main title

6 The Sun object appears surrounded by eight white boxes, as shown to the right. These boxes are called **sizing handles** and only appear when the object is selected. You use these handles to modify the height and width of the object using the mouse. The yellow diamond is an **adjustment handle** that lets you change the appearance, not the size, of most AutoShapes. For example, by dragging the adjustment handle on the Sun graphic, you can make the circle larger or smaller. To deselect the AutoShape object:
CLICK: in the title placeholder (*or anywhere else on the slide*)
The sizing handles disappear when the graphic is no longer selected.

7 Position the mouse pointer over the Sun object until the mouse pointer changes shape to a four-pronged cross and arrow. To move a graphic, position the mouse pointer in the center of the graphic and then drag it to a new location. To size a graphic, select the object and then drag its sizing handles. To size a graphic while keeping its proportions intact, hold the SHIFT key down while dragging a corner sizing handle. To begin:
CLICK: Sun graphic once to select it
Note that the sizing handles are displayed.

8 On your own, practice moving and resizing the Sun object. Before proceeding, your screen should appear similar to Figure 4.1.

**Figure 4.1**
Moving and resizing the AutoShape object

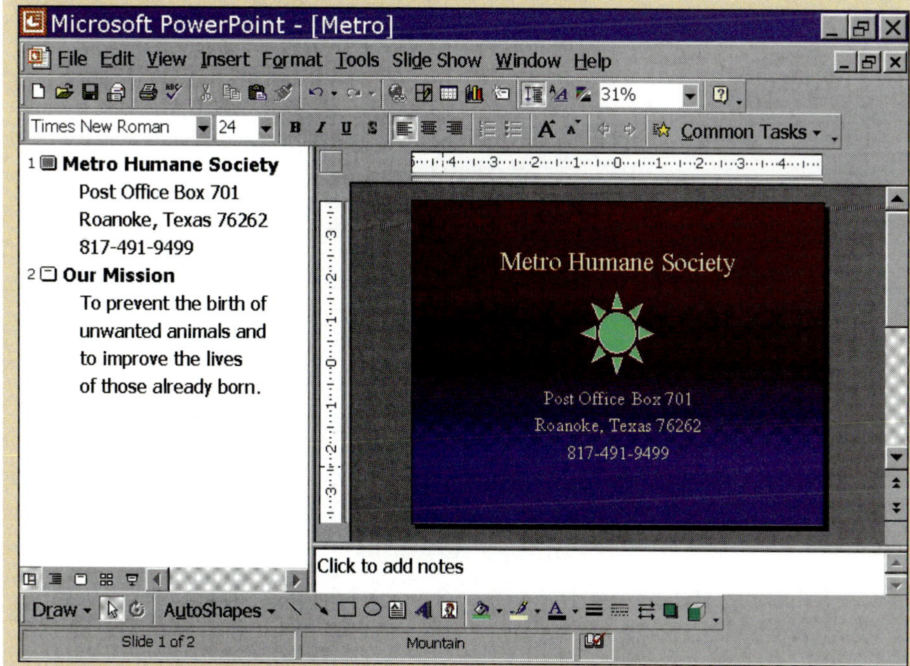


9 Save the presentation and keep it open for use in the next lesson.

POWERPOINT

## 4.1.2 Manipulating and Formatting Draw Objects

**FEATURE**
Besides sizing an object, you can enhance an AutoShape's appearance and visibility by selecting line styles and fill colors. You can also move and copy objects using standard drag and drop techniques or the Clipboard. To remove an object from the draw layer, select the object and then press the DELETE key.

**METHOD**
To display the Format AutoShape dialog box:

- DOUBLE-CLICK: an AutoShape object, or
- RIGHT-CLICK: an AutoShape object
  CHOOSE: Format AutoShape

**PRACTICE**
You now practice inserting, copying, and removing draw objects. You also apply formatting to objects using the Drawing toolbar and the Format AutoShape dialog box.

*Setup:* Ensure that you have completed the previous lesson and that the "Metro" presentation is displaying.

1 Using the Drawing toolbar, let's format the Sun object by selecting a new background fill color:
SELECT: Sun object by clicking the object once
CLICK: down arrow attached to the Fill Color button ( ) on the Drawing toolbar
SELECT: a color that resembles gray from the color palette
Note how the object has been filled with the new color.

2 Let's insert another draw object to create a border beneath the phone number in the subtitle. Do the following:
CLICK: Line button ( ) on the Drawing toolbar

3 Rather than clicking on the slide to place a default-sized line, position the mouse pointer below the first digit (8) in the telephone number. Then, by referring to Figure 4.2, click the mouse button and drag the cross-hair pointer to the right so that the line extends to just below the last digit of the phone number. When finished dragging the pointer, release the mouse button. (*Note:* Be sure to drag the mouse horizontally. Dragging slightly upward or downward will create a slanted line. Holding the SHIFT key down while dragging will help constrain the angle of the line, making it easier to draw a straight line.)

**Figure 4.2**
Inserting a line using the Drawing Toolbar

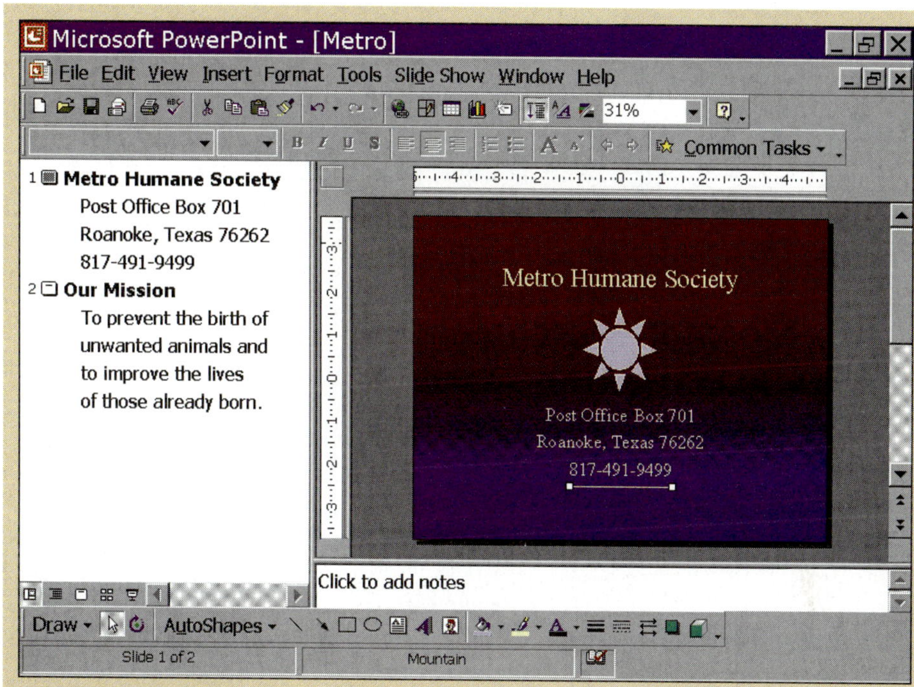


4 Let's change the line's formatting characteristics. With the line still selected:
RIGHT-CLICK: Line object once the four pronged cross and arrow are positioned over the line
CHOOSE: Format AutoShape
CLICK: *Colors and Lines* tab
The Format AutoShape dialog box appears, as shown in Figure 4.3. (*Hint:* You can also double-click the object to display the dialog box in Figure 4.3.)

**Figure 4.3**
Format AutoShape dialog box: *Colors and Lines* tab

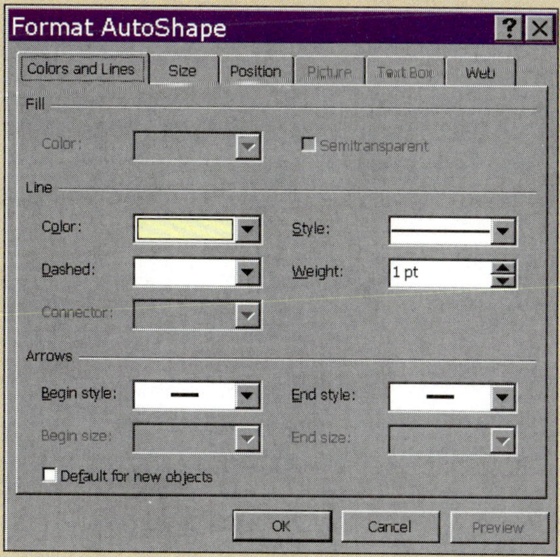

5. To change the color of the line from light yellow to light gray:
SELECT: a color that resembles light gray from the *Color* drop-down list in the *Line* area

6. To change the weight of the line to six points:
SELECT: 6 pt from the *Style* drop-down list
CLICK: OK command button
Your screen should now appear similar to Figure 4.4.

**Figure 4.4**
Formatting draw objects

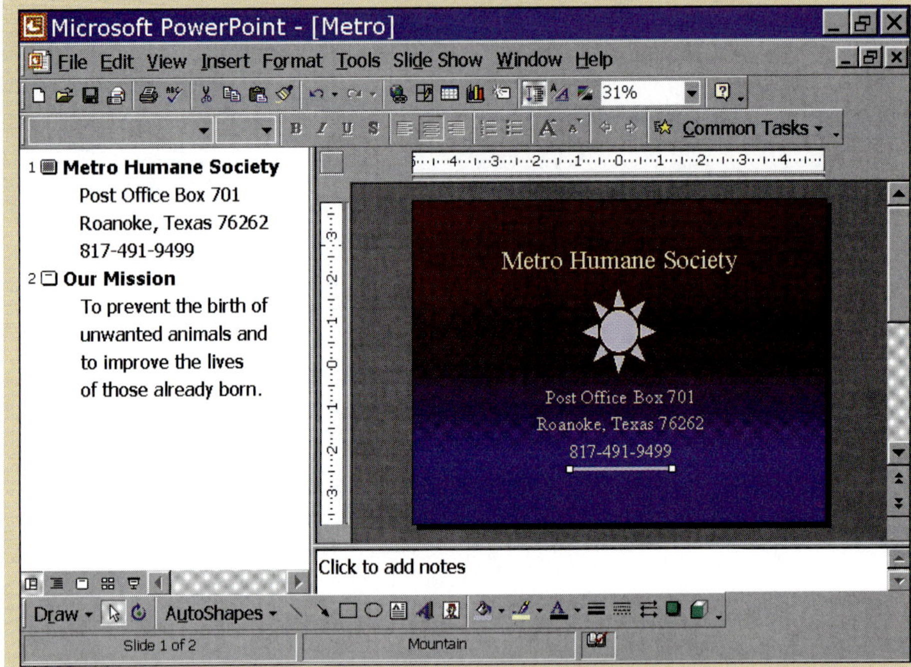


7. Let's practice using the *Size* tab of the Format AutoShape dialog box. Using this tab, you can enter exact size dimensions and change an object's rotation. With the object still selected:
RIGHT-CLICK: Line object
CHOOSE: Format AutoShape
CLICK: *Size* tab
The dialog box should now appear similar to Figure 4.5.

**Figure 4.5**
Format AutoShape dialog box: *Size* tab

Use the *Size and rotate* area to enter specific size dimensions and to change an object's rotation.

Scale an object to size using the *Height* and *Width* spin boxes.

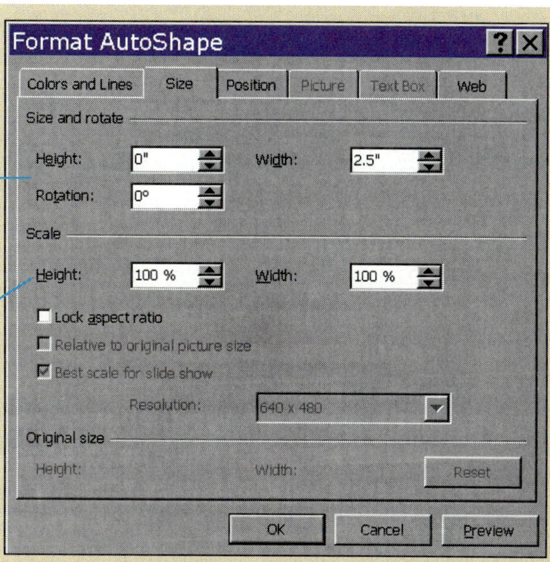


8 Let's change the width of the object:
CLICK: up arrow in the *Width* spin box until 3" appears

9 Before closing this dialog box:
CLICK: *Position* tab to view options for positioning the object
CLICK: *Web* tab to specify the text property of a Web graphic
CLICK: *Colors and Lines* tab to return to the first tab
CLICK: OK command button

10 To undo the modification you made to the line width:
CLICK: Undo button (↶)

11 In addition to sizing and moving objects, you can also copy and delete objects that you place on a slide. You will now place a copy of the Sun object to the right. To do so, position the mouse pointer over the Sun object until the mouse pointer changes to a four-pronged cross and arrow. Then, do the following to copy the object:
PRESS: CTRL key and hold it down
CLICK: the left mouse button and hold it down
DRAG: the gray Sun object to the right

12 To complete the operation, release the mouse button and then release the CTRL key. You should now see a second Sun object on the slide.

13 To delete the second Sun object, ensure that it is selected and then do the following:
PRESS: DELETE

14 Save the presentation and keep it open for use in the next lesson.

## 4.1.3 Ordering and Grouping Objects

**FEATURE**
In PowerPoint, you have control over how objects are layered on a slide. That is, you can control whether an object is positioned in front of or behind another object, or in front of or behind text. When an image is composed of multiple objects, you might want to group them together before moving, copying, or resizing the image.

**METHOD**
To change where an object appears in relation to other objects and text:

1. SELECT: an object
2. CLICK: Draw button (Draw ▾) on the Drawing toolbar
3. CHOOSE: Order
4. CHOOSE: an option from the Order menu

To create a single object out of a group of objects:

1. DRAG: with the mouse pointer to select the objects to be grouped
2. CLICK: Draw button on the Drawing toolbar
3. CHOOSE: Group

**PRACTICE**
You will now add an object to the first slide of the "Metro" presentation. Next, you will then position the object behind the existing Sun object and then group the two objects to form a single object.

*Setup:* Ensure that you've completed the previous lessons in this module and that slide 1 of the "Metro" presentation is displaying.

1 CLICK: Oval button (○) on the Drawing toolbar
POINT: to the upper-left corner of the Sun graphic
DRAG: with the mouse to the right and down until a circle covers the Sun graphic (refer to Figure 4.6)
Your screen should now appear similar to Figure 4.6.

**Figure 4.6**

A circle appears in front of the Sun graphic

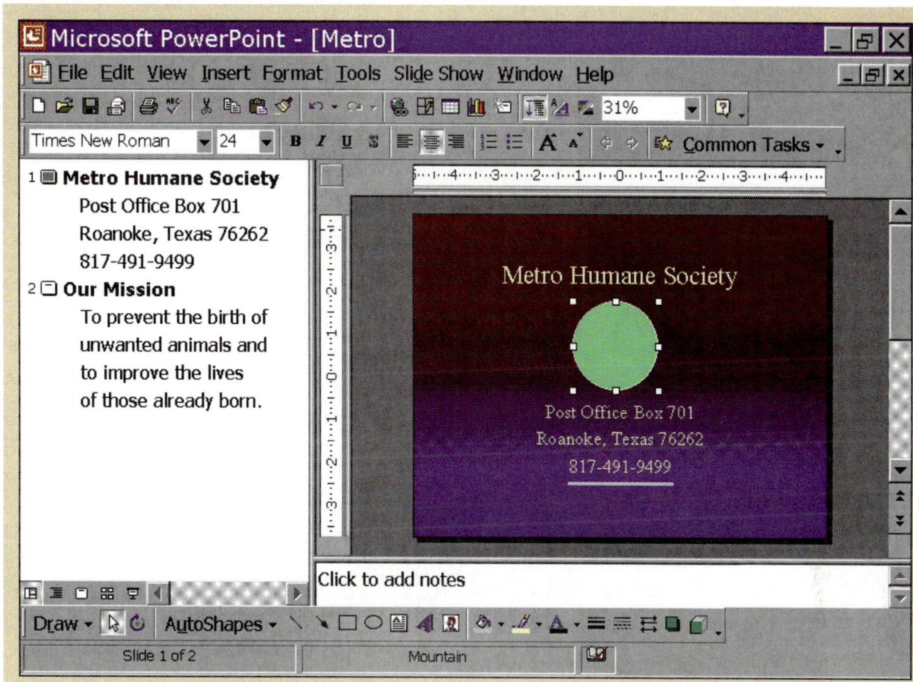


2. With the circle object still selected, let's move it behind the Sun graphic:
CLICK: Draw button on the Drawing toolbar
CHOOSE: Order, Send to Back

3. To deselect the oval object:
CLICK: away from the object
Your screen should now appear similar to Figure 4.7.

**Figure 4.7**

The circle object is now in back of the Sun graphic

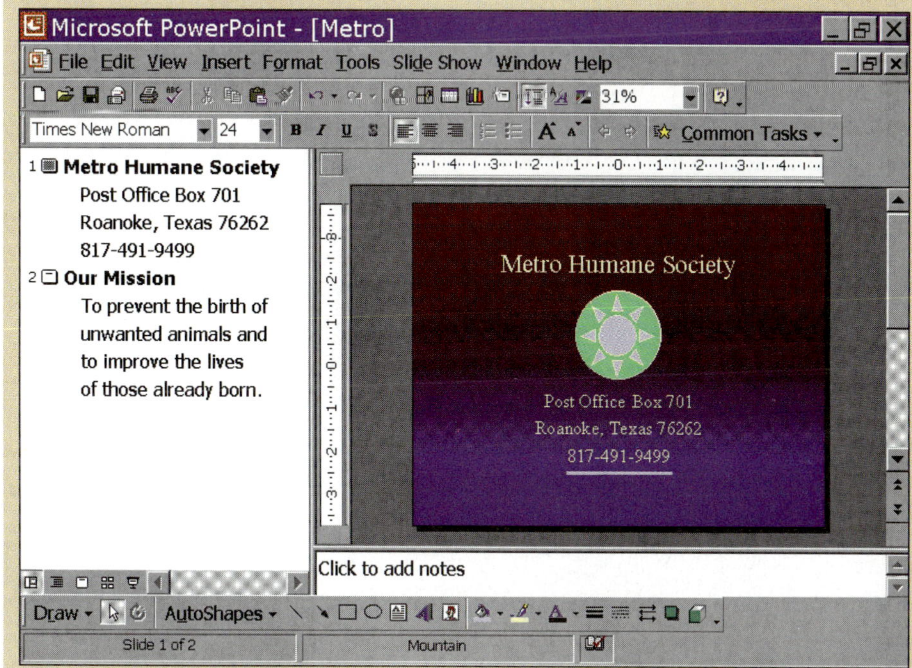

4. To create a single object out of the Sun and Oval objects, you must first select both objects. To do this, simply position above and to the left of both objects, and then:
DRAG: down and to the right ensuring that the drag box encloses both objects completely
Note that both objects are now selected, as indicated by the two sets of sizing handles.

5. To group the selected objects together:
CLICK: Draw button on the Drawing toolbar
CHOOSE: Group
The graphic should now be selected as a single group. As mentioned previously, once objects are grouped together, you manipulate them as a single object for greater ease when moving, copying, and resizing.

6. Save and then close the revised presentation.

**4.1 Self Check** When is it useful to group objects?

# 4.2 Positioning Text Anywhere

When building presentations in PowerPoint, you will most often insert text in a slide's existing title, subtitle, and bulleted list placeholders. However, when you want to label a draw object, picture, or chart, you will need greater control over where text is positioned. In this module, you learn how to add labels to draw objects and position text using text boxes.

## 4.2.1 Inserting Text In Draw Objects

**FEATURE**
When used appropriately, AutoShapes help attract your audience's attention. As such, they serve as the perfect backdrop for the words and phrases that need special emphasis.

**METHOD**

- To add text to an AutoShape:
  RIGHT-CLICK: the AutoShape
  CHOOSE: Add Text
  TYPE: *the text you want to insert*
- To invoke text wrapping inside the AutoShape:
  RIGHT-CLICK: the AutoShape
  CHOOSE: Format AutoShape
  CLICK: *Text Box* tab
  SELECT: *Word wrap text in AutoShape* check box
  CLICK: OK command button

**PRACTICE**

In this lesson, you insert text inside an AutoShape and control text wrapping.

*Setup:* Ensure that PowerPoint is loaded and that no presentations are displaying.

1. Open the PPT420 data file.

2. Save the presentation as "Desktop World" to your personal storage location.

3. Review each of the slides in this presentation. Before continuing, display the second slide.

4. Let's add the Explosion 2 AutoShape to the bottom-right corner of the current slide.
   CLICK: AutoShapes button (AutoShapes ▾) on the Drawing toolbar
   CHOOSE: Stars and Banners
   CHOOSE: Explosion 2 from the Stars and Banners submenu

5. Let's insert a default-sized Explosion graphic object:
   CLICK: near the bottom-right corner of the slide

6. While referring to Figure 4.9 on page PP-151, move and resize the Explosion object.

7. To add text to the Explosion object:
   RIGHT-CLICK: the object
   CHOOSE: Add Text
   The insertion point is now blinking inside the object.

8. TYPE: **Available now for $2250!**
   CLICK: away from the object to deselect it
   Note how the text remained on one line and extends outside the AutoShape.

9. Let's turn on the text wrapping feature so that the text will fit within the AutoShape.
RIGHT-CLICK: Explosion object
CHOOSE: Format AutoShape
CLICK: *Text Box* tab
Your screen should now appear similar to Figure 4.8.

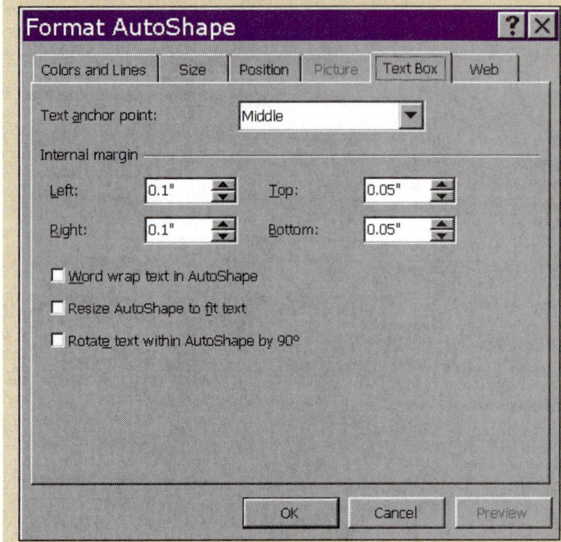


**Figure 4.8**
Format AutoShape dialog box: *Text Box* tab

10. SELECT: *Word wrap text in AutoShape* check box
CLICK: OK command button
The text should now fit within the AutoShape.

11. Let's change the formatting of the text so that it is easier to read.
SELECT: the text inside the Explosion object
CLICK: Font Color button ( ) on the Drawing toolbar
CHOOSE: dark purple from the color palette
CLICK: Bold button ( ) on the Formatting toolbar

12. CLICK: outside the Explosion object to deselect it
Your screen should now appear similar to Figure 4.9.

**Figure 4.9**
Wrapping text inside the AutoShape

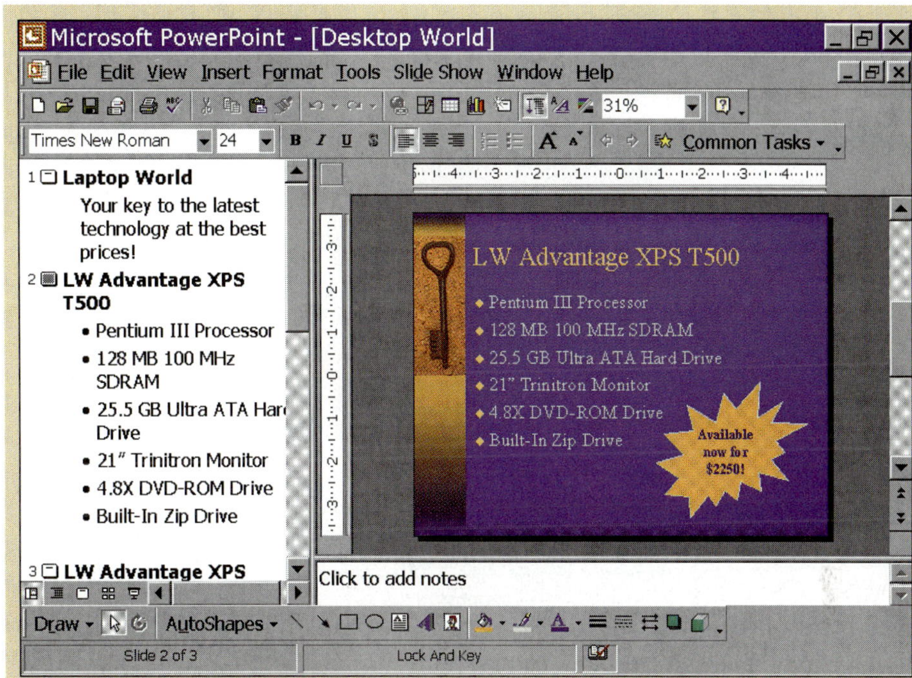


13 Save the revised presentation and keep it open for the next lesson.

## 4.2.2 Inserting Text Outside Placeholders

**FEATURE**
To position text anywhere on a slide, use a text box. A **text box,** which acts as a container for text, can contain more than one paragraph and can be formatted with its own unique character and paragraph formatting commands.

**METHOD**
1. CLICK: Text Box button (▤) on the Drawing toolbar
2. CLICK: in your document to create a text box that enlarges as you type, or
   DRAG: the mouse to establish the size of the text box

**PRACTICE**
You will now practice inserting a text box.

*Setup:* Ensure that you've completed the previous lesson and that slide 2 of the "Desktop World" presentation is displaying.

1. Let's use the Text Box tool to insert some additional text on the bottom of slide 2.
   CLICK: Text Box button (▤)

2. To insert a text box in the bottom left-hand corner of the slide that will enlarge as you type:
   CLICK: near the bottom left-hand corner of the slide
   (*Note:* You'll have an opportunity to move the text box later.)
   The insertion point should be blinking inside a text box, as shown below:

3. TYPE: **Business Lease: $77/Mo.**

4. On your own, refer to Figure 4.10 while dragging the text box into position.

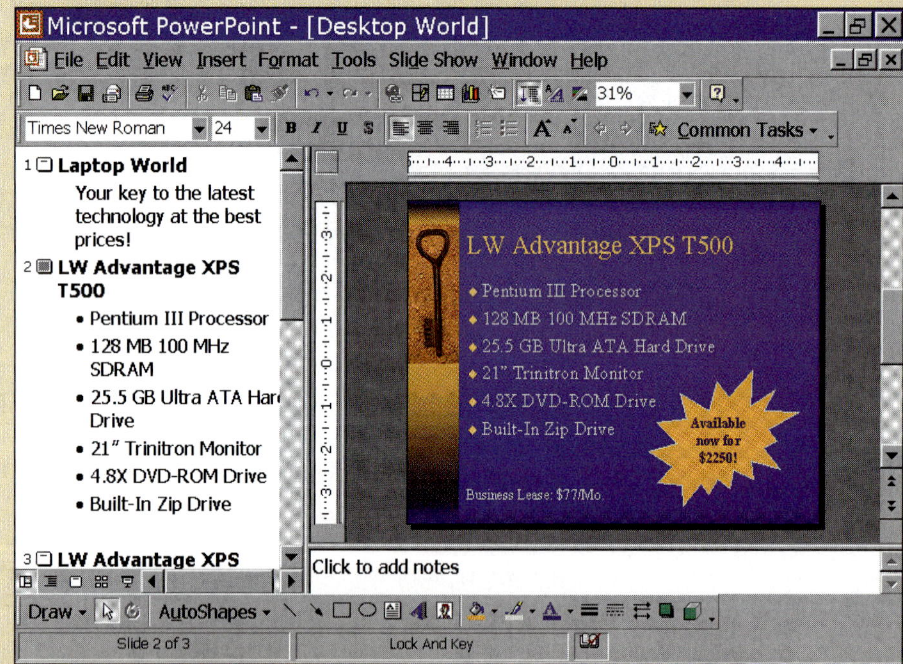


**Figure 4.10**
Inserting a text box

5. Save and then close the "Desktop World" presentation.

**4.2 Self Check** When would it be preferable to use a text box over a text placeholder?

# 4.3 Working with Masters

When you want to make a change to your presentation that affects every slide, such as changing the preset font in the Title placeholder, you don't have to edit each slide individually. Instead, you can edit the **Slide Master,** which controls the formatting of all the title and text placeholders in a presentation. Any objects you insert on the Slide Master will appear on all slides.

## 4.3.1 Making a Change that Affects Every Slide

**FEATURE**

Any changes you make to the Slide Master, including formatting the text placeholder, moving and resizing placeholders, and inserting new objects, will be visible on all slides in your presentation.

**METHOD**

1. CHOOSE: View, Master, Slide Master
2. Edit the master.
3. CLICK: Close button (Close) on the Master toolbar

**PRACTICE**

You will now open a short presentation named PPT430 and then practice editing the Slide Master.

*Setup:* Ensure that PowerPoint is loaded and that no presentations are displaying.

1 Open the PPT430 data file.

2 Save the file as "RC Melon" to your personal storage location. The presentation should appear in Slide view, similar to Figure 4.11. This presentation will be used by *R.C. Melon, Inc.*, a clothing retailer, for advertising at an upcoming clothing convention.

**Figure 4.11**

"RC Melon" presentation

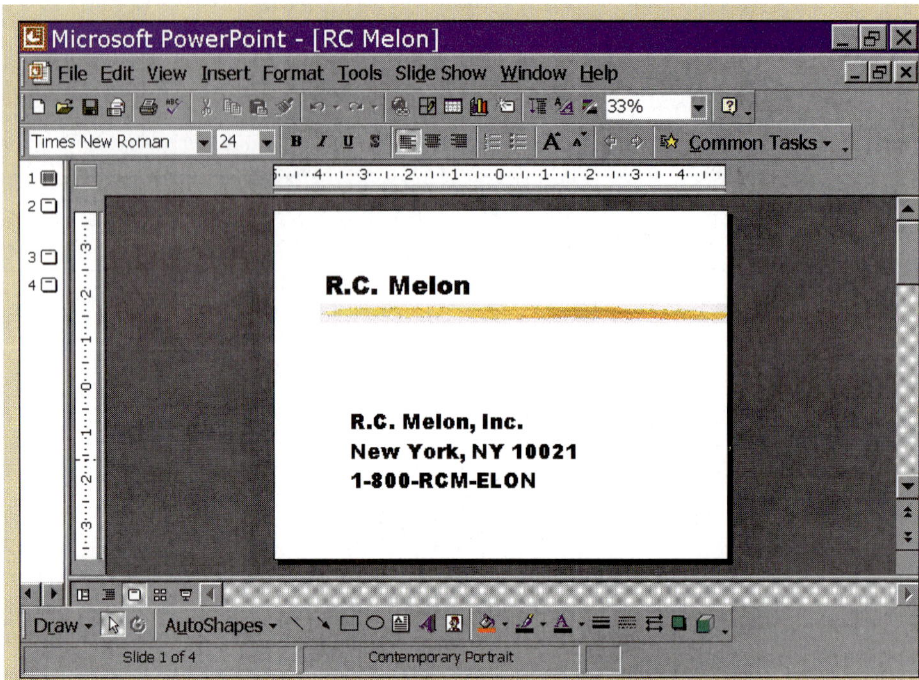


3. To get a feel for this presentation, switch to Slide Show view and then click the mouse until you've advanced through the entire presentation.

4. Let's apply italic formatting to all the titles in the presentation. The easiest way to do this involves editing the title placeholder on the Slide Master.
CHOOSE: View, Master, Slide Master
Your screen should now appear similar to Figure 4.12. (*Note:* If necessary, drag the Master toolbar out of the way so that it isn't obscuring the slide.)

**Figure 4.12**
Viewing the Slide Master

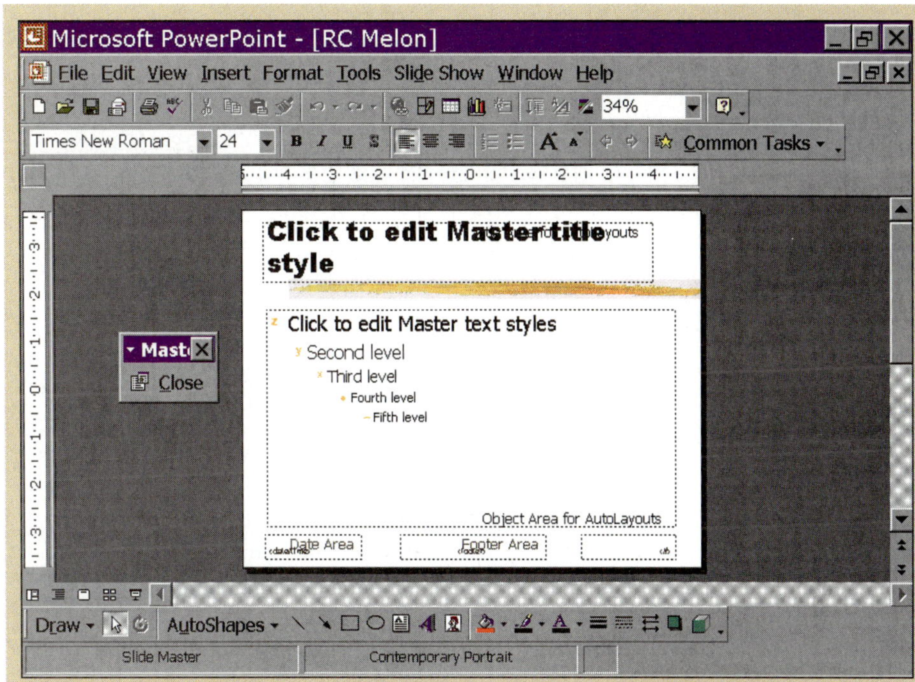


5 To edit the title placeholder, click where it says "Click to edit Master title style."

6 To apply italic formatting:
CLICK: Italic button (*I*) on the Formatting toolbar
The title on the master should now be italicized.

7 You can also modify the layout of each slide by resizing and moving a slide's placeholders. To illustrate:
SELECT: bulleted list placeholder by clicking its border once
The bulleted list placeholder should now be surrounded with sizing handles.

8 DRAG: the left-hand border to the right about an inch
(*Hint:* Use the ruler as your guide.)

9 To view the presentation:
CLICK: Close button (Close) on the Master toolbar

10 Now, view the entire presentation in Slide Show view. Note that the title placeholder on every slide is now italicized and that the bulleted items are now positioned further to the right.

11 The presentation should again be displaying in Slide view. Before proceeding, click the slide 2 icon in the Outline panel in order to display slide 2.

12. Let's change the look of the bullets on slides 2 through 4. To view the Slide Master:
CHOOSE: View, Master, Slide Master

13. To change the main bullet items, click where it says "Click to edit Master text styles."

14. CHOOSE: Format, Bullets and Numbering
The Bullets and Numbering dialog box should now appear.

15. To change the color of the bullets to orange:
CLICK: *Color* drop-down list
CLICK: Orange in the color palette

16. To change the bullet character to ❖:
CLICK: the bullet sample that contains "❖"
CLICK: OK command button

17. To view the presentation:
CLICK: Close button (Close) on the Master toolbar
Your screen should now appear similar to Figure 4.13. If you view the entire presentation, you'll notice that the new bullet symbol appears throughout the presentation.

**Figure 4.13**
The bullet symbols were modified using the Slide Master

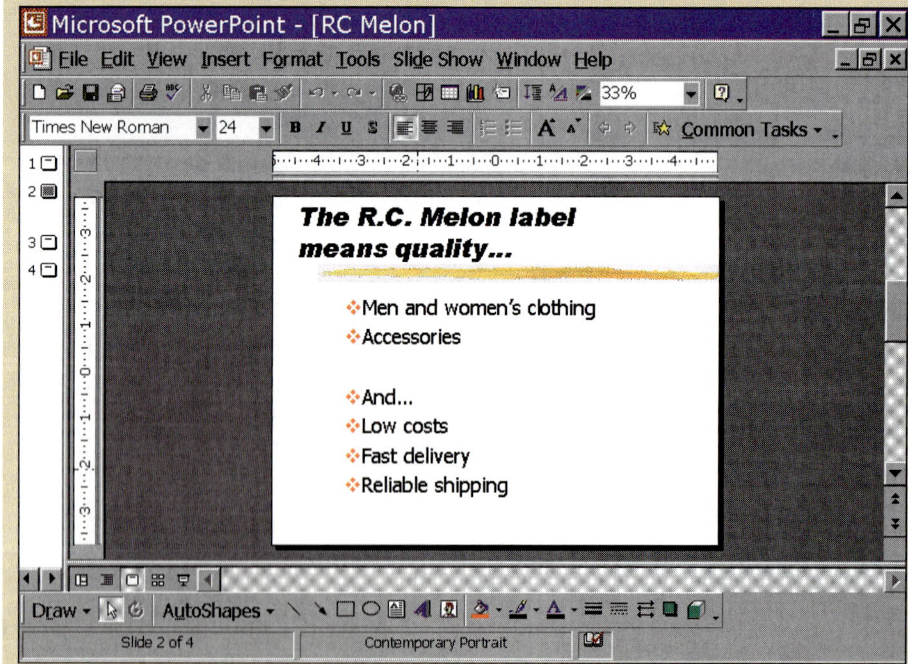


18. Save the revised presentation and keep it open for the next lesson.

## 4.3.2 Reapplying the Master to a Changed Slide

**FEATURE**
As you learned in the previous lesson, to format more than one slide at once, you edit the Slide Master. It is important to note that any changes you make to individual slides are considered *exceptions* to the master. If you later change the master or apply a design template, PowerPoint applies the new format but *retains* your exceptions. However, when you reapply a master to a slide, the exceptions are lost and the slide can be changed along with the other slides.

**METHOD**
1. CHOOSE: Format, Slide Layout
2. CLICK: Reapply command button

**PRACTICE**
You will begin by editing an individual slide in the "RC Melon" presentation. You will then reapply the master to the slide.

*Setup:* Ensure that the "RC Melon" presentation is displaying.

1 Display slide 2.

2 Let's remove the italic formatting from the title placeholder on slide 2.
SELECT: all the text in the title placeholder
CLICK: Italic button (I) to remove italic formatting
With this action, slide 2 no longer conforms to the Slide Master. This means that if you change the Title placeholder on the Slide Master, all the slides in your presentation will change *except* for slide 2.

3 To reapply the Slide Master to slide 2 so that it will change along with other slides in the future:
CHOOSE: Format, Slide Layout
Your screen should now appear similar to Figure 4.14.

**Figure 4.14**
Reapplying the master

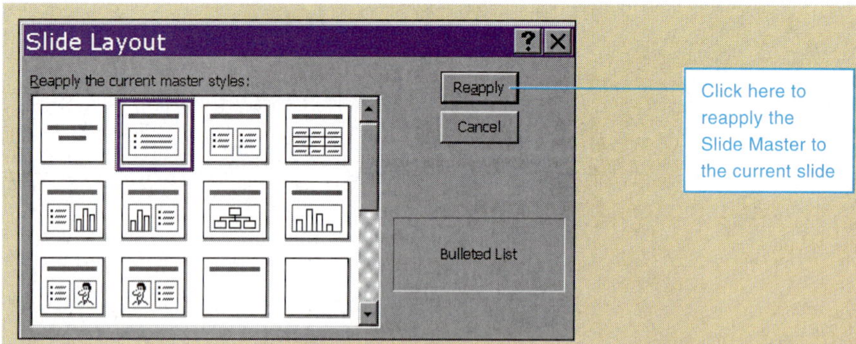


4. CLICK: Reapply command button
Note that the title placeholder is now italicized, which is in conformance with the Slide Master.

5. Save and then close the revised presentation.

**4.3 Self Check** What is the most efficient procedure for changing the way titles look in your presentation?

# 4.4 Chapter Review

Most people recognize the benefit of using formatting and graphics to improve the effectiveness of their presentations. The Drawing toolbar provides the tools for creating original graphics such as flowcharts and organization charts and for adding labels to objects. The Slide Master provides a single location for changing how fonts are used throughout a presentation and for adjusting the size and position of placeholders. In this chapter, you learned several commands for successfully formatting and jazzing up your presentations.

## 4.4.1 Command Summary

Many of the commands and procedures appearing in this lesson are summarized in the following table.

| Skill Set | To Perform This Task . . . | Do the Following . . . |
|---|---|---|
| **Modifying a Presentation** | Modify the Slide Master | CHOOSE: View, Master, Slide Master |
| | Reapply the Slide Master | CHOOSE: Format, Slide Layout<br>CLICK: Reapply command button |
| **Working with Text** | Create a text box | CLICK: Text Box button ( )<br>CLICK: on the slide to create a text box object |
| | Add text to an AutoShape | RIGHT-CLICK: the AutoShape<br>CHOOSE: Add Text |
| | Wrap text within AutoShapes | RIGHT-CLICK: the AutoShape<br>CHOOSE: Format AutoShape<br>CLICK: *Text Box* tab<br>SELECT: *Word wrap text in AutoShape* check box |
| **Working with Visual Elements** | Insert a draw object | CLICK: an object button on the Drawing toolbar<br>CLICK: on the slide to insert the object |
| | Size and move objects | SELECT: object<br>DRAG: object's handles to size, and<br>DRAG: object to move |
| | Delete an object on the draw layer | SELECT: an object<br>PRESS: DELETE |
| | Format an AutoShape object | RIGHT-CLICK: an AutoShape object<br>CHOOSE: Format AutoShape command |
| | Fill an AutoShape | CLICK: Fill Color button ( ) |
| | Scale and rotate an AutoShape | RIGHT-CLICK: an AutoShape object<br>CHOOSE: Format AutoShape command<br>CLICK: *Size* tab |
| | Change the order of objects | CLICK: Draw button (Draw)<br>CHOOSE: Order |
| | Group objects | CLICK: Draw button (Draw)<br>CHOOSE: Group |

### 4.4.2 Key Terms

This section specifies page references for the key terms identified in this chapter. For a complete list of definitions, refer to the Glossary provided immediately after the Appendix in this learning guide.

adjustment handle, *p. 141*

AutoShape, *p. 139*

draw layer, *p. 139*

sizing handles, *p. 141*

Slide Master, *p. 153*

text box, *p. 151*

## 4.5 Review Questions

### 4.5.1 Short Answer

1. What is the Slide Master?
2. Why is it significant that changes you make to individual slides are considered *exceptions* to the Slide Master?
3. What is a good reason for reapplying the Slide Master to a slide?
4. How would you go about inserting a rectangle on a slide?
5. What tool would you use to insert text in the upper-right corner of a slide?
6. What is an AutoShapes adjustment handle used for?
7. How would you go about making a duplicate copy of an AutoShape on a slide?
8. What are text boxes used for?
9. How do you add text to AutoShapes?
10. How do you reapply the Slide Master to a changed slide?

### 4.5.2 True/False

1. ____ Slides that you edit individually are considered exceptions to the Slide Master.
2. ____ To make a change that affects every slide, you should edit the Title Master.
3. ____ Text boxes can be formatted with unique character and paragraph formatting.
4. ____ It's possible to insert an AutoShape on a slide by clicking once on a slide.
5. ____ Adjustment handles are used for sizing AutoShapes.
6. ____ It's possible to add labels to AutoShapes.
7. ____ To move an object, drag the object's sizing handles.

8. ____ To scale and rotate an object, use the *Size* tab in the Format AutoShape dialog box.
9. ____ To draw AutoShape objects, click the Draw button (Draw) on the Drawing toolbar.
10. ____ To change the order of objects, click the Draw button (Draw) and then choose the Order option.

## 4.5.3 Multiple Choice

1. To change the character font for all title placeholders, you should edit the:
   a. Slide Master
   b. Title Master
   c. Handout Master
   d. Notes Master

2. To control whether an object displays in front of or behind another, use the ________ command.
   a. Group
   b. Ungroup
   c. Order
   d. Rotate

3. Which of the following should you use to enter free-form text on a slide?
   a. Text Box tool
   b. design template
   c. Text placeholder
   d. Slide Master

4. Which of the following makes it possible to edit more than one slide at once?
   a. color schemes
   b. backgrounds
   c. masters
   d. templates

5. Which of the following must you use to create lines and shapes?
   a. *Paste* option
   b. *Paste link* option
   c. Drawing toolbar
   d. Title placeholder

6. By default, lines are:
   a. white
   b. thin and dashed
   c. thin and solid
   d. None of the above

7. To select several objects at once, simply ________.
   a. drag the mouse around all objects
   b. click each object
   c. double-click each object
   d. None of the above

8. Which of the following can you use to change the shape, not the size, of an object?
   a. Slide Master
   b. adjustment handle
   c. sizing handle
   d. All of the above

9. Which of the following must you use to delete an object?
   a. Format AutoShape dialog box
   b. adjustment handle
   c. DELETE key
   d. All of the above

10. To display the Format AutoShape dialog box, ________ the AutoShape.
    a. click
    b. double-click
    c. right-click
    d. Both b and c

# 4.6 Hands-On Projects

## 4.6.1 Outdoor Adventure Tours: Cycling

This exercise practices inserting and manipulating several graphic objects on an existing presentation's draw layer.

1. Open the PPT461 presentation and save it as "Cycling" to your personal storage location.
2. Let's create a bicycle wheel using the Donut AutoShape. To begin:
   CLICK: AutoShapes button () on the Drawing toolbar
   CHOOSE: Basic Shapes
3. On the Basic Shapes submenu:
   CHOOSE: Donut ()
   The pop-up menu disappears and your mouse pointer changes to a small cross-hair as you move it over the slide area.
4. Let's place a default-sized Donut object on the draw layer:
   CLICK: to the left of the subtitle "Cycling Vacation"
   The Donut object should appear on the slide surrounded by eight sizing handles.
5. On your own, create a second Donut to the right of the first Donut repeating steps 2 through 4.
6. Move the Donuts so that they are positioned side by side, as shown below.

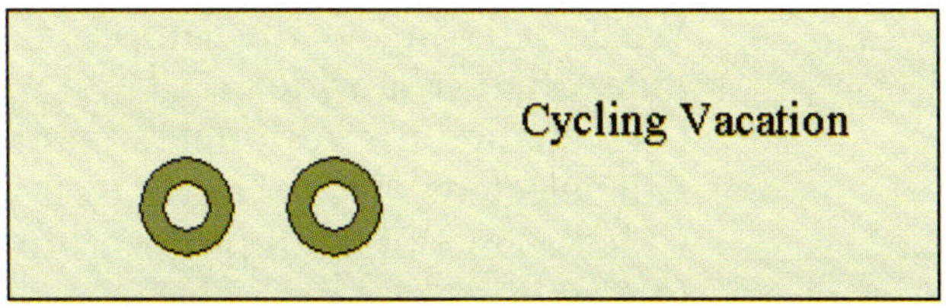


7. Let's insert a line between the bicycle tires.
   CLICK: Line button () on the Drawing toolbar
8. Rather than clicking on the slide to place a default-sized line, position the mouse pointer in the center of the first bicycle wheel. Then, click the mouse button and drag the cross-hair pointer to the right so that the line extends to the center of the second bicycle wheel. When finished dragging the pointer, release the mouse button. (*Note:* Be sure to drag the mouse horizontally in order to create a straight line.)
9. Finally, while the line is still selected, let's change the line's formatting characteristics:
   DOUBLE-CLICK: the line to display the Format AutoShape dialog box
10. To change the color of the line from dark green to pink:
    SELECT: a color that resembles pink from the *Color* drop-down list in the *Line* area

11. To change the weight of the line to 4.5 points:
    SELECT: 4½ pt from the *Style* drop-down list
    CLICK: OK command button
12. Save, print, and then close the "Cycling" presentation.

## 4.6.2 Monashee Community College: Logo

In this exercise, you will create a logo using drawing objects.

1. Begin a new presentation and select the Title Only layout for the first slide. Save the presentation as "Logo" to your personal storage location.
2. Type **Monashee Community College** in the title placeholder. In the following steps, you will create the logo shown below:

3. Let's create the blue rectangle using the Drawing toolbar.
   CLICK: Rectangle button () on the Drawing toolbar
   CLICK: in the area below the title
4. While referring to the sample, resize the rectangle so that it is taller than it is wide.
5. Let's change the rectangle's color to blue. With the rectangle still selected:
   CLICK: Fill Color drop-down arrow () on the Drawing toolbar
   CLICK: blue in the color palette
6. To insert a red text box on the right side of the rectangle:
   CLICK: Text Box button () on the Drawing toolbar
   CLICK: on a blank area of the slide
   CLICK: Fill Color drop-down arrow ()
   CHOOSE: More Fill Colors
   CLICK: red in the color palette
   CLICK: OK command button
7. The insertion point should be blinking inside the text box.
   TYPE: **MCC** in the text box
8. Select the text "MCC" and apply a Times New Roman 48-point font and the bold attribute.
9. While referring to the sample:
   DRAG: the text box so that it is positioned to the right of the rectangle

10. Let's group the logo objects:
    DRAG: over the logo to select the two objects
    CLICK: Draw button (Draw) on the Drawing toolbar
    CHOOSE: Group
11. To finalize the current slide, drag the logo so that it is centered beneath the title and between the margins.
12. Save, print, and close the "Logo" document.

## 4.6.3 Coldstream Corporation: Award Ceremony

In this exercise, you insert and format text inside an AutoShape and also use the Text Box tool.

1. Begin a new presentation and select the Blank layout for the first slide. Save the presentation as "Award" to your personal storage location.
2. Select the Stars and Banners submenu from the AutoShape button. Insert a default-sized Horizontal Scroll AutoShape in the center of the slide.
3. Increase the size of the Horizontal Scroll object while keeping its proportions intact by holding down the SHIFT key while dragging a corner sizing handle.
4. Add the text **Coldstream Corporation Award Ceremony** to the Horizontal Scroll object.
5. Use the Format AutoShape dialog box to turn on the text wrapping feature so that the text will fit within the AutoShape.
6. Rotate the Horizontal Scroll object by 10 degrees.
7. Change the text to an Arial 28-point font and apply the bold and italic attributes.
8. Change the font color to blue.
9. Change the Fill color of the Horizontal Scroll to yellow.
10. Use the Text Box tool to insert "Don't miss the social event of the year!" at the top of the slide.
11. Save, print, and close the "Award" presentation.

POWERPOINT

## 4.6.4 Spiderman Web Marketing: Design

This exercise practices editing the Slide Master and reapplying the Master to a changed slide.

1. Open the PPT464 presentation and save it as "Design" to your personal storage location.
2. View the entire presentation in Slide Show view.
3. In Slide view, use the Slide Master to apply italic formatting to all the titles of the presentation.
4. On each slide containing a bulleted list, move the left-hand border of the bulleted list placeholder to the right approximately 2 inches. (*Hint:* Use the Slide Master.)
5. Change the color of all the bullets in the presentation to purple.
6. Change all the bullets in the presentation to ❖.
7. Remove italic formatting from the title placeholder on slide 2 only.
8. Reapply the Slide Master to slide 2.
9. View the entire presentation again in Slide Show view.
10. Save, print, and then close the "Design" presentation.

## 4.6.5 On Your Own: Monster

Using a variety of draw objects, produce a slide that depicts a science-fictional monster. Use lines, arrows, labels, AutoShapes, and colors on your slide. Save your presentation as "Monster" to your personal storage location. Print your work.

## 4.6.6 On Your Own: Flow chart

Marvin's Moving Company requires a PowerPoint slide depicting the flow of work once a client has made contact with them. Using the Flowchart and Connectors AutoShapes, create a flow chart that includes the following steps:

- Contact from Client
- Issue Work Order Request
- Estimate Required?
- Yes—Contact Estimator
- No—Enter moving date in computer, then issue Confirmation Notice

Save your presentation as "Flow Chart" and print your work.

# 4.7 Case Problems: Walters Import Cars

After completing Chapter 4, Karl Walters is ready to modify Lucky Lou's previously created PowerPoint presentation for the upcoming Car Show. First, Karl will use the Slide Master to consistently change the formatting and layout on every slide. He will then insert text on a slide without using a text placeholder. Finally, Karl will insert and modify several graphic objects using the Drawing toolbar.

In the following case problems, assume the role of Karl Walters and perform the same steps that he identifies. You may want to re-read the chapter opening before proceeding.

1. Karl opens the PPT471 presentation and saves it as "Walters" to his personal storage location. After viewing the presentation, he reaches for his sunglasses and decides to create a more consistent and subdued tone. Using the Slide Master, Karl removes the italic, underline, and text shadow attributes from the Master title placeholder. He decreases the Master title font size to 44 points and changes the font color to white.

   For the main bullet item, he alters the bullet shapes from ⚒ to ■ and alters the bullet color from red to black. He removes the bold, italic, and underline attributes, and applies an Arial 32-point font. He also changes the font color from pink to black. Karl saves his changes.

2. Karl views the presentation in Slide Show view and notices that the title of the last slide has not accepted the master slide changes. The last slide was most likely modified individually and is now considered an exception to the master. For consistency, Karl reapplies the Slide Master to the final slide by using the Format, Slide Layout menu command. Karl sighs as he removes his sunglasses and saves his changes.

3. To acknowledge the change in ownership, Karl changes all occurrences of the text "Lucky Lou's Car Dealership" to "Walters Import Cars." He removes the cloverleaf clip art image from the first slide. On the third slide he replaces the clip art image with an import sports car and saves his changes.

   Eager to add text outside of a placeholder, Karl uses the Text Box to insert "Visit our new showroom!" at the bottom of the third slide. He formats the text using an Arial, 32-point font and changes the font color to purple. He saves his changes.

4. Karl is ready to add several graphics using the Drawing toolbar. He begins by adding a new slide with a Blank layout at the end of the presentation. He selects a Cloud Callout AutoShape from the Callouts submenu. He inserts a default-sized Cloud Callout graphic in the center of the slide. He increases the size of the graphic proportionally by holding down the SHIFT key while dragging a corner sizing handle.

   Karl inserts the text "Formerly Lucky Lou's Car Dealership" in the cloud graphic. He ensures that the Word wrap feature inside the AutoShape has been selected. He changes the font color to white, the font size to 28 points, and adds the bold attribute.

   To insert a rectangle that covers the cloud graphic, Karl clicks the Rectangle button on the Drawing toolbar and drags from the upper-left corner of the cloud graphic to the right and down. He changes the fill color of the rectangle to purple. He then changes the order of the two graphics by sending the rectangle to the back. Finally, Karl groups the cloud graphic and the rectangle graphic to achieve the following result.

Ready for the upcoming Car Show, Karl saves and prints a copy of the presentation.

# Notes

# Notes

# Notes

# Notes

# Microsoft PowerPoint 2000

*Preparing to Deliver a Presentation*

## CHAPTER FIVE

## Chapter Outline



## Learning Objectives

After completing this chapter, you will be able to:

- Add electronic effects to online presentations
- Insert hyperlinks and publish a presentation to the World Wide Web
- Prepare speaker notes, audience handouts, and overhead transparencies

Case Study

## Kool Kids Klothing

Viviana Morton owns a home-based business selling children's clothing. Her husband, Brian, created a PowerPoint presentation for her to use at her next home party and at an upcoming trade show.

Viviana would like to add some interest to her presentation using electronic effects. She frequently forgets to mention important items during her presentations and would therefore like to create speaker notes to assist her during her home parties. Viviana would like to use overhead transparencies and give her audience printed notes of the presentation. Brian has also suggested that she display her presentation on the World Wide Web.

In this chapter, you and Viviana learn how to add online effects including preset and custom animation, transitions, and hyperlinks. You will create headers and footers, speakers notes, audience handouts, and overhead transparencies. You will also learn how to preview a presentation as a Web page and then save it into HTML format for Web publishing.



# 5.1 Designing Online Presentations

Once you decide to deliver a presentation electronically using a computer, you have several options for making the presentation interesting, entertaining, and complete. In the following lessons, you learn how to enhance your online presentations with animation and transitions. You can apply most effects in Normal or Slide Sorter view. The Slide Sorter toolbar, labeled in Figure 5.1, provides shortcuts to several electronic effects.

**Figure 5.1**
Slide Sorter toolbar

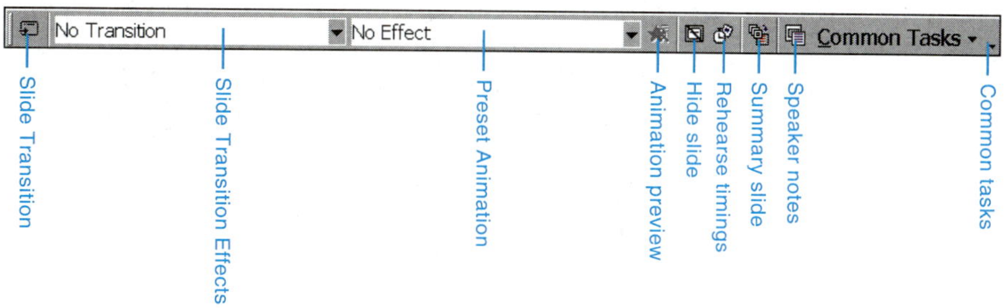

## 5.1.1 Animating Text and Objects

**FEATURE**

Visual and sound effects, called *animation*, are used to entertain and focus your audience on important points. Most slide objects can be animated. You can control how objects should appear on your slides (for example, from the left or right) and what sound should accompany the object. For example, you can apply a whoosh sound to text as it drops into place one letter at a time or the sound of screeching brakes as paragraphs race in from the left.

**METHOD**

- To create basic animations:
  SELECT: the object or placeholder that you want to animate
  CHOOSE: Slide Show, Preset Animation
  CHOOSE: an option on the menu
- To create custom animations:
  Display the slide that contains the objects you want to animate.
  CHOOSE: Slide Show, Custom Animation

**PRACTICE**

In this lesson, you open a seven-slide presentation and then practice adding animation.

*Setup:* Ensure that no presentations are open in the application window.

1. Open the PPT510 data file.

2. Save the presentation as "Small Business" to your personal storage location.

3. To familiarize yourself with the content of the presentation, view the entire presentation using Slide Show view. Note that the presentation contains quite a bit of text. In the following steps, you'll counteract the text-heavy nature of this presentation with interesting animations.

4. Before continuing, ensure that slide 1 is displaying in Normal view.

5. Let's use the Preset Animation command to animate the title on the first slide.
   CLICK: in the main title placeholder
   CHOOSE: Slide Show, Preset Animation
   Your screen should now appear similar to Figure 5.2.

**Figure 5.2**
The Preset Animation menu

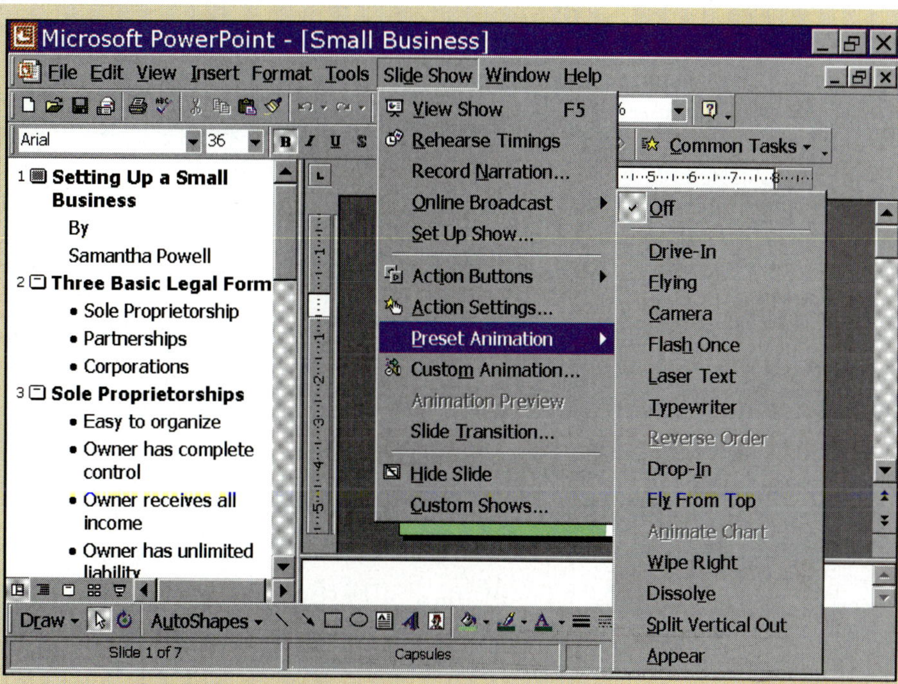


6. CHOOSE: Typewriter

7. To view the effect in action:
CHOOSE: View, Slide Show
CLICK: the left mouse button once to activate the animation
The letters appeared one by one and were accompanied by a typewriter sound effect.

8. To return to Normal view:
PRESS: ESC

9. Let's turn off the animation that we just applied to the first slide.
CHOOSE: Slide Show, Preset Animation
CHOOSE: Off

10. Let's apply custom animation to all the titles on the remaining slides. Instead of editing each slide individually, we're going to edit the Slide Master.
CHOOSE: View, Master, Slide Master

11. CHOOSE: Slide Show, Custom Animation
The Custom Animation dialog box should now appear, as shown in Figure 5.3.

**Figure 5.3**

Custom Animation dialog box: *Order & Timing* tab

Select the object you want to animate in this list box.

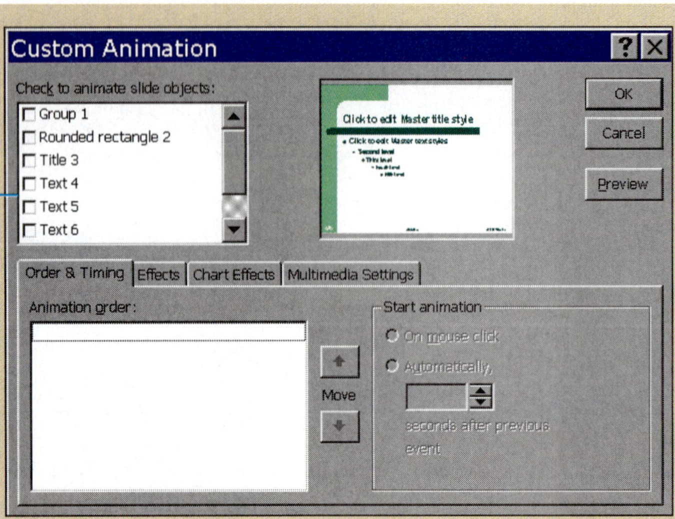


12 To animate a particular slide object, you must select it in the *Check to animate slide objects* list box. Because the text in the list box isn't very descriptive, it's sometimes difficult to tell what object is being referenced. However, if you click an object's name (not its check box), the object will appear selected in the preview area. To illustrate:
CLICK: the text "Title 3" in the list box (not its check box)
Note that the title placeholder is selected in the preview area.
CLICK: the text "Text 4" in the list box
The bulleted list placeholder is now selected in the preview area.

13 To animate the title placeholder:
SELECT: Title 3 check box
A check should now appear in the Title 3 check box. Note that the title is also selected in the preview area.

14 We'll come back to the *Order & Timing* tab later. For now, let's look at the *Effects* tab.
CLICK: *Effects* tab
The dialog box should now appear similar to Figure 5.4. According to the default selections in the dialog box, animated titles will display *all at once*, appear from the *left* side of the screen, and incorporate the *Fly* effect. Additionally, *no sound* will accompany the titles and they won't appear dimmed after animation.

**Figure 5.4**

Custom Animation dialog box: *Effects tab*

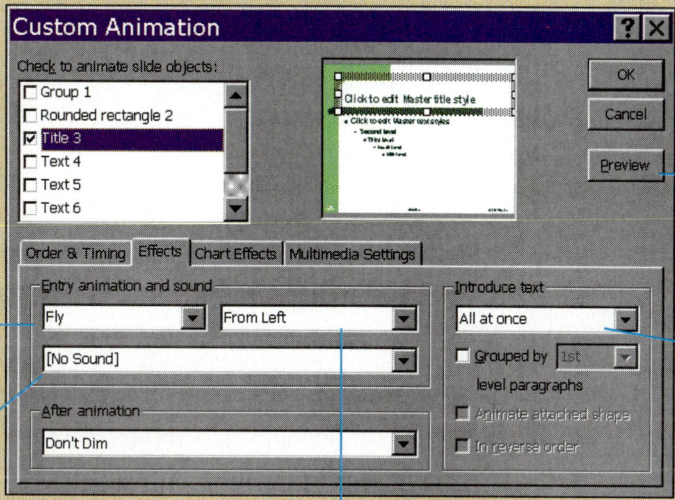


15 To preview these default settings:
CLICK: Preview command button
To change any of the default settings, use the drop-down lists in the *Entry animation and sound* area.

16 Let's review the settings in the *Order & Timing* tab.
CLICK: *Order & Timing* tab

17 Note that the *On mouse click* option button is currently selected in the *Start animation* area. With this option selected, the title won't display until the user clicks the mouse. Let's change this setting so that the title appears automatically once the slide is displayed.
SELECT: *Automatically* option button
When more than one animation event is scheduled on a slide or when creating a self-running slide show, you may want to include a time factor in the *Automatically* spin box. For this exercise, let's leave the spin box unchanged.

18 To leave the Custom Animation dialog box:
CLICK: OK command button

19 To close the Slide Master:
CLICK: Close (Close) on the Master toolbar
The presentation should now appear in Normal view.

20 On your own, view the animated titles by switching to Slide Show view. (*Note:* slide 1 isn't animated because you turned animation off in step 9.)

21 Save the presentation and keep it open for use in the next lesson.

## 5.1.2 Adding Slide Transitions

**FEATURE**

*Transitions* are the special effects you see when you go from one slide to the next. Previously only available in higher-end multimedia authoring programs, transitions can now be easily inserted into any of your PowerPoint presentations. The easiest way to apply transition effects is using the Slide Sorter toolbar.

**METHOD**

1. Display the presentation in Slide Sorter view.
2. Select one or more slides. To select multiple slides, press SHIFT while clicking each slide.
3. CLICK: Slide Transition Effects drop-down arrow (No Transition)
4. SELECT: a transition from the drop-down list

**PRACTICE**

You will now apply transition effects to all the slides in the "Small Business" presentation.

*Setup:* Ensure that you have completed the previous lesson and that the "Small Business" presentation appears in Normal view.

1 To switch to Slide Sorter view:
CHOOSE: View, Slide Sorter

2 To select all the slides in the presentation:
CHOOSE: Edit, Select All

3 In this step, you will apply a random transition effect to the presentation. What this means is that PowerPoint will decide what transition effect to apply each time you display another slide.
CLICK: Slide Transition Effects drop-down arrow (No Transition)
CHOOSE: Random Transition (located last in the drop-down list)

4 Display the presentation in Slide Show view.

5. To apply a fixed transition to slide 2:
CLICK: outside any miniature slide to deselect all slides
CLICK: slide 2
CLICK: Slide Transition Effects drop-down arrow (No Transition)
SELECT: Box In from the drop-down list

6. Display the presentation in Slide Show view.

7. Switch to Normal view.

8. Save and then close the revised presentation.

**5.1 Self Check** In an electronic slide show, what are transitions used for?

# 5.2 Using PowerPoint's Web Features

Most commonly, you will print a presentation for your reference or for inclusion in an audience handout. However, the Internet is a strong publishing medium unto itself. With the proper access, anyone can become an author and publisher. This section not only introduces you to previewing and printing presentations using traditional tools but also to publishing presentations electronically on the World Wide Web.

For those of you new to the online world, the **Internet** is a vast collection of computer networks that spans the entire planet, made up of many smaller networks connected by standard telephone lines, fiber optics, and satellites. The term **Intranet** refers to a private and usually secure local or wide area network that uses Internet technologies to share information. To access the Internet, you need a network or modem connection that links your computer to your account on the university's network or to an Independent Service Provider (ISP).

Once you are connected to the Internet, you can use Web browser software, such as Microsoft Internet Explorer or Netscape Navigator, to access the **World Wide Web.** The Web provides a visual interface for the Internet and lets you search for information by simply clicking on highlighted words and images, known as **hyperlinks.** When you click a link, you are telling your computer's Web browser to retrieve a page from a Web site and display it on your screen. Not only can you publish your presentations on the Web, you can incorporate hyperlinks directly within a presentation to facilitate navigating between documents.

## 5.2.1 Inserting Hyperlinks

**FEATURE**
Hyperlinks are useful for moving directly to another slide in the current presentation, displaying a slide in a different presentation, or opening a Web page. The simplest way to insert a hyperlink is to type it in. For example, if you type an HTML address, or URL, such as **www.mhhe.com** on a slide, PowerPoint will by default format it as a hyperlink. PowerPoint will also format e-mail addresses such as **person@mcgraw-hill.com** as hyperlinks. To format existing objects as hyperlinks, including text, graphics, and tables, you must use the Insert Hyperlink button ( ).

**METHOD**
- In Normal view:
  TYPE: a valid URL or e-mail address
- To format an existing object as a hyperlink:
  CLICK: Insert Hyperlink button ( ), or
  CHOOSE: Insert, Hyperlink

**PRACTICE**
You will now insert practice inserting hyperlinks.

*Setup:* Ensure that no presentations are displaying.

1. Open the PPT520 data file.

2. Save the presentation as "Chili Cookoff" to your personal storage location.

3. Let's format the text "Rocklin High School" as a hyperlink to Rocklin's Web site.
   SELECT: Rocklin High School

4. To format the selection as a hyperlink:
   CLICK: Insert Hyperlink button ( )
   The Insert Hyperlink dialog box should appear (Figure 5.5). By default, the *Existing File or Web Page* button is selected on the *Link to* bar on the left side of the dialog box.

**Figure 5.5**
Insert Hyperlink dialog box

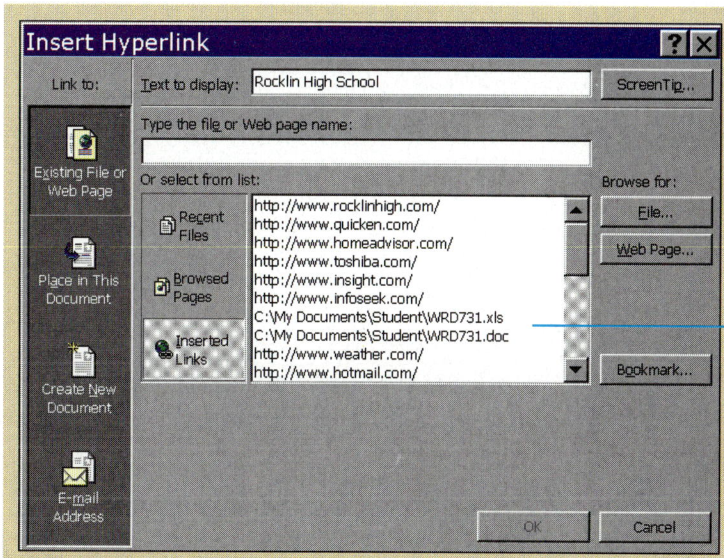


This list will be different on your computer.

5 The insertion point is blinking in the *Type the file or Web page name* text box.
TYPE: **www.rocklinhigh.com**
Notice that PowerPoint automatically formatted the address as "http://www.rocklinhigh.com."

6 CLICK: OK command button
The text "Rocklin High School" is now formatted as a hyperlink. You can only activate the hyperlink in Slide Show view.

7 View the presentation in Slide Show view. If you move the mouse pointer over the text "Rocklin High School" on the first slide, the mouse pointer will change to a hand, indicating that the text is formatted as a hyperlink.

8 Save the revised presentation and keep it open for the next lesson.

## 5.2.2 Publishing to the Web

**FEATURE**
PowerPoint makes it easy to convert a presentation for display on the World Wide Web. The process involves saving the presentation in **HTML** (Hypertext Markup Language) format for publishing to a Web server. Once saved using the proper format, you may upload the files to your company's Intranet or to a Web server.

## METHOD

- To preview how a presentation will appear as a Web page:
  CHOOSE: File, Web Page Preview
- To save a presentation into HTML format for Web publishing:
  CHOOSE: File, Save as Web Page

## PRACTICE

You will now practice saving the "Chili Cookoff" presentation in an HTML format.

*Setup:* Ensure that you've completed the previous lesson and that the "Chili Cookoff" presentation is displaying.

1. To save the current presentation as a Web page:
CHOOSE: File, Save as Web Page
The Save As dialog box appears with some additional options, as shown in Figure 5.6. Notice that "Web Page" appears as the file type in the *Save as type* drop-down list box.

**Figure 5.6**
Save As dialog box for a Web page

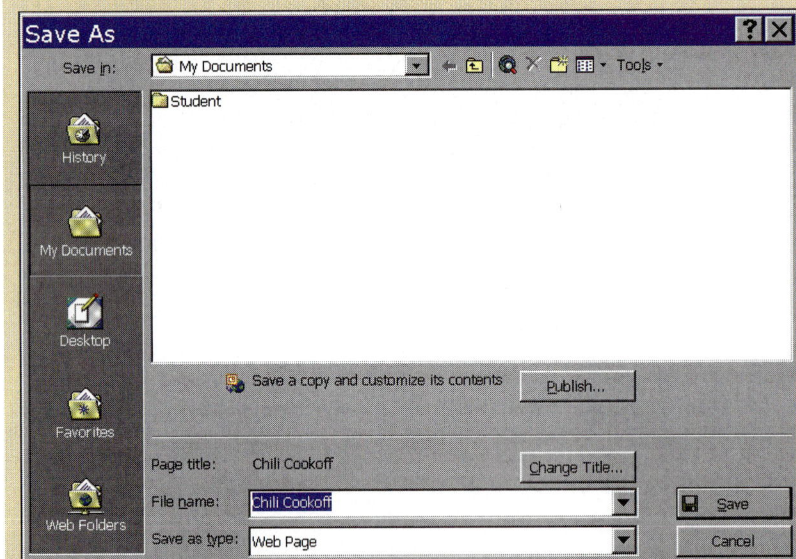


2. Using the *Save in* drop-down list box or the Places bar:
SELECT: *your storage location*, if not already selected
(*Note:* To publish or post your presentation Web page to an Intranet or to the Internet, you can click the Web Folders button ( ) in the Places bar and then select a server location.)

3. To proceed with the conversion to HTML:
CLICK: Save command button
The document is saved as "Chili.htm" to your personal storage location.

4 To preview how the presentation will appear in a Web browser:
CHOOSE: File, Web Page Preview
After a few moments, the presentation appears displayed in a Web browser window. Figure 5.7 shows the presentation displayed using Internet Explorer.

**Figure 5.7**
Viewing a document Web page

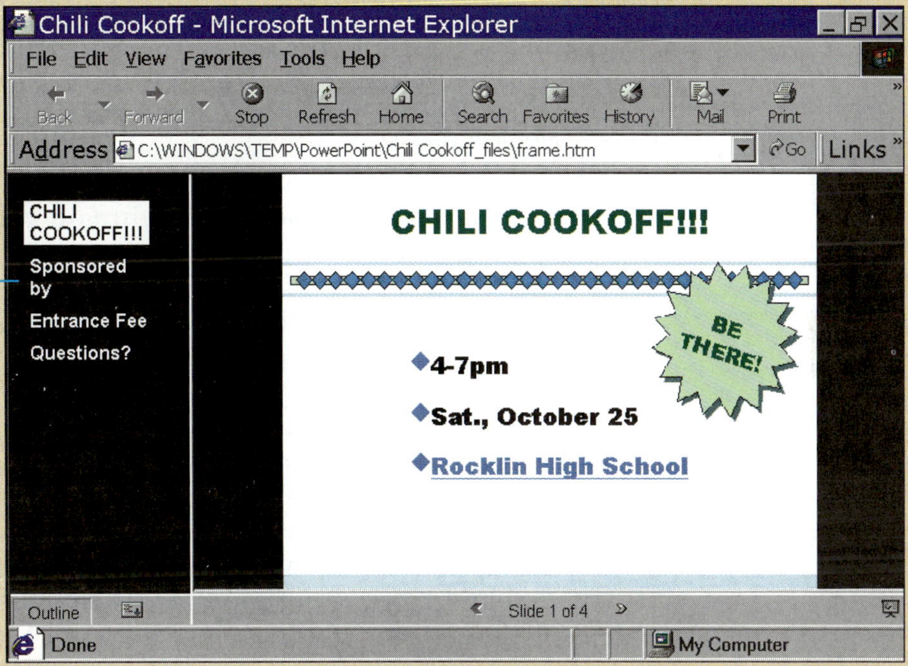


Navigate the online presentation by clicking the slide titles in the left window pane.

5 To view the slides, click their titles in the left window frame.

6 To close the Web browser window:
CLICK: its Close button (☒)

7 Close the "Chili" presentation.



**In Addition**
**Sending a Presentation via E-Mail**

To send a PowerPoint presentation via e-mail, your computer must use Outlook 2000 or Outlook Express 5.0 or later as its default mail editor. Then, simply choose File, Send To, Mail Recipient from PowerPoint's Menu bar and provide information in the header area. To e-mail a PowerPoint presentation as an attachment, choose File, Send To, Mail Recipient (as Attachment) from PowerPoint's Menu bar. The options that are available when e-mailing presentations from PowerPoint will vary depending on what e-mail program you're using.

**5.2 Self Check** How would you go about creating a Web presentation?

# 5.3 Preparing Slides and Supplements for Printing

One of the greatest skills that you can possess is a talent for public speaking. Whatever career choice you've made or will make, the time will come when you must present an opinion, train a co-worker, or give an impromptu speech at your son or daughter's kindergarten class. In the real world, however, some people would rather streak across the field during the Super Bowl than say a few words in front of their peers!

Here are some techniques to help you combat your platform jitters and pull off a winning presentation:

- Prepare your presentation materials thoroughly.
- Practice your delivery in front of the mirror or using a tape recorder.
- Polish your delivery (e.g., remember to make eye contact).
- Psyche yourself up and project positive thoughts.
- Visualize yourself doing an excellent job!

When preparing to give a presentation, allot yourself approximately two minutes to present each slide. Therefore, a 30-minute presentation will have about 15 slides. You may feel that you need more content than this to "save you" for half an hour, but the actual time that it takes to present a slide to an audience is rarely less than two minutes. You do not want to put all your information into your slide presentation anyway. Otherwise, you might as well just distribute handouts to the audience and send them on their way. Remember, the audience is there to listen to what you will say and how you will say it! Every successful speaker communicates his or her interest and enthusiasm in a topic and remains courteous to the audience at all times.

## 5.3.1 Inserting Headers and Footers

**FEATURE**

The Header and Footer command provides an easy way to insert the current slide number, date, time, or other text on every slide in a presentation. The Slide Master determines where this information appears on a slide.

## METHOD

1. CHOOSE: View, Header and Footer
2. CLICK: *Slide* tab to add information to slides, or
   CLICK: *Notes and Handouts* tab to add information to notes pages and handouts
3. SELECT: the options you want
4. CLICK: Apply to add information to the current slide, or
   CLICK: Apply to All to add information to all slides

## PRACTICE

In this lesson, you use the Headers and Footers command.

*Setup:* Ensure that no presentations are displaying.

1 Open the PPT530 data file.

2 Save the presentation as "College Training" to your personal storage location.

3 CHOOSE: View, Header and Footer
CLICK: *Slide* tab
Your screen should now appear similar to Figure 5.8.

**Figure 5.8**
Header and Footer dialog box: *Slide* tab

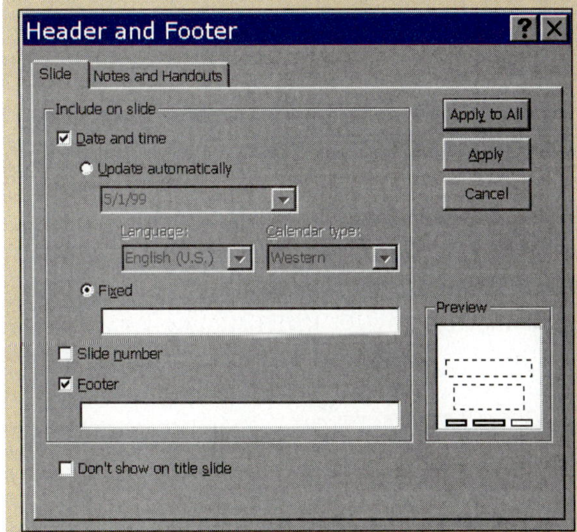


4 To insert the same date on every slide, ensure that the *Fixed* option button is selected and then do the following:
CLICK: in the text box located below the *Fixed* option button
TYPE: **1/15/2000**

5 To insert the current slide number on the slide:
SELECT: *Slide number* check box

6. To insert footer text:
CLICK: in the text box located below the *Footer* check box
TYPE: **Prepared by James Clifford**

7. To insert this information on every slide:
CLICK: Apply to All command button
The inserted information now appears on every slide.

8. Save the revised presentation and keep it open for the next lesson.

## 5.3.2 Printing Speaker Notes

**FEATURE**
In preparing for a presentation, you should consider creating cheat sheets or crib notes to help you when delivering the presentation. These notes help you avoid a common pitfall among novice presenters—putting too much text on the slides. Keep your slides brief and to the point. Use the notes pages in PowerPoint to store reminders to yourself, relevant facts, and anecdotes. You might also use notes pages to provide your audience with additional information related to each slide.

**METHOD**
1. In Normal view, display the slide you want to add notes to.
2. CLICK: in the notes pane
   TYPE: ***notes***
3. To enlarge the notes pane for easier typing:
   DRAG: the border on the top of the notes pane upward
4. To print notes pages:
   CHOOSE: File, Print
   SELECT: Notes Pages from the *Print what* drop-down list

**PRACTICE**
In this lesson, you add notes to the "College Training" presentation and then print them.

*Setup:* Ensure that the "College Training" presentation is displaying.

1. Display slide 1 in Normal view.

2. To enlarge the size of the notes pane:
DRAG: the border on the top of the notes pane upward until the pane reaches a height of approximately 3 inches (refer to Figure 5.9)

3. To add notes to the first slide:
CLICK: in the notes pane
TYPE: **Welcome to MPC College.**
PRESS: ENTER twice
TYPE: **And welcome to our first computer-training orientation meeting. We are anxious to share with you the elements of our training program and to take you on a tour of our training facilities.**
PRESS: ENTER twice
TYPE: **Please feel free to ask questions at any point during the presentation.**
Your screen should now appear similar to Figure 5.9.

**Figure 5.9**
Using the notes pane

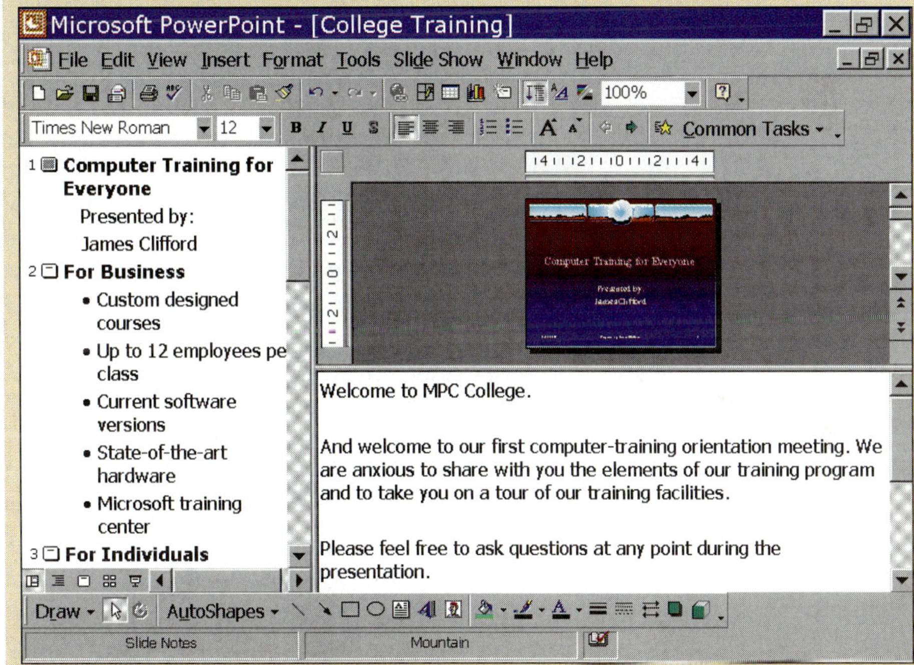


4. To print the notes pages:
CHOOSE: File, Print
SELECT: Notes Pages from the *Print what* drop-down list

5. To print just the current slide:
SELECT: Current Slide option in the *Print range* area
CLICK: OK command button

6. Before proceeding:
DRAG: the border on the top of the notes pane downward until the pane reaches a height of approximately one-half inch.

7. Save the presentation and keep it open for use in the next lesson.

## 5.3.3 Printing Audience Handouts

**FEATURE**
Preparing handouts for your audience is a courtesy. In PowerPoint, a handout is essentially a printout of the slides in your presentation. In the Print dialog box, you can choose to include two, three, four, six, or nine slides on a handout page. Keep in mind that when you include fewer slides on the page, there's more room for your audience to take notes.

**METHOD**
1. CHOOSE: File, Print
2. SELECT: Handouts from the *Print what* drop-down list
3. SELECT: the number of slides you want on the handout from the *Slides per page* drop-down list
4. SELECT: *Horizontal* or *Vertical* option in the *Order* area

**PRACTICE**
In this lesson, you print audience handouts.

*Setup:* Ensure that you have completed the previous lesson and that the "College Training" presentation appears in Normal view.

1 To print the handouts:
CHOOSE: File, Print
SELECT: Handouts from the *Print what* drop-down list

2 To print six slides per page:
SELECT: 6 from the *Slides per page* drop-down list (this may already be the current selection)
Note that the *Horizontal* option is selected by default in the *Order* area, meaning that slide 2, for example, will appear to the right of slide 1, rather than below it. Let's leave this setting unchanged.

3 To proceed:
CLICK: OK command button
Since this presentation only contains five slides, only a single page should have been printed.

4 Save the presentation and keep it open for use in the next lesson.

## 5.3.4 Preparing Overhead Transparencies

**FEATURE**

If the circumstances of your presentation don't lend themselves to online delivery from your computer screen or from an electronic projection device, consider creating overhead transparencies. Depending on whether your printer supports color printing, you can choose to print transparencies in color, shades of gray, or black and white. Before printing, you must format your presentation for overhead transparencies using the Page Setup dialog box.

**METHOD**

1. To format your presentation for overhead transparencies:
   CHOOSE: File, Page Setup
2. SELECT: Overhead from the *Slides sized for* drop-down list
   CLICK: OK command button
3. CHOOSE: File, Print
4. If your printer doesn't support color:
   SELECT: *Grayscale* or *Pure black and white* check box
5. If your printer supports color, make sure that the *Grayscale* and *Pure black and white* check boxes aren't selected.
6. CLICK: OK command button

**PRACTICE**

You will now prepare overhead transparencies for the "College Training" presentation.

*Setup:* Ensure that you have completed the previous lesson and that the "College Training" presentation appears in Normal view.

1 To create overhead transparencies:
CHOOSE: File, Page Setup
The Page Setup dialog box should now appear (Figure 5.10).

**Figure 5.10**
Page Setup dialog box

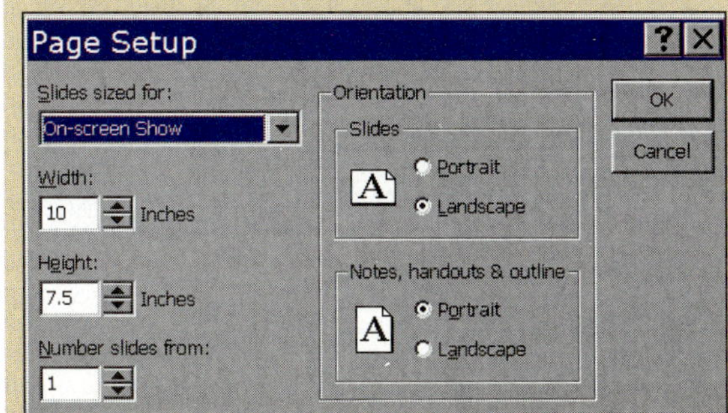


2 SELECT: Overhead from the *Slides sized for* drop-down list
CLICK: OK command button

3. Before outputting slides to transparencies, you'll want to insert transparency film in your printer. For this exercise, however, paper will be fine.
CHOOSE: File, Print
Let's leave the current dialog box selections unchanged.

4. CLICK: OK command button

5. Save and then close the presentation.

**In Addition**
**Creating 35mm Slides**

If you are in the United States and have established an online Internet connection, you can send your presentation directly to Genigraphics, a company that specializes in the output of color 35mm slides and other types of color output. Simply choose File, Send to Genigraphics from the Menu bar and then follow the instructions presented by the Genigraphics wizard. If you're not located in the United States, contact your local service bureau and then ask them for instructions on how to convert your PowerPoint presentation to 35mm slides.

## 5.3.5 Asking the Office Assistant for Help

**FEATURE**
The Office Assistant is your personal and customizable computer guru. When you need to perform a task that you're unsure of, such as creating handouts, call up the Assistant and then type your question into the balloon area. When you click the Search button, the Office Assistant analyzes your request and provides a suggested list of helpful topics. Furthermore, the Assistant watches your keystrokes and mouse clicks to ensure that you are using the software productively and efficiently.

**METHOD**
To display the Office Assistant:

- CLICK: Office Assistant button (?), or
- CHOOSE: Help, Show Office Assistant

To hide the Office Assistant:

1. RIGHT-CLICK: *the Assistant character*
2. CHOOSE: Hide from the pop-up menu

**PRACTICE**
You now practice using the Office Assistant.

*Setup:* Ensure that no presentations are displaying.

1 To display a new presentation:
CLICK: New button ( )
CLICK: Title Slide layout
CLICK: OK command button

2 Let's ask the Office Assistant how to create overhead transparencies.
CLICK: Office Assistant button ( )
An Assistant character appears on the screen.

3 Using the mouse (and referring to Figure 5.11):
DRAG: the Assistant character to the middle of the Outline pane
(*Note:* Clicking on the Office Assistant with the left mouse button will toggle the balloon's display on and off. For this exercise, ensure that the balloon is displayed.)

**Figure 5.11**
Displaying and moving the Office Assistant

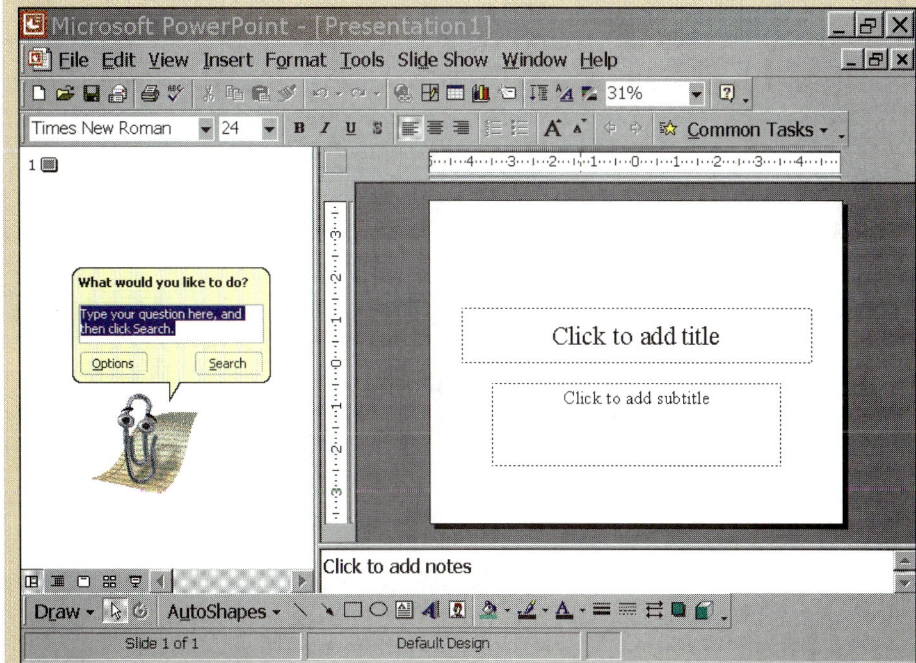


4 To ask the desired question:
TYPE: **How do I create handout pages?**
CLICK: Search button

5 The Assistant requests that you clarify the request. To do so:
CLICK: *Create handouts* option

6. After a few moments, the Help system is launched and the desired topic is displayed (Figure 5.12). To remove the Assistant character from the screen:
RIGHT-CLICK: the Assistant character
CHOOSE: Hide
(*Note:* You may need to click the Microsoft PowerPoint Help button on the taskbar to display the Help window.)

**Figure 5.12**
Displaying the Help system

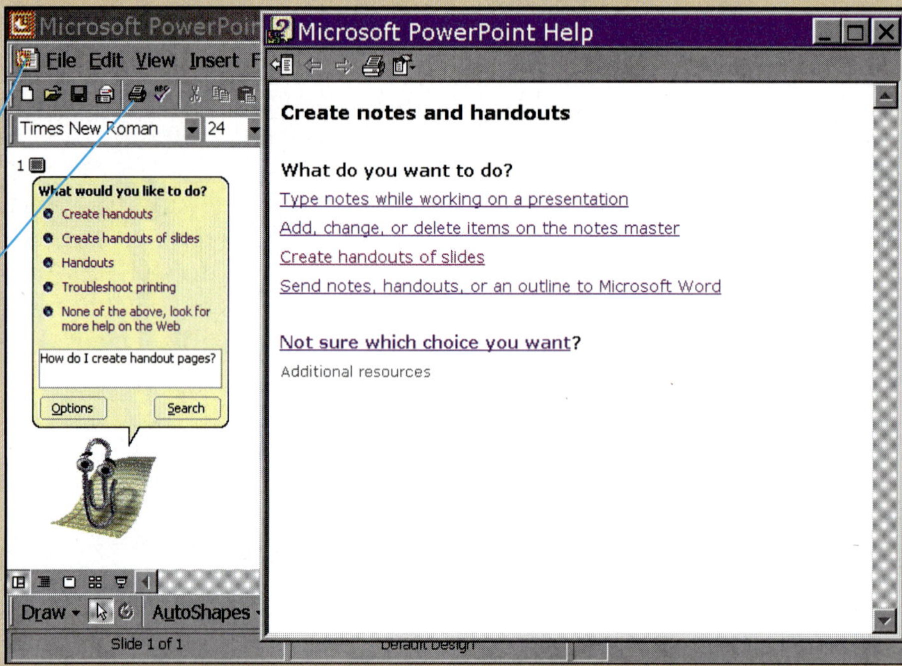


7. To close the Help system window:
CLICK: its Close button (☒)

8. Close the presentation without saving the changes.

**In Addition**
Using the Office Clipboard

In Microsoft Office 2000 applications, the Windows and Office Clipboards enable you to copy items from one location to another. Whereas the **Windows Clipboard** can store only a single item at once, the enhanced **Office Clipboard** can store up to 12 items. The Office Clipboard is automatically activated when you copy two items without an intervening paste. You can also activate the Office Clipboard by right-clicking any Office toolbar and then selecting the Clipboard option. Each copied item is represented by a representative icon on the Clipboard toolbar. Note that the Windows Clipboard continues to work once the Office Clipboard is activated. The last item that was copied to the Office Clipboard will always be located in the Windows Clipboard.

Whereas the contents of the Windows Clipboard are pasted by clicking the Paste button ( ) on the Standard toolbar or using the Paste Special command, the contents of the Office Clipboard are pasted using buttons on the Clipboard toolbar. Using the Clipboard toolbar, you can paste the items into any one of the Office 2000 applications individually or as a group. You can also clear the entire contents of the Office Clipboard with a button on the Clipboard toolbar.

**5.3 Self Check** What is the procedure for creating audience handouts?

# 5.4 Chapter Review

If you plan to deliver your presentation online, consider adding animation, transitions, or hyperlinks to hold the attention of your audience. In preparing for a presentation in front of a live audience, consider creating speaker notes that you can refer to when delivering the presentation. Other items that can aid your delivery are audience handouts, transparencies, and 35mm slides.

## 5.4.1 Command Summary

Many of the commands and procedures appearing in this lesson are summarized in the following table.

| Skill Set | To Perform This Task . . . | Do the Following . . . |
|---|---|---|
| **Creating a Presentation** | Insert headers and footers | CHOOSE: View, Header and Footer |
| **Customizing a Presentation** | Animate text and objects | SELECT: an object or placeholder<br>CHOOSE: Slide Show, Preset Animation |
| | Create custom animations | CHOOSE: Slide Show, Custom Animation |
| | Add slide transitions | SELECT: one or more slides in Slide Sorter view<br>CLICK: Slide Transition Effect drop-down arrow (No Transition)<br>SELECT: a transition effect |
| | Add speaker notes | TYPE: notes in the Notes pane |
| **Creating Output** | Print speaker notes | CHOOSE: File, Print<br>SELECT: Notes Pages from the *Print what* drop-down list |
| | Print audience handouts | CHOOSE: File, Print<br>SELECT: Handouts from the *Print what* drop-down list |
| | Preparing to print overhead transparencies | CHOOSE: File, Page Setup<br>SELECT: Overhead from the *Slides sized for* drop-down list |
| **Managing Files** | Insert a hyperlink to a Web address | TYPE: **Web address**<br>PRESS: ENTER (or the Space Bar) |
| | Convert existing objects to hyperlinks | CLICK: Insert Hyperlink button ( ) |
| | Save a presentation to HTML | CHOOSE: File, Save as Web Page |
| | Preview a Web page | CHOOSE: File, Web Page Preview |
| | Display the Office Assistant | CLICK: Office Assistant button ( ), or<br>CHOOSE: Help, Show Office Assistant |

*Continued*

| Skill Set | To Perform This Task . . . | Do the Following . . . |
|---|---|---|
| **Managing Files *Continued*** | Insert headers and footers | CHOOSE: View, Header and Footer |
| | Hide the Office Assistant | RIGHT-CLICK: *the Assistant character*<br>CHOOSE: Hide from the pop-up menu |

### 5.4.2 Key Terms

This section specifies page references for the key terms identified in this session. For a complete list of definitions, refer to the Glossary provided immediately after the Appendix in this learning guide.

HTML, *p. 183*

hyperlinks, *p. 181*

Internet, *p. 181*

Intranet, *p. 181*

World Wide Web, *p. 181*

## 5.5 Review Questions

### 5.5.1 Short Answer

1. How do you add preset animations to slide objects?
2. What is a slide transition?
3. How do you insert a URL as a hyperlink?
4. How do you format an existing object as a hyperlink?
5. What is the procedure for converting a presentation to HTML?
6. What is the procedure for printing notes pages?
7. What is the procedure for printing audiencc handouts?
8. How would you go about formatting your presentation for overhead transparencies?
9. What is the Office Assistant?
10. How do you hide the Office Assistant?

## 5.5.2 True/False

1. ____ The Slide Sorter toolbar provides shortcuts to several electronic effects.
2. ____ Transitions can only be added in Normal view.
3. ____ In PowerPoint, it's possible to enhance objects with sound effects.
4. ____ To view a slide's animations, you must switch to Normal view.
5. ____ An intranet uses Internet technologies for sharing information.
6. ____ The Insert Hyperlink button () is used for adding transitional effects to slide presentations.
7. ____ In PowerPoint, you can add headers and footers to slides, notes pages, and handouts.
8. ____ Hiding the Office Assistant can only be accomplished by exiting PowerPoint.
9. ____ It's possible to preview how a presentation will look in your browser.
10. ____ To create custom animations, choose Slide Show, Custom Animation from PowerPoint's Menu bar.

## 5.5.3 Multiple Choice

1. Which of the following can answer your PowerPoint questions?
   a. Page Setup dialog box
   b. transitions
   c. animations
   d. Office Assistant

2. Which of the following must you use to format a presentation for overhead transparencies?
   a. Page Setup dialog box
   b. transitions
   c. animations
   d. Office Assistant

3. Which of the following are used to entertain and focus your audience on important points?
   a. Page Setup dialog box
   b. transitions
   c. animations
   d. Office Assistant

4. Which of the following displays when you move from one slide to the next?
   a. Page Setup dialog box
   b. transitions
   c. animations
   d. Office Assistant

5. Which of the following can you use to open Web pages?
   a. Office Assistant
   b. hyperlinks
   c. Slide Sorter toolbar
   d. All of the above

6. Which of the following provides a visual interface for the Internet?
   a. hyperlinks
   b. World Wide Web
   c. intranet
   d. Both a and b

7. To create a slide footer, choose:
   a. View, Footer
   b. View, Header and Footer
   c. Insert, Header and Footer
   d. Both a and b

8. Which of the following are commonly found on Web pages?
   a. hyperlinks
   b. Internet
   c. intranet
   d. All of the above

9. In PowerPoint, you can print:
   a. slides
   b. handouts
   c. notes pages
   d. All of the above

10. Which of the following provides several shortcuts to electronic effects?
    a. Page Setup dialog box
    b. Office Assistant
    c. Slide Sorter toolbar
    d. All of the above

# 5.6 Hands-On Projects

## 5.6.1 Outdoor Adventure Tours: Wilderness

This exercise practices creating preset and custom animations.

1. Open the PPT561 file and save the presentation as "Wilderness" to your personal storage location.
2. Use Slide Show view to familiarize yourself with the content of the presentation.
3. Ensure that slide 1 is displaying in Normal view. Let's use the Preset Animation command to animate the title on the first slide:
   CLICK: in the main title placeholder
   CHOOSE: Slide Show, Preset Animation
   CHOOSE: Drive-In
4. To view the effect in action:
   CHOOSE: View, Slide Show
   CLICK: the left mouse button once to activate the animation
   Notice how the title appeared from the right and was accompanied by a braking vehicle sound effect.
   PRESS: ESC to return to Normal view
5. Let's apply custom animation to the second slide. Ensure that slide 2 is displaying in Normal view
   CHOOSE: Slide Show, Custom Animation
6. To animate the photographer graphic:
   SELECT: Object 3 check box
   A check should now appear in the Object 3 check box. Note that the graphic is also selected in the preview area.
7. To select an effect:
   CLICK: *Effects* tab
   SELECT: Camera from sound drop-down list
   CLICK: Preview command button.
8. Let's change the settings in the *Order & Timing* tab.
   CLICK: *Order & Timing* tab
   SELECT: *Automatically* option button
   CLICK: OK command button
9. Finally, let's add a custom animation to every slide using the Slide Master:
   CHOOSE: View, Master, Slide Master
   CHOOSE: Slide Show, Custom Animation

10. To make the top rectangle crawl slowly upwards on each slide:
SELECT: Rectangle 3 check box to animate the upper slide rectangle
CLICK: *Effects* tab to select an effect
SELECT: the Crawl and From Bottom effects in the *Entry animation and sound* area
CLICK: OK command button
11. On your own, view the animated slides by returning to the first slide and switching to Slide Show view.
12. Save and close the "Wilderness" presentation.

## 5.6.2 Monashee Community College: Electronic Publishing Certificate Program

In this exercise, you will create and print speaker notes to assist while delivering a presentation, insert a footer on every slide, and print an audience handout.

1. Open the PPT562 presentation.
2. Save the presentation as "Electronic Publishing" to your personal storage location.
3. Display slide 1 in Normal view. To enlarge the typing area of the notes pane:
DRAG: the border on the top of the notes pane upward until the pane reaches a height of approximately 3 inches
4. To add notes to the first slide:
CLICK: in the notes pane
TYPE: **Good evening and thank you for coming to our Electronic Publishing Information session.**
5. Move to the second slide and add the following notes:
TYPE: **This evening you will be introduced to the people involved with Monashee Community College's Electronic Publishing Program.**
PRESS: ENTER twice
TYPE: **We will first describe the program in detail and then explain the application process. Finally, several students will share their experiences of the program with you.**
PRESS: ENTER twice
TYPE: **Please save your questions until the end of the presentation.**
6. To return the notes pane to its original size:
DRAG: the border on the top of the notes pane downward until the pane reaches a height of approximately one-half inch.

7. To print the notes page of the current slide only:
   CHOOSE: File, Print
   SELECT: Notes Pages from the *Print what* drop-down list
   SELECT: Current Slide option in the *Print range* area
   CLICK: OK command button
8. Let's add a footer to every slide.
   CHOOSE: View, Header and Footer
   CLICK: *Slide* tab
9. To insert the current slide number on the slide:
   SELECT: *Slide number* check box
10. To insert footer text:
    CLICK: in the text box located below the *Footer* check box
    TYPE: **Electronic Publishing Certificate Program**
    CLICK: Apply to All command button to insert this information on every slide.
11. Let's print an audience handout with all six slides appearing on one sheet.
    CHOOSE: File, Print
    SELECT: Handouts from the *Print what* drop-down list
    SELECT: 6 from the *Slides per page* drop-down list
    CLICK: OK command button
12. Save your changes and close the "Electronic Publishing" presentation.

## 5.6.3 Coldstream Corporation: Environmental Control

In this exercise, you will insert and preview several hyperlinks, save the presentation into HTML format for Web publishing, and then print the final slide.

1. Open the PPT563 presentation and save it as "Environment" to your personal storage location.
2. Move to the last slide and format the text "Coldstream's Web site" as a hyperlink to www.coldstream.com.
3. View the presentation in Slide Show view. Note how the mouse pointer changes to a hand over the text "Coldstream's Web site," indicating that the text is formatted as a hyperlink.
4. Return to the last slide in Normal view. Insert a second list item by typing **www.environment** and pressing ENTER at the bottom of the slide. Note how PowerPoint formatted the text by default as a hyperlink.
5. Preview how the presentation will appear as a Web page using the File, Web Page Preview menu command.
6. Save the presentation into HTML format for Web publishing to your personal storage location.
7. Print the last slide only and then close the "Environment" presentation.

## 5.6.4 Spiderman Web Marketing: Services

In this exercise, you will apply preset and custom animation and slide transitions. You will add and print speaker notes and insert a hyperlink. Finally, you will print an audience handout and preview the presentation as a Web page.

1. Open the PPT564 presentation and save it as "Spiderman Services" to your personal storage location.
2. Apply the Laser Text preset animation to the main title on the first slide.
3. To the second slide, apply a custom animation so that the Text 2 slide object incorporates the Checkerboard Entry animation and is accompanied by a Clapping sound.
4. Use Slide Sorter view to add the Box In slide transition to every slide.
5. Add speaker notes to the third slide with the text "Discuss recent Internet awards." Print the speaker notes of this slide only.
6. On the first slide, insert the hyperlink www.spiderman.com below the subtitle.
7. Print an audience handout that includes six slides per page and appears vertically on the page.
8. Preview the presentation as a Web page.
9. Save and close the "Spiderman Services" presentation.

## 5.6.5 On Your Own: Hometown

You have been asked to make a presentation about your hometown to your son's primary school class. Create a five-slide presentation indicating the location, population, history, and attractions of a real or fictional town or city. Create and print speaker notes, audience handouts, and a set of overhead transparencies in the event that the computer projection unit fails. Save your presentation as "Hometown" to your personal storage location.

### 5.6.6 On Your Own: School Fair

Your "Hometown" presentation (created in the last exercise) to your son's class was such a hit that the school has asked to use the presentation at their next school fair. Modify the presentation to have online effects such as animation, transitions, timing, and hyperlinks. Use the Office Assistant to refresh your memory on how to insert a footer with the current date on every slide. Save this presentation as "School Fair" to your personal storage location.

## 5.7 Case Problems: Kool Kids Klothing

Now that Viviana has learned some techniques for preparing to deliver a presentation, she is ready to animate her presentation using electronic effects. She will also insert the same footer on each slide, create and print speaker notes, an audience handout, and an overhead transparency. Finally she will preview and save her presentation as a Web page.

In the following case problems, assume the role of Viviana and perform the same steps that she identifies. You may want to re-read the chapter opening before proceeding.

1. Viviana opens the PPT571 presentation and saves it as "Kool Kids" to her personal storage location. To add visual interest, she adds the following preset and custom animation. On the first slide she selects the "camera" preset animation for the photo graphic, and the "dissolve" preset animation for the subtitle. In order to add custom animation to every slide, she selects the Slide Master and adds the Spiral effect to the Group 1 slide object.

   Using Slide Sorter view, she adds the Blinds Vertical slide transition to each slide. To the last slide she inserts a hyperlink to her Web site URL www.koolkids.com. Viviana saves the revised presentation.

2. Viviana adds the following speakers notes to the first slide:

   **Welcome to Kool Kids Klothing. My name is Viviana Morgan and I am a Kool Kids Klothing consultant. I would like to tell you about our upcoming Open House.**

   She moves to the second slide and adds the following text in the Notes pane:

   **I hope you can make it on August 20 to see some very exciting children's clothing.**

   Viviana prints the notes page of the first slide only. She saves her changes.

3. Viviana decides to add a footer to each slide, except for the first slide, that contains only the text "Kool Kids Klothing." She then creates and prints a one-page audience handout that displays all six slides horizontally at once. She then formats the presentation for overhead transparencies and prints the first three slides as Grayscale. She saves her changes.

4. Viviana is ready to publish this presentation to the Web. She first previews her presentation as a Web page. Then using the File, Save as Web Page menu command, she saves her presentation into HTML format for Web publishing. She can't wait to show off her "Kool" presentation!

# Notes

# Notes

# Notes

# MICROSOFT POWERPOINT 2000

## *Customizing Presentations*

CHAPTER

SIX

# Chapter Outline



# Learning Objectives

After completing this chapter, you will be able to:

- Customize a presentation's color scheme and backgrounds
- Create new design templates
- Enhance a presentation with action settings, action buttons, animated GIF pictures, and sound clips
- Share data among the Office 2000 applications using the techniques of pasting, linking, and embedding
- Use the Custom Show command to create mini-presentations within larger presentations

## Case Study

## Jade Beach Juice Company

Trevor Campbell and Kaity Kerr's juice business began humbly at a beachside concession stand. Trevor and Kaity constantly experimented and created new flavors of juice drinks by squeezing and blending different combinations of fruits. Despite progressing from hand-squeezed juices to an electric juicer, Trevor and Kaity could not keep up with the growing number of customers who raved about their delicious drinks. One of their secrets was that they selected only the freshest and finest fruits. "Jade Beach Juice Company" was soon created and production moved from a simple beach stand to several warehouses with over 100 employees. To obtain further financial assistance, Trevor and Kaity have created a PowerPoint presentation to explain their business to potential financiers. After creating the presentation, they both realize that they must customize their presentation to better reflect their business and to retain their viewers' interest.

In this chapter, you, along with Trevor and Kaity, learn how to change the entire look of a presentation by customizing its color scheme and background. You learn how to incorporate interactive effects using action settings and buttons, and multimedia effects using animated GIF pictures and sound clips. You also practice integrating PowerPoint with the other Office 2000 applications and targeting your presentation to different audiences using custom shows.



# 6.1 Changing the Look of a Presentation

How your presentation looks can directly affect your audience's response to your message. If your message is buried in inconsistent design elements and varied colors, you risk losing the attention of your audience. An easy way to give your presentation a consistent look is to apply one of PowerPoint's preexisting design templates.[1] Of course, you may find it necessary to adjust the current design scheme to meet your particular requirements. By customizing a presentation's Slide Master[2], color scheme, or slide backgrounds, you can give your presentation a unique look. But always remember to exercise restraint so that your creativity doesn't overpower your message.

---

[1]As discussed in Chapter 2, a design template determines the formatting, fonts, colors, and slide backgrounds used in a presentation.

[2]We discussed changing the Slide Master in Chapter 4.

## 6.1.1 Changing Color Schemes

**FEATURE**

The colors you use in a presentation can influence how an audience responds to your message. Fortunately for us, Microsoft hired professional artists to compile PowerPoint's numerous color schemes. A **color scheme** is a set of eight colors that you can apply to individual slides, notes pages, and audience handouts. By using color schemes, you ensure that all the colors in your presentation are balanced and work well together. Also, color schemes make it easy to apply a new set of colors to your presentation, just as using templates makes it easy to change its overall design. Once applied, you can easily customize a color scheme to your particular needs.

**METHOD**

- To apply an alternate color scheme:
  CHOOSE: Format, Slide Color Scheme
  SELECT: a scheme in the *Color schemes* area
  CLICK: Apply to All command button
- To customize a selected color scheme:
  CHOOSE: Format, Slide Color Scheme
  CLICK: *Custom* tab
  SELECT: the object you want to change in the *Scheme colors* area
  CLICK: Change Color command button
  SELECT: an alternate color in the Standard palette
  CLICK: OK command button
  CLICK: Apply to All command button

**PRACTICE**

In this lesson, you apply a new color scheme and then customize it to meet your needs.

*Setup:* Ensure that PowerPoint is loaded.

1. Open the WRD610 data file.

2. Save the presentation as "Puppy" to your personal storage location. Your screen should now appear similar to Figure 6.1. The "Blends" design template has been applied to this presentation.

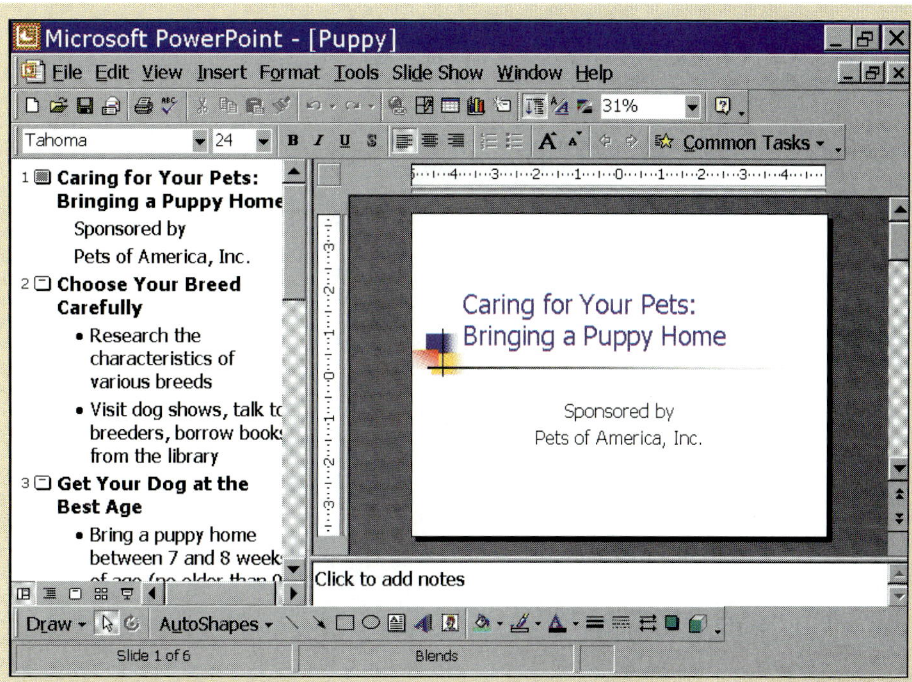


**Figure 6.1**
The first slide of the "Puppy" presentation

**3** Advance through the slides in this presentation in order to become familiar with their contents.

**4** Let's apply an alternate color scheme to the presentation.
CHOOSE: Format, Slide Color Scheme
The dialog box in Figure 6.2 should now appear. Note that the seven color schemes you see in the dialog box are all part of the "Blends" design template.

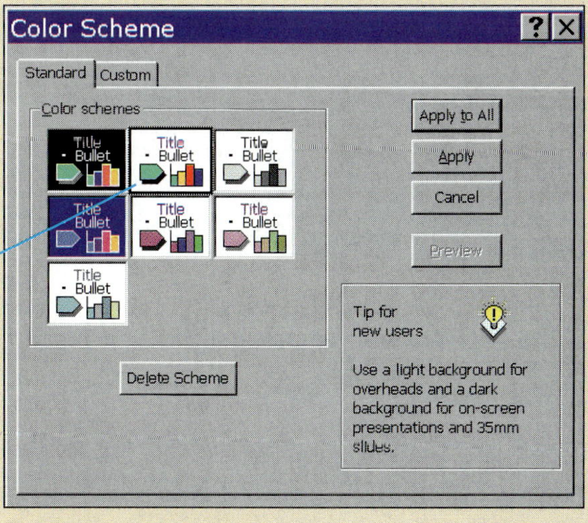


The scheme located in the center-top row is currently applied to your presentation.

**Figure 6.2**
Color Scheme dialog box

5. To experiment with how your slides would look with a few of the other schemes, do the following:
CLICK: a color scheme
CLICK: Preview command button
DRAG: Color Scheme dialog box downward and out of the way to reveal more of the preview image

6. DRAG: Color Scheme dialog box back to its original position

7. Repeat steps 5 and 6 to view a few more color schemes.

8. To apply an alternate color scheme to the presentation:
SELECT: the color scheme that has a black background (located in the first column of the first row)
CLICK: Apply to All command button
The new color scheme has now been applied to every slide in the presentation. Figure 6.3 shows the first slide of the presentation.

**Figure 6.3**
Applying an alternate color scheme

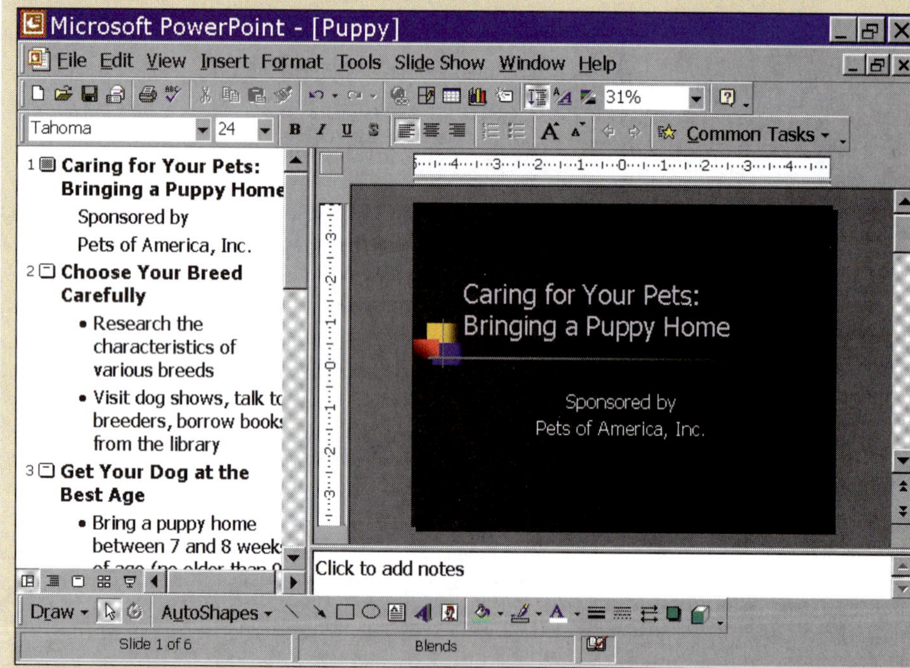


9. On your own, view the revised presentation.

10 You may find that a predefined color scheme works well for you and needs no revisions. However, if this isn't the case, you can easily change the colors that are used for individual slide objects. To illustrate:
CHOOSE: Format, Slide Color Scheme
CLICK: *Custom* tab
The Color Scheme dialog box should appear similar to Figure 6.4. (Note that you can change the background fill color using this dialog box. In the next lesson, we show you another method for changing a slide's background color.)

**Figure 6.4**
Color Scheme dialog box: *Custom* tab

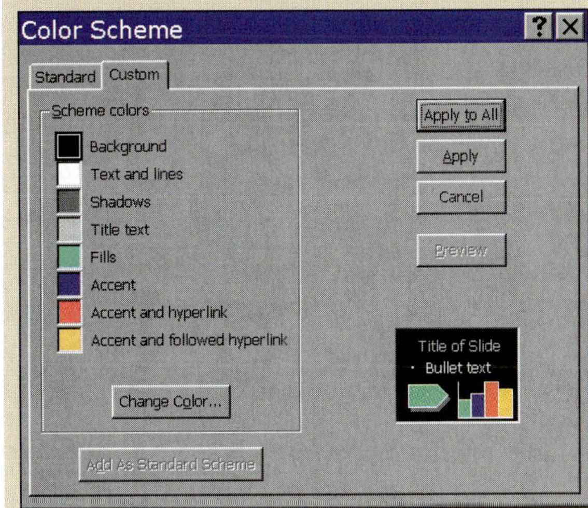


11 To modify the foreground or text color for the Title placeholder:
CLICK: *Title Text* color box in the *Scheme Colors* area
CLICK: Change Color command button
The Title Text Color dialog box now appears (Figure 6.5), displaying PowerPoint's default color palette. You can select different colors by pointing to them in the palette and then clicking. (*Note*: You can mix your own colors using the *Custom* tab.)

**Figure 6.5**
Title Text Color dialog box

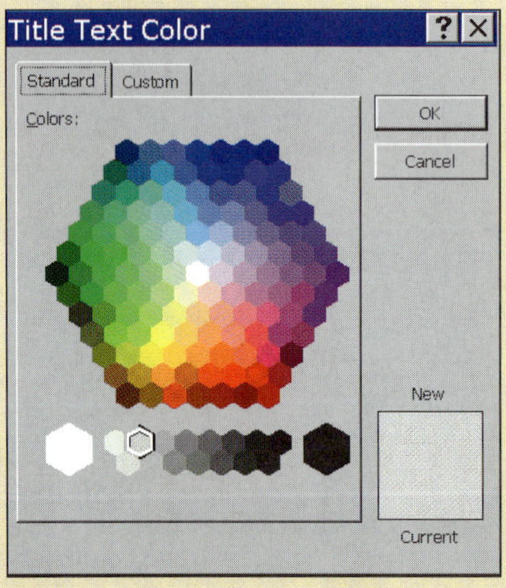


12 Light gray is the currently selected color for title text. To change the color to bright green:
CLICK: bright green in the color palette
CLICK: OK command button

13 To apply the new color to every slide in the presentation:
CLICK: Apply to All command button
All the titles in the presentation are now bright green.

14 To reapply the original color scheme to the entire presentation:
CHOOSE: Format, Slide Color Scheme
CLICK: *Standard* tab
SELECT: the original color scheme (top row, center)
CLICK: Apply to All command button

15 Keep the presentation open for use in the next lesson.

## 6.1.2 Customizing Slide Backgrounds

**FEATURE**
You can customize the background of your presentation in several different ways. You can easily change the background fill color or apply an alternate fill effect to the background. If your background currently includes graphics that are overwhelming your message, you can omit them from the Slide Master. When selecting or modifying a background, keep in mind that you should pick darker backgrounds for 35mm slides and on-screen presentations, and light background colors for overhead transparencies.

**METHOD**

- To change the current background color:
  CHOOSE: Format, Background
  CLICK: drop-down arrow in the *Background fill* area
  SELECT: a color from the existing color palette, or
  CHOOSE: More Colors and then select an alternate color from the Standard palette
- To apply an alternate fill effect to the background:
  CHOOSE: Format, Background
  CLICK: drop-down arrow in the *Background fill* area
  CHOOSE: Fill Effects and then make selections using the *Gradient*, *Texture*, *Pattern*, and *Picture* tabs

**PRACTICE**

You will now customize the background of an existing presentation.

*Setup:* Ensure that the "Puppy" presentation is displaying.

1 To practice changing the background of the "Puppy" presentation, do the following:
CHOOSE: Format, Background
CLICK: drop-down arrow in the *Background fill* area
SELECT: Mustard from the color palette
CLICK: Apply to All command button
(*Note:* You can change a presentation's background color using the Color Scheme dialog box or the Background dialog box.) The background should have changed from white to mustard.

2 To choose from a wider selection of colors:
CHOOSE: Format, Background
CLICK: drop-down arrow in the *Background fill* area
CHOOSE: More Colors
The Standard color palette should now appear.

3 To change the background color to light gray:
SELECT: light gray from the palette located near the bottom of the dialog box
CLICK: OK command button
CLICK: Apply to All command button

4 Let's get creative and apply some fill effects to the background.
CHOOSE: Format, Background
CLICK: drop-down arrow in the *Background fill* area
CHOOSE: Fill Effects
The Fill Effects dialog box should now appear (Figure 6.6). The *Gradient* tab is currently selected.

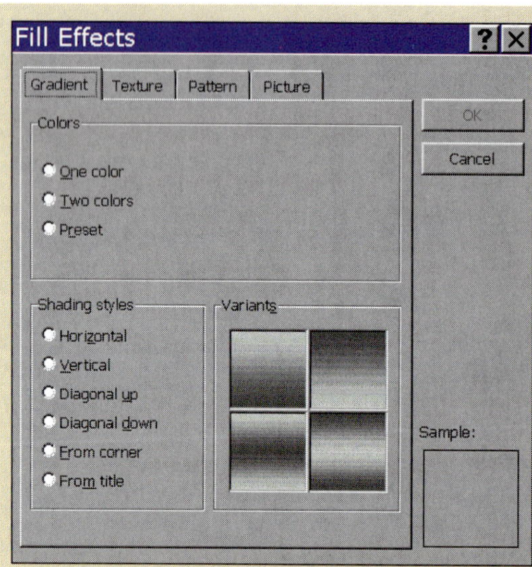


**Figure 6.6**
Fill Effects dialog box: *Gradient* tab

5. To apply a horizontal gradient to the presentation that appears lighter toward the top of the slide and darker toward the bottom, do the following:
SELECT: *Horizontal* option button in the *Shading styles* area
CLICK: sample box located in the upper-left corner of the *Variants* area, if it isn't selected already
CLICK: OK command button
CLICK: Apply to All command button
Figure 6.7 shows the first slide of the presentation with a horizontal gradient.

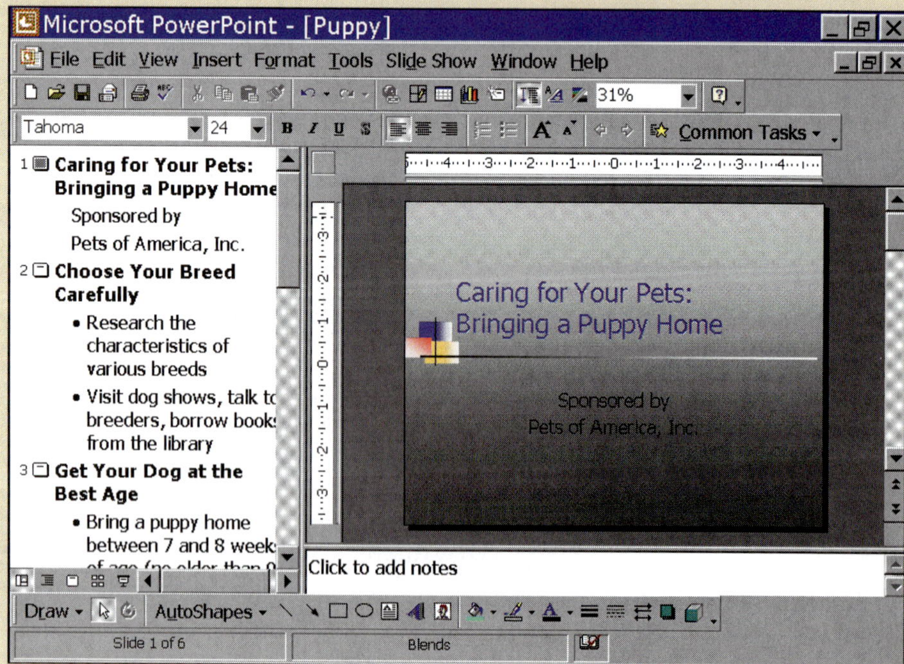


**Figure 6.7**
Applying a single-color horizontal gradient

6 Let's modify the horizontal gradient to display with two colors.
CHOOSE: Format, Background
CLICK: drop-down arrow in the *Background fill* area
CHOOSE: Fill Effects
SELECT: *Two colors* option button in the *Colors* area

7 Let's leave the first color (light gray) unchanged. For the second color, do the following:
CLICK: *Color 2* drop-down arrow
SELECT: Mustard from the color palette
CLICK: OK command button
CLICK: Apply to All command button
Figure 6.8 shows the first slide of the presentation with a two-color horizontal gradient.

**Figure 6.8**
Applying a two-color horizontal gradient

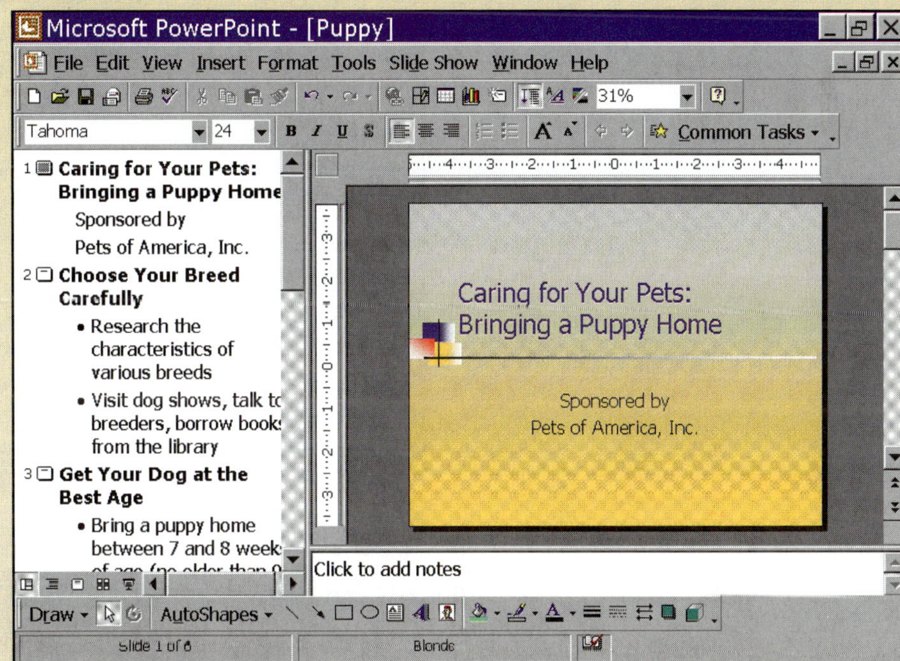


8 Now, let's apply one of PowerPoint's textured fills to the presentation's background.
CHOOSE: Format, Background
CLICK: drop-down arrow in the *Background fill* area
CHOOSE: Fill Effects
CLICK: *Texture* tab
Your screen should now appear similar to Figure 6.9.

**Figure 6.9**
Fill Effects dialog box: *Texture* tab

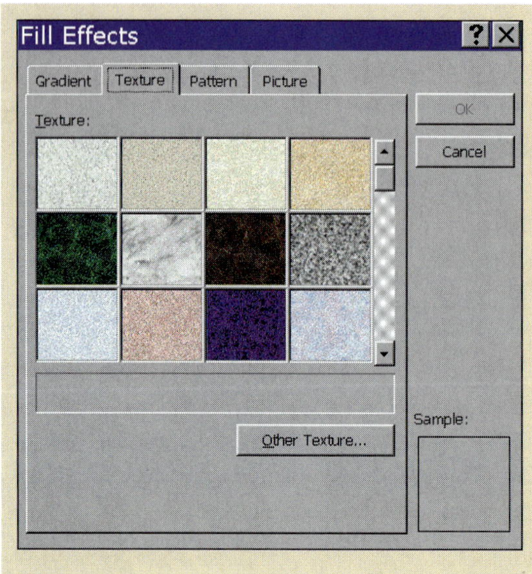


9 In the *Texture* dialog box, drag the vertical scroll bar downward to view the available fills.

10 To apply the "Woven mat" fill to the presentation:
CLICK: Woven mat fill in the *Texture* list box (located in the fourth column of the fourth row)
CLICK: OK command button
CLICK: Apply to All command button
Unfortunately, this background makes the text of your presentation unreadable.

11 A simple way to reverse the last command is to use the Undo command.
CHOOSE: Edit, Undo Background

12 To change the background from a gradient fill to a more discreet pattern, let's use the *Pattern* tab of the Fill Effects dialog box. Do the following:
CHOOSE: Format, Background
CLICK: drop-down arrow in the *Background fill* area
CHOOSE: Fill Effects
CLICK: *Pattern* tab
A wide selection of patterns is available in the dialog box (Figure 6.10).

**Figure 6.10**

Fill Effects dialog box: *Pattern* tab

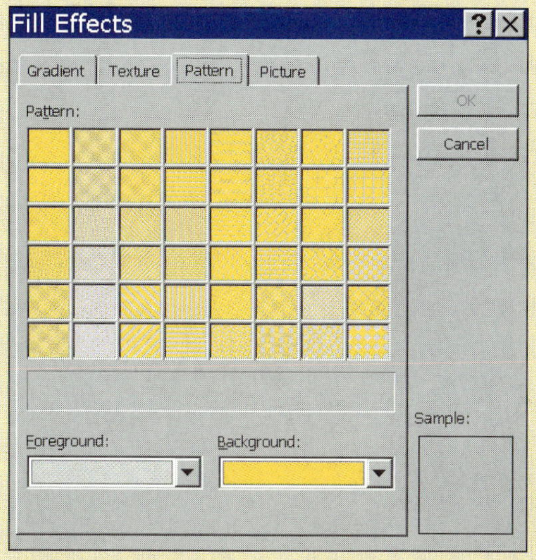


13 To apply the "Narrow horizontal" pattern to every slide in the presentation:
CLICK: Narrow horizontal in the *Pattern* area (located in the fourth column of the fourth row)
CLICK: OK command button
CLICK: Apply to All command button
Narrow horizontal lines should now appear in the presentation's background.

14 Let's perform one more task. To remove the background graphics from display in the presentation, do the following:
CHOOSE: Format, Background
SELECT: *Omit background graphics from master* check box
CLICK: Apply to All command button
As you scroll through the presentation, note that no background graphics appear.

15 To redisplay the background graphics:
CHOOSE: Edit, Undo Background

16 Save the revised presentation and keep it open for the next lesson.

## 6.1.3 Creating a New Design Template

**FEATURE**

Not only do design templates make it possible for nondesigners to create professional-looking presentations with ease, but they help ensure a consistent look across multiple presentations. If one of PowerPoint's existing design templates works nicely for you, except for a few alterations, consider creating a new template from the existing template. You can also create a new design template from an existing presentation or create a design template entirely from scratch by starting with a blank presentation.

**METHOD**

1. Open an existing presentation or design template, or start a blank presentation.
2. Edit the presentation or template to suit your needs.
3. CHOOSE: File, Save As
4. TYPE: **a name** for the new template in the *File name* text box
5. SELECT: Design Template from the *Save as type* drop-down list
6. Specify a save location for the new template.

**PRACTICE**

In this lesson, you create a new design template from an existing presentation.

*Setup:* Ensure that the "Puppy" presentation is displaying.

1 Let's create a new design template from the "Puppy" presentation.
CHOOSE: File, Save As
TYPE: **Horizontal Lines** in the *File name* text box
SELECT: Design Template from the *Save as type* drop-down list

2 By default, the new template will be saved in the Templates folder along with PowerPoint's existing design templates.
CLICK: Save command button

3 Close the "Horizontal Lines" template.

4 Let's start a new presentation and then apply the "Horizontal Lines" template.
CLICK: New button (🗋) on the Standard toolbar
CLICK: OK command button in the New Slide dialog box to insert a title slide

5 To apply the "Horizontal Lines" template to the presentation:
CHOOSE: Format, Apply Design Template
SELECT: Horizontal Lines in the list box
The Apply Design Template dialog box should now appear similar to Figure 6.11.

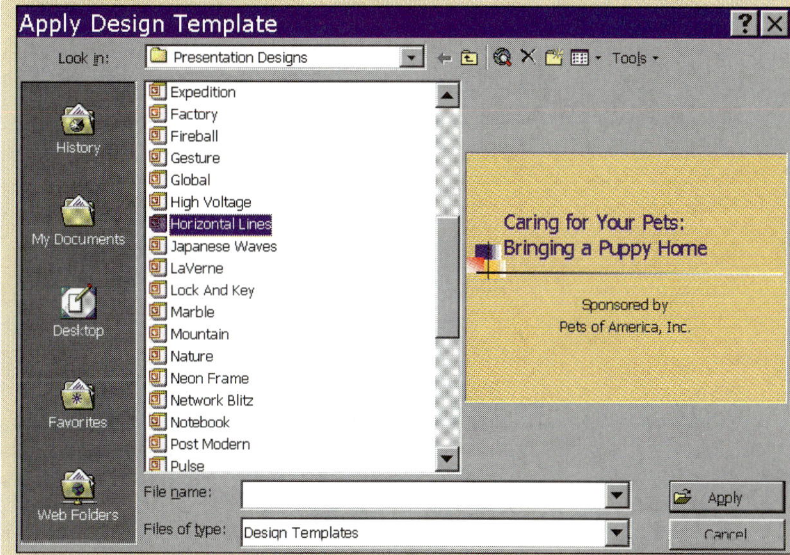


**Figure 6.11**
The template you created appears in the templates list

6 CLICK: Apply command button

7 Close the current presentation without saving.

**In Addition**
Setting Tabs

Tabs enable you to neatly arrange text and numbers on a page. The four basic types of tabs are left, center, right, and decimal. (By default, PowerPoint supplies left-aligned tabs every inch.) To set a new tab, select a tab type using the Tab Alignment button (L) located on the left side of the Ruler. Then click the desired location on the Ruler to set the tab stop. To remove a tab, drag a tab stop down and off the Ruler.

**6.1 Self Check** What is the procedure for adding texture to a presentation's background?

# 6.2 Incorporating Interactive and Multimedia Effects

PowerPoint provides several ways for making your online presentations both easier to navigate and more interesting. You can move directly to other slides in a presentation, for example, by simply clicking on highlighted words and images, known as *hyperlinks*, or on ready-made symbols, called **action buttons.** When used wisely, these interactive effects, along with such multimedia effects as animation, sound, and video, greatly enhance your presentations.

## 6.2.1 Using Action Settings

**FEATURE**

Not only do hyperlinks make it easier for presenters to move directly to content that supports the current discussion, but they give your audience greater control over the flow of information when the presentation is delivered in a self-running environment.[3] In Chapter 5, you learned how to insert hyperlinks using the Insert Hyperlink dialog box. The Action Settings dialog box provides an even easier method for inserting hyperlinks to other locations within the same presentation.

**METHOD**

1. SELECT: the text or object that you want to format as a hyperlink
2. CHOOSE: Slide Show, Action Settings
3. SELECT: *Hyperlink to* option button
4. CHOOSE: the slide you want to hyperlink to from the *Hyperlink to* drop-down list
5. CLICK: OK command button

**PRACTICE**

In this lesson, you practice inserting hyperlinks to other slides within an existing presentation.

*Setup:* Ensure that no presentations are displaying.

1 Open the PPT620 data file.

2 Save this six-slide presentation as "Small Business" to your personal storage location.

[3]We discuss how to create self-running slide shows in Chapter 7.

3 Advance through the slides in this presentation to become familiar with their contents.

4 Let's use the Action Settings dialog box to format each of the bullets on slide 2 as hyperlinks to slides containing additional information. To begin, display slide two in Normal view.

5 To link the first bulleted item (Sole Proprietorship) to slide 3, which contains additional information on sole proprietorships, do the following:
SELECT: the first bulleted item
CHOOSE: Slide Show, Action Settings
The Action Settings dialog box should now appear (Figure 6.12).

**Figure 6.12**
Action Settings dialog box

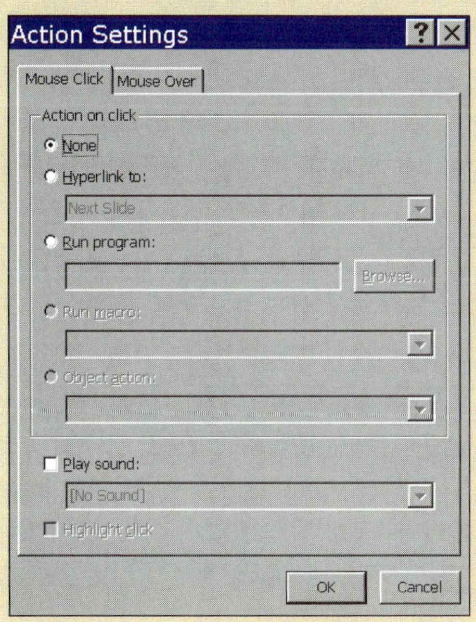


6 To establish a link to the next slide:
SELECT: *Hyperlink to* option button
Note that "Next Slide," our desired setting, already appears in the *Hyperlink to* drop-down list.

7 To proceed:
CLICK: OK command button
Note that the text "Sole Proprietorships" on slide 2 appears formatted as a hyperlink.

8. To link the second bulleted item (Partnerships) to slide 4, which contains additional information on partnerships, do the following:
SELECT: the second bulleted item
CHOOSE: Slide Show, Action Settings
SELECT: *Hyperlink to* option button
CHOOSE: Slide from the *Hyperlink to* drop-down list
The Hyperlink To Slide dialog box should now appear (Figure 6.13).

**Figure 6.13**

Hyperlink To Slide dialog box

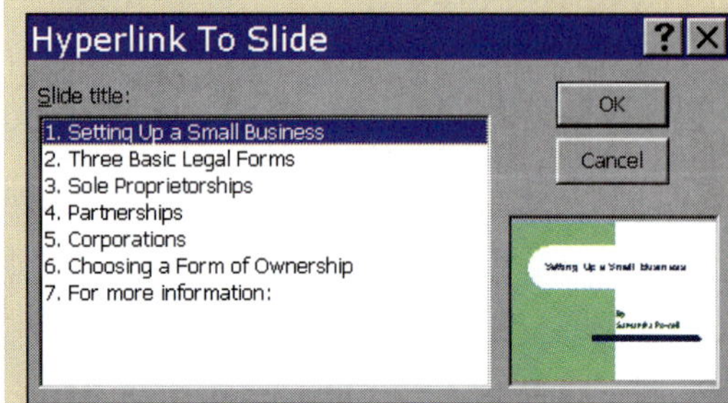


9. SELECT: slide 4 in the *Slide title* list box
CLICK: OK command button
CLICK: OK command button to display the current slide

10. On your own, link the third bulleted item (Corporations) to slide 5, which contains additional information on corporations.

11. Display the presentation in Slide Show view and then practice using the inserted hyperlinks.

12. Save the revised presentation and keep it open for use in the next lesson.

## 6.2.2 Inserting Action Buttons

**FEATURE**

Similar to hyperlinks, action buttons are commonly used for navigating to other slides in a presentation. They can also (a) be programmed to run other programs, called *macros*[4], (b) open, edit, or run embedded objects, such as another presentation, or (c) play sounds.

[4]We discuss creating and editing macros in Chapter 8.

**METHOD**

1. CHOOSE: Slide Show, Action Buttons
2. CLICK: a symbol in the displayed menu
3. Use the *Mouse Click* tab to define what happens when the button is clicked, or the *Mouse Over* tab to define what happens when the user positions the mouse pointer over the button.
4. CLICK: OK command button

**PRACTICE**

In this lesson, you insert an action button on the final slide of the "Small Business" presentation that links back to the first slide.

*Setup:* Ensure that the "Small Business" presentation is displaying in Normal view.

1 Display the last slide in the "Small Business" presentation in Normal view.

2 To insert an action button on this slide, do the following:
CHOOSE: Slide Show, Action Buttons
The Action Buttons menu contains several symbols, as shown to the right.

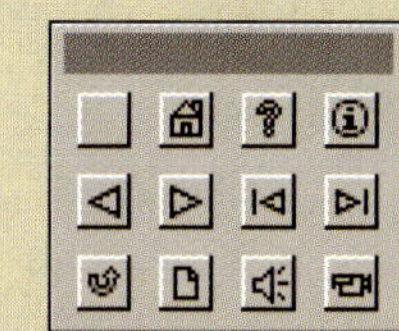

3 CHOOSE: Action Button: Beginning () from the menu

4 To insert the action button on the slide in its default size, do the following:
CLICK: on the slide
(*Note:* You can size and move action buttons using the same techniques for manipulating other types of graphics objects.) The Action Settings dialog box automatically appears, with "First Slide" displaying in the *Hyperlink to* drop-down list box.

5 To accept the current settings in the Action Settings dialog box:
CLICK: OK command button

6 On your own, move and resize the inserted action button by referring to Figure 6.14.

**Figure 6.14**

Inserting an action button

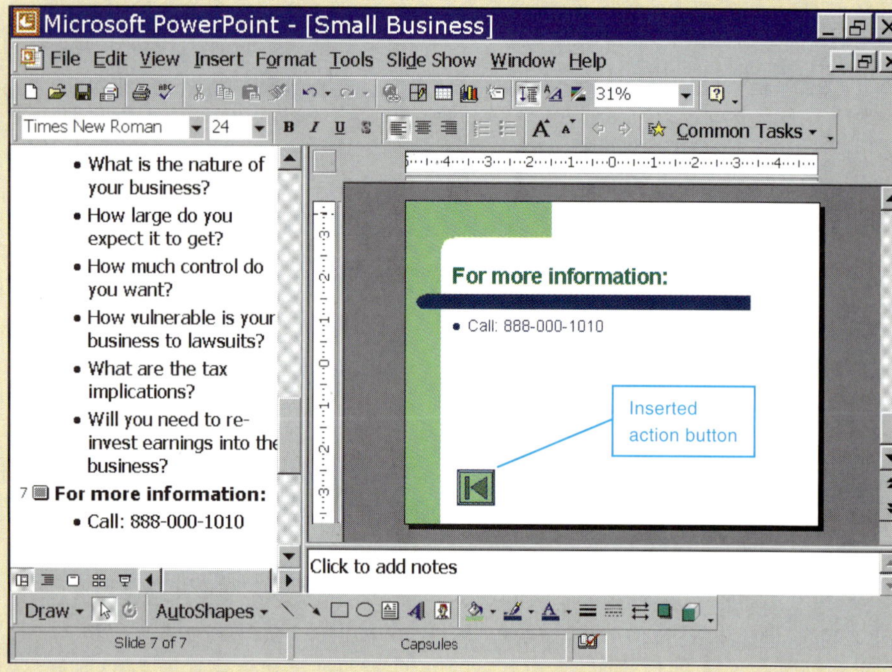


7 To practice using the action button, display the last slide of the presentation in Slide Show view and then click the inserted action button. The first slide of the presentation should appear.

8 PRESS: ESC to display the presentation in Normal view (*Note:* Once inserted, you can change the action performed when you click an action button by right-clicking the button and then choosing Action Settings.)

9 Save the revised presentation and keep it open for use in the next lesson.

## 6.2.3 Inserting Animated GIF Pictures

**FEATURE**

**Animated GIF pictures** contain a series of GIF (Graphics Interchange Format) images. When displayed in rapid sequence in a PowerPoint presentation or on a Web page, they achieve an animated effect. Several animated GIF pictures are included in the Clip Gallery for easy insertion in your presentations. To view an animated GIF, you must display your presentation in Slide Show view. Note that you can't crop or otherwise edit an animated GIF object in any way using PowerPoint's Picture toolbar. Instead, you must use a program designed especially for editing animated GIF files.

**METHOD**

- To insert an animated GIF file from the Clip Gallery:
  CHOOSE: Insert, Movies and Sounds, Movie from Gallery
  CLICK: the animated GIF file you want to insert
  CLICK: Insert Clip button (▣) on the shortcut menu
- To insert an animated GIF file from a file:
  CHOOSE: Insert, Movies and Sounds, Movie from File and then navigate to where the animated GIF file is stored
  DOUBLE-CLICK: the animated GIF file you want to insert

**PRACTICE**

In this lesson, you insert an animated GIF picture on the first slide of the "Small Business" presentation.

*Setup:* Ensure that the "Small Business" presentation is displaying in Normal view.

1 Display the first slide of the "Small Business" presentation in Normal view.

2 Would you believe that an animated GIF picture of Samantha Powell (the author of this "Small Business" presentation) exists in the Clip Gallery? For our purposes, it exists indeed. To insert Samantha's picture on the current slide, do the following:
CHOOSE: Insert, Movies and Sounds, Movie from Gallery
The *Motion Clips* tab is currently selected.

3 Samantha's picture is located in the Business category.
CLICK: Business category
CLICK: Maximize button (□) of the Insert Movie dialog box
Your screen should now appear similar to Figure 6.15. (*Note:* If no clips appear in the window, talk to your instructor or lab assistant. It's possible that these clips weren't installed on your computer.)

**Figure 6.15**

Insert Movie dialog box

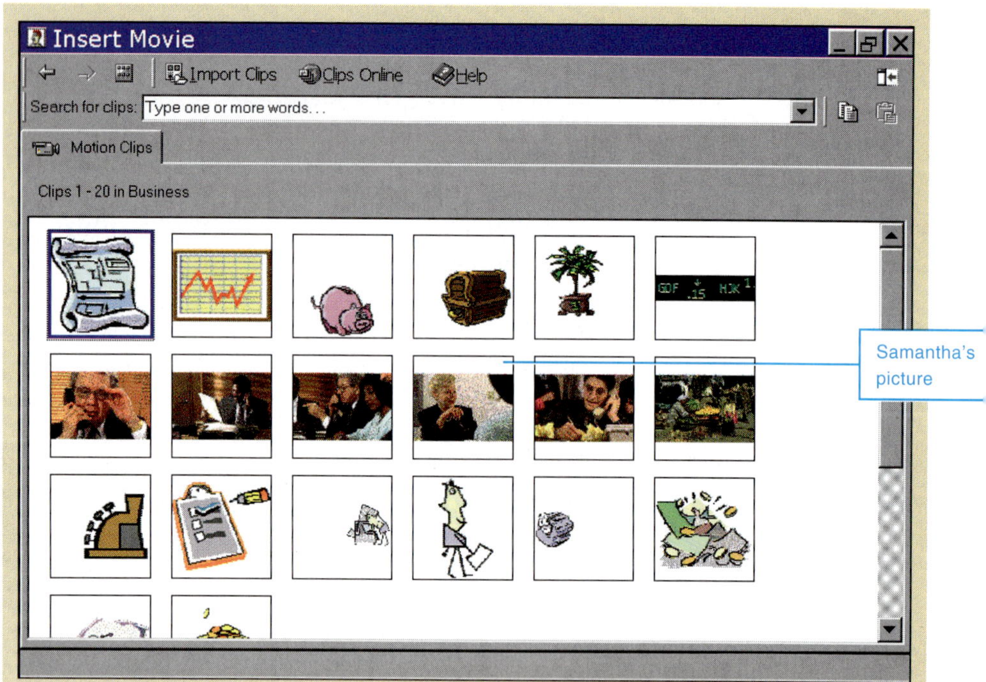


4. CLICK: Samantha's picture (refer to Figure 6.15)
CLICK: Insert Clip button on the shortcut menu

5. Close the Insert Movie dialog box by clicking its Close button.

6. Move and resize the inserted picture until the first slide looks similar to Figure 6.16. (*Hint:* For greater control over sizing and moving objects, press and hold down the ALT key while dragging.)

**Figure 6.16**

Inserting an animated GIF picture

7. To view the animated GIF file in action, switch to Slide Show view. In this movie, Samantha moves her glasses back and forth.

8. PRESS: ESC to view the presentation in Normal view

9. Save the revised presentation and keep it open for use in the next lesson.

**In Addition**
Inserting Video Clips

The procedure for inserting video clips on a slide is the same as for inserting animated GIF pictures.

## 6.2.4 Inserting Sound Clips

**FEATURE**

Sound clips are inserted as icons on slides. In Slide Show view, you play sound clips by clicking their icons. You can also specify that a sound clip play automatically upon displaying a slide, or that it play repeatedly in a continuous loop. To experience sound in a presentation, your computer must be configured with a sound card and speakers.

**METHOD**

1. CHOOSE: Insert, Movies and Sounds
2. To insert sound from the Clip Gallery:
   CHOOSE: Sound from Gallery
   CLICK: the sound clip you want to insert
   CLICK: Insert Clip button (▣) on the shortcut menu
3. To insert sound from a file:
   CHOOSE: Sound from File and then navigate to where the sound file is stored
   DOUBLE-CLICK: the sound file to insert a sound icon on the slide
4. In the displayed dialog box:
   CLICK: Yes to play the sound clip automatically when the next slide is displayed, or
   CLICK: No to require the user to click the sound icon in order to play the clip

**PRACTICE**

In this lesson, you insert a sound clip on the first slide of the "Small Business" presentation.

*Setup:* Ensure that the "Small Business" presentation is displaying in Normal view.

1 Display the first slide of the "Small Business" presentation. Since this slide will likely be displaying for a while as your audience assembles, let's make things more interesting by adding some music.

2 CHOOSE: Insert, Movies and Sounds, Sound from Gallery
The *Sounds* tab is currently selected.

3 The sound we want to insert is located in the Business category.
CLICK: Business category
CLICK: Maximize button (▢) in the Insert Sound dialog box
Your screen should now appear similar to Figure 6.17. (*Note:* If no clips appear in the window, talk to your instructor or lab assistant. It's possible that these clips weren't installed on your computer.)

**Figure 6.17**
Insert Sound dialog box

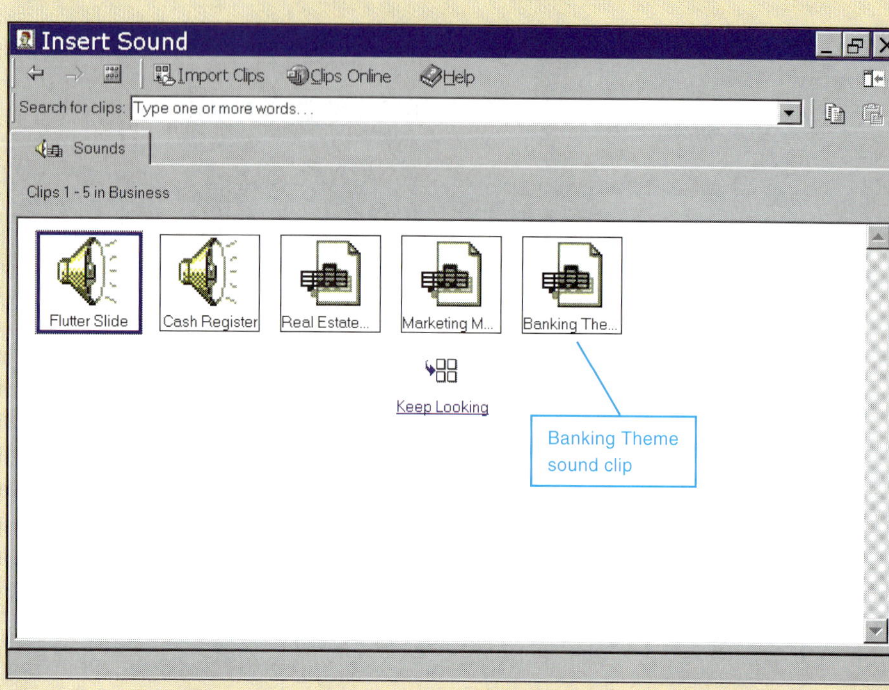


4 CLICK: Banking Theme clip (refer to Figure 6.17)
CLICK: Insert Clip button (▣) on the shortcut menu

5 Close the Insert Sound dialog box by clicking its Close button (☒).

6 In response to the displayed dialog box:
CLICK: Yes command button to play the sound automatically upon viewing the first slide
The sound is inserted as a small icon on the slide.

7 To format the sound clip so that it plays over and over:
RIGHT-CLICK: the sound icon
CHOOSE: Edit Sound Object
The Sound Options dialog box should appear (Figure 6.18).

**Figure 6.18**
Sound Options dialog box

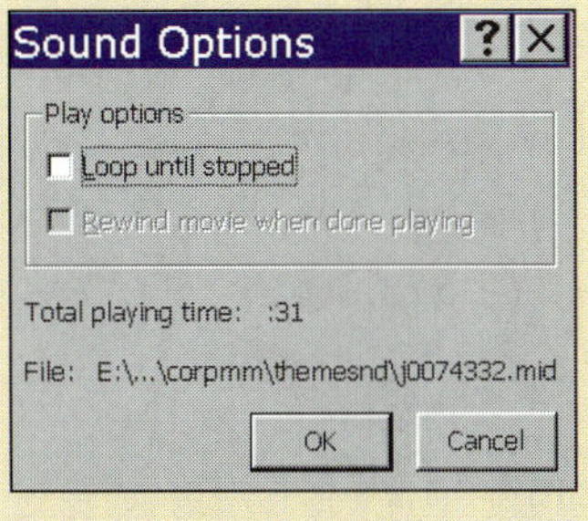


8 SELECT: *Loop until stopped* check box
CLICK: OK command button

9 Since you want the sound clip to play every time you display the first slide, let's hide the sound icon from view:
DRAG: the icon so that it is located on top of Samantha's picture
RIGHT-CLICK: the icon
CHOOSE: Order, Send to Back from the right-click menu
The sound icon is no longer visible.

10 To experience the sound clip, switch to Slide Show view. The clip will continue to play until you either exit the slide show or display the next slide.

11 When you've heard enough:
PRESS: ESC to view the presentation in Normal view

12 Save and then close the revised presentation.



**6.2 Self Check** What is an animated GIF file?

# 6.3 Integrating PowerPoint with Office 2000

When you paste information from the Windows or Office Clipboards into a document, such as a PowerPoint presentation, Office uses HTML (HyperText Markup Language) as its default data format. HTML, as you may already know, is the language of the World Wide Web. Microsoft selected HTML as the default data format so that your text formatting, tables, and other formats will remain unchanged when you copy items among the Office applications. There may be times, however, when you don't want to use HTML as the data format, such as when you don't want to retain your original formatting. In this case, you can use the Paste Special command and then select an alternate data format.

When sharing data among applications, not only do you have to consider the format of the shared data, you also have to decide on how you want the source data (what you're copying) and the copied data to be related. Table 6.1 describes three ways to share data among Office 2000 applications. Each method involves copying the desired data from the **source document,** the document in which the data was first entered, into the **destination document,** or the document that receives the data.

**Table 6.1**
Three methods for sharing data among Office 2000 applications

| Method | Description |
|---|---|
| Pasting | The simplest method for sharing information is to copy the desired data from the source document and then paste it into the destination document. **Pasting** data involves inserting a static representation of the source data into the destination document. |
| Linking | In **linking,** you not only paste the data, you also establish a dynamic link between the source and destination documents. Thereafter, making changes in the source document updates the destination document automatically. |
| Embedding | **Embedding** data involves inserting a source document into a destination document as an object. Unlike pasted data, an embedded object is fully editable within the client application. Unlike linked data, an embedded object does not retain a connection to its source document; everything is contained in the destination document. |

In this module, we explore the methods of pasting, linking, and embedding data among applications. You also learn how to edit shared objects and export a PowerPoint presentation to Word.

## 6.3.1 Pasting Data from Word to PowerPoint

**FEATURE**

Pasting is used to transfer data from one application to another. There is no linking of documents or embedding of objects when you paste data. The data is simply copied from the source document to the Clipboard and then inserted into the destination document.

**METHOD**

1. Copy data from a Word source document to the Clipboard.
2. Select the desired target location in the PowerPoint presentation.
3. CHOOSE: Edit, Paste, or
   CLICK: Paste button ()

**PRACTICE**

You will now practice pasting data from an existing Word document into a PowerPoint presentation.

*Setup:* Ensure that PowerPoint is loaded and that Word is installed on your computer.

1. Launch Word and then open the PPT631 Word file.

2. Save the file as "Student Memo" to your personal storage location. This document contains a table that you'll copy into a PowerPoint presentation.

3. In PowerPoint, open the open the PPT630 presentation file.

4. Save the file as "OCC Study" to your personal storage location. The objective of this presentation is to provide students with several tips for becoming a better student.

5. View the "OCC Study" presentation in Slide Show view to become familiar with its contents. Note that the final slides of the presentation (slides 8 and 9) currently contain lots of blank space. In this module, you'll copy a Word table to slide 8 and an Excel chart to slide 9.

6. To switch back to Word:
CLICK: "Student Memo" Word button on the taskbar

7. Scroll downward until you see the table. Your screen should now appear similar to Figure 6.19.

**Figure 6.19**
Word table

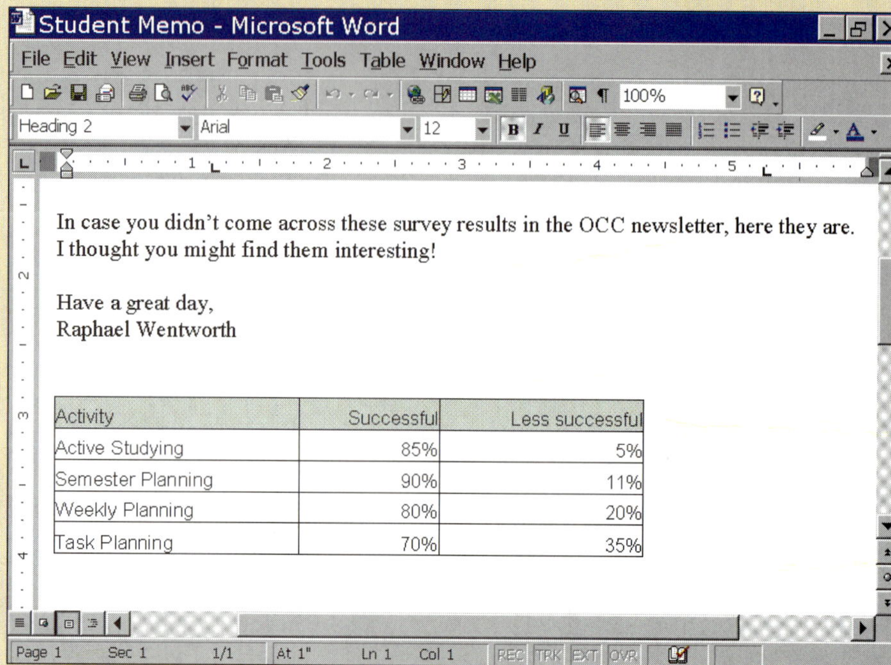


8. To copy the table to the Clipboard:
SELECT: the entire table
CLICK: Copy button () on the Standard toolbar

9. To make the PowerPoint application window active:
CLICK: "OCC Study" PowerPoint button on the taskbar

10. To prepare for the next step, display slide 8 of the presentation in Normal view.

11. To paste the Word table onto slide 8:
CLICK: Paste button ()

**12** To get a closer look at the slide, do the following:
CLICK: Slide View button (▣) (located below the outline pane)
CHOOSE: 50% from the Zoom drop-down list on the Standard toolbar
Your screen should now appear similar to Figure 6.20. The pasted data is automatically divided into separate table cells and directly editable. Also note that because the default data format for pasted data is HTML, the formatting of the Word text is retained in the PowerPoint presentation. Unfortunately, an Arial 10-point font is too small to be seen on a PowerPoint slide!

**Figure 6.20**
Pasting a Word table into PowerPoint

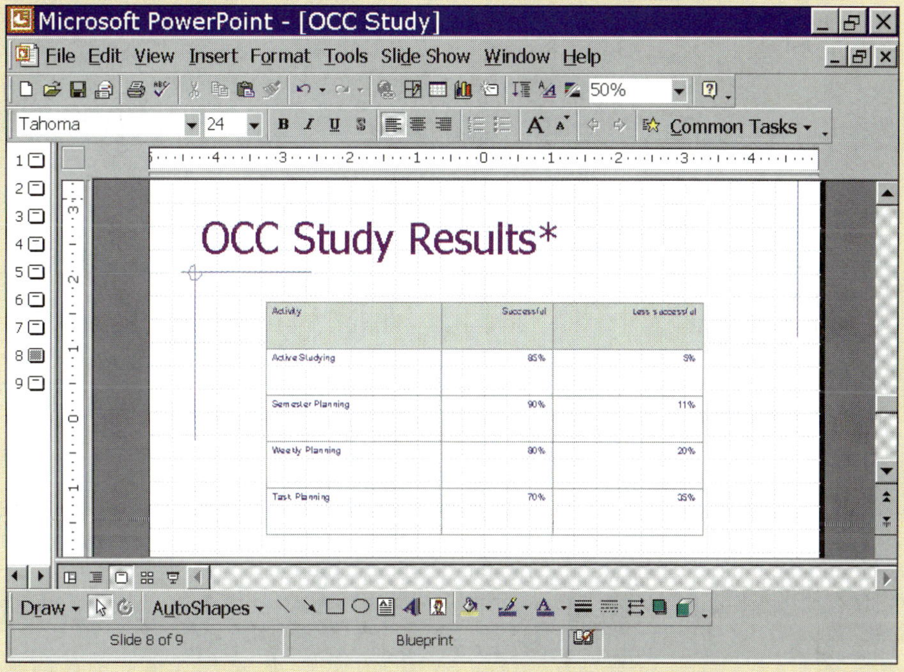


**13** To prepare for the next lesson, let's delete the pasted table from the PowerPoint slide. To do this:
CLICK: near the upper-left corner of the table
The table should be surrounded with sizing handles.
PRESS: DELETE

**14** With slide 8 displaying in an enlarged view, continue to the next lesson.

## 6.3.2 Linking a Word Table to a PowerPoint Slide

**FEATURE**

You link files when the information you need from a source document is either maintained by other users or needs to be incorporated into multiple documents. For successful linking to occur, the source documents must always be accessible, whether stored on the same computer as the destination document or via a network connection.

**METHOD**

1. Copy data from the Word source document to the Clipboard.
2. In the PowerPoint destination document, position the insertion point where you want to insert the data.
3. CHOOSE: Edit, Paste Special
4. SELECT: *Paste link* option button
5. SELECT: a data format in the *As* list box
6. CLICK: OK command button

**PRACTICE**

Your objective in this lesson is to copy and link a Word table to a PowerPoint presentation.

*Setup:* Ensure that you've completed the previous lesson in this module. The "Student Memo" document should be open in Word and the "OCC Study" presentation should be open in PowerPoint. The PowerPoint window is the active window and slide 8 is displaying.

1 If you completed the last lesson, the Word table you copied is still stored in the Clipboard. To paste the table onto slide 8 of the "OCC Study" presentation and establish a link to the Word document, do the following:
CHOOSE: Edit, Paste Special from the PowerPoint menu
Microsoft PowerPoint's Paste Special dialog box appears, as shown in Figure 6.21. You can select the desired format for pasting the Clipboard contents from the *As* list box (Table 6.2). Note that "HTML Format" is the currently selected option.

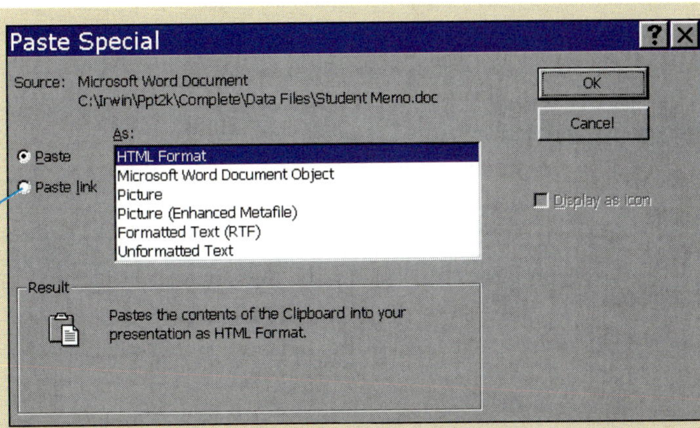


**Figure 6.21**
PowerPoint's Paste Special dialog box

Select this option button to establish a link between the source and destination data.

**Table 6.2**
Data format options

| Data Format | Description |
|---|---|
| HTML Format | The data is inserted in an HTML format so that text attributes and other formatting are retained. |
| Microsoft Word Document Object | The data is inserted as an embedded Word object that you can edit by double-clicking. |
| Picture | The data is inserted as a picture object for printing on high-quality printers. |
| Picture (Enhanced Metafile) | The data is inserted as an enhanced metafile. |
| Formatted Text (RTF) | The data is inserted as an editable Word table. |
| Unformatted Text | The data is inserted as text, with no formatting applied. |

2 To review the various data formats:
CLICK: once on each option in the *As* list box and read the description appearing in the *Result* area

3 To establish a link between the source and the destination documents:
SELECT: *Paste link* option button
CLICK: OK command button
The information is inserted on the slide and the link is established.

4. To insert the object using the HTML data format:
SELECT: HTML Format in the *As* list box

5. Move and resize the table until your screen appears similar to Figure 6.22.

**Figure 6.22**
Linking data from a Word document to a PowerPoint slide

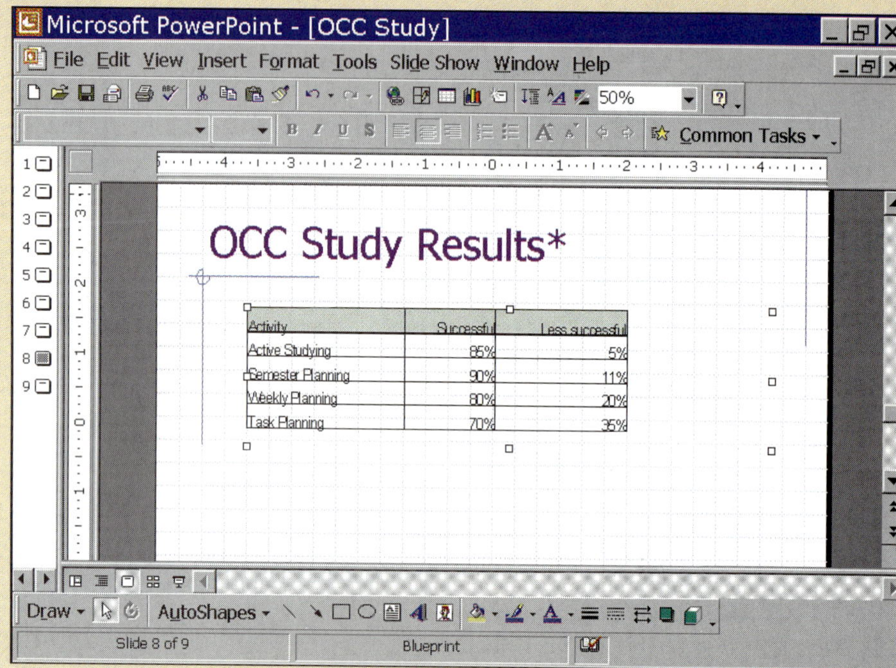


6. Locate the value for Task Planning in the "Successful Students" column. To demonstrate dynamic linking, let's change this value from 70% to 90% in the Word table. To do so:
CLICK: "Student Memo" Word button on the taskbar

7. In the Word table:
SELECT: 70% (located in the last row of the Successful column)
TYPE: **90%**
You have now updated the Word source document.

8. To view slide 8 in the PowerPoint presentation:
CLICK: "OCC Study" PowerPoint button on the taskbar
The updated value (90%) now displays in the table. (*Note:* If the value didn't update automatically, right-click the linked table object and then choose Update link from the right-click menu.)

9. Save the revised "OCC Study" presentation and keep it open for use in the next lesson.

10. Switch to and then save the revised "Student Memo" document.

11. Close Word.

## 6.3.3 Embedding an Excel Chart on a PowerPoint Slide

**FEATURE**

Embedding data enables you to place a fully editable version of the source data into the destination document. Moreover, when editing an embedded object, you use the actual commands and tools of the original **server application** (the application that was used to create the data originally) from within the current application window. Understandably, a document containing embedded objects will require more disk space than one containing links.

**METHOD**

1. Copy data from the Excel source document to the Clipboard.
2. In the PowerPoint destination document, position the insertion point where you want to insert the data.
3. CHOOSE: Edit, Paste Special
4. SELECT: Microsoft Excel Chart Object in the *As* list box
5. CLICK: OK command button

**PRACTICE**

Your current objective is to embed an Excel chart in a PowerPoint presentation.

*Setup:* Ensure that you've completed the previous lessons in this module. In PowerPoint, slide 8 of the "OCC Study" presentation should be displaying in an enlarged view.

1 To display slide 9 of the "OCC Study" presentation:
CLICK: Next Slide button (▾) on the vertical scroll bar
In this lesson, you will embed an Excel chart on this slide.

2 Load Excel and then open the PPT633 worksheet file.

3 Save the worksheet as "OCC Results" to your personal storage location. Your screen should appear similar to Figure 6.23.

**Figure 6.23**
"OCC Results" worksheet

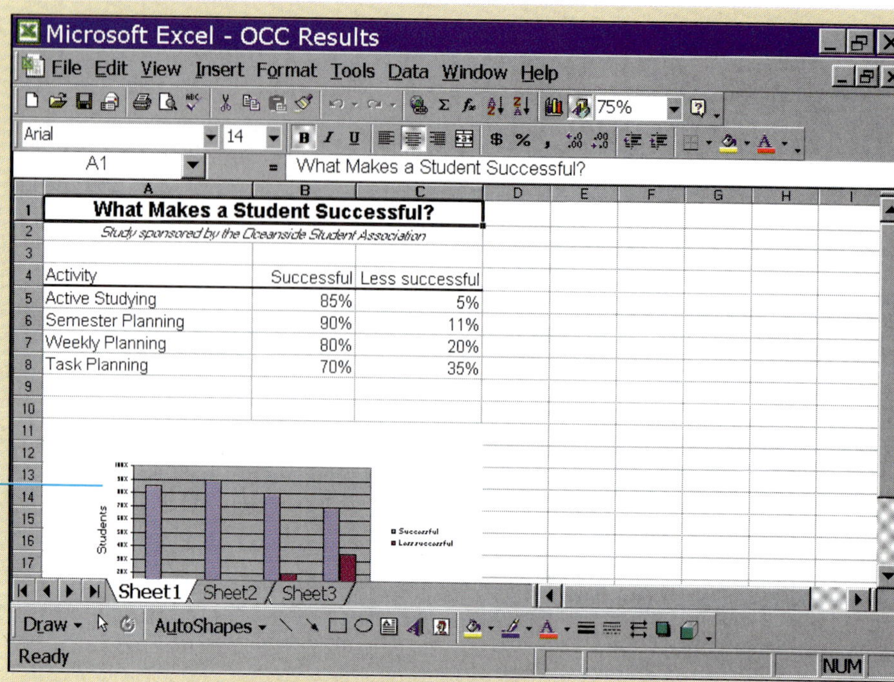


In this lesson, you copy this chart to a PowerPoint slide.

4. To copy the chart to the Clipboard:
CLICK: near the upper-left corner of the chart object
CLICK: Copy button ( )

5. To switch back to PowerPoint:
CLICK: "OCC Study" PowerPoint button on the taskbar

6. To embed the worksheet object onto the PowerPoint slide:
CHOOSE: Edit, Paste Special
SELECT: Microsoft Excel Chart Object in the *As* list box
CLICK: OK command button
The embedded object appears on the PowerPoint slide with sizing handles. Unlike with linked objects, any changes you make in the source document won't affect this embedded chart.

7. On the PowerPoint slide, move and resize the object until your screen appears similar to Figure 6.24.

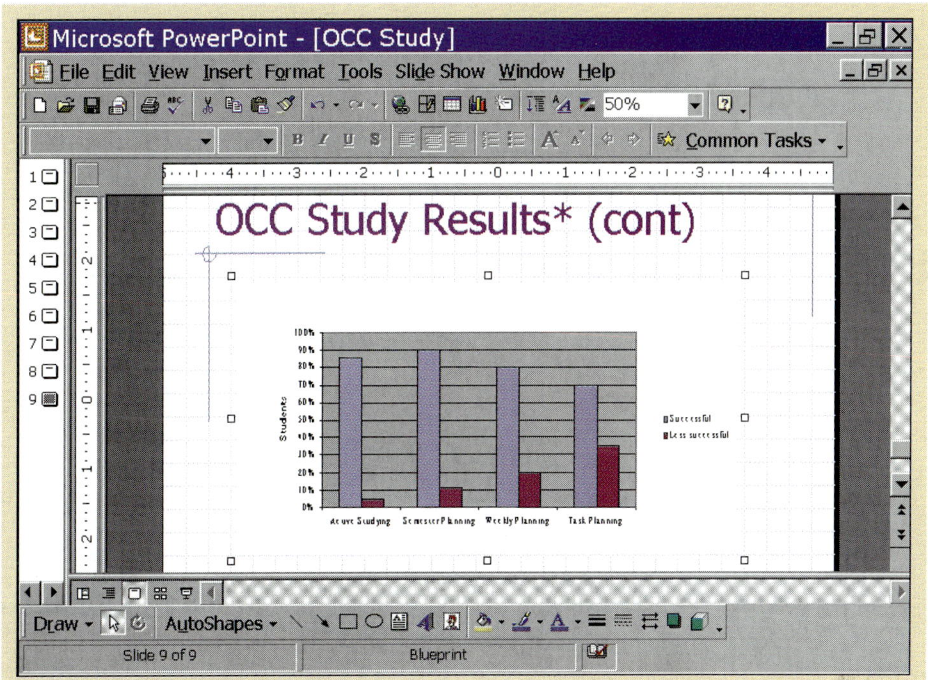


**Figure 6.24**
Embedding an Excel chart on a PowerPoint slide

8 In the next lesson, you learn more about editing linked and embedded objects. For now, save the revised "OCC Study" presentation to your personal storage location.

9 Switch to and then close Excel.

## 6.3.4 Editing Shared Objects

**FEATURE**

A feature called *Visual Editing* makes it easy to update an embedded object in place. To edit an embedded object, such as an Excel chart in PowerPoint, you simply double-click the object. Rather than being launched into the server application (Excel) to perform the changes, you remain where you are (PowerPoint) and the current application's menus and toolbars are replaced with those of the server application. In other words, you don't have to exit the current application to change the embedded object. In contrast, when you double-click a linked object, the server application is launched and the source document is opened. Also, by default, linked objects are updated automatically when the destination document is opened.

## METHOD

- To edit an embedded object:
  DOUBLE-CLICK: the object and then make any necessary changes
  CLICK: outside the object when you're finished making changes
- To edit a linked object:
  DOUBLE-CLICK: on the object to launch the server application and then make any necessary changes
- If a linked object isn't updated automatically in the destination document, do the following:
  RIGHT-CLICK: the linked object
  CHOOSE: Update Link from the right-click menu

## PRACTICE

You will now practice editing an embedded object. (*Note:* You practiced editing a linked object in lesson 6.3.2.)

*Setup:* Ensure that you've completed the previous lessons in this module and that slide 9 of the "OCC Study" presentation is displaying in PowerPoint.

1. To modify the embedded chart that's located on slide 9 of the "OCC Study" presentation:
   DOUBLE-CLICK: the object
   Your screen should now appear similar to Figure 6.25. Note that PowerPoint's Menu bar and toolbars are replaced by Excel's. Also, the embedded object itself is bounded by a frame and sheet tabs.

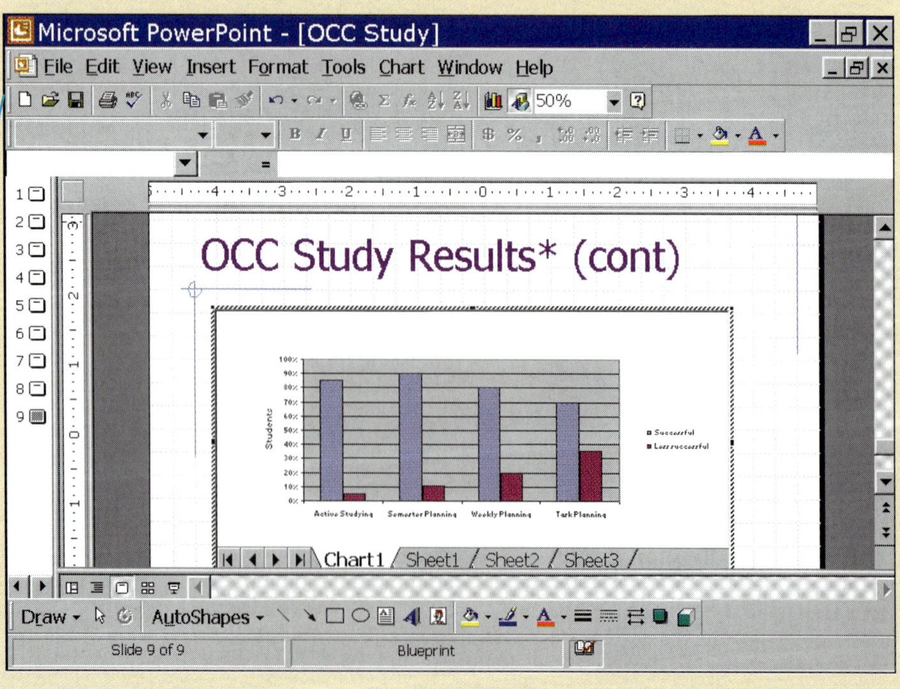


**Figure 6.25**
Editing an embedded Excel object in PowerPoint

PowerPoint's Menu bar and toolbars have been replaced by Excel's.

2 To practice editing an embedded object, you will now increase the font used for the legend.
RIGHT-CLICK: the legend (located on the right side of the chart)
CHOOSE: Format Legend from the right-click menu
CLICK: *Font* tab in the Format Legend dialog box
SELECT: the current value in the *Size* text box
TYPE: **6**
CLICK: OK command button
The legend text should now be easier to read.

3 To finish editing the embedded object:
CLICK: the mouse pointer outside the object to deselect the object
Note that the object's hatched border disappears and that PowerPoint's Menu bar and toolbars are now displaying.

4 Save the revised presentation and keep it open for use in the next lesson.



## 6.3.5 Exporting an Outline to Word

**FEATURE**
You can easily convert your PowerPoint outlines, notes, or handouts to Word. When you convert an outline to Word, Word sets up heading styles by referring to the headings in the PowerPoint outline. In Word, a *heading style* is a format given to a heading. For the best printing results in Word, when your notes or handouts contain graphics, we recommend viewing them first in PowerPoint using the Grayscale Preview button (▣) on the Standard toolbar and then making any color adjustments as necessary.

**METHOD**
CHOOSE: File, Send To, Microsoft Word

**PRACTICE**
You will now export a PowerPoint outline to Word.

*Setup:* Ensure that the "OCC Study" presentation is displaying in PowerPoint.

1 To export the outline of the "OCC Study" presentation to Word:
CHOOSE: File, Send To, Microsoft Word
The Write-Up dialog box will now appear (Figure 6.26). Using this dialog box you can select what you want to export to Word and how you want the content formatted.

**Figure 6.26**

Write-Up dialog box

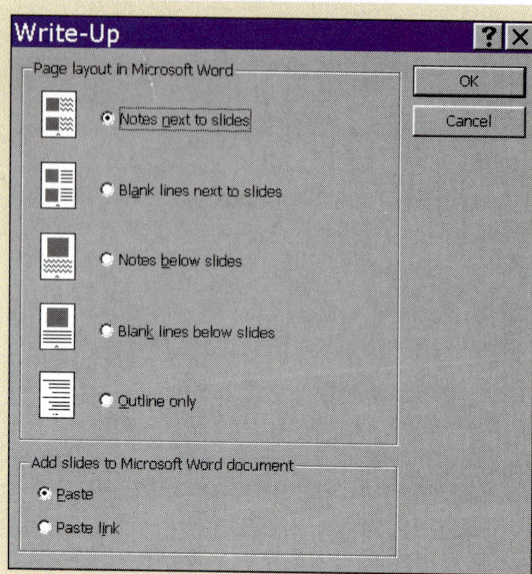


**2** To export your outline to Word:
SELECT: *Outline only* option button
CLICK: OK command button
Word should launch and the outline of your presentation should appear in Print Layout view. Note the awkward filename in the Title bar. You'll change the name of this document shortly.

**3** To switch to Outline view:
CHOOSE: View, Outline
Your screen should now appear similar to Figure 6.27.

**Figure 6.27**

PowerPoint outline displaying in Word

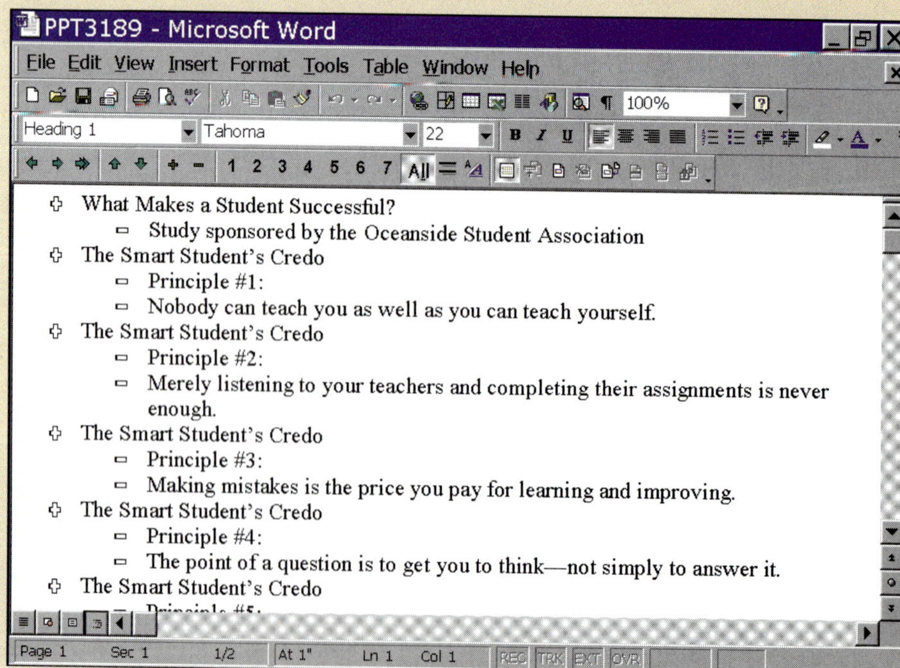

4. Save the document as "PowerPoint Outline" to your personal storage location.
5. Close Word.
6. In PowerPoint, close the "OCC Study" presentation.

**In Addition**
Saving a Slide as a Graphic

To save an existing slide as a graphic that you can insert in other documents and presentations, choose File, Save As and then choose a graphics format from the *Save as type* drop-down list.

**6.3 Self Check** When you paste data, what is the default data format? HTML.



# 6.4 Working with Custom Shows

PowerPoint's Custom Show command makes it possible to adapt a single presentation to multiple audiences rather than creating several presentations that contain only minor differences. To use this command, you must divide your presentation into groups of slides, called **custom shows.** Then, when delivering the presentation, you simply display the custom shows that target the needs of your audience. For example, your job might be to deliver a presentation to two types of prospective students—those attending classes on the main campus and those taking classes via the Internet. To accommodate your needs, you've divided your presentation into an introductory group of slides that you will show both audiences and a more targeted group of slides for students interested in distance education.

In this module, you learn how to divide a presentation into custom shows, deliver a presentation that contains custom shows, and create an agenda slide that references your custom shows. You also learn how to hide slides that you either don't have time to display or that don't contribute to your current objective.

## 6.4.1 Dividing a Presentation into Custom Shows

**FEATURE**

Once a presentation has been divided into custom shows, you can easily adapt the presentation to the needs of your audience, displaying only those slides that are relevant and skipping those that are not. Before dividing a presentation into custom shows, make sure that your presentation contains all the slides that you want to include in the shows.

**METHOD**

1. CHOOSE: Slide Show, Custom Shows
2. CLICK: New command button
3. TYPE: **a name** for the custom show in the *Slide show name* text box
4. PRESS: CTRL and hold it down
5. CLICK: the slides you want to add to the show in the *Slides in presentation* area
6. Release the CTRL key when you're finished selecting slides.
7. CLICK: OK command button

**PRACTICE**

In this lesson, you divide an existing presentation into three custom shows.

*Setup:* Ensure that PowerPoint is loaded and that no presentations are displaying.

1 Open the PPT640 data file.

2 Save the presentation as "OCC Info" to your personal storage location. This eleven-slide presentation is intended for prospective students of Oceanside Community College.

3 On your own, peruse the "OCC Info" presentation in order to become familiar with its contents. As you advance through the presentation, keep the following in mind:

— The first slide of the presentation is the title slide.
— Slides 2–4 describe OCC at a very high level. The information on these slides is relevant to all students.
— Slides 5–8 provide administration-related information that applies to all students.
— Slides 9–11 of the presentation target students interested in learning more about distance education.

By referring to the previous groupings, you'll now divide this presentation into three custom shows named "Intro Slides," "Admin Slides," and "Distance Ed" slides, respectively.

**4** Let's add slides 2–4 to a custom slide show named "Intro Slides." Do the following:
CHOOSE: Slide Show, Custom Shows
CLICK: New command button
The Define Custom Show dialog box should now appear (Figure 6.28).

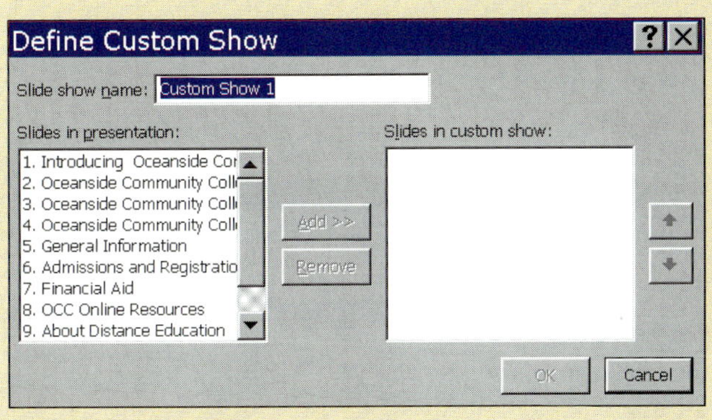


**Figure 6.28**
Define Custom Show dialog box

**5** To give a name to the custom show:
TYPE: **Intro Slides** in the *Slide show name* text box

**6** To select slides 2–4 for inclusion in the custom show:
PRESS: CTRL and hold it down
CLICK: slides 2, 3, and 4 in the *Slides in presentation* list box

**7** To add the selected slides to the custom show:
CLICK: Add command button
The three selected slides should now appear in the *Slides in custom show* list box.

**8** To continue:
CLICK: OK command button
Note that a custom show named "Intro Slides" appears in the Custom Shows dialog box.

**9** Now, let's add slides 5–8 to a custom show named "Admin Slides."
CLICK: New command button
TYPE: **Admin Slides** in the *Slide show name* text box
PRESS: CTRL and hold it down
CLICK: slides 5, 6, 7, and 8 in the *Slides in presentation* list box
CLICK: Add command button
CLICK: OK command button

10 To create one more custom show named "Distance Ed" that contains slides 9–11, do the following:
CLICK: New command button
TYPE: **Distance Ed** in the *Slide show name* text box
PRESS: CTRL and hold it down
CLICK: slides 9, 10, and 11 in the *Slides in presentation* list box
CLICK: Add command button
CLICK: OK command button
The Custom Shows dialog box should now appear similar to Figure 6.29.

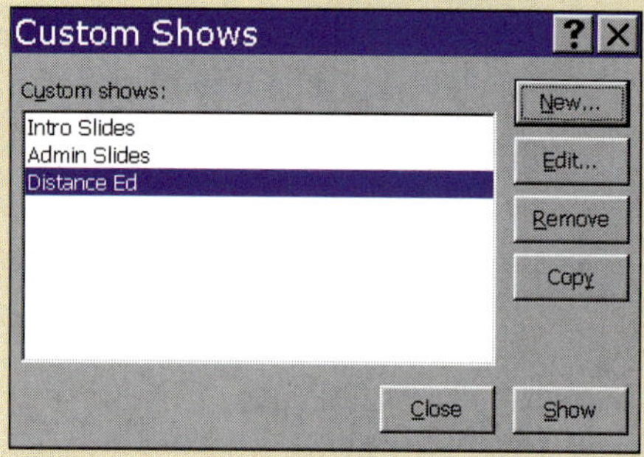


**Figure 6.29**
The "OCC Study" presentation contains three custom shows

11 To leave the Custom Shows dialog box:
CLICK: Close command button

12 Save the revised "OCC Info" presentation and keep it open for use in the next lesson.

## 6.4.2 Starting Custom Shows

**FEATURE**
Once created, you have several options for starting custom shows. You can jump to custom shows using hyperlinks or action buttons that you've inserted directly on a slide; or during the presentation, you can right-click a slide and then jump to a particular show using the right-click menu.

**METHOD**
- CLICK: hyperlinks or action buttons that jump to a particular custom show
- RIGHT-CLICK: a slide in Slide Show view
  CHOOSE: Go, Custom Show from the right-click menu
  CHOOSE: the custom show you want to display

**PRACTICE**

You will now display the "OCC Info" presentation in Slide Show view and practice starting custom shows using the right-click menu.

*Setup:* Ensure that the "OCC Info" presentation is displaying in Normal view.

1. Display the first slide of the "OCC Info" presentation in Normal view.

2. To start the slide show:
CHOOSE: View, Slide Show
The first slide in the presentation should now appear.

3. Let's say that time is running short and you've decided not to display the first few introductory slides. To jump directly to the first slide in the "Admin Slides" show:
RIGHT-CLICK: the first slide
CHOOSE: Go, Custom Show
Your screen should now appear similar to Figure 6.30.

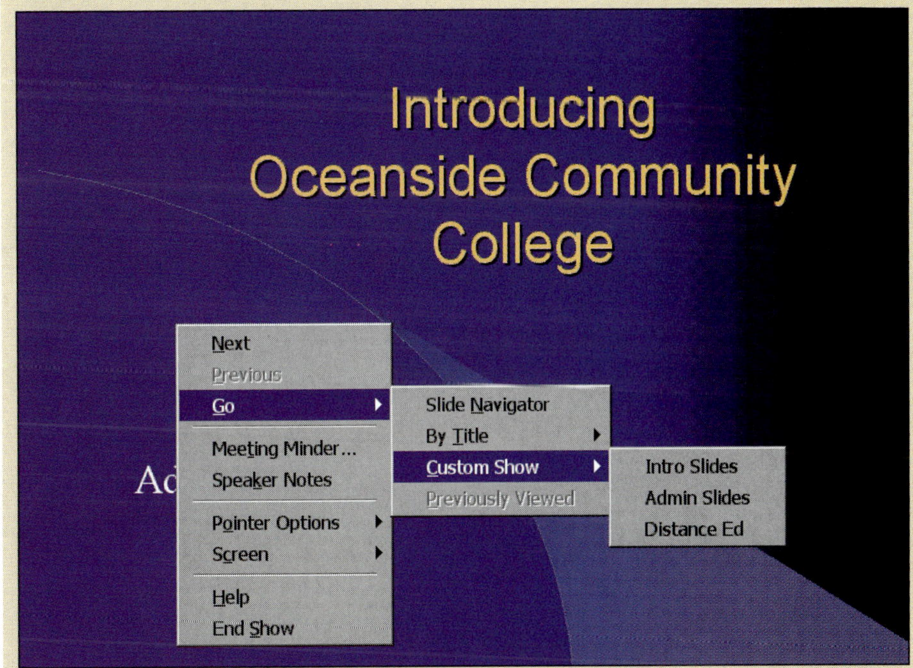


**Figure 6.30**
Starting a custom show

4. CHOOSE: Admin Slides
The first slide in the "Admin Slides" show should now display. If you continuing clicking with the mouse button, the rest of the slides in the "Admin Slides" show will display in sequence, followed by any other slides in the presentation.

POWERPOINT

5 To illustrate moving to the "Distance Ed" show, do the following:
RIGHT-CLICK: the displayed slide
CHOOSE: Go, Custom Show, Distance Ed
The first slide in the "Distance Ed" show should now display.

6 To prepare for the next lesson:
PRESS: ESC to exit Slide Show view
DRAG: the vertical scroll box to the top of the scroll bar

## 6.4.3 Creating a Summary Slide

**FEATURE**
In PowerPoint, summary slides are useful for listing and optionally navigating to the major sections in a presentation. Summary slides contain bullets displaying the titles of any slides you select in Slide Sorter view. If you perform the additional step of formatting the bullets as hyperlinks, you can easily jump from one location in your presentation to another and optionally redisplay the summary slide upon viewing a particular section.

**METHOD**
1. Switch to Slide Sorter view.
3. PRESS: CTRL and hold it down
4. SELECT: any slides whose titles you want to include on the summary slide
5. Release the CTRL key when you're finished selecting slides.
6. CLICK: Summary Slide button (▣) on the Slide Sorter toolbar to insert a summary slide before the first selected slide

**PRACTICE**
In this lesson, you create a summary slide for the "OCC Info" presentation.

*Setup:* Ensure that the first slide in the "OCC Info" presentation is displaying in Normal view.

1 To switch to Slide Sorter view:
CHOOSE: View, Slide Sorter

2 In this step, you begin building a summary slide by selecting the first slide in each of the custom shows stored in this presentation.
CLICK: slide 2
PRESS: CTRL and hold it down
CLICK: slides 5 and 9 and then release the CTRL key

3 To insert the summary slide before slide 2, which is the first selected slide:
CLICK: Summary Slide button ( ) on the Slide Sorter toolbar
Note that a slide was inserted before slide 2.

4 Let's change the title of the inserted slide from "Summary Slide" to "Agenda."
CHOOSE: View, Normal
SELECT: "Summary Slide" title
TYPE: **Agenda**

5 Let's edit the first bulleted item so that it links to the "Intro Slides" custom show.
SELECT: the first bulleted item
CHOOSE: Slide Show, Action Settings
SELECT: *Hyperlink to* option button
CHOOSE: Custom Show from the *Hyperlink to* drop-down list
The Link to Custom Show dialog box appears in Figure 6.31.

**Figure 6.31**
Link to Custom Show dialog box

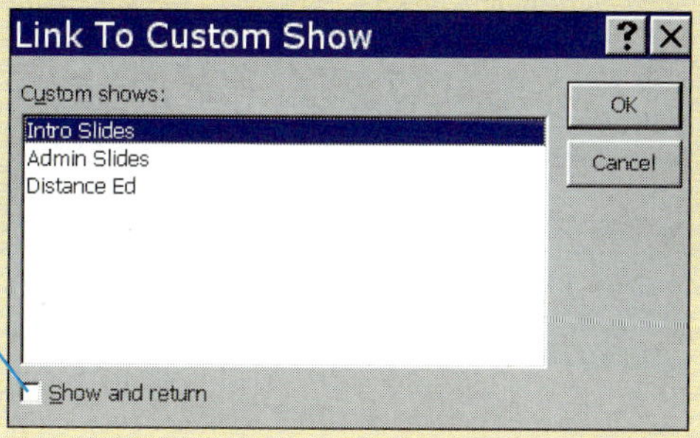


Select this check box to redisplay the agenda slide after the custom show ends.

6 CHOOSE: Intro Slides in the Link to Custom Show dialog box

7 So that the agenda slide will reappear after viewing the "Intro Slides" show:
SELECT: *Show and return* check box
CLICK: OK command button
CLICK: OK command button to redisplay the agenda slide

8 To edit the second bulleted item so that it hyperlinks to the "Admin Slides" custom show, do the following:
SELECT: the second bulleted item
CHOOSE: Slide Show, Action Settings
SELECT: *Hyperlink to* option button
CHOOSE: Custom Show from the *Hyperlink to* drop-down list
CHOOSE: Admin Slides in the Link to Custom Show dialog box
SELECT: *Show and return* check box
CLICK: OK command button
CLICK: OK command button to redisplay the agenda slide

POWERPOINT

9. On your own, edit the third bulleted item so that it links to the "Distance Ed" custom show. Make sure to select the *Show and return* check box. The completed Agenda slide should now appear similar to Figure 6.32.

**Figure 6.32**

Creating an agenda slide that links to custom shows

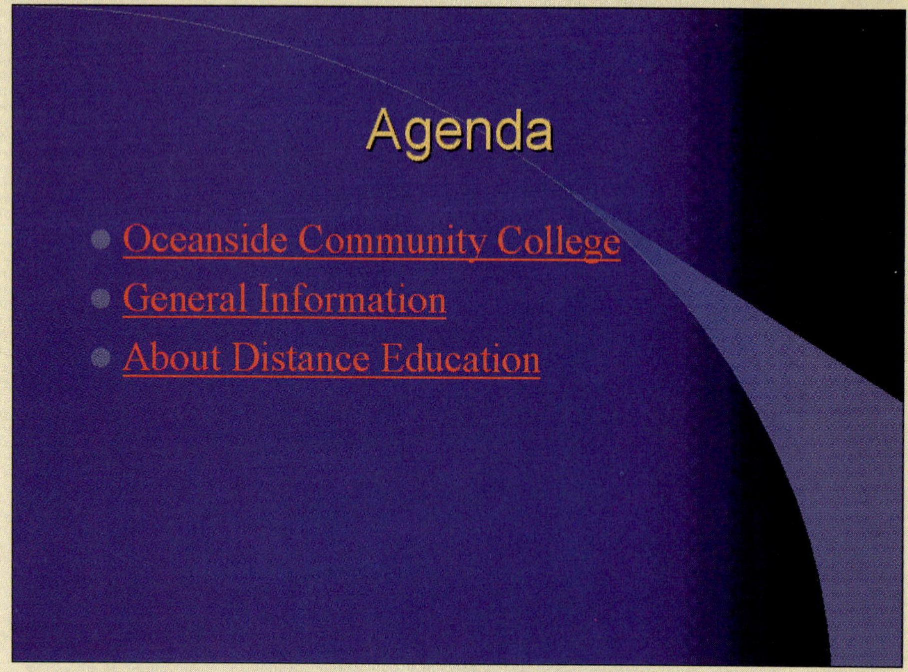


10. Save the revised "OCC Info" presentation.
11. Before continuing, display slide 1 of the presentation in Normal view.
12. To practice using the agenda slide, do the following:
    CHOOSE: View, Slide Show
    CLICK: on the first slide to display the agenda slide
13. On your own, practice navigating through the presentation using the hyperlinks on the agenda slide. Note that upon viewing the final slide in a custom show, the agenda slide redisplays.
14. PRESS: ESC to display the presentation in Normal view
15. Keep the presentation open for use in the next lesson.

**In Addition**
Creating New Slides from a Summary Slide

To create separate slides from an existing summary slide, first create a copy of the slide using the Edit, Duplicate command. Then, in the Outline pane, select the slide's bullets located on the duplicate slide and press SHIFT + TAB. This action will promote the bulleted points into separate slides.

## 6.4.4 Hiding Slides

**FEATURE**
When targeting a presentation to multiple situations and audiences, you may find the need to hide one or more slides. Although they remain in the presentation, hidden slides don't appear when you run the slide show.

**METHOD**

- SELECT: the slide you want to hide in Normal view
  CHOOSE: Slide Show, Hide Slide
- CLICK: Hide Slide button (▣) in Slide Sorter view

**PRACTICE**
This lesson practices hiding a slide in the "OCC Info" presentation.

*Setup:* Ensure that the "OCC Info" presentation is displaying.

1. Display slide 2, the agenda slide, in Normal view.
2. To hide this slide from view:
   CHOOSE: Slide Show, Hide Slide
3. Display slide 1 in Normal view.
4. To view the presentation:
   CHOOSE: View, Slide Show
   CLICK: on the first slide to advance the show
   Note that the agenda slide was skipped over.
5. PRESS: ESC to return to Normal view
6. To unhide the agenda slide, display slide 2 in Normal view.
7. CHOOSE: Slide Show, Hide Slide to reverse the setting
8. Save and then close the "OCC Info" presentation.

POWERPOINT

**6.4 Self Check** In PowerPoint, what is a custom show?

# 6.5 Chapter Review

PowerPoint's presentation and design templates simplify the job of creating engaging presentations. Still, you may want to further customize a presentation to meet your targeted needs. To retain your presentation's basic design but give it a new look, consider customizing the current color scheme or applying a new one. You can also select different colors for the background or apply customized fill effects. Once you customize a presentation to your needs and preferences, you may want to save it as a design template so that it can be used as the basis for future presentations. To further engage your audience, consider customizing your presentations with interactive and multimedia effects, custom slide shows, and objects created in other Office 2000 applications.

## 6.5.1 Command Summary

Many of the commands and procedures appearing in this chapter are summarized in the following table.

| Skill Set | To Perform This Task . . . | Do the Following . . . |
|---|---|---|
| **Creating a Presentation** | Create a new design template | CHOOSE: File, Save As<br>SELECT: Design Template from the *Save as type* drop-down list |
| | Create a summary slide | SELECT: the desired slides in Slide Sorter view<br>CLICK: Summary Slide button |
| **Modifying a presentation** | Apply an alternate color scheme | CHOOSE: Format, Slide Color Scheme<br>CLICK: a scheme in the *Color schemes* area |
| | Customize a selected color scheme | CHOOSE: Format, Slide Color Scheme<br>CLICK: *Custom* tab |
| | Change the current background color | CHOOSE: Format, Background<br>CLICK: the color drop-down list<br>CLICK: one of the displayed colors (or choose More Colors) |

*Continued*

| Skill Set | To Perform This Task . . . | Do the Following . . . |
|---|---|---|
| **Modifying a presentation *Continued*** | Insert links to other slides within the current presentation | SELECT: text or an object<br>CHOOSE: Slide Show, Action Settings<br>SELECT: *Hyperlink to* option button and then make a selection from the *Hyperlink to* drop-down list |
| | Insert an action button | CHOOSE: Slide Show, Action Buttons<br>CLICK: an action symbol and then customize the button using the Action Settings dialog box |
| | Insert an animated GIF picture from the Clip Gallery | CHOOSE: Insert, Movies and Sounds, Movie from Gallery |
| | Insert an animated GIF picture from a file | CHOOSE: Insert, Movies and Sounds, Movie from File |
| | Create a presentation within a presentation | CHOOSE: Slide Show, Custom Show<br>TYPE: **a name** for the custom show<br>CLICK: New command button<br>SELECT: the slides you want to add to the custom show<br>CLICK: OK command button |
| | Hide slides | CHOOSE: Slide Show, Hide Slide in Normal view, or<br>CLICK: Hide Slide button (▣) in Slide Sorter view |
| **Working with Visual Elements** | Add textured backgrounds | CHOOSE: Format, Background<br>CLICK: the color drop-down list<br>CHOOSE: Fill Effects |
| | Insert a sound clip from the Clip Gallery | CHOOSE: Insert, Movies and Sounds, Sound from Gallery |
| **Creating Output** | Save a slide as a graphic | CHOOSE: File, Save As<br>SELECT: a graphics format from the *Save as type* drop-down list |

*Continued*

| Skill Set | To Perform This Task . . . | Do the Following . . . |
|---|---|---|
| **Using Data from Other Sources** | Insert a sound clip from a file | CHOOSE: Insert, Movies and Sounds, Sound from File |
| | Pasting data from Word to PowerPoint | SELECT: data in Word<br>SELECT: the desired target location in PowerPoint<br>CLICK: Paste button (📋) in PowerPoint |
| | Linking a Word table to a PowerPoint slide | SELECT: Word table and then copy it to the Clipboard<br>SELECT: the desired target location in PowerPoint<br>CHOOSE: Edit, Paste Special<br>SELECT: *Paste link* option button |
| | Embedding an Excel chart on a PowerPoint slide | SELECT: Excel chart and then copy it to the Clipboard<br>SELECT: the desired target location in PowerPoint<br>CHOOSE: Edit, Paste Special<br>SELECT: Microsoft Excel Chart Object in the *As* list box |
| | Export an outline to Word | CHOOSE: File, Send To, Microsoft Word |

## 6.5.2 Key Terms

This section specifies page references for the key terms identified in this session. For a complete list of definitions, refer to the Glossary provided immediately after the Appendix in this learning guide.

action button, *p. 224*

animated GIF pictures, *p. 228*

color scheme, *p. 212*

custom show, *p. 247*

destination document, *p. 234*

embedding, *p. 234*

linking, *p. 234*

pasting, *p. 234*

server application, *p. 241*

source document, *p. 234*

# 6.6 Review Questions

## 6.6.1 Short Answer

1. What are action settings used for?
2. What is an action button?
3. List three categories of fill effects that you can apply to a presentation.
4. When should you save a presentation as a template?
5. What procedure would you use to export a PowerPoint outline to Word?
6. How do you apply an alternate color scheme to a presentation?
7. How do you edit an embedded object?
8. In Slide Show view, how do you jump to a custom show?
9. In PowerPoint, what is a summary slide?
10. What is an embedded object?



## 6.6.2 True/False

1. ____ Color schemes can be applied to individual slides and entire presentations.
2. ____ When customizing a color scheme, you can only choose from colors stored in the current color scheme.
3. ____ Every custom show you create is stored in its own file.
4. ____ To edit a linked object, double-click it.
5. ____ Summary slides are inserted before the first slide you select in Slide Sorter view.
6. ____ Although hidden slides remain in the current presentation, they don't show in Slide Show view.
7. ____ In PowerPoint, a color scheme is composed of eight colors that work well together.
8. ____ The Action Settings dialog box can be used to insert hyperlinks on slides.
9. ____ In PowerPoint, the only way to play a sound clip is to click its corresponding icon in Slide Show view.
10. ____ When an object needs to be updated by several users, it is advisable to embed the object.

## 6.6.3 Multiple Choice

1. Which of the following should you use if the information you rely upon is shared among multiple users on a network?
   a. embedded objects
   b. linked objects
   c. grouped objects
   d. All of the above

2. Which of the following should you use to embed an object on a slide?
   a. *Paste* option button
   b. *Paste link* option button
   c. Drawing toolbar
   d. Title placeholder

3. To apply a color scheme to the current slide, click:
   a. Apply
   b. Apply to All
   c. Insert
   d. Insert All

4. Which menu command enables you to create a linked object?
   a. Edit, Paste
   b. Insert, Slides from Outline
   c. Edit, Paste Special
   d. Insert, New Slide

5. Which of the following can you apply to a presentation's background?
   a. patterns
   b. textures
   c. gradient fills
   d. All of the above

6. To save a presentation as a template, choose:
   a. File, New
   b. File, Save As
   c. View, Slide Master
   d. None of the above

7. When selecting background colors, light background colors are best for:
   a. 35mm slides
   b. on-screen presentations
   c. overhead transparencies
   d. All of the above

8. Which of the following can you use to insert hyperlinks on slides?
   a. Insert Hyperlink dialog box
   b. Action Settings dialog box
   c. both a and b
   d. None of the above

9. Which of the following tabs in the Fill Effects dialog box enables you to apply shading that goes from light to dark?
   a. *Gradient* tab
   b. *Texture* tab
   c. *Pattern* tab
   d. *Picture* tab

10. Which of the following can you use to program action buttons?
    a. Insert Hyperlink dialog box
    b. Action Settings dialog box
    c. Define Custom Show dialog box
    d. All of the above



# 6.7 Hands-On Projects

## 6.7.1 Outdoor Adventure Tours: Finalizing a Presentation

This exercise practices changing color schemes and background colors, creating a summary slide, adding an action button, and creating a design template.

1. Open the PPT671 data file and save it as "Outdoor Trade Show" to your personal storage location.
2. Review the slides to become familiar with their content.
3. To change the color scheme:
   CHOOSE: Format, Slide Color Scheme
   SELECT: the middle scheme in the second row
   CLICK: Apply to All command button
4. To apply a background texture to all the slides:
   CHOOSE: Format, Background
   CLICK: drop-down arrow in the *Background fill* area
   CHOOSE: Fill Effects
   CLICK: *Texture* Tab
   CLICK: Green Marble fill and apply this fill to all slides
5. Note that the background graphics prevent most of the marble fill from displaying. To remove the background graphics:
   CHOOSE: Format, Background
   CLICK: *Omit background graphics* check box and apply this setting to all slides

6. To change the color of the text and lines on all slides:
   CHOOSE: Format, Slide Color Scheme
   CLICK: *Custom* tab and then click the Text and Lines box
   CLICK: Change Color command button
   SELECT: a medium yellow color and then apply the new text color to all slides
7. To save the current setup as a design template:
   CHOOSE: File, Save As
   TYPE: **Green Marble** as the file name
   SELECT: Design Template from the *Save as type* drop-down list
   CLICK: Save command button to complete the action
8. To create a new summary slide as the second slide in the presentation, switch to Slide Sorter view and then do the following:
   CLICK: slide 2
   PRESS: CTRL and hold it down
   CLICK: on slides 3 through 7, then release the CTRL key
   CLICK: Summary Slide button ( ) on the Slide Sorter toolbar
9. Switch back to Normal view and examine the new slide that was inserted after the first slide.
10. To remove the bullets from in front of the numbered lines:
    SELECT: numbered lines
    CLICK: Bullets button ( ) on the Formatting toolbar
11. To add an action button at the end of the presentation, display the last slide and then do the following:
    CHOOSE: Slide Show, Action Button
    CLICK: on the first button (Custom)
    CLICK: on the slide to position the button
12. To configure the button to return the user to the summary slide:
    SELECT: *Hyperlink to* option in the Action Settings dialog box
    SELECT: Slide from drop-down list box
    SELECT: Summary Slide from the list of slides
    CLICK: OK command button to complete the Action Button
13. Adjust the size and position of the Action Button to a small discreet square in the lower-right corner of the slide.
14. Switch to the Slide Show view and then test the action button.
15. Save the revised presentation as "Outdoor Trade Show," overwriting the previous version.
16. Close the presentation.

## 6.7.2 Monashee Community College: Embellishing a Presentation

In this exercise, you embellish a presentation using a gradient background fill, a sound clip, and an action clip. You will also paste information from a Word document onto the last slide.

1. Open the PPT672 data file and then save it as "Monashee Troubleshooting" to your personal storage location.
2. Review the slides to become familiar with their content.
3. To change the background color of the slide to a different gradient fill:
   CHOOSE: Format, Background
   SELECT: drop-down arrow in the *Background fill* area and then choose Fill Effects
   SELECT: *Color 1* drop-down arrow and then change the color to a slightly darker shade of blue
   SELECT: *Diagonal up* option button
   SELECT: the variant located in the top-right corner and then apply your selections to all slides
4. To insert an animated clip on the first slide, move to the first slide in the presentation and then:
   CHOOSE: Insert, Movies and Sounds, Movie from Gallery
   CLICK: Science and Technology category
   CLICK: first clip in the category and insert it on the slide
5. Size and position the clip so that it forms a 4-inch square in the bottom-right corner of the slide.
6. To insert a sound clip on the last slide, move to the last slide of the presentation and then:
   CHOOSE: Insert, Movies and Sounds, Sound from Gallery
   CLICK: Industry Category and then insert the Technobop sound clip
   CLICK: Yes command button to have the clip sound automatically when the slide is displayed
7. Position the sound clip icon in the bottom-right corner of the slide.
8. Switch to Slide Show view to preview the animation and sound clip, then return to Normal view.
9. Open the Word document named PPT672a, then copy the names at the bottom of the memo to the Clipboard.
10. To insert these names as credits on the last slide of the presentation, return to the PowerPoint presentation and then:
    CLICK: in the text area of the last slide
    CHOOSE: Edit, Paste Special and select the HTML Format to paste the text into the last slide

POWERPOINT

11. To change the format of the four names:
    SELECT: all the names
    CLICK: Bullets button (☰) to remove the bullets from the lines
    CLICK: Center button (☰)
12. To hide slide 9 since it is not applicable to this audience, move to slide 9 and then:
    CHOOSE: Slide Show, Hide Slide
13. Switch to Slide Show view and then review the entire presentation.
14. Save and then close the revised "Monashee Troubleshooting" presentation.

## 6.7.3 Coldstream Corporation: Adding Interactive Elements

You will now practice creating a summary slide, inserting hyperlinks, adding an action button, and linking an Excel chart to your presentation.

1. Open the PPT673 data file and then save it as "Coldstream Workplace Issues" to your personal storage location.
2. Review the slides to become familiar with the content.
3. Create a summary slide for slides 2 through 6.
4. Change the title of the summary slide from "Summary" to "Workshop Categories."
5. Set a hyperlink from the Leadership Partnering category to the slide with the same title.
6. Set hyperlinks for each of the remaining four topic categories.
7. Open the PPT673a data file.
8. Select the chart located on the Workshops worksheet and then copy the chart to the Clipboard.
9. Switch back to the PowerPoint presentation, move to the last slide, and then click in the text area.
10. Use the Edit, Paste Special command to link the contents of the Clipboard as a Microsoft Excel Chart object.
11. Close the Excel workbook.
12. To add an action button to all slides that will return the user to the summary slide, view the Slide Master.
13. CHOOSE: Slide Show, Action Buttons and then select the Custom button
14. Configure the button as a hyperlink to the Workshop Categories slide.
15. Reduce the size of the button and place it at the lowest point of the bottom-right corner of the slide. Then, close the Slide Master.
16. To edit the 1999 Skills figures in the original Excel workbook, double-click on the linked chart on the last slide. Change the figure from 108 to 118.

17. Save the revised Excel workbook as "Coldstream Workshop" to your personal storage location.
18. Change to Slide Show view, testing all hyperlinks and action buttons.
19. Save and then close the revised "Coldstream Workplace Issues" presentation.

## 6.7.4 Spiderman Web Marketing: Creating a Custom Show

In this exercise, you create a custom slide show and practice embedding an Excel chart.

1. Open the PPT674 data file and then save it as "Spiderman Web Info" to your personal storage location.
2. Review the slides to become familiar with the content.
3. Create a custom show named "Benefits & Customers" that includes slides 2, 5, 6, 7, and 8.
4. Add an action button to the first slide that will display the "Benefits & Customers" slide custom show when clicked.
5. Move to the last slide of the presentation and add an action button that will return the user to the first slide.
6. Apply the "Laverne" design template to your presentation.
7. Open the Excel workbook named PPT674a from your data files location.
8. Select the chart object and then copy the information to the Clipboard.
9. Switch back to the PowerPoint presentation, then move to the slide titled Product Companies.
10. Use the Paste Special command to embed the contents of the Clipboard as an embedded Excel Chart object.
11. To remove the border and fill from the embedded chart object, double-click on the object to access Excel's chart object toolbars and menus.
12. Double-click again on the white area of the chart to open the Format Chart Area dialog box.
13. SELECT: *None* option button in the *Border* area
    SELECT: *None* option button in the *Area* area
    CLICK: outside the chart object to return to PowerPoint
14. Adjust and position the chart so that it is easily viewed on the screen.
15. Switch to Slide Show view and then preview the presentation.
16. Save and then close the revised "Spiderman Web Info" presentation.

POWERPOINT

### 6.7.5 On Your Own: Victor's Video Rentals

Victor has asked you to create a simple presentation promoting his video rental store. He wants potential customers to know about his store's convenient location, low video rental prices, and large selection of children's videos. To make the presentation more interesting, incorporate interactive and multimedia effects in the presentation, such as action settings, action buttons, an animated GIF picture, and a sound clip. Save your presentation as "Video Rentals" to your personal storage location.

### 6.7.6 On Your Own: Weather Forecast

To practice sharing data between PowerPoint and other Office 2000 applications, create a three-slide presentation that incorporates data from an Excel worksheet named PPT676.xls. Name the first slide "Pasted weather" and then copy and paste the colored data from PPT676.xls file onto the first slide of the presentation. Name the second slide "Embedded weather" and embed the same Excel data on the second slide. Name the third slide "Linked weather" and link the Excel data to the third slide. Finally make several changes to the original Excel data and check which slide displays the changes. Save your presentation as "Weather" to your personal storage location.

## 6.8 Case Problems: Jade Beach Juice Company

Trevor Campbell and Kaity Kerr have come a long way since they began selling freshly squeezed fruit juices from a rented stall on the beach. They had no idea that their liquid creations would some day be sold across the country with international orders beginning to trickle in. As the Jade Beach Juice Company continues to expand in all directions, so has the need to procure financial backing. Trevor and Kaity have scheduled several appointments with potential financiers and plan to use a PowerPoint presentation to explain their company. After previewing the presentation, Trevor would like to change the look of the presentation to better reflect their juices. Kaity wants to incorporate action settings and buttons and to create custom shows for each of their scheduled appointments.

In the following case problems, assume the roles of Trevor and Kaity and perform the same steps that they identify. You may want to re-read the chapter opening before proceeding.

1. Trevor opens the PPT681 presentation and saves it as "Jade Beach Juice" to his personal storage location. After reviewing the presentation, he decides to apply a "juicier" color scheme to the entire presentation. Trevor selects and previews each of the color schemes on the *Standard* tab of the Color Scheme dialog box. The color scheme with a yellow background (located in the second column of the first row) reminds him of his favorite drink, a Banana Peach Smoothy, so he applies it to all of the slides.

   To create a thirst-quenching effect, Trevor would like to create juice drops as the fill effect on the background of every slide. He applies a textured fill that resembles water droplets to all the slides in the presentation. Trevor also decides to brighten the color used for shadows, changing it from beige to bright orange on every slide. Pleased with the new look, Trevor saves the revised presentation. He then saves the presentation as a design template named "Juice" and closes the presentation.

2. Kaity opens the "Jade Beach Juice" presentation and then saves it as "Jade Beach Juice-2" to her personal storage location. After viewing the presentation, Kaity feels strongly that the second slide should contain an outline of all the topics contained in the presentation. She switches to Slide Sorter view and selects all of the slides except for the first one. Using the Summary Slide button, she creates a new slide. She changes the slide's title from "Summary Slide" to "Outline."

   Kaity ponders how to navigate with greater ease to each of the topic headings listed on the outline slide. Following Trevor's suggestion, she creates a hyperlink from each of the topic headings on the second slide to its corresponding slide within the presentation. Rather than clicking the mouse to activate the hyperlink, Kaity prefers to simply position the mouse pointer over the hyperlink. Kaity saves the revised presentation.

POWERPOINT

3. Delighted at how easy it is to move around the presentation, Kaity decides to add forward action buttons to the bottom-right corner of the first three slides. By clicking the action button, the next slide automatically appears.

   On the bottom-right corner of the last slide, Kaity adds a home action button that returns to the first slide. Dissatisfied with the default color of the action buttons, Kaity discovers that by right-clicking the action button and selecting "Format AutoShape" from the right-click menu, she can select a more appropriate fill color, such as yellow. Kaity saves the revised presentation as "Jade Beach Juice-3" to her personal storage location.

4. Since Trevor and Kaity will be delivering this presentation to several different financial institutions, they have decided to create three custom shows. Trevor entitles the first custom show "Banks" and includes slides 1, 5, and 7. The second custom show is called "Credit Unions" and consists of slides 1, 3, 4, and 6. "Government Grants" is the name of the third custom show and contains slides 2, 3, 4, and 7.

   Kaity practices starting each of the three custom shows using the right-click menu in Slide Show view. To start the "Government Grants" custom show, Trevor creates an action button in the top-left corner of the first slide. To conform to the presentation's other action buttons, Trevor changes the fill color of the action button to yellow. Trevor saves the revised presentation as "Jade Beach Juice-4" to his personal storage location.

   Parched from their vigorous work, they sip on their latest creation, a Pineapple Raspberry Coconut Twist.

# Notes

# Notes

# Microsoft PowerPoint 2000

*Delivering Presentations*

## Chapter Seven

## Chapter Outline



## Learning Objectives

After completing this chapter, you will be able to:

- Customize the size and orientation of slides to your output format
- Prepare presentations for delivery on another computer
- Capture meeting minutes during a presentation
- Deliver a self-running presentations
- Format presentations for display on the Web and then post them to a Web server
- Subscribe to a Web presentation and learn more about presentation broadcasting

## Case Study

## Galveston Genealogy Club

Ernest Williamson has always been interested in travel and history. Several years ago Ernest had the opportunity to travel extensively throughout Europe and Asia. During his journey he was fortunate to locate and meet several long-lost relatives. Ernest became fascinated with his family history and, after returning home, began recording as much family information as he could. Despite his busy career as an Aircraft Maintenance Engineering instructor at the local college, Ernest now devotes much of his free time to this new hobby. In fact, he was recently elected President of the Galveston Genealogy Club.

Ernest has discovered that genealogy is one of the fastest-growing hobbies around the world. Through the use of computers and Internet connections, genealogical information is located and shared with ease. As president of the Galveston Genealogy Club, Ernest is frequently asked to make presentations to new members who are eager to learn how to trace their family history. Ernest is familiar with creating a basic presentation in PowerPoint; however, he would like to learn more about delivering on-screen and Web presentations. He has also heard about presentation broadcasting and intends to explore this option.

In this chapter, you and Ernest learn how to adjust slide size and orientation, prepare presentations for use on other computers, record meeting minutes, and format and post presentations for the Web. You will also learn about presentation broadcasting.

# 7.1 Delivering On-Screen Presentations

In Chapter 5, we discussed several ways you can prepare a presentation for delivery, including adding animation, transitions, and hyperlinks, as well as preparing speaker notes, audience handouts, and overhead transparencies. In this module, we describe a few more preparation procedures and then describe how to deliver your on-screen presentations on any computer, regardless of whether PowerPoint is installed. We also describe how to use the Meeting Minder utility for incorporating meeting feedback during your presentations.

## 7.1.1 Adjusting Slide Size and Orientation

**FEATURE**

The Page Setup dialog box provides options for customizing your presentation to your desired output format. By default, PowerPoint sizes your slides for display on-screen and applies a landscape orientation. If you change nothing in the Page Setup dialog box, your slides will also print nicely on letter-sized paper (8.5 by 11 inches) and overhead transparencies. If, however, you would like to switch from landscape to portrait orientation or size your presentation for display on legal- or custom-sized paper, 35mm slides, or banners, you will want to use the Page Setup dialog box. The Page Setup dialog box can also be used to change the starting slide number for those times when your presentation will become a part of a larger presentation.

**METHOD**

1. CHOOSE: File, Page Setup
2. Make your selections.
3. CLICK: OK command button

**PRACTICE**

In this lesson, you size an existing on-screen presentation for display on 35mm slides.

*Setup:* Ensure that PowerPoint is loaded and that no presentations are displaying.

1. Open the PPT710 data file.

2. Save the presentation as "Community Center" to your personal storage location. This presentation was created by the Moraga Community Center to describe its course offerings.

3. In this lesson, you prepare the "Community Center" presentation for a co-worker who will be using 35mm slides. To begin:
   CHOOSE: File, Page Setup
   The Page Setup dialog box should now appear (Figure 7.1). Note that "On-screen Show" currently appears in the *Slides sized for* drop-down list. Also note that the *Landscape* option button is selected in the *Slides* area.

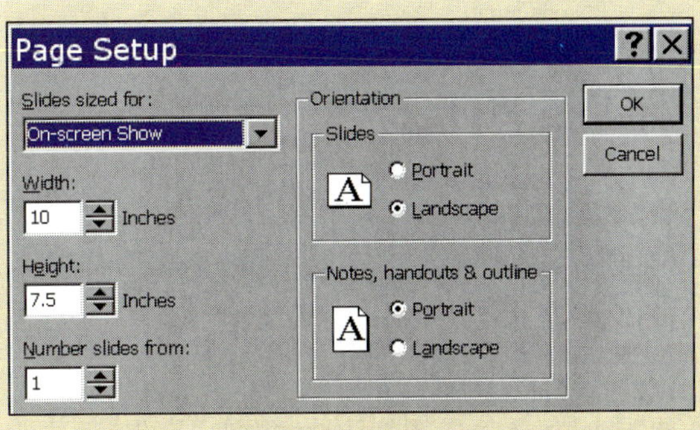


**Figure 7.1**
Page Setup dialog box

4 To optimize the size of the slides for display on 35mm slides, do the following:
SELECT: 35mm Slides from the *Slides sized for* drop-down list
Note that the dimensions in the *Width* spin box automatically changed from 10 to 11.25.

5 To leave all the other settings in the dialog box unchanged:
CLICK: OK command button

6 Save the presentation as "35mm Slides" to your personal storage location. At this point, if you are in the United States and have established an online Internet connection, you can send your presentation directly to Genigraphics, a company that specializes in the output of color 35mm slides and other types of color output. Simply choose File, Send to Genigraphics from the Menu bar and then follow the instructions presented by the **Genigraphics Wizard.** If you're not located in the United States, contact your local service bureau and ask them for instructions on how to convert your PowerPoint presentation to 35mm slides.

7 To prepare for the next lesson, close the "35mm Slides" presentation and then open the "Community Center" presentation.

## 7.1.2 Delivering Presentations on Another Computer

**FEATURE**

The **Pack and Go Wizard** is useful for those times when you must deliver a presentation on a computer that isn't your own. This wizard packages one or more presentations into a single file and stores them on one or more diskettes. The wizard also includes the PowerPoint Viewer program in case the computer you'll be presenting on doesn't have PowerPoint installed. For an added sense of security and to ensure that the presentation looks the same on another computer, the Pack and Go Wizard lets you include linked files and embed TrueType fonts. Lastly, the wizard compresses the presentation so that it takes a lesser number of diskettes to take your show on the road!

**METHOD**

1. CHOOSE: File, Pack and Go
2. Then follow the steps presented by the wizard.

**PRACTICE**

In this lesson, you prepare an existing presentation for delivery on another computer.

*Setup:* Ensure that you've completed the previous lesson and that the "Community Center" presentation is displaying.

1 CHOOSE: File, Pack and Go Wizard
The initial Pack and Go Wizard dialog box appears (Figure 7.2).

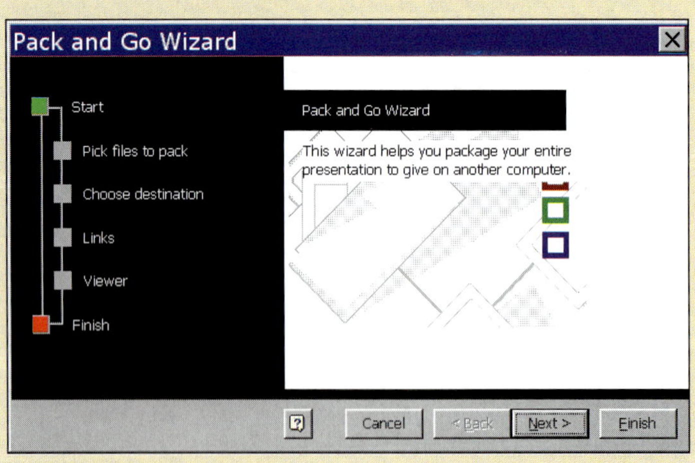


**Figure 7.2**
The Pack and Go Wizard dialog box

2 To proceed:
CLICK: Next command button

3 In this step, you select to package the active presentation. Since this check box is already selected:
CLICK: Next command button

4 In most cases you will want to store your packed presentations on diskettes for easy transport to your delivery computer. However, for this lesson, since you might not have access to a diskette, let's store the packaged presentation in our personal storage location. Do the following:
SELECT: *Choose destination* option button
CLICK: Browse option button

5 Using the *Look in* drop-down list or the Places bar, navigate to your personal storage location.

6 CLICK: Select command button
The path to your personal storage location should now appear in the *Choose destination* text box.

7 To proceed:
CLICK: Next command button
The Pack and Go Wizard dialog box should now appear similar to Figure 7.3.

**Figure 7.3**
Including linked files and embedding TrueType fonts

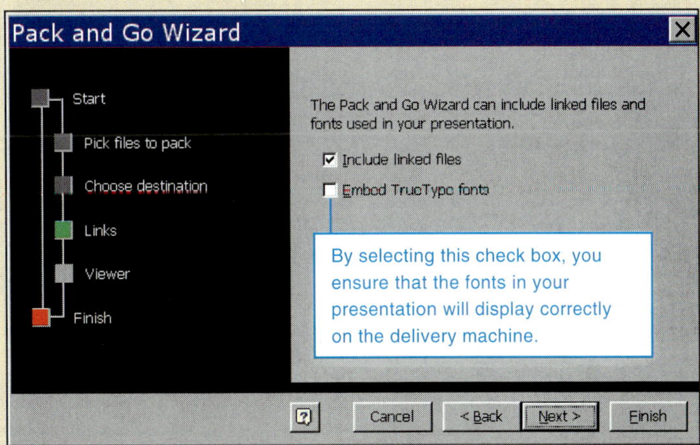


8 If it isn't already selected:
SELECT: *Embed TrueType fonts* check box

9 To proceed without changing current selections:
CLICK: Next command button

10. If your delivery computer doesn't have an installed version of PowerPoint, you need to select the *Viewer for Windows 95 or NT* option button. To continue without making a selection:
CLICK: Next command button
The final wizard dialog box should now appear. Note the message indicating that your presentation will be compressed to your personal storage location.

11. CLICK: Finish command button
The presentation, in a compressed format, is being copied to the storage area. After a few seconds, a dialog box will display indicating that the presentation has been successfully packed.

12. To respond to the displayed dialog box:
CLICK: OK command button
To unpack a presentation that has been copied onto a diskette, you insert your packed diskette in the delivery computer's disk drive and then use Windows Explorer to view the files on the diskette. Double-click the file named "pngsetup" and then select a folder on the hard disk where the presentation should be copied. If your computer has an installed version of PowerPoint, you will be asked if you want to run the presentation right now. Otherwise, double-click the PowerPoint Viewer program, named "ppview32," and then select the presentation you want to run.

13. Keep the "Community Center" presentation open for use in the next lesson.

**In Addition**
Using the Projector Wizard

When presenting on-screen presentations to large audiences, you'll need to connect an electronic projection device to your desktop or laptop computer. To optimize your presentation for display on your particular projection device, you will want to launch PowerPoint's **Projector Wizard**. You can access this wizard by choosing Slide Show, Set Up Show from PowerPoint's Menu bar. To find out more about using this tool, consult PowerPoint's online Help system.

## 7.1.3 Capturing Meeting Minutes

**FEATURE**

When using a presentation as a basis for group discussion, the Meeting Minder utility can be very useful. With this utility, you can incorporate meeting feedback and action items directly into your presentation.

**METHOD**

1. Display the presentation in Slide Show view.
2. RIGHT-CLICK: anywhere on the screen
3. CHOOSE: Meeting Minder from the right-click menu
4. Use the *Meeting Minutes* tab to collect audience feedback and the *Action Items* tab to collect a list of action items for display on a final slide.

**PRACTICE**

You will now run the "Community Center" slide show and practice incorporating meeting feedback and action items using the Meeting Minder utility.

*Setup:* Ensure that you completed the previous lessons in this module and that slide 1 of the "Community Center" presentation appears in Normal view.

1 Let's pretend that you're delivering the "Community Center" presentation to your co-workers for the sole purpose of obtaining feedback. In such a setting, the Meeting Minder utility is very useful.
CHOOSE: View, Slide Show
The title slide should now appear.

2 To proceed to the third slide, entitled "Adult Classes"
CLICK: left mouse button twice

3 At this point, let's pretend that one of your co-workers has feedback that you would like to record.
RIGHT-CLICK: anywhere on the slide
CHOOSE: Meeting Minder from the right-click menu
Your screen should now appear similar to Figure 7.4.

POWERPOINT

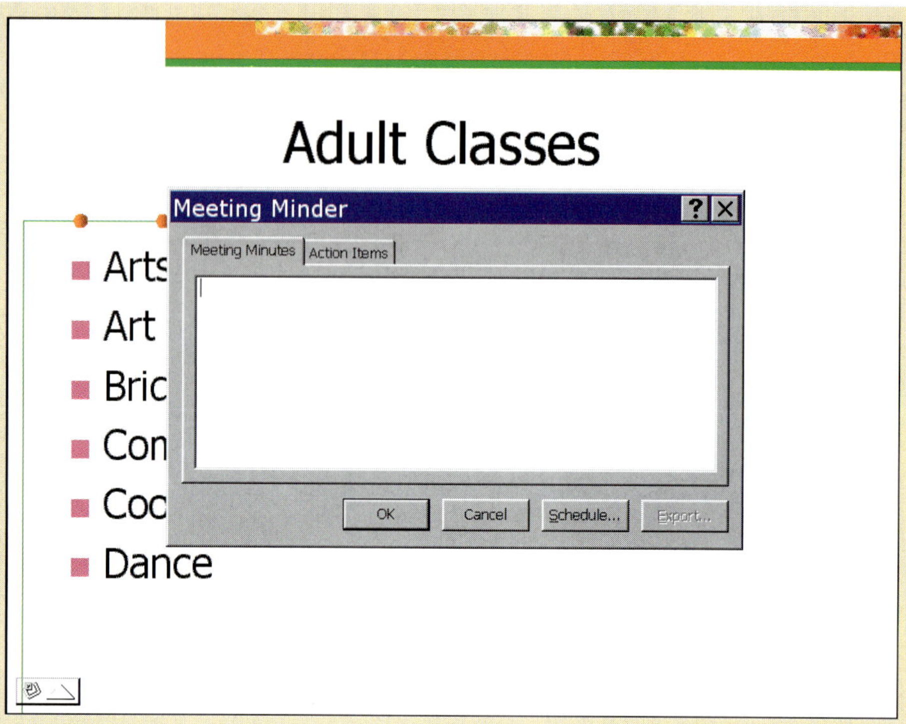


**Figure 7.4**
Meeting Minder: *Meeting Minutes* tab

4 TYPE: **Roger thinks we should add Chess to our list of adult classes.**

5 To add an action item that will be inserted on the final slide of the presentation:
CLICK: *Action Items* tab
Your screen should now appear similar to Figure 7.5.

**Figure 7.5**
Meeting Minder: *Action Items* tab

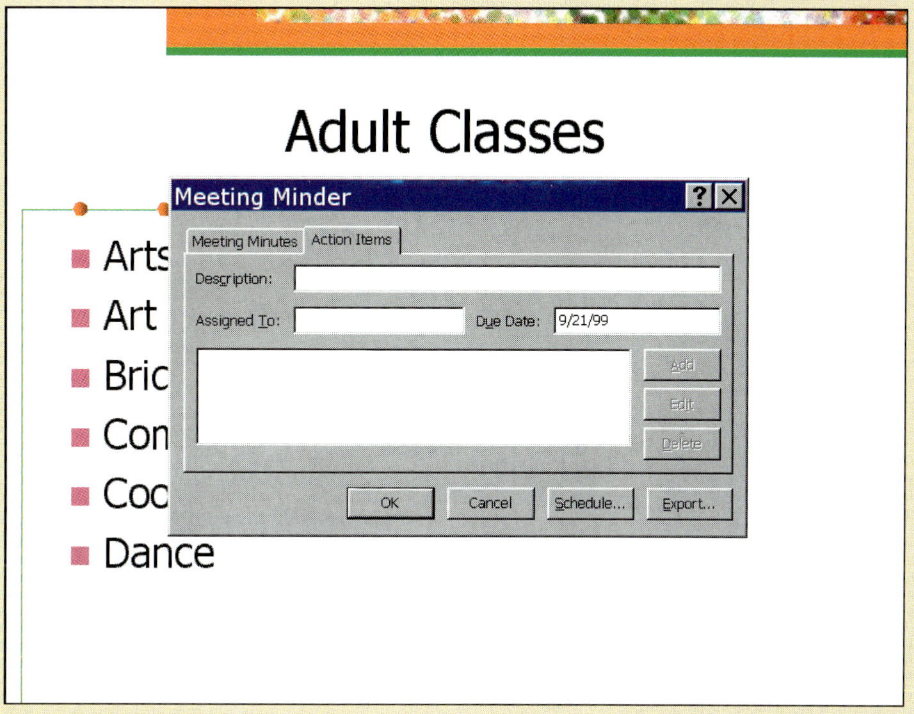


POWERPOINT

6 TYPE: **Explore adding Chess to the list of adult classes. Find instructors.** in the *Description* text box
PRESS: TAB to move the insertion point to the *Assigned To* text box
TYPE: **Roger**
CLICK: Add command button

7 To proceed with the presentation:
CLICK: OK command button

8 Let's pretend that another co-worker has a suggestion that you would like to record.
RIGHT-CLICK: anywhere on the slide
CHOOSE: Meeting Minder from the right-click menu

9 PRESS: CTRL + END to move the insertion point to the end of the minutes
PRESS: ENTER to move the insertion point to the next line
TYPE: **Sylvia thinks we should add a group of Health classes.**

10 To add an action item:
CLICK: *Action Items* tab

11 TYPE: **Explore adding Health classes to the adult curriculum.** in the *Description text* box
PRESS: TAB to move the insertion point to the Assigned To text box
TYPE: **Sylvia**
CLICK: Add command button
The Meeting Minder dialog box should now appear similar to Figure 7.6.

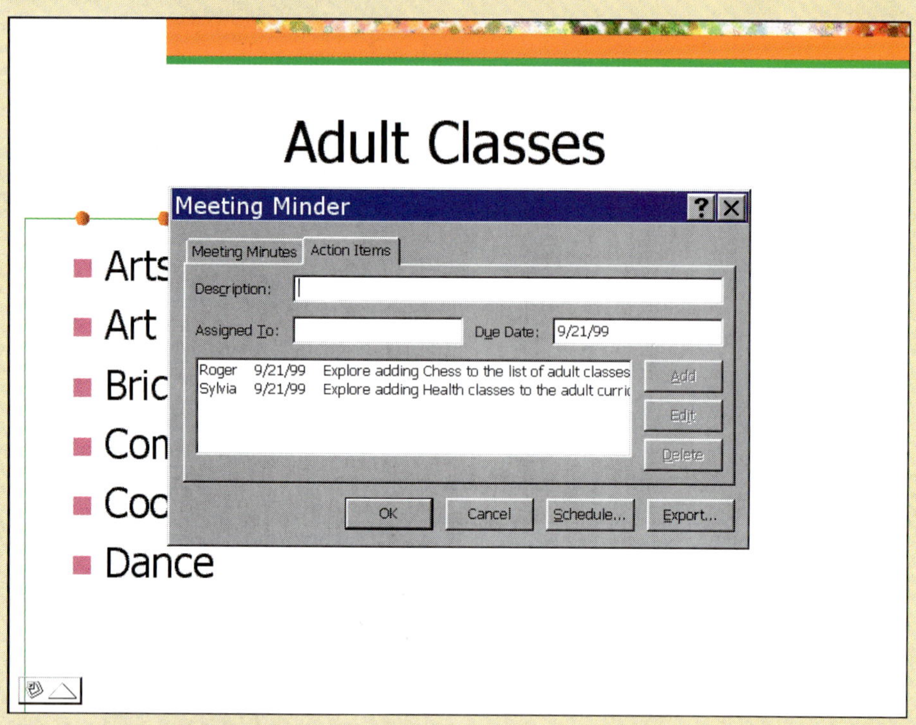


**Figure 7.6**
Adding action items

12 To proceed with the presentation:
CLICK: OK command button

13 Advance through the presentation by clicking the left mouse button—upon viewing the "Registering for Classes" slide, click the left mouse button once more. The final slide should now appear, as shown in Figure 7.7.

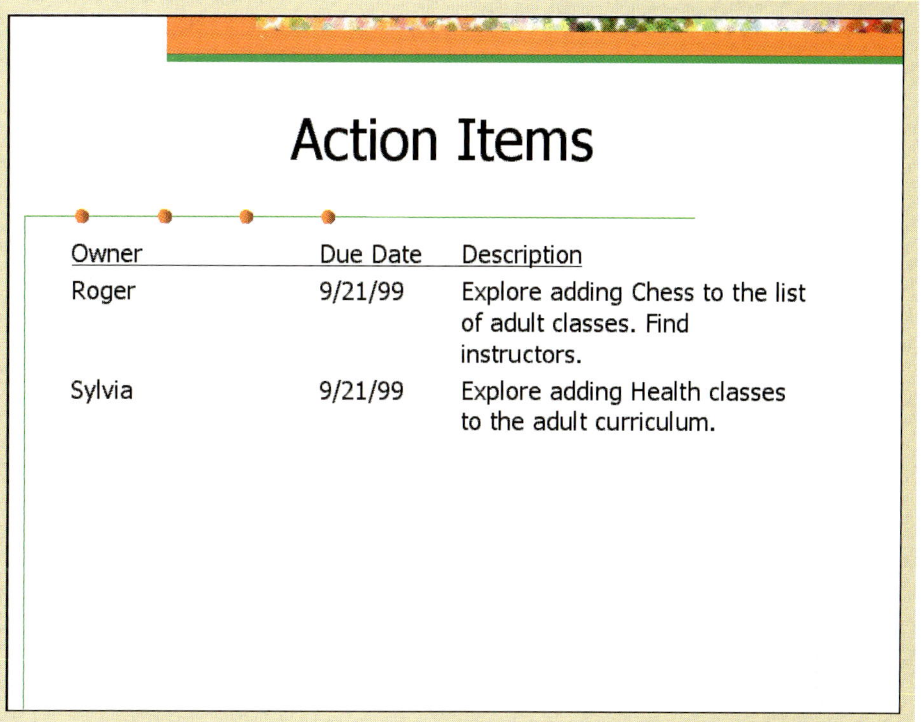


**Figure 7.7**
Action items slide

14. CLICK: the left mouse button once more
The presentation should once again be displaying in Normal view.

15. Save the revised presentation and keep it open for use in the next lesson.

**In Addition**
**Exporting Meeting Minutes**

To export a copy of your meeting minutes to Microsoft Word or Microsoft Outlook, display the Meeting Minder dialog box in Slide Show view and then click the Export command button. If the command button is not immediately enabled, click the *Action Items* tab and then click on one of the items in the displayed list. To complete the export operation, select a check box in the Meeting Minder Export dialog box.

## 7.1.4 Delivering Self-Running Presentations

**FEATURE**

Self-running presentations are typically found in trade-show kiosks and typically run in a continuous loop; that is, once the last slide is displayed, the presentation begins again with the first slide. Before you can deliver a self-running presentation, you must build timings into the presentation. These timings tell PowerPoint how long each slide should stay on the screen during Slide Show view.

**METHOD**

- To set timings by rehearsing them as you go:
  CHOOSE: Slide Show, Rehearse Timings
  CLICK: Advance button ( ) when you're ready to display the next slide
- To set timings manually:
  SELECT: the slide(s) you want to set timings for
  CHOOSE: Slide Show, Slide Transition
  TYPE: `a timing value` in the *Automatically after* text box
  CLICK: Apply or Apply to All command buttons
- To set a presentation to run in a continuous loop:
  CHOOSE: Slide Show, Set Up Show
  SELECT: *Loop continuously until 'Esc'* check box
  CLICK: OK command button

**PRACTICE**

In this lesson, you rehearse timings for the "Community Center" presentation and then set up the presentation to run in a continuous loop.

*Setup:* Ensure that you've completed the previous lessons in this module and that the first slide of the "Community Center" presentation is displaying in Normal view.

1 To build timings into the slide show, you will use the Rehearse timings toolbar, which appears labeled below:

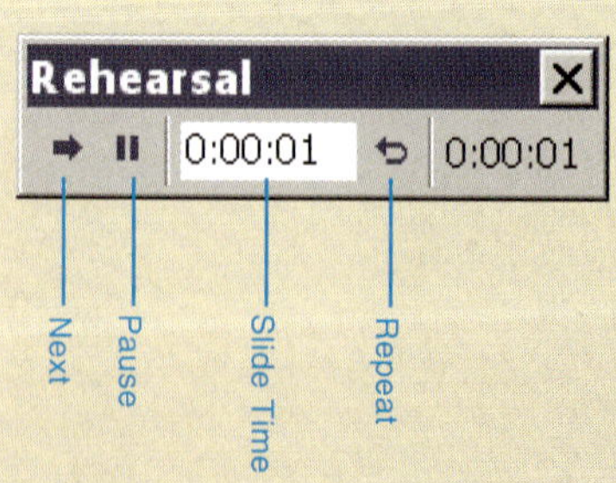


To display the toolbar and then rehearse timings:
CHOOSE: Slide Show, Rehearse Timings

2. To set timings:
CLICK: Advance button (➡) after the clock reaches three seconds
CLICK: Advance button (➡) every three seconds for each remaining slide

3. When the slide show is finished, PowerPoint displays a dialog box showing the total number of seconds that have elapsed. To record the timings:
CLICK: Yes command button

4. To review the timings in Slide Sorter view:
CLICK: Yes command button

5. To set up the presentation to run in a continuous loop:
CHOOSE: Slide Show, Set Up Show
The dialog box in Figure 7.8 should appear.

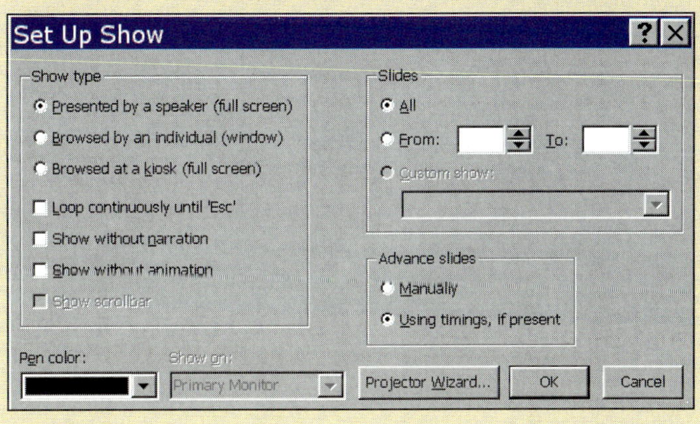


**Figure 7.8**
The Set Up Show diaog box

6. SELECT: *Loop continuously until 'Esc'* check box

7. Ensure that the *Presented by a speaker (full screen)* and *Using Timings, if present* option buttons are selected.

8. CLICK: OK command button

9. Display the presentation in Slide Show view and then sit back and watch! Note that slide 1 appears after slide 16 when the presentation loops back to the beginning.

10. To exit Slide Show view:
PRESS: ESC
Your self-running slide show is complete.

11. Save and then close the revised "Community Center" presentation.

**7.1 Self Check** What capabilities does the Meeting Minder utility provide?

# 7.2 Delivering Web Presentations

Office provides several features for customizing documents for display on the Web. For example, using PowerPoint you can add navigational controls to your Web presentations, enable or disable animation, and resize graphics to fit in the browser window. To make Web pages available for others to see using their browsers, you must post (or copy) them to a special computer called a **Web server.** If the designated Web server is configured with **Microsoft Office Server Extensions (OSE),** the process for accessing the Web server becomes similar to accessing a local hard drive or network server. That is, using the familiar Explorer, Open, and Save As dialog boxes, workgroup members can save files, open, and search for files on their company's internal Web site. Additionally, users can subscribe to and collaborate on important files using Office 2000's discussion features.

In the following lessons, you format an existing presentation for display on the Web and then post the presentation to an OSE-enabled Web server. You also learn how to subscribe to a presentation, a useful feature when your presentation requires collaboration from several people.

## 7.2.1 Formatting Presentations for the Web

**FEATURE**

In Chapter 5, you saved a presentation to HTML without changing any of the presentation's current formatting. In this lesson, you save another presentation to HTML, but in the process you embed TrueType fonts, format the presentation for display in a specific browser, and change the title that will display in the browser's Title bar. You will also customize the look of your published presentation and review other settings that affect how PowerPoint deals with supporting files and pictures.

**METHOD**

1. CHOOSE: File, Save as Web Page
2. To ensure that the fonts in your presentation will display the same on your published Web page:
   CLICK: Tools drop-down arrow in the dialog box's toolbar
   CHOOSE: Embed TrueType Fonts

3. CLICK: Publish command button and change selections as necessary
4. CLICK: Web Options command button to change the formatting and other settings for your published presentation
   CLICK: OK command button
5. CLICK: Change command button to change the Web page title, if necessary
   TYPE: **the title** you want to appear in your Web browser
   CLICK: OK command button
6. CLICK: Publish command button

**PRACTICE**

In this lesson, you save an existing presentation as a Web page and change several settings that affect its appearance on the Web.

*Setup:* Ensure that PowerPoint is loaded and that no presentations are displaying.

1 Open the PPT720 presentation.

2 Save the presentation as "Tour" to your personal storage location. This presentation was created by INTRAV Tours to describe an upcoming trip to the Mediterranean.

3 To save this presentation in an HTML format:
CHOOSE: File, Save as Web Page
The Save As dialog box will now appear.

4 To embed TrueType fonts:
CLICK: Tools drop-down arrow in the dialog box's toolbar
CHOOSE: Embed TrueType Fonts

5 If you click the Save command button right now, the presentation will be saved in an HTML format using several default settings. To customize the contents of the presentation, you must click the Publish command button.
CLICK: Publish command button
The Publish as Web Page dialog box should now appear (Figure 7.9).

**Figure 7.9**

Publish as Web Page dialog box

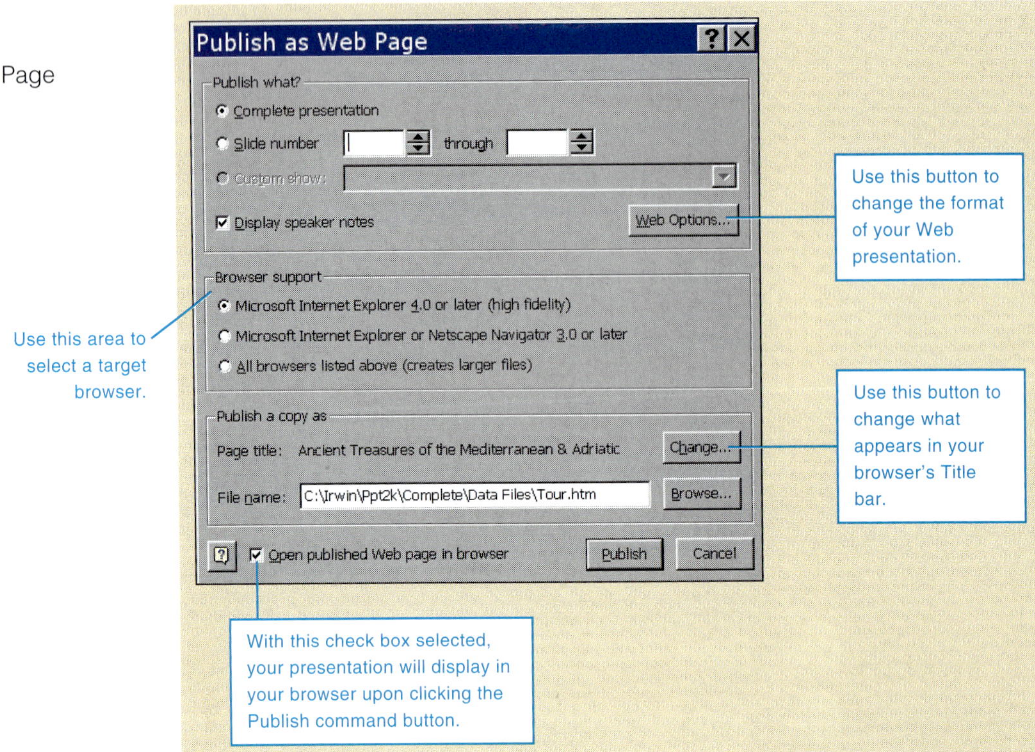


6 Assuming your presentation will be viewed using Microsoft Internet Explorer 4.0 or later, do the following:
SELECT: *Microsoft Internet Explorer 4.0 or later* option button, if it isn't already selected

7 To change the title that will appear in your browser's Title bar:
CLICK: Change command button
TYPE: **Mediterranean Tour** in the Set Page Title dialog box
CLICK: OK command button
Note that the new title is now reflected in the *Publish a copy as* area of the dialog box.

8 To change some of the formatting for the Web page:
CLICK: Web Options command button
The Web Options dialog box should now appear (Figure 7.10). (*Note:* You can also access this dialog box by choosing Tools, Options from the Menu bar, clicking the *General* tab, and then clicking the Web Options command button.)

**Figure 7.10**
Web Options dialog box: *General* tab

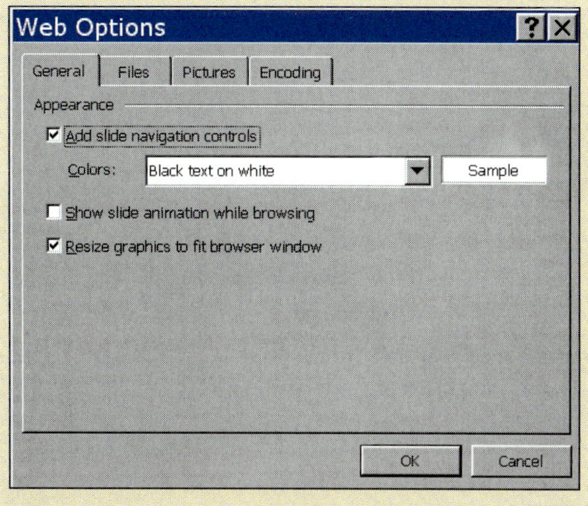


9 To change the colors used for the navigation controls that will be used in the published presentation, do the following:
SELECT: Presentation colors (text color) from the *Colors* drop-down list

10 Do the following to review the other settings in this dialog box:
CLICK: *Files* tab and then review the current settings
CLICK: *Pictures* tab and then review the current settings
CLICK: *Encoding* tab and then review the current settings
CLICK: OK command button
The Publish as Web Page dialog box should reappear.

11 Note that the *Open published Web page in browser* check box is selected. As a result, when you click the Publish command button in the next step, your presentation will automatically display in your browser.

12 To proceed with publishing the presentation and then displaying it in your browser, do the following:
CLICK: Publish command button
Assuming you're using Internet Explorer as your browser, your screen should now appear similar to Figure 7.11. (*Note:* If necessary, maximize the browser window.)

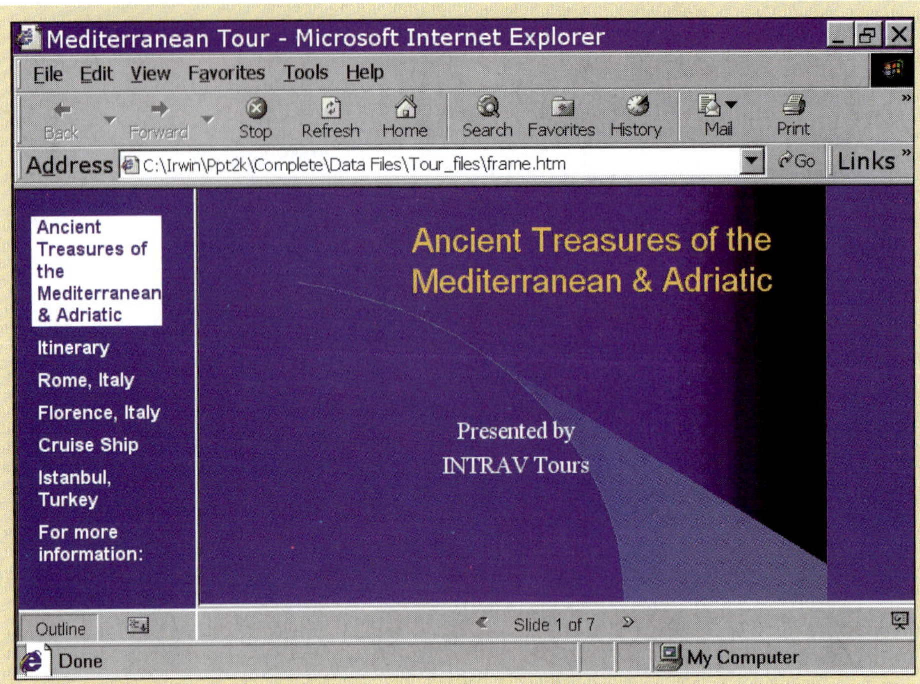


**Figure 7.11**

Viewing the Web presentation in Internet Explorer

13. Practice navigating the presentation using the navigation frame, located on the left side of the Web page.

14. Close Internet Explorer. The "Tour" presentation should be displaying in Normal view.

15. Close the "Tour" presentation.

## 7.2.2 Posting Presentations to the Web

**FEATURE**

With access to an OSE-enabled Web server (and an assigned username and password), workgroup members can publish Office documents to the Internet or the company's Intranet using the familiar Explorer windows and Open and Save As dialog boxes. For easy access to your Web server and to help organize files, you should first create a folder, called a **Web folder,** on your server computer.

**METHOD**

- To create a Web folder:
  DOUBLE-CLICK: My Computer icon () on the Windows desktop
  DOUBLE-CLICK: Web Folders icon ()
  DOUBLE-CLICK: Add Web Folder icon and then follow the instructions in the Add Web Folder wizard

- To save a file to a Web folder:
  CHOOSE: File, Save As (or choose File, Save as Web Page)
  CLICK: Web Folders button on the Places bar
  DOUBLE-CLICK: the desired Web folder in the list area
  CLICK: Save command button

**PRACTICE**

You will now create a Web folder and then save a file to it.

*Setup:* Ensure that you've completed the previous lesson and that no presentations are displaying. If you don't have access to an OSE-enabled Web server or don't have a password and user name, you should review, rather than perform, the following practice steps.

1. Minimize any open applications so you can view the Windows desktop.

2. To create a Web folder:
   DOUBLE-CLICK: My Computer icon ( ) on the Windows desktop

3. Locate the Web Folders icon ( ) in the My Computer window and then:
   DOUBLE-CLICK: Web Folders icon ( )

4. In the Web Folders window:
   DOUBLE-CLICK: Add Web Folder icon
   The Add Web Folder wizard is launched. Your screen should now appear similar to Figure 7.12.

**Figure 7.12**
Add Web Folder wizard

POWERPOINT

5. You must now identify a location, or Web address, on your Web server for the new Web folder.
TYPE: **your Web server address**
CLICK: Next command button
(*Note:* At this point, the Add Web Folder wizard will check that your chosen Web server is OSE-enabled.)

6. You must now name the Web folder.
TYPE: **Web folder name** (for example, "Presentations")
CLICK: Finish command button
A Web folder icon, with the name you assigned, should be displaying in the Web Folders window.

7. Close the Web Folders window by clicking its Close button (☒).

8. Let's open the Web page you created in the last lesson.
CHOOSE: File, Open
SELECT: Web Pages from the *Files of type* drop-down list
DOUBLE-CLICK: "Tour" in the file listing
The HTML version of the "Tour" presentation should be displaying in Normal view.

9. To save the Web page to the folder you just created:
CHOOSE: File, Save As
CLICK: Web Folders button in the Places bar
DOUBLE-CLICK: the desired Web Folder in the list area to the right
At this point, your computer will need to establish an Internet connection.

10. Next, you will be prompted to provide your user name and password. Figure 7.13 provides an example of this dialog box. If you know your user name and password, type them in now and then click the OK command button when you're finished. After a few moments, the contents of the selected Web folder will appear. If the Web folder is new, it will be empty. Figure 7.14 shows the contents of a Web folder named "Presentations" that contains several items.

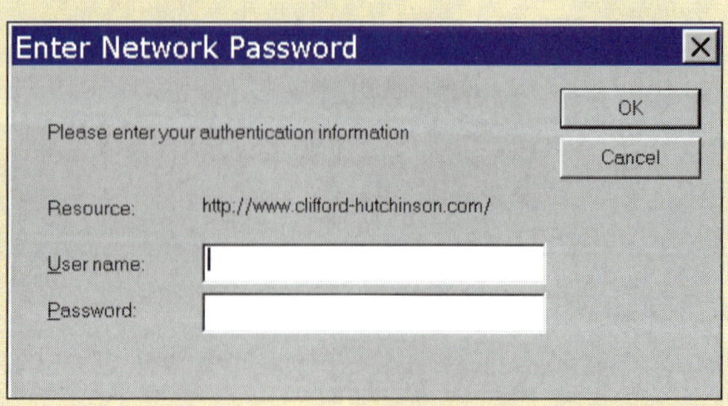


**Figure 7.13**
Enter Network Password dialog box

**Figure 7.14**

Viewing the contents of the "Presentations" Web folder located on a Web server

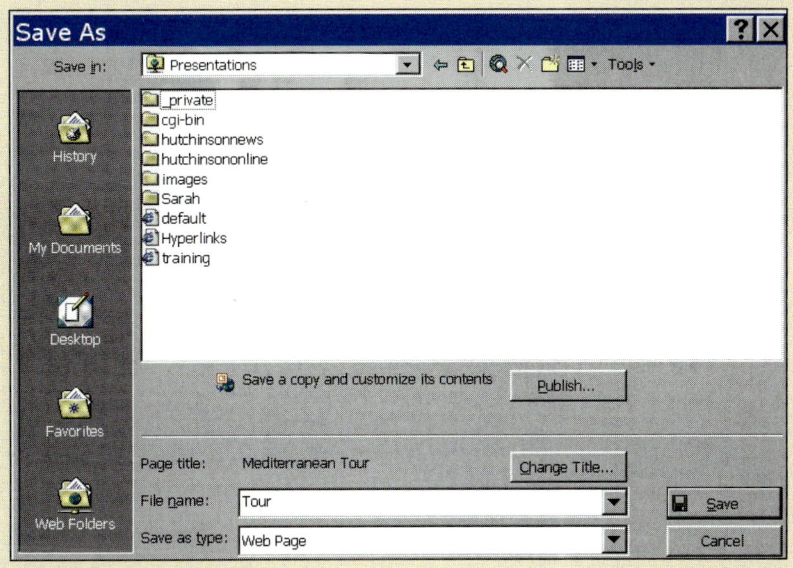


11 To execute the Save command:
CLICK: Save command button
A dialog box will display briefly indicating that the file is being transferred from your computer to the Web server.

12 To view the posted page in your browser, launch your browser software. Then, type the following into the Address bar: server computer name, a slash (/), and the posted filename followed by the ".htm" extension.
TYPE: **address in the Address bar** (for example, www.clifford-hutchinson.com/tour.htm)
PRESS: ENTER
Figure 7.15 shows the "Tour" page displaying in Internet Explorer after the page was copied to the "www.clifford-hutchinson.com" address on a Web server.

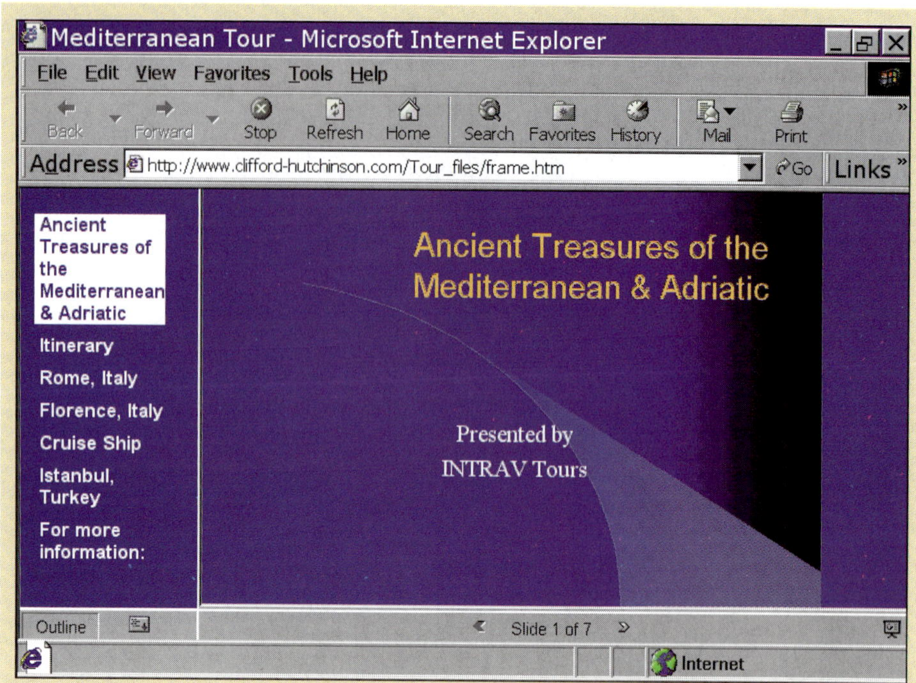


**Figure 7.15**
The Web page was copied to the Web server

13. Close your browser window.

## 7.2.3 Subscribing to Web Presentations

**FEATURE**
In business, a single presentation often represents the work of many people, each of whom has contributed his or her expertise to a particular section of the presentation. With access to PowerPoint 2000 and an OSE-enabled Web server, you can easily collaborate with others on presentations stored on your Web server. By subscribing to a Web presentation, you can receive notification by e-mail when a remark has been added to the presentation or the presentation itself has changed.

**METHOD**
1. On your OSE-enabled Web server, open the document or folder that you want to be notified about.
2. CHOOSE: Tools, Online Collaboration, Web Discussions
3. CLICK: Subscribe button on the Discussions toolbar
4. SELECT: the type of changes you want to be notified about, where you want to be notified, and how often you want to be notified
5. CLICK: OK command button

**PRACTICE**

In this lesson, you subscribe to the "Tour" presentation that you posted to your Web server in the last lesson.

*Setup:* Ensure that you've completed the previous lessons in this module and that the HTML version of the "Tour" presentation is displaying in Normal view. If you weren't able to complete the last lesson or if you don't have access to a Web server that supports Microsoft Office Server Extensions, you should review, rather than perform, the following practice steps.

1. To initiate the subscription process, open the "Tour" file that's stored on your Web server.
2. CHOOSE: Tools, Online Collaboration, Web Discussions
   The Discussions toolbar will display.
3. CLICK: Subscribe button on the Discussions toolbar
4. In the resulting dialog box, select the types of changes you want to be notified about, where you want to be notified, and how often you want to be notified.
5. CLICK: OK command button to register your settings
6. Close the "Tour" presentation.



**7.2 Self Check** In what ways do Microsoft Office Server Extensions (OSE) enhance the capabilities of a Web server?

# 7.3 About Presentation Broadcasting

Similar to broadcasting a television program that others view at the scheduled time, you can use PowerPoint 2000 to broadcast presentations on the Web. This capability is ideal when your audience is either very large or scattered in remote locations. A **presentation broadcast** is delivered over the Web and viewed using Web browser software, not PowerPoint. Once notified of an upcoming broadcast, audience members simply point their browsers to the designated Web address at the scheduled time and begin viewing the show. Depending on the settings defined by your presenter, you may even be able to chat online with others who are viewing the show.

## 7.3.1 Scheduling Broadcasts

**FEATURE**

Scheduling a broadcast presentation involves informing your audience of the time and location (Web address) of the presentation. You can either use Microsoft Outlook to schedule the broadcast, just as you would schedule any other meeting, or you can use your own e-mail program. If you use your own e-mail program to schedule the broadcast, a hyperlink will be inserted in the e-mail message to the Web location of the scheduled broadcast. If your presentation is intended for over fifteen people or if it includes video, your presentation must be run from a Netshow Web server.

**METHOD**

1. CHOOSE: Slide Show, Online Broadcast
2. CHOOSE: Set Up and Schedule
3. SELECT: *Set up and schedule a new broadcast* option button
   CLICK: OK command button to display the Schedule a New Broadcast dialog box
4. CLICK: *Description* tab and then type what you want users to see on the lobby page, the page audience members see upon visiting the broadcast (presenter's name, subject of the presentation, any last-minute information)
5. CLICK: *Broadcast Settings* tab to set various broadcast options, unless they've already been set by your system administrator
6. CLICK: Schedule Broadcast command button
7. Your e-mail program will now launch. If you're using Microsoft Outlook, schedule the broadcast as you would schedule a meeting. Using an alternate e-mail program, type the broadcast date and time in the message.

## 7.3.2 Delivering Broadcasts

**FEATURE**

Delivering a broadcast involves copying your presentation to the server you specified when scheduling the broadcast and then typing in any last-minute comments. You should perform this procedure at least 30 minutes prior to the scheduled broadcast time. Your presentation will automatically be copied in an HTML format to your designated Web server.

**METHOD**

1. CHOOSE: Slide Show, Online Broadcast
2. CHOOSE: Begin Broadcast to copy your presentation to the designated Web server

3. CLICK: *Audience Message* option button, if you have any last-minute comments
   CLICK: Update command button
4. CLICK: Start command button to begin the broadcast

**7.3 Self Check** Why is it useful to be able to broadcast presentations?



# 7.4 Chapter Review

This chapter focused on several procedures related to delivering on-screen and Web-based presentations. To deliver one or more presentations on another computer, consider using the Pack and Go Wizard to compress your source files to 3.5-inch diskettes. In the case that PowerPoint isn't installed on your delivery computer, you can select to include the PowerPoint Viewer program along with your compressed files. Once your presentation is underway, it's easy to collect meeting feedback using the Meeting Minder utility and automatically insert an action-items slide at the end of the presentation!

With PowerPoint 2000 (or another Office application) and an OSE-enabled Web server, the Web provides another viable delivery method. You can easily post a presentation to your Web server using the same procedure you would use to save it to your local hard drive or company network. You can also open and search for files and provide feedback to other workgroup members using Office's discussion features. Further, in case it isn't possible for your audience to gather in a single location, you can alert audience members that your presentation will be broadcast at a designated time on the Web.

## 7.4.1 Command Summary

Many of the commands and procedures appearing in this chapter are summarized in the following table.

| Skill Set | To Perform This Task . . . | Do the Following . . . |
|---|---|---|
| **Creating a Presentation** | Format a presentation for the Web | CHOOSE: File, Save as Web Page<br>CLICK: Publish command button<br>CLICK: Web Options command button |
| **Modifying a Presentation** | Rehearse slide timings | CHOOSE: Slide Show, Rehearse Timings |

*continued*

| Skill Set | To Perform This Task . . . | Do the Following . . . |
|---|---|---|
| **Modifying a Presentation *Continued*** | Set slide timings manually | SELECT: one or more slides in Slide Sorter view<br>CHOOSE: Slide Show, Slide Transition<br>TYPE: a timing value in the *Automatically after* text box |
| | Create a self-running presentation | CHOOSE: Slide Show, Set Up Show<br>SELECT: *Loop continuously until 'Esc'* check box |
| **Creating Output** | Adjust slide size and orientation | CHOOSE: File, Page Setup |
| | Size your presentation for 35mm slides | CHOOSE: File, Page Setup<br>SELECT: 35mm Slides from the *Slides sized for* drop-down list |
| **Delivering a Presentation** | Use the Pack and Go Wizard | CHOOSE: File, Pack and Go |
| | Incorporate meeting feedback | RIGHT-CLICK: a slide in Slide Show view<br>CHOOSE: Meeting Minder |
| **Managing Files** | Save embedded fonts | CHOOSE: File, Save As (or File, Save as Web Page)<br>CLICK: Tools drop-down arrow<br>CHOOSE: Embed TrueType Fonts |
| | Save an HTML presentation for a target browser | CHOOSE: File, Save as Web Page<br>CLICK: Publish command button<br>SELECT: an option in the *Browser support* area |
| | Create a Web folder | DOUBLE-CLICK: My Computer icon ()<br>DOUBLE-CLICK: Web Folders icon ()<br>DOUBLE-CLICK: Add Web Folder icon and then follow the wizard prompts |

*continued*

| Skill Set | To Perform This Task . . . | Do the Following . . . |
|---|---|---|
| **Managing Files *Continued*** | Save and open pages on Web servers | CLICK: Web Folders button on the Places bar in the Open or Save As dialog box<br>DOUBLE-CLICK: the desired Web folder in the list area<br>CLICK: Save (or Open) command button |
| **Collaborating with Workgroups** | Subscribe to a presentation | CHOOSE: Tools, Online Collaboration, Web Discussions<br>CLICK: Subscribe button on the Discussions toolbar<br>SELECT: the type of changes you want to be notified about, where you want to be notified, and how often you want to be notified<br>CLICK: OK command button |
| | Schedule a presentation broadcast | CHOOSE: Slide Show, Online Broadcast<br>CHOOSE: Set Up and Schedule<br>SELECT: *Set up and schedule a new broadcast* option button |
| | Deliver a presentation broadcast | CHOOSE: Slide Show, Online Broadcast<br>CHOOSE: Begin Broadcast<br>CLICK: Start command button |

## 7.4.2 Key Terms

This section specifies page references for the key terms identified in this session. For a complete list of definitions, refer to the Glossary provided immediately after the Appendix in this learning guide.

Genigraphics Wizard, *p. 275*

Microsoft Office Server Extensions (OSE), *p. 286*

Pack and Go Wizard, *p. 276*

presentation broadcast, *p. 295*

Projector Wizard, *p. 278*

Web folder, *p. 290*

Web server, *p. 286*

# 7.5 Review Questions

## 7.5.1 Short Answer

1. What is the reason for embedding TrueType fonts in a presentation?
2. What problem does the PowerPoint Viewer program solve?
3. What is a self-running presentation?
4. What is a presentation broadcast?
5. What is a Web server?
6. What are Web folders used for?
7. What is involved in delivering a presentation broadcast?
8. Using PowerPoint, when might you want to use the Page Setup dialog box?
9. What does the Pack and Go Wizard do?
10. What must you do to a presentation before it can run in a continuous loop?

## 7.5.2 True/False

1. ____ Using PowerPoint, it's possible to optimize a Web presentation for display in a target browser.
2. ____ To take advantage of PowerPoint's discussion features, your Web server must be OSE-enabled.
3. ____ Presentation broadcasts alert you when changes have been made to files stored on your Web server.
4. ____ Using the Page Setup dialog box, you can select to send your electronic slides to Genigraphics for conversion to 35mm slides.
5. ____ The procedure for saving to a Web folder is much more complicated than saving to a local hard drive.
6. ____ The Genigraphics Wizard is useful for preparing your presentation for display on another computer.
7. ____ When saving a presentation to HTML, it's possible to customize what appears in your browser's Title bar.
8. ____ A Web folder is essentially a shortcut to a location on a Web server.
9. ____ The Pack and Go Wizard lets you choose whether to embed TrueType fonts.
10. ____ It's possible to embed TrueType fonts using the Save As dialog box.

## 7.5.3 Multiple Choice

1. Which of the following is helpful in converting your electronic slides into 35mm slides?
   a. Pack and Go Wizard
   b. Genigraphics Wizard
   c. Page Setup dialog box
   d. Both b and c

2. Which of the following can you use to compress a presentation for storage on a diskette?
   a. Pack and Go Wizard
   b. Genigraphics Wizard
   c. Page Setup dialog box
   d. Both b and c

3. To change a slide's orientation, you must use the ______________.
   a. Page Setup dialog box
   b. Meeting Minder utility
   c. Projector Wizard
   d. None of the above

4. When saving a presentation to HTML, which of the following can you do to customize your presentation?
   a. add slide navigation controls
   b. select a target browser
   c. customize what appears in your browser's Title bar
   d. All of the above

5. To receive notification when a presentation stored on your Web server has been updated, you must ______________.
   a. create a Web folder
   b. subscribe to the presentation
   c. schedule a presentation broadcast
   d. deliver a presentation broadcast

6. To activate the Meeting Minder utility, you right-click the current slide in ______________.
   a. Normal view
   b. Slide Sorter view
   c. Slide Show view
   d. All of the above

7. What must you have access to before you can broadcast presentations on the Web?
   a. PowerPoint 2000
   b. OSE-enabled Web server
   c. Web folders
   d. Both a and b

8. To take advantage of PowerPoint's presentation broadcasting capabilities, your Web server must have ______________ installed on it.
   a. video and animation
   b. Web folders
   c. Microsoft Office Server Extensions
   d. All of the above

9. Before setting up a presentation to loop continuously, you must build ______________ into the presentation.
   a. animation
   b. transitions
   c. timings
   d. All of the above

10. Which of the following can you use to automatically insert a list of action items on the final slide of a presentation?
   a. Genigraphics Wizard
   b. Pack and Go Wizard
   c. Meeting Minder utility
   d. Projector Wizard

# 7.6 Hands-On Projects

## 7.6.1 Outdoor Adventure Tours: Finalizing an On-Screen Presentation

This exercise practices using the Page Setup dialog box, rehearsing timings, creating a self-running presentation, and manually changing the timing of the slide transitions.

1. Open the PPT761 data file.
2. Save the presentation as "Outdoor Extremes" to your personal storage location.
3. Review the slides to become familiar with their content.
4. To change the slide setup to a landscape, on-screen format:
   CHOOSE: File, Page Setup
   SELECT: On-screen Show in the *Slides Sized for* box
   SELECT: *Landscape* option button in the *Slides* area
   CLICK: OK command button
5. To rehearse timings for each slide:
   CHOOSE: Slide Show, Rehearse Timings
   Allow approximately three seconds for the first and last slides and five seconds for slides 2 to 8. Record the new show timings when prompted at the end.

6. To set up the slide show for an individual viewer:
   CHOOSE: Slide Show, Set Up Show
   SELECT: *Browsed by an individual* option button in the *Show type* area
   SELECT: *Loop continuously until 'Esc'* check box
   SELECT: *Using Timings, if present* option button in the *Advance slides* area
   CLICK: OK command button
7. Switch to the Slide Show view to test the show.
8. To change the slide show setup to display as a full screen:
   CHOOSE: Slide Show, Set Up Show
   SELECT: *Presented by a speaker* option button in the *Show type* area
   CLICK: OK command button
9. Switch to the Slide Show view to test the revised slide-show format.
10. To change the timing of the first slide to two seconds, ensure that the presentation is displaying in Slide Sorter view and then:
    CLICK: on the first slide
    CHOOSE: Slide Show, Slide Transition
    SELECT: the contents of the *Automatically after* text box
    TYPE: **2** in the *Automatically after* text box
    CLICK: Apply command button
11. Use the same technique to change the timing of the final slide to six seconds.
12. Save and then close the revised "Outdoor Extremes" presentation.



## 7.6.2 Monashee Community College: Delivering A Presentation

In this exercise, you will use the Page Setup dialog box on an existing presentation, adjust presentation timings, package the presentation, and publish the presentation as a Web page.

1. Open the PPT762 data file.
2. Save the data file as "Monashee Credo" to your personal storage location.
3. Review the slides to become familiar with their content.
4. To adjust the size of the formatted presentation:
   CHOOSE: File, Page Setup
   SELECT: On-screen Show in the *Slides sized for* section
   CLICK: OK command button
5. To set timings for the slide show:
   CHOOSE: Slide Show, Rehearse Timings
   Adjust each slide so that it displays for two to three seconds and record the new timings when prompted.

6. To set up the presentation so that it can be browsed at a kiosk:
   CHOOSE: Slide Show, Set Up Show
   SELECT: *Browsed at a kiosk* option button in the *Show type* area
   SELECT: *Using timings, if present* in the *Advance slides* area
   CLICK: OK command button
7. To compress and pack the presentation for distribution to other sites:
   CHOOSE: File, Pack and Go.
8. Proceed through the steps of the Wizard, making the following choices at the appropriate steps:
   SELECT: *Active Presentation* check box
   SELECT: *Choose Destination* option button and then specify your personal storage location
   SELECT: *Embed TrueType fonts* check box
   SELECT: *Don't include the Viewer* option button
9. To prepare to save the presentation as a Web Page:
   CHOOSE: File, Save As Web Page.
10. To change the Page title:
    CLICK: Change Title command button
    TYPE: **Monashee Instructor Credo** in the *Page title* text box
    CLICK: OK command button to return to the Save As dialog box
11. To open the Publish as Web Page dialog box:
    CLICK: Publish command button
12. Adjust the settings to include the following features and then press the Publish command button:
    - Publish the complete presentation
    - Do not display the Speakers Notes
    - Include support for all browsers listed
    - Edit the *File name* location in the *Publish a copy as* area
    - Open published Web page in browser
13. Review the presentation in the browser and then close the browser window.
14. Close any presentations that are still displaying in PowerPoint.

## 7.6.3 Coldstream Corporation: Gathering Meeting Feedback

You will now add minutes and action items and then export the minutes to a Word document. You will also create a Web folder and save the presentation as a Web page.

1. Open the PPT763 data file.
2. Save the presentation as "Coldstream Presentation Ideas" to your personal storage location.
3. Review the slides to become familiar with their content.

4. Set up the slide show to be presented by a speaker using manual settings.
5. Switch to Slide Show view and then mimic presenting the Slide show to an audience, incorporating the following minutes and action items:

| *Slide* | *Minutes* | *Action Item* | |
|---|---|---|---|
| 2 | Questions about different award mechanisms | Peter– | Investigate New Award System |
| 4 | Much discussion about possibility of non-traditional markets | Janice– | Investigate Secondary School Programs |
| | | Dave– | Survey Nonprofit Agencies |
| 8 | General feeling that this section needs thorough reworking | Pat– | Chair review committee for next fiscal |

6. When the slide show is complete, begin the process of exporting a copy of the minutes to Microsoft Word. (*Hint:* Display the Meeting Minder dialog box and then click the Export command button. If the command button is not immediately enabled, switch to the *Action Items* tab and click on one of the items in the displayed list.)
7. Set the Export options so that items are sent to Microsoft Word.
8. CLICK: Export Now command button
9. Print a copy of the minutes and action items and then close Word without saving the document.
10. Return to PowerPoint and then close the Meeting Minder dialog box.
11. Save the presentation as a Web page named "Coldstream Presentation Ideas." Use the Change Title and Publish command buttons to make the following changes to the settings:
    Page Title: Coldstream Presentation Ideas
    Browser Support: All listed browsers
12. If you have access to an OSE-enabled Web Server, create a Web folder named "Coldstream" on your server computer.
13. Save the presentation again as a Web page to the new "Coldstream" Web folder.
14. In PowerPoint, close any presentations that remain open.

7.7

POWERPOINT

# Notes

4. Finally, Ernest is ready to post the presentation named "Web Genealogy" from the previous exercise to the Web. He first identifies a Web address on his Web server and then creates a Web folder entitled "Advertisement." Ernest then saves the "Web Genealogy" file to the Web folder.

   After launching his browser software, Ernest views the posted page in his browser. Proud of his accomplishments, Ernest feels like his great-great-great grandfather, Sir Malcolm Williamson, who owned one of the first printing presses in England.

# Notes

# Notes

# Notes

**MICROSOFT POWERPOINT 2000**

*Developing Applications in PowerPoint*

# CHAPTER EIGHT

# Chapter Outline



# Learning Objectives

After completing this chapter, you will be able to:

- Automate everyday procedures by recording and running macros
- Use the Visual Basic Editor to modify recorded macros
- Protect your computer from macro viruses and prevent unauthorized users from altering your files
- Streamline PowerPoint's Menu bar and toolbars to your specific work habits and patterns

Case Study

## Door-to-Door Moving Services

For more than 20 years, Door-to-Door Moving Services has been synonymous with household moving. It has become one of the world's leading van lines due to its single-minded focus on two important elements—customer satisfaction and value. Linda Hallibeck is proud to be joining the Door-to-Door team. After a grueling interview process, she landed the job of office and technology manager.

Aside from having management responsibilities over several key personnel, Linda is directly responsible for making sure that the laptop computers used by the company's sales representatives are functioning properly and contain all the necessary software. A proficient Office and PowerPoint 2000 user, Linda's first task is to automate many of the procedures that the company's sales representatives currently perform manually so the procedures can be executed more easily.

In this chapter, you and Linda learn how to automate routine procedures using macros. You also learn how to customize menus and toolbars in order to create a more efficient work environment.



# 8.1 Creating Macros

Many of the tasks you perform in PowerPoint are repetitive, such as enhancing selections of text, applying design templates, or printing. For our benefit, PowerPoint has assigned many of these monotonous tasks to toolbar buttons and "Auto" commands. However, there are still specific tasks that you may have to perform time and time again that are not included as buttons on a toolbar. For these activities, PowerPoint allows you to store and play back keystrokes and commands. In addition to saving you an enormous amount of time, these stored instructions, called **macros,** also improve the consistency and accuracy of repetitive procedures. Using a macro, you can execute a sequence of instructions by simply clicking a button, pressing a key combination, or selecting a name from a list box.

By incorporating macros into a presentation, you make it easier to use for yourself and for others. Any procedures you perform repeatedly are perfectly suited for macros. A few examples include opening a file, printing it, and then closing it; adding customized bullets to a selection of text; and formatting a presentation to a specific layout in order to match your output requirements. Instead of having to remember all of the steps required to perform such procedures, with macros you only have to remember a few simple keystrokes or which button to click. Furthermore, you can use macros to automate complicated or time-consuming procedures for personnel who are not familiar with PowerPoint. This chapter leads you through recording macros and performing some simple editing of macro code.

## 8.1.1 Recording a Macro

**FEATURE**

Microsoft PowerPoint and the other Office 2000 applications share a common programming language, called **Visual Basic for Applications (VBA),** for writing macros. If the word "programming" sends you into a tizzy, you can relax. PowerPoint's **Macro Recorder** enables you to create simple macros without knowing anything about VBA or programming. The Macro Recorder records your actions, such as choosing menu commands or clicking toolbar buttons, and then writes the required VBA programming code for you. If a macro is not performing to your satisfaction, you can simply record it again or edit the macro's generated code. Before starting the macro recording process, it's best to plan the steps that you want to perform and store in the macro.

**METHOD**

1. CHOOSE: Tools, Macro, Record New Macro
2. Enter a name, shortcut key, and description in the Record Macro dialog box.
3. SELECT: a location from the *Store macro in* drop-down list box
4. CLICK: OK command button to start recording
5. Perform the steps that you want to record.
6. CLICK: Stop button (■) to end recording

**PRACTICE**

In this exercise, you create a macro that automatically inserts an action button on the current slide.

*Setup:* Ensure that PowerPoint is loaded and that no presentations are displaying.

1. Open the PPT810 student file.

2. Save the presentation as "Practice with Macros" to your personal storage location.

3. After reviewing the contents of the presentation, display the first slide.

4. To create a macro for this presentation:
CHOOSE: Tools, Macro, Record New Macro
The Record Macro dialog box should now appear, as shown in Figure 8.1.

**Figure 8.1**
Record Macro dialog box

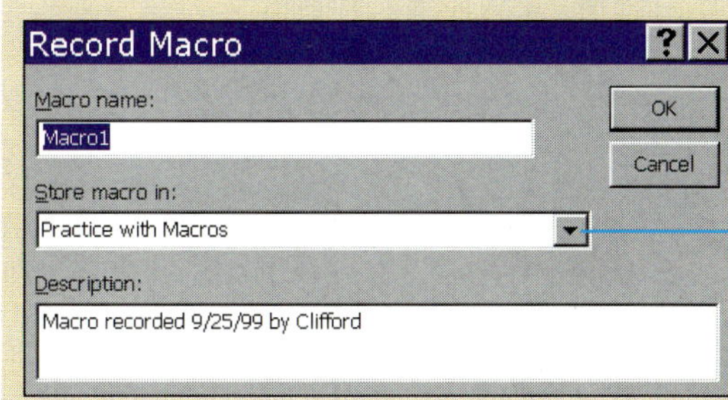


By default, your macros will be stored in the current presentation. To store a macro in another open presentation, select the desired presentation from the *Store macro* in drop-down list.

5 To enter the name that you want to assign to the macro:
TYPE: **ForwardButton** in the *Macro name* text box
(*Note:* An acceptable macro name begins with a letter and does not contain spaces.)

6 We also strongly advise that you include a concise description of the macro in the *Description* text box. Not only will the description help you differentiate between similar macros in the future but the description also appears in the Customize dialog box when you add macros to toolbars and menus. By default, PowerPoint includes the current date and your name in the *Description* text box. To insert an additional paragraph in the *Description* text box, do the following:
CLICK: in the *Description* text box
PRESS: END
PRESS: ENTER
TYPE: **This macro inserts an action button that displays the next slide when clicked.**

7 To begin recording the macro:
CLICK: OK command button
The Stop Recording button (below) now floats above the application window in a small Stop Recording toolbar.

Stop Recording button

8 The following list of actions will be recorded in the macro:
CHOOSE: Slide Show, Action Buttons
CLICK: Forward or Next action button (▷)
CLICK: on the current slide
CLICK: OK command button in the Action Settings dialog box
DRAG: the action button to the bottom-right corner of the current slide
DRAG: the corner sizing handle inward to reduce the size of the action button to about half its original size

POWERPOINT

9. To stop recording:
CLICK: Stop Recording button in the dialog box
Believe it or not, you've just recorded a macro!

10. Save the revised presentation.

11. Continue to the next lesson where you will get an opportunity to play back the macro.

**In Addition**
Creating an Automatic Macro

An automatic macro or **automacro** is a special type of macro that executes without your interaction. Instead, it is initiated by something that happens in PowerPoint. Although you create an automacro as you would any other macro, the name that you give the macro determines how it operates. The most commonly used automacro, named "Auto_Open," runs automatically when you open a presentation. If, for whatever reason, you want to stop the Auto_Open macro from executing, hold down the SHIFT key when opening the presentation.

## 8.1.2 Playing Back a Macro

**FEATURE**
To access a recorded macro, it must either be stored in the current document or in another open presentation. Running a macro is similar to playing a tape on a tape recorder. PowerPoint provides a number of different methods for running, or executing, your macros. You can execute a macro by selecting its name from a dialog box, by pressing a key combination, by clicking a toolbar or command button, or by selecting a custom command from the menu. Macros can also run automatically when you perform procedures such as opening a document.

**METHOD**
1. CHOOSE: Tools, Macro, Macros
2. SELECT: a macro in the list box
3. CLICK: Run command button

**PRACTICE**
In this lesson, you learn how to run macros using the Macro dialog box.

*Setup:* Ensure that you've completed the previous lesson and that the second slide in the "Practice with Macros" presentation is displaying.

1. To insert a Forward action button on the second slide, do the following:
CLICK: Next Slide button () to advance to the second slide

2. To execute the "ForwardButton" macro:
CHOOSE: Tools, Macro, Macros
The Macro dialog box should now appear (Figure 8.2). (*Note:* You can also press ALT + F8 to display the Macro dialog box.)

**Figure 8.2**
Macro dialog box

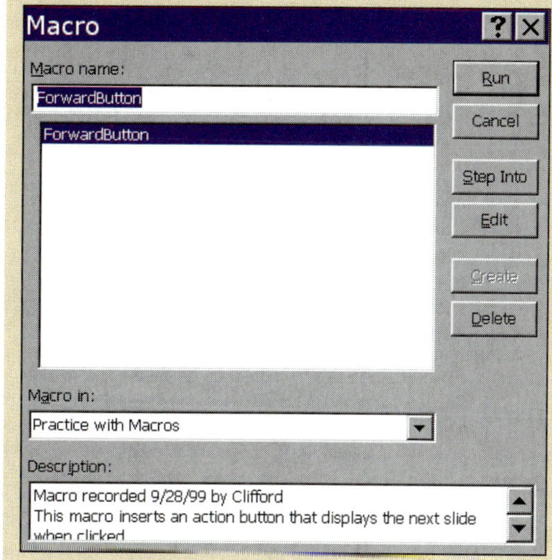


3. To run the macro, you select its name in the Macro dialog box and then click Run. You can also double-click the macro name in the list box. Do the following:
SELECT: ForwardButton (it should already be selected)
CLICK: Run command button
The Forward action button should have been inserted on the current slide.

4. On your own, display the next slide in the presentation and then execute the "ForwardButton" macro. Again, the action button was inserted on the current slide. (*Note:* For macros that take longer to execute, PowerPoint provides the ESC key as a panic button to interrupt or halt a macro's execution before it finishes processing.)

5. Now, let's run a macro that's stored in the PPT812 data file. Open the PPT812 data file now. (*Note:* A dialog box may display warning you that the presentation file contains macros. If this is the case, click the Enable Macros command button. We describe this dialog box in the next lesson.)

6. Using the Window menu, redisplay the "Practice with Macros" presentation.

7. To access a macro named "CitrusDesign" that is stored in the PPT812 presentation, do the following:
PRESS: ALT + F8 to display the Macro dialog box directly
SELECT: PPT812 from the *Macro in* drop-down list
DOUBLE-CLICK: CitrusDesign macro in the list box
The CitrusDesign macro was automatically executed, which applied the Citrus design template to the "Practice with Macros" presentation.

8. Save the revised "Practice with Macros" presentation and then continue to the next lesson.

## 8.1.3 Protecting Your Work from Macro Viruses

**FEATURE**

A **virus** is a program that was created with the intention of doing harm to your computer system. Viruses can mess up or delete your software applications and documents, or worse, turn your computer's hard disk into an unsalvageable mess. To protect against viruses, we recommend that you purchase or download a virus-protection program and then run it regularly, such as every time you turn on your computer. One type of virus, called a **macro virus,** can be prevented directly from within PowerPoint.

**METHOD**

To view or change the current macro virus protection level:

1. CHOOSE: Tools, Macro, Security
2. SELECT: an alternate security level, if desired
3. CLICK: OK command button

**PRACTICE**

In this lesson, you open the "Practice with Macros" presentation that contains a macro and then review PowerPoint's security levels.

*Setup:* Ensure that you've completed the previous lessons in this module and that no presentations are displaying.

1. Open the "Practice with Macros" presentation from your personal storage location.

2. Depending on what the chosen security level is on your computer, the dialog box in Figure 8.3 may display.

**Figure 8.3**
Opening a presentation that contains macros

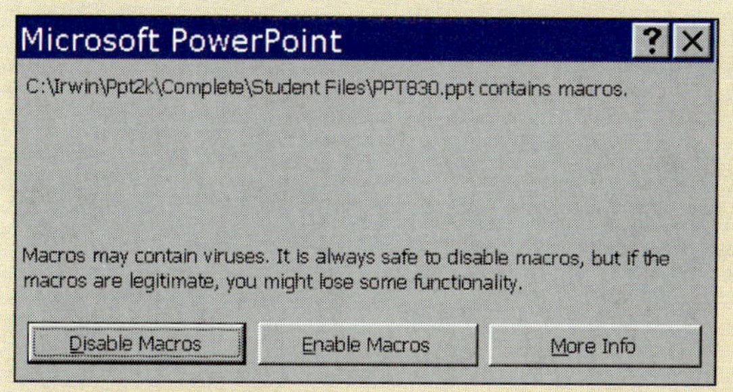


If the dialog box in Figure 8.3 is displaying:
CLICK: Enable Macros command button

3 Let's see what security level is selected on your computer.
CHOOSE: Tools, Macro, Security
The Security dialog box should now appear (Figure 8.4).

**Figure 8.4**
Security dialog box

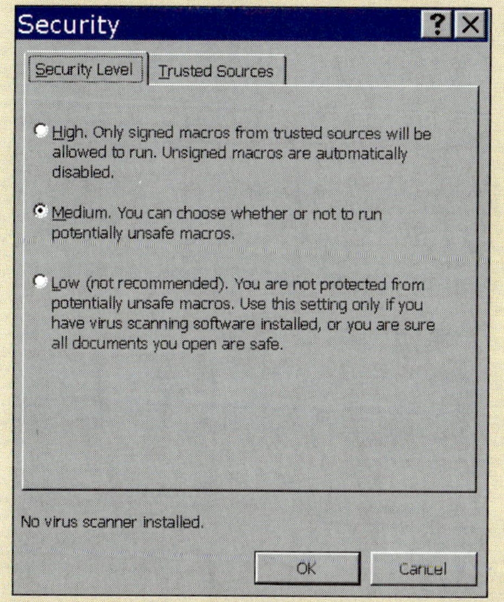


4 Review the descriptions of each security level in the Security dialog box. When the *Medium* option button is selected, PowerPoint will always display a warning dialog box (shown in step 2) each time you attempt to open a document that contains macros.

5 To leave the settings in the Security dialog box unchanged:
CLICK: Cancel command button

6 Keep the "Practice with Macros" presentation open for use in the next lesson.

## 8.1.4 Deleting a Macro

**FEATURE**

Creating and running the simple macro from the last two lessons should provide some perspective on how easy it is to work with macros in PowerPoint. When you have finished testing or using a macro and no longer need it, you should delete the macro from the presentation in which it is stored.

**METHOD**

1. CHOOSE: Tools, Macro, Macros
2. SELECT: the desired macro in the *Macro name* list box
3. CLICK: Delete command button
4. CLICK: Yes command button to confirm the deletion
5. CLICK: Close command button

**PRACTICE**

In this lesson, you delete the "ForwardButton" macro from the "Practice with Macros" document.

*Setup:* Ensure that you've completed the previous lessons in this module and that the "Practice with Macros" document is displaying.

1 CHOOSE: Tools, Macro, Macros

2 SELECT: the "ForwardButton" macro in the *Macro name* list box
CLICK: Delete command button
CLICK: Yes command button to confirm the deletion

3 Save and then close the revised "Practice with Macros" presentation.

4 Close any other presentations that are currently open without saving.

**8.1 Self Check** What is the procedure for playing back a recorded macro?

# 8.2 Editing Macros

The Macro Recorder is an excellent tool for quickly storing sequences of instructions that can be played back immediately. But there will be times when you need to edit your macros. You may have chosen the wrong command during the recording process; you may need to change some data that you entered; you may want to expand the macro with a few additional steps; you may even want to consolidate several smaller macros into one comprehensive routine. Rather than re-recording a macro, you can easily modify the macro's code using the **Visual Basic Editor.** The Editor is a special utility that enables you to create, edit, and print macros. In this module, we describe launching the Visual Basic Editor and then editing and printing a recorded macro.

## 8.2.1 Launching the Visual Basic Editor



**FEATURE**

Although the Editor is a separate program from Office 2000, it is fully integrated with PowerPoint. It knows, for example, which document to associate a particular macro module with. The Editor also provides access to all of the tools you need to write macros from scratch.

**METHOD**

1. CHOOSE: Tools, Macro, Macros
2. SELECT: the macro in the list box
3. CLICK: Edit command button

**PRACTICE**

In this lesson, you create a new presentation for storing a collection of macros. After creating the first macro, you then launch the Visual Basic Editor to edit the macro.

*Setup:* Ensure that PowerPoint is loaded and that no presentations are displaying.

1 To begin a blank presentation:
CLICK: New button (□) on the Standard toolbar
CLICK: OK command button to insert a Title slide

2 Save the blank presentation as "Macros" to your personal storage location.

3. Let's record a macro you can use to start new presentations. This macro will apply the Global design template and insert your name and title in the Subtitle placeholder. To begin:
CHOOSE: Tools, Macro, Record New Macro
TYPE: **NewPresentation** in the *Macro name* text box

4. To insert an additional paragraph in the *Description* text box, do the following:
CLICK: in the *Description* text box
PRESS: END
PRESS: ENTER
TYPE: **Applies a design template and inserts information in the Subtitle placeholder.**
CLICK: OK command button to begin recording the macro

5. The following list of actions will be recorded in the macro:
CHOOSE: Format, Apply Design Template
DOUBLE-CLICK: Global template in the list box
CLICK: in the Subtitle placeholder
TYPE: ***your name*** (substitute your actual name)
PRESS: ENTER
TYPE: **Managing Director, Global Telecom**
CLICK: outside the Subtitle placeholder

6. To stop recording:
CLICK: Stop Recording button in the dialog box

7. Save the "Macros" presentation and keep it open for use in the next few steps.

8. Let's start a blank presentation and then run the "NewPresentation" macro that we just created.
CLICK: New button (□) on the Standard toolbar
CLICK: OK command button to insert a Title slide

9. To test the "NewPresentation" macro on this blank presentation:
PRESS: ALT + F8 to display the Macro dialog box directly
SELECT: Macros from the *Macro in* drop-down list
DOUBLE-CLICK: NewPresentation macro in the list box
The Global template was automatically applied to the blank presentation and text was automatically inserted in the subtitle.

10. Close the current document without saving. The "Macros" document should now be displaying.

**11** To launch the Visual Basic Editor so that you can edit the "New-Presentation" macro:
CHOOSE: Tools, Macro, Macros
SELECT: NewPresentation in the list box, if it isn't selected already
CLICK: Edit command button
The Visual Basic Editor has now launched in a separate window.

**12** Maximize the Visual Basic Editor window, if it isn't maximized already. Your screen may now appear similar to Figure 8.5, although don't worry if your screen looks different.

**Figure 8.5**
The Visual Basic Editor window

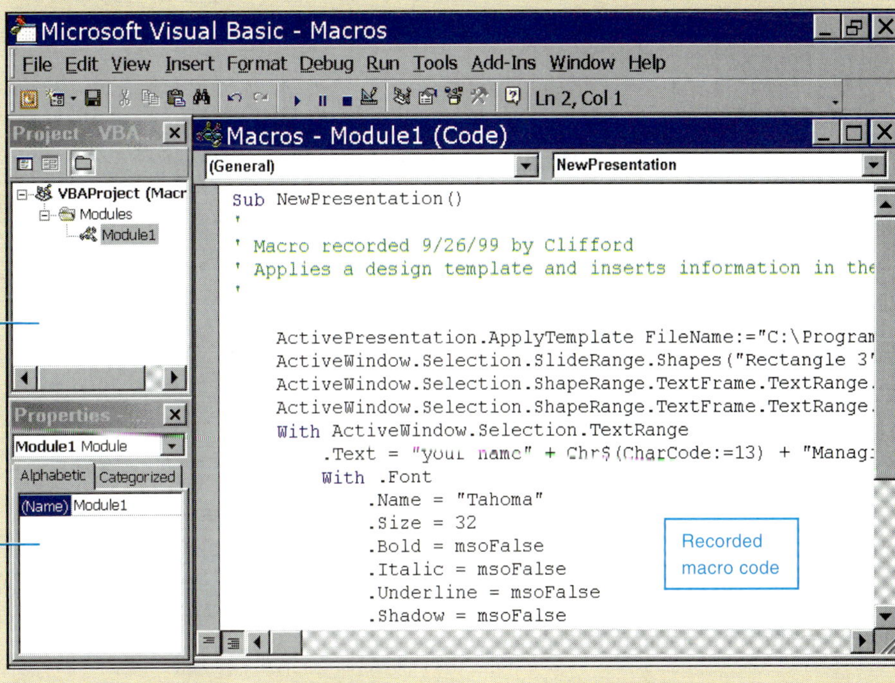


Project Explorer window

Properties window

**13** Let's customize the viewing area for use in the next few modules. While referring to the labels in Figure 8.5, do the following:
CLICK: Close button (☒) of the Project Explorer window
CLICK: Close button (☒) of the Properties window
CLICK: Maximize button (☐) of the Code window, if it is not already maximized
Your screen should appear similar to Figure 8.6 before proceeding.

**Figure 8.6**
Viewing macro code

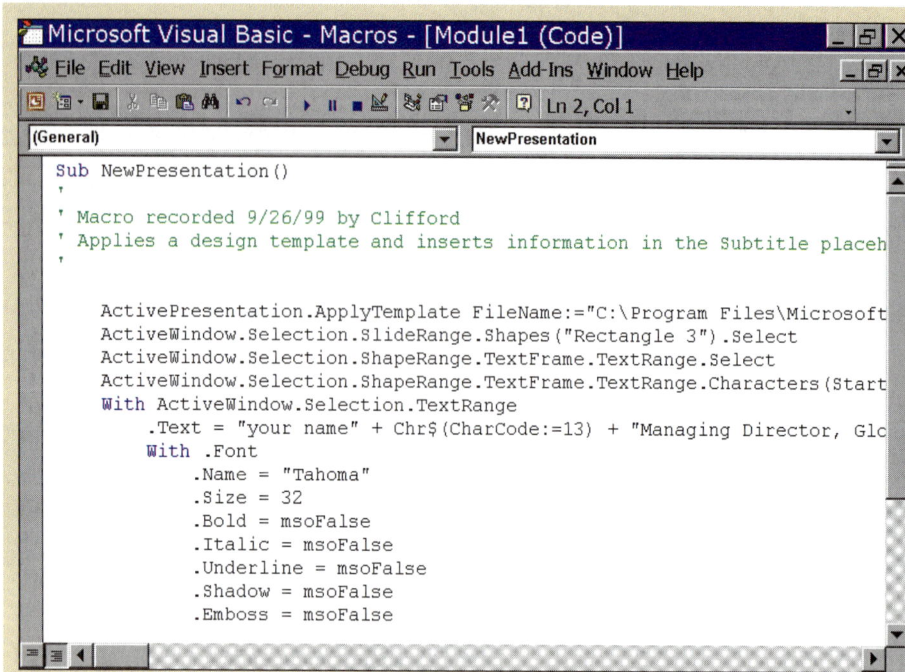


14. Without changing the current screen display, continue to the next lesson.

## 8.2.2 Modifying a Recorded Macro

**FEATURE**

Remember that you need not record over a macro in order to change a few steps or selections. Using the Visual Basic Editor, it is not difficult to modify a macro's programming code. Once you have finished editing a macro, you will want to save your changes.

**METHOD**

1. Edit the macro code, as desired.
2. CHOOSE: File, Save Macros from the Menu bar in the Visual Basic Editor

**PRACTICE**

In this section, you practice editing a macro.

*Setup:* Ensure that you've completed the previous lesson and that the code of the "NewPresentation" macro is displaying in the Editor window.

1. In the next few steps, you will change the information that the macro is inserting in the subtitle placeholder. To begin, locate the ".Text = "*your name*" line and then do the following:
SELECT: "Managing Director" on the current line (you may have to scroll the code window to the right)
TYPE: **Vice-President**

2. Now, to increase the font size of the subtitle text from 32 to 36, first locate the ".Size = 32" line and then do the following:
DOUBLE-CLICK: 32
TYPE: **36**

3. To save the revised macro:
CHOOSE: File, Save Macros

4. To close the Editor window and return to your document:
CHOOSE: File, Close and Return to Microsoft PowerPoint

5. Let's try out the revised "NewPresentation" macro to see if your edits were registered.
CLICK: New button ( ) to begin a new presentation
CLICK: OK command button to insert a Title slide
PRESS: ALT + F8 to display the Macro dialog box directly
SELECT: Macros from the *Macro in* drop-down list
DOUBLE-CLICK: NewPresentation macro in the list box
Note that your text changes are now displayed in the presentation.

6. CLICK: in the changed text to verify that the macro is applying the correct font size

7. Close the current presentation without saving.

8. The "Macros" presentation should be displaying. Keep this presentation open for use in the next lesson.

## 8.2.3 Printing Your Macros

**FEATURE**

Although we're sure you will agree that working in the Visual Basic Editor is a most enjoyable experience, nothing will impress your friends more than a printout of your macro programming code. Kidding aside, printing your macros can be especially helpful when you need to jot down a few handwritten notes describing a particular block of code or maybe you need to fax a copy to an associate for review. Perhaps you just want to edit a macro while riding the bus or train to work. A printout will also provide you with a hardcopy backup of your work, in case you accidentally lose the electronic version.

**METHOD**

1. Display the Visual Basic Editor window.
2. CHOOSE: File, Print
3. SELECT: *Current Module* option button (or another option)
4. CLICK: OK command button

**PRACTICE**

In this lesson, you print the macro stored in the "Macros" presentation.

*Setup:* Ensure that you've completed the previous lessons in this module and that the "Macros" presentation is displaying.

1 To print a copy of your macro code:
PRESS: ALT + F11 to display the Visual Basic Editor directly
CHOOSE: File, Print
The dialog box shown in Figure 8.7 should appear.

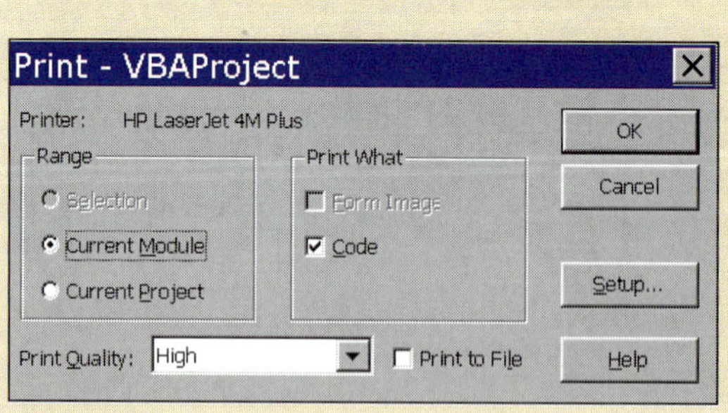


**Figure 8.7**
Print dialog box in the Visual Basic Editor

2 To proceed with printing using the default selections:
CLICK: OK command button
The macro code is sent to the printer immediately.

3. Close the Visual Basic Editor window.
4. Close the "Macros" presentation, saving your changes.

**8.2 Self Check** What is the Visual Basic Editor used for?

# 8.3 Customizing Your Workspace

On installing Microsoft PowerPoint, the Menu bar and toolbars are set up in a default configuration. As you gain experience with PowerPoint and create macros for automating everyday procedures, you may want to customize PowerPoint to your preferred way of working. Fortunately, PowerPoint's environment is extremely flexible and easily customized. For example, you can modify the existing interface elements, such as the Menu bar, and create entirely new menu options and toolbars. Whatever your efforts involve, your overall objective should be to make it easier to access the commands and procedures you use most often.



## 8.3.1 Modifying the Menu Bar

**FEATURE**

Microsoft Office 2000 introduced the use of personalized menus and toolbars for dynamically presenting the commands you use most often. In the first chapter of this book, you turned this feature off so that all the default commands would appear in the Menu bar. You can further customize PowerPoint's menus by adding, arranging, and removing commands. For example, rather than selecting macros from the Macro dialog box, you can create new menu commands that run specific macros. This feature can make the macros you create very accessible, especially to new users.

**METHOD**

1. CHOOSE: Tools, Customize
2. CLICK: *Commands* tab
3. SELECT: a category in the *Categories* list box
4. DRAG: a command from the *Commands* list box to the desired location on an existing menu
5. CLICK: Close command button

**PRACTICE**

In this lesson, you will open an existing presentation and then add a new option to the File pull-down menu.

*Setup:* Ensure that PowerPoint is loaded and that no presentations are displaying.

1. Open the PPT830 data file. (*Note:* If a warning dialog box appears, click the Enable Macros command button.) Although this presentation appears empty, it contains two macros that you will use in this module.

2. Save the document as "My Workspace" to your personal storage location.

3. To display the Customize dialog box for modifying PowerPoint's menu:
CHOOSE: Tools, Customize
CLICK: *Commands* tab
The dialog box shown in Figure 8.8 appears. Whenever this dialog box is displayed, all of the toolbar buttons and menu commands are disabled automatically to allow for editing.

**Figure 8.8**
Customize dialog box: *Commands* tab

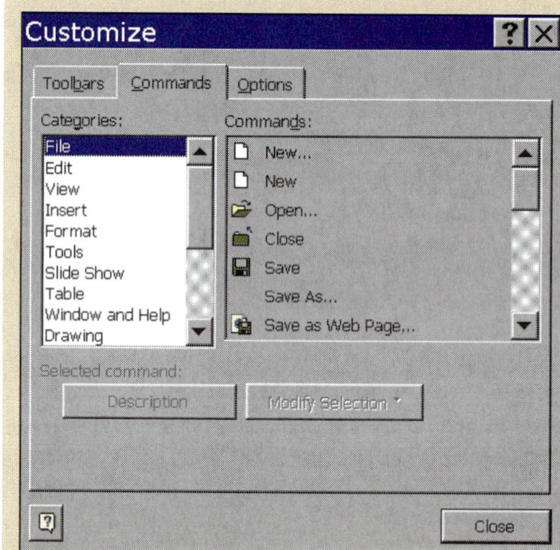


4. The *Commands* tab provides a centralized listing of all of PowerPoint's menu commands. To add a command to the Menu bar or a toolbar, you simply drag the command from the Commands list box. In this step, you will add a command called "Publish as Web Page" to the File menu. Do the following:
SELECT: File in the *Categories* list box, if it isn't already selected
SELECT: Publish as Web Page in the *Commands* list box (this command is located beneath the Save as Web Page command)

5 To place this command onto the File menu, drag the Publish as Web Page option over top of the File command in the Menu bar. Note that the File pull-down menu appears automatically. You can now position the command immediately below the Save as Web Page command using the black insertion line as your guide. Your screen should appear similar to Figure 8.9 before proceeding.

**Figure 8.9**
Adding a command to the Menu bar

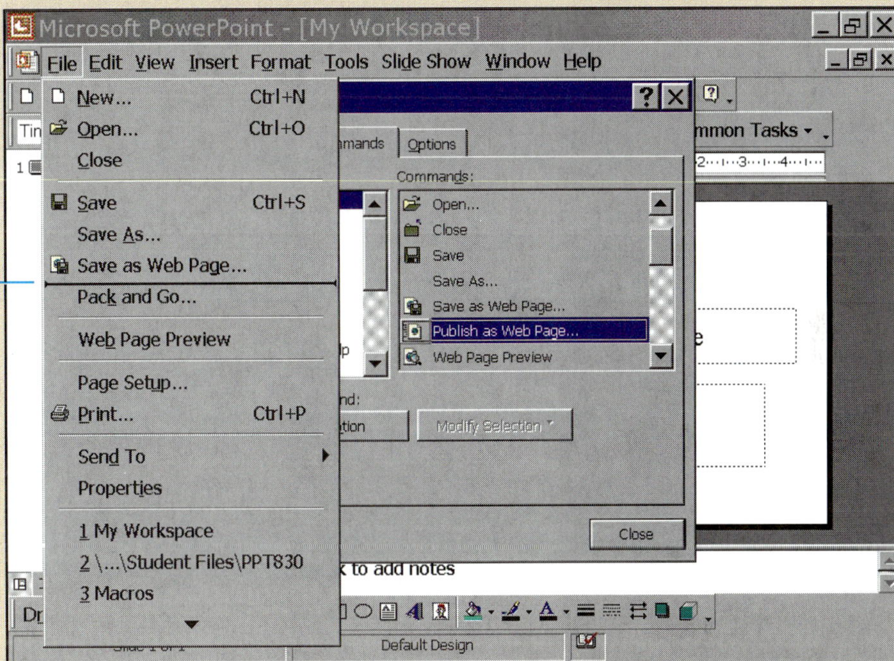


Drag the "Publish as Web Page" option from the *Commands* list box to this position on the File menu.

6 Release the mouse button to complete the drag and drop operation. Note that the command remains selected on the File menu.

7 With the command still selected on the File menu:
CLICK: Modify Selection command button in the Customize dialog box
A pop-up menu appears with options that allow you to change the name of the command and the appearance of its icon or button image.

8 To rename the menu command:
CHOOSE: Name
SELECT: the existing text in the attached text box, if it isn't selected already
TYPE: **Customize a Web Page**
PRESS: ENTER
Note that the renamed menu option appears in the File menu.

9 To complete the editing:
CLICK: Close command button in the Customize dialog box

10. Save the revised document.
11. To test the new command, do the following:
CHOOSE: File, Customize a Web Page
The Publish a Web Page dialog box should display with options for customizing your presentation for the Web.
12. CLICK: Cancel command button in the dialog box
13. Continue to the next lesson.

## 8.3.2 Manipulating Toolbars

**FEATURE**

Toolbars allow you to organize multiple commands and features into compact and conveniently located button strips. The Standard toolbar itself gives you single-click access to over 20 commands. In addition to dozens of useful built-in toolbars, PowerPoint allows you to create custom toolbars that are suited to your personal needs and preferences. You can add existing menus and buttons to a custom toolbar or create new buttons that run macros. In fact, a toolbar can contain buttons, menus, drop-down list boxes, and a variety of other interface controls.

Did you know that PowerPoint's menu is actually a toolbar? Like all toolbars, you can display the Menu bar docked alongside the application window or *floating* in its own window, complete with a Title bar and Close button (☒). There are four docking areas for toolbars, alongside the top and bottom horizontal window borders and the left and right window borders.

**METHOD**

- To float a toolbar, drag it away from the four docking areas using the move handle that appears at the far left-hand side of a docked toolbar.
- To dock a toolbar, drag it by its Title bar to the top, bottom, left, or right wall in the application window.
- To display or hide a toolbar, choose View, Toolbars or right-click on a displayed toolbar and then choose the toolbar's name.

**PRACTICE**

In this lesson, you practice manipulating the display and appearance of toolbars.

*Setup:* Ensure that you've completed the previous lesson and that the "My Workspace" presentation is displaying.

1 Do the following:
DRAG: the move handle of the Standard toolbar toward the center of the application window

2 When you release the mouse button, the Standard toolbar appears in its own window.

3 To size the toolbar, position the mouse on the Standard toolbar's right-hand border until the pointer changes to a horizontal double-headed arrow. Then, drag the toolbar's border to half its original width, as shown below, and then release the mouse button.

4 On your own, drag the Standard toolbar by its Title bar back to its original position between the Menu bar and the Formatting toolbar.

5 To view the most commonly used toolbars in PowerPoint:
CHOOSE: View, Toolbars
You should see a minimum of 13 toolbars listed in the cascading menu. The toolbars that are active and displayed in the application window are shown with a check mark (✔) in the menu.

6 Let's activate a new toolbar:
CHOOSE: Picture
The Picture toolbar should now appear in its own window, at the same location where it was last activated.

7 Close the Picture toolbar by clicking its Close button (☒).

## 8.3.3 Customizing a Toolbar

**FEATURE**
Besides having the ability to control where toolbars are positioned in the application window, you can modify the location of buttons in a toolbar, size buttons, add and delete buttons, and create new buttons that are assigned to run macros. Moving buttons on a toolbar offers limited scope for personalizing your system. However, removing buttons that you don't often use and replacing them with frequently used commands and features can improve your productivity tenfold.

**METHOD**

To add, delete, and modify toolbar buttons:

1. CHOOSE: Tools, Customize
2. DRAG: buttons and commands within a toolbar to change the order; away from a toolbar to delete it; or onto a toolbar to add it
3. RIGHT-CLICK: a toolbar button to display editing commands
4. CLICK: Close command button when finished

To reset a toolbar to its default configuration:

1. CHOOSE: Tools, Customize
2. CLICK: *Toolbars* tab
3. SELECT: the desired toolbar in the Toolbars list box
4. CLICK: Reset command button
5. CLICK: OK command button to confirm

**PRACTICE**

In this lesson, you modify the contents of a toolbar.

*Setup:* Ensure that you've completed the previous lessons in this module and that the "My Workspace" presentation is displaying.

1 To customize a toolbar, you access the Customize dialog box. Do the following:
CHOOSE: Tools, Customize
CLICK: *Toolbars* tab
The dialog box shown in Figure 8.10 appears.

**Figure 8.10**
Customize dialog box: *Toolbars* tab

2 As mentioned previously, when the Customize dialog box is displayed all of the toolbar buttons and menu commands are disabled. Therefore, you can move and remove buttons on a toolbar by simply clicking and dragging them. To illustrate, do the following:
CLICK: Bold button (B) on the Formatting toolbar
The button appears surrounded by a thick border.

3 To remove this button from the toolbar:
DRAG: Bold button (B) away from the toolbar and into the presentation area

4 Release the mouse button to complete the button removal. (*Note:* You can also change the order of buttons on a toolbar by dragging them to their new locations.)

5 To size a drop-down list button on the Formatting toolbar:
CLICK: Font drop-down list button (Times Roman)

6 Position the mouse pointer over the right vertical border of the button until the mouse pointer changes shape. Then, drag the border to the right to increase its width. Release the mouse button to view the results.

7 To add a button for changing the current security level:
CLICK: *Commands* tab in the Customize dialog box
SELECT: Tools in the *Categories* list box
SELECT: Security in the *Commands* list box

8 Drag the Security option from the *Commands* list box and position it, using the black insertion line as your guide, to the right of the Open button on the Standard toolbar.

9 Release the mouse button. You will see that the Security button appears in the toolbar.

10 Fortunately, PowerPoint provides a command that lets you reset the toolbars back to their original settings. To do so:
CLICK: *Toolbars* tab

11 To reset the Standard toolbar, ensure that it is highlighted in the list box and then:
CLICK: Reset command button
CLICK: OK command button to reset any changes made to the Standard toolbar

12 To reset the Formatting toolbar, highlight "Formatting" in the Toolbars list box by clicking its name. (*Note:* Don't deselect the Formatting check box.)

13 CLICK: Reset command button
CLICK: OK command button to reset any changes made to the Formatting toolbar
Note that the Standard and Formatting toolbars are now reset to their default configurations.

14 To close the Customize dialog box and accept the changes:
CLICK: Close command button

15 Keep the "My Workspace" presentation open for use in the next lesson.

## 8.3.4 Creating a New Toolbar

**FEATURE**

There may be circumstances where creating a new toolbar is easier than modifying the existing ones. For example, you would not change PowerPoint's default settings if there are less experienced users who access your computer and would be confused by such modifications. In this case, creating a toolbar with your personal command favorites can give you the versatility you need without creating problems for others. But be prepared: once your friends and associates see what you can do with PowerPoint, they'll be asking you to create personal toolbars for them too!

**METHOD**

1. CHOOSE: Tools, Customize
2. CLICK: *Toolbars* tab
3. CLICK: New command button
4. TYPE: **a name for the toolbar**
5. DRAG: the desired commands from the *Commands* list box to the empty toolbar palette

**PRACTICE**

In this exercise, you create a custom toolbar and then populate it with buttons and commands.

*Setup:* Ensure that you've completed the previous lessons in this module and that the "My Workspace" presentation is displaying.

1 As always, you must first display the Customize dialog box:
CHOOSE: Tools, Customize
CLICK: *Toolbars* tab

**2** To create a new toolbar:
CLICK: New button in the dialog box
The New Toolbar dialog box appears, as shown below:

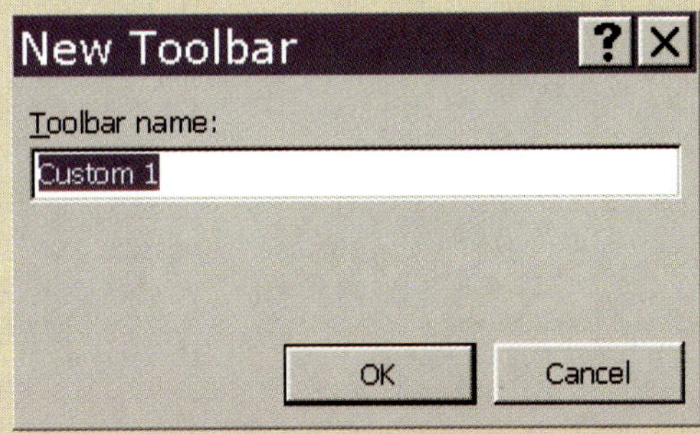


**3** The name is currently selected in the *Toolbar name* text box. To specify a new name:
TYPE: **Personal**
CLICK: OK command button
By performing this command, a new option called "Personal" now appears selected in the *Toolbars* list box. You will also notice a small empty toolbar palette appears, floating in the application window.

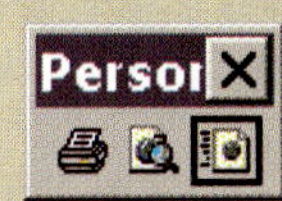


**4** To add commands to your new Personal toolbar, locate the following commands on the *Commands* tab and then drag them to the new toolbar palette. When completed, your toolbar should appear similar to the graphic on the right:

| Categories | Commands |
|---|---|
| File | Print |
| File | Web Page Preview |
| File | Publish as Web Page |

**5** Let's add some buttons to the toolbar that can run our macros:
SELECT: Macros in the *Categories* list box
SELECT: Size35mm macro

**6** Drag the "Size35mm" macro from the Commands list box and position it to the right of the Publish as Web Page button on the Personal toolbar.

7. To rename the macro button:
RIGHT-CLICK: the button
CHOOSE: Name from the right-click menu
SELECT: the existing text in the attached text box, if it isn't selected already
TYPE: 35mm
PRESS: ENTER
Note that the renamed button appears on the toolbar.

8. On your own, add the "SizeOnscreen" macro to your personal toolbar and then change the name of the button to "Onscreen." The Personal toolbar should now appear similar to the following:

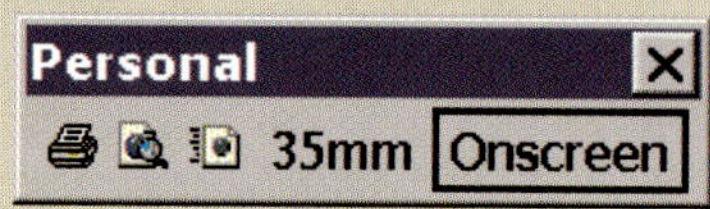


9. To exit the Customize dialog box:
CLICK: Close button

10. On your own, test the buttons on your new Personal toolbar.

11. Close the Personal toolbar.

12. Save and then close the "My Workspace" presentation.

**In Addition**
**Permanently Removing a Custom Toolbar**

To permanently remove a custom toolbar, display the *Toolbars* tab in the Customize dialog box. Select the custom toolbar in the *Toolbars* list box and then click the Delete command button. Click the OK command button to confirm the removal and then close the Customize dialog box.

**8.3 Self Check** What procedure would you use to remove a button from the Standard toolbar?

# 8.4 Chapter Review

This chapter introduces macros for automating the tasks you perform in PowerPoint, not only for yourself but also for less experienced users. Using the Macro Recorder, you record routine tasks, which are then translated into Visual Basic for Applications (VBA) code. You also learn to run, modify, and print macros, and protect your computer from macro viruses. To boost your productivity and make your applications easier to use for novices, you customize PowerPoint's Menu bar and toolbars. You also create a custom toolbar for holding your favorite commands and macros.

## 8.4.1 Command Summary

Many of the commands and procedures appearing in this chapter are summarized in the following table.

| Skill Set | To Perform This Task . . . | Do the Following . . . |
|---|---|---|
| **Using Macros** | Record a new macro | CHOOSE: Tools, Macro, Record New Macro |
| | Run a macro | CHOOSE: Tools, Macro, Macros<br>SELECT: *a macro*<br>CLICK: Run command button |
| | Protect your work from macro viruses | CHOOSE: Tools, Macro Security |
| | Edit a macro using the Visual Basic Editor | CHOOSE: Tools, Macro, Macros<br>SELECT: *a macro*<br>CLICK: Edit command button |
| **Working with Toolbars** | Customize the Menu bar and toolbars | CHOOSE: Tools, Customize |
| | Toggle the display of a toolbar on and off | CHOOSE: View, Toolbars<br>CHOOSE: *the desired toolbar* |
| | Create a new toolbar | CHOOSE: Tools, Customize<br>CLICK: *Toolbars* tab<br>CLICK: New command button |

POWERPOINT

### 8.4.2 Key Terms

This section specifies page references for the key terms identified in this chapter. For a complete list of definitions, refer to the Glossary provided at the end of this learning guide.

automacro, *p. 318*

macros, *p. 315*

Macro Recorder, *p. 316*

macro virus, *p. 320*

virus, *p. 320*

Visual Basic Editor, *p. 323*

Visual Basic for Applications (VBA), *p. 316*

## 8.5 Review Questions

### 8.5.1 Short Answer

1. What is VBA?
2. What is a macro?
3. When naming a macro, why is it advisable to complete the *Description* text box?
4. Why might you want to edit an existing macro?
5. What is a macro virus?
6. How do you assign a macro to a toolbar button?
7. What is the procedure for deleting a macro?
8. What is the procedure for launching the Visual Basic Editor?
9. Explain the process of renaming an existing toolbar button.
10. What is the procedure for displaying or hiding an existing toolbar?

### 8.5.2 True/False

1. ____ Before you can create macros in PowerPoint, you must have a good understanding of Visual Basic for Applications (VBA).
2. ____ Macro names can include spaces.
3. ____ It is possible to assign a macro to the Menu bar and toolbars.
4. ____ PowerPoint's Macro Recorder records your actions and then writes the required VBA programming code for you.
5. ____ In PowerPoint, it's possible to store macros directly in presentations.

6. ____ It's possible to run a macro located in another open presentation in the current presentation.
7. ____ Macro viruses are programs that were created with malicious intentions.
8. ____ In PowerPoint, although it's possible to move and delete buttons on a toolbar, it's not possible to resize buttons.
9. ____ PowerPoint's Menu bar is actually a toolbar that you can move and resize in the application window.
10. ____ Even after adding buttons to one of PowerPoint's predefined toolbars, it's possible to restore the toolbar to its original configuration.

## 8.5.3 Multiple Choice

1. Which of the following refers to a programming language that is shared by the Office 2000 applications?
   a. Office's Macro Recorder
   b. VBA
   c. procedures
   d. All of the above

2. The ______________ makes it easy to create macros in PowerPoint without knowing how to use a programming language.
   a. Macro Recorder
   b. Tape Recorder
   c. Macro Assembly Language
   d. Macro Wizard

3. The ______________ is a special Office 2000 utility that enables you to create, edit, and print macros.
   a. Visual Toolbox
   b. Edit Tool Bar
   c. Macro Editor
   d. Visual Basic Editor

4. In PowerPoint, it's possible to customize toolbars by ______________ toolbar buttons.
   a. renaming
   b. moving
   c. removing
   d. All of the above

5. It's possible to run macros stored in ______________.
   a. the current presentation
   b. open presentations
   c. closed presentations
   d. Both a and b

6. Which of the following help improve the accuracy with which repetitive procedures are performed?
   a. macro printouts
   b. customized toolbars
   c. macros
   d. All of the above

7. Which of the following is located on the Stop Recording toolbar?
   a. Stop Recording button
   b. Pause Recording button
   c. Start Recording button
   d. Both a and b

8. To print your macros, you must display the ______________.
   a. PowerPoint application window
   b. Visual Basic Editor utility
   c. Macros dialog box
   d. All of the above

9. To customize the Menu bar or a toolbar:
   a. Choose Tools, Customize from PowerPoint's Menu bar
   b. Choose Tools, Customize from the Visual Basic Editor's Menu bar
   c. Either a or b
   d. None of the above

10. To return a predefined PowerPoint toolbar to its original configuration, click the ______________ button in the *Toolbars* tab of the Customize dialog box.
    a. Default
    b. Reset
    c. Original configuration
    d. Normal

# 8.6 Hands-On Projects

## 8.6.1 Outdoor Adventure Tours: Creating and Running a Macro

This exercise practices using the macro recorder to create a macro, running a macro, launching the Visual Basic Editor, and printing the macro code.

1. Open the PPT861 data file location and save it as "Outdoor Star Macro" to your personal storage location.
2. To display the drawing toolbar:
   RIGHT-CLICK: any toolbar
   CHOOSE: Drawing, if it isn't already selected
3. To start recording a macro that will add a yellow-star Autoshape to the lower-right corner of the current slide:
   CHOOSE: Tools, Macro, Record New Macro
   TYPE: **YellowStar** in the *Macro name* box
   TYPE: ***Your Name*** where appropriate in the *Description* text box
   TYPE: **Adds a Yellow Star to lower-right corner of current slide** on a new line in the *Description* text box
   CLICK: OK command button
4. To record the macro, perform the following steps:
   CLICK: AutoShapes button on the Drawing toolbar
   CHOOSE: Stars and Banners, 5-Point Star
   CLICK: in the lower-right corner of the slide to place the AutoShape
   DRAG: sizing handle to enlarge the star to approximately 1-inch square
   CLICK: down arrow attached to the Fill Color button () on the Drawing toolbar
   CHOOSE: More Fill Colors
   SELECT: bright yellow in the color palette
   CLICK: OK command button
   CLICK: down arrow attached to the Line Color button ()
   CHOOSE: No Line
5. Stop recording the macro.
6. Move to the next slide in the presentation to practice running your macro.
   CHOOSE: Tools, Macro, Macros
   SELECT: YellowStar macro
   CLICK: Run command button
7. To launch the Visual Basic Editor to display the macro code:
   CHOOSE: Tools, Macro, Macros
   SELECT: YellowStar Macro
   CLICK: Edit command button

POWERPOINT

8. To print a copy of the macro:
   CHOOSE: File, Print to display the Print dialog box
   CLICK: OK command button without changing any of the default selections
9. Close the Visual Basic Editor.
10. Save and then close the revised presentation.

## 8.6.2 Monashee Community College: Editing Macro Code

In this exercise, you practice editing macro code and adding a menu item.

1. Open the PPT862 data file, enabling the macros, if prompted.
2. Save the presentation as "Monashee Footer" to your personal storage location.
3. Review the slides to become familiar with their content. Note that no footers are displayed on any of the slides.
4. To display the macros stored in this presentation:
   CHOOSE: Tools, Macro, Macros
5. To run the MonasheeFooter macro:
   SELECT: Monashee Footer from the list of macros
   CLICK: Run command button
6. Review the slides and note that a footer with the college name and slide number has been added to every slide after the first slide.
7. To access the macro code so that it can be edited:
   CHOOSE: Tools, Macro, Macros
   SELECT: MonasheeFooter from the list of macros
   CLICK: Edit command button
8. In the macro, two lines of code contain the phrase "Monashee College." Locate these lines now.
9. Insert the word **Community** between "Monashee" and "College" in both lines of code.
10. Save the revisions to the macro, then close the Visual Basic Editor and return to the presentation.
11. Run the MonasheeFooter macro again.
12. Review the presentation to ensure that the college name in the footer has been changed.
13. To add the macro to the end of the Menu bar:
    CHOOSE: Tools, Customize
    SELECT: Macros in the *Categories* list box
    DRAG: MonasheeFooter from the *Commands* list box to the Menu bar, positioning it to the right of the Help menu item
14. To edit the name of the menu item:
    RIGHT-CLICK: the MonasheeFooter menu item

15. Insert a space between "Monashee" and "Footer" in the *Name* text box and then press ENTER.
16. To leave the Customize dialog box:
    CLICK: Close command button
17. Save and then close the revised presentation.

## 8.6.3 Coldstream Corporation: Working with Toolbars

You will now practice creating a new toolbar, modifying an existing toolbar, and resetting a built-in toolbar to its original configuration.

1. Open the PPT863 data file, enabling macros if prompted.
2. Save the presentation as "Coldstream Toolbars" to your personal storage location.
3. Customize the Formatting toolbar by removing the following buttons:
   –Text Shadow
   –Increase Font Size
   –Decrease Font Size
4. Now, add the following commands from the Format category to the right side of the Formatting toolbar:
   –Increase Paragraph Spacing
   –Decrease Paragraph Spacing
   –Change Case
5. Rearrange the new buttons so that the Change Case button is positioned to the right of the Underline button and the Paragraph Spacing buttons are placed to the right of the Align Right button.
6. Create a new toolbar named "Coldstream" that includes the following commands:

| Category | Command |
|---|---|
| File | Page Setup |
| File | Save As Web Page |
| Slide Show | Rehearse Timings |
| Slide Show | Set up Show |
| Macros | ColdstreamFooter |
| Macros | SpecialTex |

7. Change the name of the ColdstreamFooter button to **Footer**.
8. Test the new toolbar.
9. Drag the new Coldstream toolbar so that it is docked at the bottom of the application window.

10. To return the Formatting toolbar to its original configuration, open the Customize dialog box, click on the Formatting toolbar name, then click the Reset command button.
11. Save and then close the revised "Coldstream Toolbars" presentation.

### 8.6.4 Spiderman Web Marketing: Managing Macros and Toolbars

In this exercise, you practice setting security levels, recording and deleting macros, printing macro code, and deleting a toolbar.

1. Close all open presentations.
2. Use the Tools, Macro, Security command to change your computer's security settings to High.
3. Open the PPT864 data file. Although this presentation contains macros, note that there was no warning about macros when the presentation was opened.
4. Save the presentation as "Spiderman Business" to your personal storage location.
5. Open the Macros dialog box and select the "TurnHere" macro from the list. Note that the Run command button is disabled because of the High security settings.
6. Close the current presentation.
7. Change the current security level to Medium.
8. Reopen the "Spiderman Business" presentation, enabling the macros when prompted.
9. Open the Macros dialog box and run the "TurnHere" macro.
10. Record a new macro named "SpiderPreferred" that does the following:
    –Applies the Checkers design template
    –Changes the current color scheme, selecting the color scheme located in the middle of the first row and applying it to all slides
    –Changes the background fill, selecting the Newsprint texture (located in the first row of the first column) and applying it to all slides
11. Open the Macros dialog box and delete the "SpecialText" and "Turn Here" macros.
12. Open the Visual Basic Editor and print a copy of the macro code.
13. Open the Customize dialog box and review the list of toolbars. If the Coldstream toolbar is included in the list, select the toolbar and then delete it.
14. Save and then close the revised "Spiderman Business" presentation.

### 8.6.5 On Your Own: Collecting Your Favorite Macros

For this exercise, you create a presentation for storing macros that you think will be useful in building future presentations. Ideas include macros for printing your presentation, formatting text selections, applying design templates, inserting action buttons, or hiding slides. Play back each macro to make sure it is running properly and then print a copy of all the macros stored in the presentation. Save the presentation as "Favorite Macros" to your personal storage location and then close the presentation.

### 8.6.6 On Your Own: Optimizing Your Work Area

Start a new presentation and then customize the Menu bar and toolbars to your preferred way of working. In your presentation, describe the changes you made to your work area, giving reasons for each of your actions. Save the presentation as "Your Name's Work Area," substituting your actual name in the filename. Print and then close the presentation.



## 8.7 Case Problems: Door-to-Door Moving Services

Each day, hundreds of families in locations around the world trust Door-to-Door Moving Services with possessions they have accumulated over a lifetime. At Door-to-Door, it is the responsibility of the local sales representative to deliver premove counseling and explain all costs involved. Per a recent change in company policy, sales representatives are now required to present this information using PowerPoint slide shows stored on a laptop computer. To make it easier for the sales representatives to work with PowerPoint, Linda has decided to update their laptops with several macros. She is also eager to customize PowerPoint's Menu bar and toolbars to make the most often used commands more accessible.

In the following case problems, assume the role of the primary character, Linda, and perform the same steps that she identifies. You may want to re-read the chapter opening before proceeding.

1. To give sales representatives greater control over the look of the standard pre-sales presentation, Linda has decided to embellish it with several macros. She begins by opening the PPT870 presentation and then saving it as "Pre-Sales" to her personal storage location. She then records the following macros, storing them in the "Pre-Sales" presentation:

| **Macro Name** | **What It Does** |
|---|---|
| ARTSY | Applies the Artsy design template |
| CITRUS | Applies the Citrus design template |
| FIREBALL | Applies the Fireball design template |

She then saves the revised presentation and keeps it open in order to complete the next task.

2. Linda decides to use the Visual Basic Editor to change the "Fireball" macro so that it applies the Bold Stripes design template instead of the Fireball template. After starting the Visual Basic Editor, she performs the following steps:
–Locate the "Sub Fireball ()" line, which is the very first line of the macro. This line identifies the name of the macro.
–Select the text "Fireball" and then type "BoldStripes" to change the name of the macro.
–Locate the "ActivePresentation" line and then scroll the display to the right until you see the name "Fireball.pot."
–Select the text "Fireball.pot" and then type "Bold Stripes.pot" to change the name of the template.
Next, Linda saves the revised macro and closes the Visual Basic Editor. She then plays back the "BoldStripes" macro to ensure that it runs correctly. Finally, she saves the revised presentation as "Pre-Sales2" to her personal storage location and keeps the presentation open in order to complete the next task.

3. To make the three design macros more accessible, Linda creates a new pull-down menu on the Menu bar named "Design Options." To accomplish this, she opens the Customize dialog box and then selects the *Commands* tab. In the *Categories* list box, she selects the New Menu option and drags the option from the *Commands* list to the right side of the Menu bar.

   After renaming the new menu option "Design Options," she then adds the "Artsy," "Citrus," and "BoldStripes" macros to the pull-down menu. (*Hint:* Click the "Design Options" menu option and then drag the macro to the drop-down menu that displays below. Until you've copied the first macro, the drop-down menu will display as a small box.) After trying out the new Design Options menu, she saves the presentation as "Pre-Sales3" to her personal storage location. She decides to keep the presentation open in order to complete the next task.

4. Linda decides to create two more macros in the open presentation, as described below:

| Macro Name | What It Does |
|---|---|
| Landscape | Applies landscape orientation |
| Portrait | Applies portrait orientation |

Next, she creates a new toolbar named "Door-to-Door" and adds the following buttons:

| Button | Where It Is Located |
|---|---|
| Landscape | In the Macros category |
| Portrait | In the Macros category |
| Slide Show | In the View category |
| Notes Page | In the View category |
| Print | In the File category |

Linda is pleased with what she has accomplished thus far. When the new toolbar is used in conjunction with the new Menu bar option created in the last exercise, it should be much easier for the company's sales representatives to perform these routine tasks in the future.

# Notes

# Notes

# Notes

# Answers to Self Check Questions

| | |
|---|---|
| **1.1 Self Check** | What is an adaptive menu? This type of menu displays only the most commonly-used commands. By default, the adaptive-menu feature is enabled in all Office 2000 applications. |
| **1.2 Self Check** | What is the difference between Slide Sorter and Slide Show view? In Slide Sorter view, you view several slides at once in the application window. In Slide Show view, you view an individual slide outside the application window. |
| **1.3 Self Check** | In the Save As dialog box, what is the Places bar used for? The Places bar provides convenient access to commonly used storage locations. |
| **1.4 Self Check** | What procedure enables you to print multiple copies of a presentation? Choose File, Print and then specify an alternate value in the *Number of copies* spin box. |
| **2.1 Self Check** | What is the Slide Finder tool used for? The Slide Finder tool is used to insert slides from other presentations into the current presentation. |
| **2.2 Self Check** | What is the procedure for moving and resizing object placeholders? To move a placeholder, position the mouse pointer over the placeholder until a four-headed arrow appears. Then drag the placeholder to a new location. You resize placeholders by dragging the object's sizing handles. |
| **2.3 Self Check** | What are organization charts used for? Organization charts are used to show a hierarchy of formal relationships. |
| **2.4 Self Check** | How can you go to a specific slide in Slide Show view? Right-click anywhere on the slide and then choose Go, Slide Navigator from the right-click menu. Then, click the slide you want to display and click the Go To command button. |
| **3.1 Self Check** | How would you go about changing a bulleted list to a numbered list? Select the bulleted text and then click the Numbering button ( ). |
| **3.2 Self Check** | What is the procedure for changing the width of a table column? Position the mouse pointer over a column border until a double-headed arrow appears. Then drag the border to the left or right. |

POWERPOINT

| | |
|---|---|
| **3.3 Self Check** | What is the procedure for correcting spelling errors using the right-click menu? Position the mouse pointer over a misspelled word and then right-click to display a list of suggested correct spellings. Select the correct spelling from the right-click menu. |
| **4.1 Self Check** | When is it useful to group objects? Grouping is ideal when you want to move, copy, or resize a multiple-object image as a single unit. |
| **4.2 Self Check** | When would it be preferable to use a text box over a text placeholder? Although placeholders help provide a uniform structure to a presentation, they are more confining than text boxes. Text boxes are ideal for positioning text anywhere on a slide. |
| **4.3 Self Check** | What is the most efficient procedure for changing the way titles look in your presentation? Edit the title placeholder on the Slide Master. |
| **5.1 Self Check** | In an electronic slide show, what are transitions used for? Transitions are the special effects you see when going from one slide to the next. They help make electronic presentations more interesting. |
| **5.2 Self Check** | How would you go about creating a Web presentation? To create a Web presentation, create the presentation and then choose File, Save as Web Page. |
| **5.3 Self Check** | What is the procedure for creating audience handouts? To create an audience handout, choose View, Master, Handout Master to customize the look of the handout pages. To print handouts, choose File, Print and then choose Handouts from the *Print what* drop-down list. |
| **6.1 Self Check** | What is the procedure for adding texture to a presentation's background? To add texture to a presentation's background, use the *Texture* tab of the Background dialog box. Select a texture in the scroll box and then press ENTER or click OK. |
| **6.2 Self Check** | What is an animated GIF file? Animated GIF files contain a series of GIF (Graphics Interchange Format) images. When displayed in rapid sequence, they achieve an animated effect. |
| **6.3 Self Check** | When you paste data, what is the default data format? HTML. |
| **6.4 Self Check** | In PowerPoint, what is a custom show? A custom show is a named group of slides within a presentation. |

| | |
|---|---|
| **7.1 Self Check** | What capabilities does the Meeting Minder utility provide? With this utility, you can incorporate meeting feedback and action items directly in your presentation. |
| **7.2 Self Check** | In what ways do Microsoft Office Server Extensions (OSE) enhance the capabilities of a Web server? With access to an OSE-enabled Web server, users can manage files on the Web server using the familiar Explorer, Open, and Save As dialog boxes. In addition, users can take advantage of Office's Web discussion features. |
| **7.3 Self Check** | Why is it useful to be able to broadcast presentations? The ability to broadcast presentations over the Web is useful when your audience is either very large or scattered in remote locations. |
| **8.1 Self Check** | What is the procedure for playing back a recorded macro? To play back a recorded macro, display the Macros dialog box, select the macro you want to execute, and then click the Run command button. |
| **8.2 Self Check** | What is the Visual Basic Editor used for? The Visual Basic Editor is used for creating, editing, and printing macros. |
| **8.3 Self Check** | What procedure would you use to remove a button from the Standard toolbar? Choose Tools, Customize and then drag the unwanted button from the Standard toolbar. |

# Glossary

**action button** In PowerPoint, a ready-made symbol that you insert on slides that perform an action when clicked in Slide Show view. You determine what action is performed when the action button is clicked.

**adaptive menus** The dynamic menu bars and toolbars that are personalized to the way you work. Office 2000 watches the tasks that you perform in an application and then displays only those commands and buttons that you use most often.

**adjustment handle** A tiny yellow diamond that lets you change the appearance, not the size, of most AutoShapes.

**animated GIF picture** A file that contains a series of GIF images. When displayed in rapid sequence, they achieve an animated effect.

**application window** In Microsoft Windows, each running application program appears in its own application window. These windows can be sized and moved anywhere on the Windows desktop.

**AutoContent Wizard** A PowerPoint feature that assists you in beginning new presentations by providing content and design suggestions.

**AutoFit feature** With this feature enabled, PowerPoint automatically resizes placeholders to accommodate inserted text.

**AutoLayout** A preset slide layouts. PowerPoint provides twenty-four AutoLayouts from which you can choose.

**automacro** Special type of macro that executes without your interaction, such as when you begin a new document.

**AutoShape** Ready-made shape that you can insert in your document and then move, resize, and otherwise format to meet your needs.

**cell** In a table, the intersection of a column and a row.

**clip art image** Computer graphic that you can insert into your document to make it more interesting or entertaining.

**color scheme** Set of eight matching colors that help define the look of a presentation.

**custom show** A group of named slides in a presentation.

POWERPOINT

**design template** A presentation whose background, color schemes, typefaces, and other formatting options can be applied to another presentation.

**destination document** An Office document that contains data copied from another application.

**draw layer** Invisible surface floating above (and mostly independent of) the slide layer. Used for holding objects, such as lines, arrows, and clip art images.

**embedding** A method for sharing data in Office 2000 application. Embedded data is fully editable within the destination document and doesn't retain a connection to its source document.

**font** All the symbols and characters of a particular style of print.

**Genigraphics Wizard** Used for sending your PowerPoint slides to Genigraphics, a company that specializes in the output of color 35mm slides.

**HTML** An acronym for Hypertext Markup Language, which is the standardized markup language used in creating documents for display on the World Wide Web.

**hyperlink** In terms of Internet technologies, a text string or graphics that when clicked take you to another location, either within the same document or to a separate document stored on your computer, an Intranet resource, or onto the Internet.

**Internet** A worldwide network of computer networks that are interconnected by standard telephone lines, fiber optics, and satellites.

**Intranet** A private local or wide area network that uses Internet protocols and technologies to share information within an institution or corporation.

**justification** In PowerPoint, a description of how text and objects are aligned (left, center, right, full) in a placeholder.

**linking** A method for sharing data in Office 2000 application. In linking, you not only paste the data, you also establish a dynamic link between the source and destination documents.

**macro** Group of VBA programming instructions.

**Macro Recorder** Word feature for recording your actions and then writing the required VBA programming code for you.

**macro virus** Macro program that was created with the intention of doing harm to your computer system.

**Microsoft Clip Gallery** The location where clip art, sound and movie clips are stored and organized for all Microsoft Office applications.

**Microsoft Graph** An Office 2000 miniapplication that lets you create charts and graphs for insertion in the current document.

**Microsoft Office Server Extensions (OSE)** When installed on a Web server, OSE extensions make it possible for Office 2000 users to use familiar procedures to save files to, search for, and open files on the Internet or their company's internal Web site. Additionally, with access to an OSE-enabled Web server, users can take advantage of Office 2000's Web discussion features.

**Microsoft Organization Chart** An Office 2000 miniapplication for creating organization charts that you can embed in the current document.

**Normal view** In this view mode, the Outline, Slide, and Notes panes appear. This view mode provides one place for viewing the different parts of your presentation.

**Notes pane** Visible in Normal view, this location is used for typing reminder notes and information you want to share with your audience.

**organization chart** Schematic drawing showing a hierarchy of formal relationships.

**Outline pane** In PowerPoint, this location is used for typing text and rearranging a presentation.

**Outline view** This view mode enlarges the Outline pane to fill most of the screen.

**Pack and Go Wizard** Used for compressing one or more presentations into a single file across one or more diskettes.

**password** In PowerPoint, a string of up to 15 characters that the user must type in before either opening or modifying a file.

**pasting** A method for sharing data in Office 2000 application. Pasting data involves inserting a static representation of the source data into the destination document.

**placeholder** Marks the location of a slide object and provides instructions for editing the object.

**Places bar** The strip of icon buttons appearing in the Open and Save As dialog boxes that allow you to display the most common areas for retrieving and storing files using a single mouse click.

**presentation broadcast** A presentation that has been scheduled for delivery on the Web. Broadcast presentations are viewed using browser software, not Microsoft PowerPoint.

**Projector Wizard** Used for optimizing your presentation for display on your designated projection device.

**server application** When sharing data among Office applications, this term refers to the application that was used to create the shared data.

**sizing handles** Tiny boxes that surround selected objects. You resize objects by dragging their sizing handles.

**Slide Finder** Tool used for inserting slides from existing presentations in the current presentation. The contents of presentations are displayed using slide snapshots.

**Slide Master** This slide holds the formatting specifications for the placeholders and background of all slides.

**Slide pane** In PowerPoint, this location is used for seeing how your slide will look and for editing the slide directly.

**Slide Show view** In this view mode, your presentation is displayed as an on-screen slide show, complete with transitions and special effects.

**Slide Sorter view** This mode for viewing a presentation displays multiple slides at once using small thumbnail representations. This mode gives you an immediate feeling for the continuity or flow of a presentation.

**Slide view** This view mode enlarges the Slide pane to fill most of the screen.

**source document** Original document in which information is created for transfer to a destination document.

**text box** A container for text, graphics, tables, or other objects. You can position text boxes anywhere on a slide.

**virus** Program that was created with the intention of doing harm to your computer system.

**Visual Basic Editor** Special Office 2000 utility program that enables you to create, edit, and print macros.

**Visual Basic for Applications (VBA)** Programming language shared by Office 2000 for recording and writing macros.

**Web folder** Shortcut to a location on a Web server.

**Web server** Special computer for storing Web pages.

**World Wide Web** A visual interface to the Internet based on *hyperlinks*. Using Web browser software, you click on hyperlinks to navigate resources on the Internet.

# Appendix: Microsoft Windows Quick Reference

## Using the Mouse and Keyboard

Microsoft Windows provides a graphical environment for working in your application, such as Microsoft Word, Excel, Access, or PowerPoint. As you work with Windows applications, you will find that there are often three different ways to perform the same command. The most common methods for performing commands include:

| | |
|---|---|
| • Menu | Choose a command from the Menu bar or from a right-click menu. |
| • Mouse | Position the mouse pointer over a toolbar button and then click once. |
| • Keyboard | Press a keyboard shortcut (usually CTRL + *letter*). |

Although you may use a Windows application with only a keyboard, much of a program's basic design relies on using a mouse. Regardless of whether your mouse has two or three buttons, you will use the left or primary mouse button for selecting screen objects and menu commands and the right or secondary mouse button for displaying right-click menus.

The most common mouse actions include:

| | |
|---|---|
| • Point | Slide the mouse on your desk to position the tip of the mouse pointer over the desired object on the screen. |
| • Click | Press down and release the left mouse button quickly. Clicking is used to select a screen object, activate a toolbar command, and choose menu commands. |
| • Right-Click | Press down and release the right mouse button. Right-clicking the mouse pointer on a screen object displays a context-sensitive menu. |
| • Double-Click | Press down and release the mouse button twice in rapid succession. Double-clicking is used to select screen objects or to activate an embedded object for editing. |
| • Drag | Press down and hold the mouse button as you move the mouse pointer across the screen. When the mouse pointer reaches the desired location, release the mouse button. Dragging is used to select a group of screen objects and to copy or move data. |

You may notice that the mouse pointer changes shape as you move it over different parts of the screen. Each mouse pointer shape has its own purpose and may provide you with important information. There are four primary mouse shapes that appear in Windows applications:

| | | |
|---|---|---|
| | arrow | Used to choose menu commands and click toolbars buttons. |
| | hourglass | Informs you that the application is occupied and requests that you wait. |
| | I-beam | Used to set the position of the insertion point and to modify and edit text. |
| | hand | Used to select hyperlinks in the Windows-based Help systems, in Microsoft Office documents, and on the Web. |

Aside from being the primary input device for entering information, the keyboard offers shortcut methods for performing some common commands and procedures.

## Starting Windows

Because Windows is an operating system, it is loaded into the computer's memory when you first turn on the computer. To start Windows, you must do the following:

1. Turn on the power switches to the computer and monitor. After a few seconds, the Windows desktop will appear. (*Note*: If you are attached to a network, a dialog box may appear asking you to enter your User name and Password. Enter this information now or ask your instructor for further instructions.)
2. A Welcome dialog box may appear providing information about the operating system's major features. If the Welcome dialog box appears on your screen:
   CLICK: Close button (☒) in the top right-hand corner of the Welcome window
3. If additional windows appear open on your desktop:
   CLICK: Close button (☒) in the top right-hand corner of each window

# Parts of a Dialog Box

A dialog box is a common mechanism in Windows applications for collecting information before processing a command. In a dialog box, you indicate the options you want to use and then click the OK button when you're finished. Dialog boxes are also used to display messages or to ask for the confirmation of commands. The following shows an example of the Print dialog box, which is similar across Windows applications.

Print dialog box

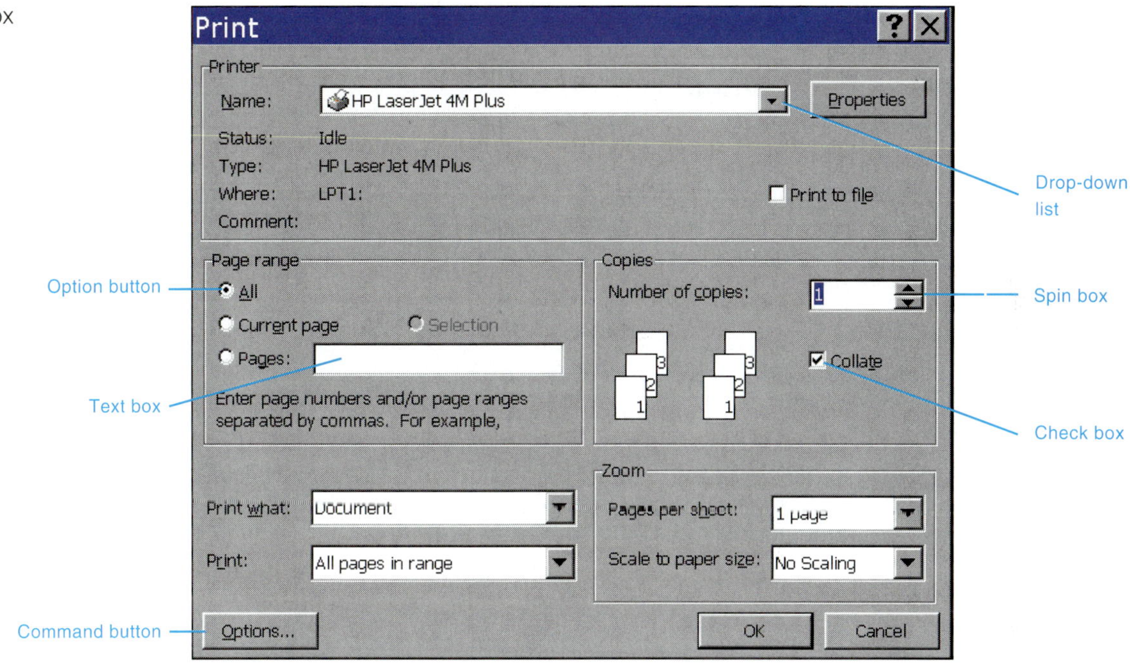


A dialog box uses several types of controls or components for collecting information. We describe the most common components in the following table.

Dialog box components

| *Name* | *Example* | *Action* |
|---|---|---|
| Check box | ☑ Always ☐ Never | Click an option to turn it on or off. The option is turned on when an "✔" appears in the box. |
| Command button | OK<br>Cancel | Click a command button to execute an action. Click OK to accept your selections or click Cancel to exit the dialog box. |

*Continued*

| *Name* | *Example* | *Action* |
|---|---|---|
| Drop-Down list box |  | Make a choice from the list that appears when you click the down arrow next to the box; only the selected choice is visible. |
| List box |  | Make a choice from the scrollable list; several choices, if not all, are always visible. |
| Option button |  | Select an option from a group of related options. |
| Slide box | 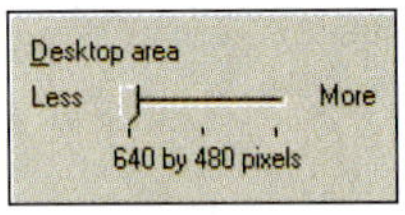 | Drag the slider bar to make a selection, like using a radio's volume control. |
| Spin box |  | Click the up and down arrows to the right of the box until the number you want appears. |
| Tab |  | Click a named tab at the top of the window to access other pages of options in the dialog box. |
| Text box |  | Click inside the text box and then type the desired information. |

Most dialog boxes provide a question mark icon (?) near the right side of the Title bar. If you have a question about an item in the dialog box, click the question mark and then click the item to display a pop-up help window. To remove the help window, click on it once.

# Getting Help

Windows applications, such as Microsoft Office 2000 applications, provide a comprehensive library of online documentation. This section describes these help features and how to find more detailed information.

# Obtaining Context-Sensitive Help

In Windows applications, you can often retrieve context-sensitive help for menu options, toolbar buttons, and dialog box items. *Context-sensitive help* refers to a program's ability to present helpful information reflecting your current position in the program. The help information is presented concisely in a small pop-up window that you can remove with the click of the mouse. This type of help lets you access information quickly and then continue working without interruption. The following table describes some methods for accessing context-sensitive help while working in Windows applications.

Displaying context-sensitive Help information

| *To display...* | *Do this...* |
| --- | --- |
| A description of a dialog box item | Click the question mark button ([?]) in a dialog box's Title bar and then click an item in the dialog box. Alternatively, you can often right-click a dialog box item and then choose the What's This? command from the shortcut menu. |
| A description of a menu command | Choose the Help, What's This? command from the menu and then choose a command using the question mark mouse pointer. Rather than executing the command, a helpful description of the command appears in a pop-up window. |
| A description of a toolbar button | Point to a toolbar button to display a pop-up label called a ToolTip. |

# Getting Help in Office 2000

## Getting Help from the Office Assistant

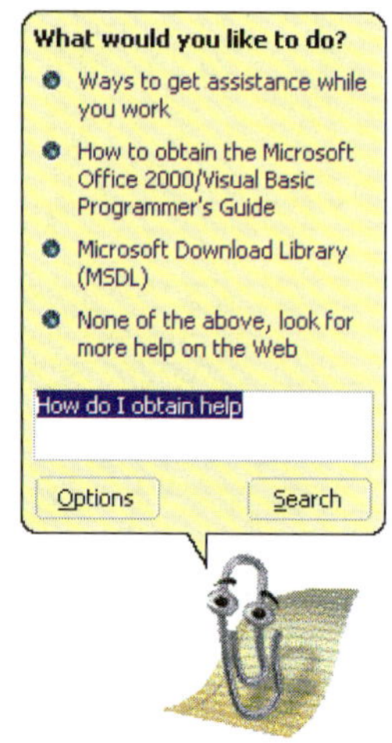


In Office 2000 applications, the Office Assistant is your personal computer guru and is available by default when your application is first installed. When you need to perform a task that you're unsure of, simply click the Assistant character and then type a phrase such as "How do I obtain help" in the Assistant balloon. The Assistant analyzes your request and provides a resource list of suggested topics, as shown to the right. Simply click a topic to obtain additional information.

The Assistant also watches your keystrokes and mouse clicks as you work and offers suggestions and shortcuts to make you more productive and efficient. If you find the Office Assistant to be distracting, you can turn it off by choosing "Hide the Office Assistant" from the Help menu. To redisplay it, simply choose "Microsoft *Application* Help" or "Show the Office Assistant" from the Help menu.

## Getting Help from the Help Window

You may prefer to obtain a complete topical listing of your application's Help system. To do this, you must first disable the Office Assistant by clicking the Options button in the Assistant balloon, clearing the *Use the Office Assistant* check box, and then pressing ENTER. Once the Office Assistant is disabled, simply choose "Microsoft *Application* Help" from the Help menu to display the Help window. If the *Contents*, *Answer Wizard*, and *Index* tabs don't appear, click Show ( ) in the window's toolbar.

The Help window, shown below, provides three different tools, each on its own tab, to help you find the information you need quickly and easily. You can read the Help information you find onscreen or print it out for later reference by clicking the Print button ( ) in the window's toolbar. To close the Help window, click its Close button ( ).

Example Help window

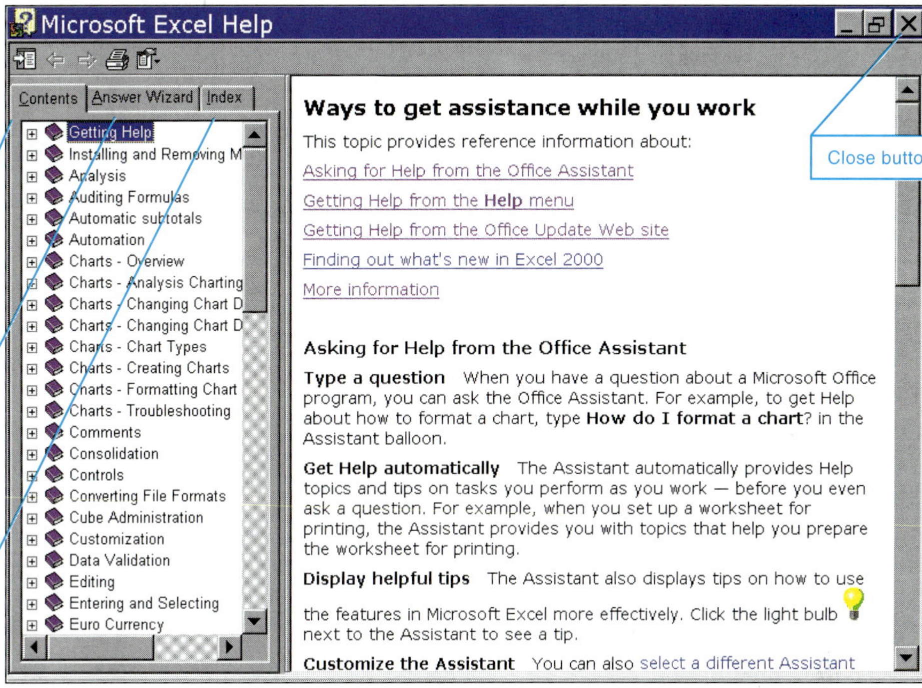


The *Contents* tab is currently selected. Use this tab to display the Table of Contents for the entire Help system.

The *Answer Wizard* tab enables you to obtain help information by typing in questions.

The *Index* tab enables you to display topics by selecting keywords or typing in words and phrases.

Close button

## Getting Help from the Office Update Web Site

Microsoft's Office Update Web site provides additional technical support and product enhancements. You can access this site from any Office application by choosing "Office on the Web" from the Help menu.

# Index



POWERPOINT

## N



## O

## P

POWERPOINT

**MOUS Certification Objectives**

Following are charts listing the Microsoft Office User Specialist (MOUS) Certification Objectives for both the Core/Level 1 MOUS exam as well as the Expert MOUS exam. The chart below lists the MOUS certification skill and describes where this skill is covered in the Advantage Series Text.

**Microsoft PowerPoint 2000**
**Total Objectives: 50**

| Standardized Coding Number | Activity | ICV Performance based? | Lesson # |
|---|---|---|---|
| **PP2000.1** | **Creating a presentation** | | |
| PP2000.1.1 | Delete slides | **Yes** | **124** |
| PP2000.1.2 | Create a specified type of slide | **Yes** | **124** |
| PP2000.1.3 | Create a presentation from a template and/or a Wizard | **Yes** | **122** |
| PP2000.1.4 | Navigate among different views (slide, outline, sorter, tri-pane) | **Yes** | **125** |
| PP2000.1.5 | Create a new presentation from existing slides | **Yes** | **211** |
| PP2000.1.6 | Copy a slide from one presentation into another | No | **211** |
| PP2000.1.7 | Insert headers and footers | **Yes** | **531** |
| PP2000.1.8 | Create a Blank presentation | No | **120, 232** |
| PP2000.1.9 | Create a presentation using the AutoContent Wizard | **Yes** | **121** |
| PP2000.1.10 | Send a presentation via e-mail | No | **522** |
| **PP2000.2** | **Modifying a presentation** | | |
| PP2000.2.1 | Change the order of slides using Slide Sorter view | **Yes** | **212** |
| PP2000.2.2 | Find and replace text | No | **334** |
| PP2000.2.3 | Change the layout for one or more slides | **Yes** | **221, 222** |
| PP2000.2.4 | Change slide layout (Modify the Slide Master) | **Yes** | **431, 432** |
| PP2000.2.5 | Modify slide sequence in the outline pane | No | **212** |
| PP2000.2.6 | Apply a design template | **Yes** | **223** |
| **PP2000.3** | **Working with text** | | |
| PP2000.3.1 | Check spelling | No | **332, 333** |
| PP2000.3.2 | Change and replace text fonts (individual slide and entire presentation) | **Yes** | **431, 432** |
| PP2000.3.3 | Enter text in tri-pane view | **Yes** | **123** |
| PP2000.3.4 | Import Text from Word | **Yes** | **331** |
| PP2000.3.5 | Change the text alignment | **Yes** | **314** |
| PP2000.3.6 | Create a text box for entering text | **Yes** | **422** |
| PP2000.3.7 | Use the Wrap text in AutoShape feature | No | **421** |
| PP2000.3.8 | Use the Office Clipboard | No | **535** |
| PP2000.3.9 | Use the Format Painter | **Yes** | **315** |
| PP2000.3.10 | Promote and Demote text in slide & outline panes | **Yes** | **123** |
| **PP2000.4** | **Working with visual elements** | | |
| PP2000.4.1 | Add a picture from the ClipArt Gallery | **Yes** | **231** |
| PP2000.4.2 | Add and group shapes using WordArt or the Drawing Toolbar | No | **411, 413** |
| PP2000.4.3 | Apply formatting | **Yes** | **412** |
| PP2000.4.4 | Place text inside a shape using a text box | **Yes** | **422** |
| PP2000.4.5 | Scale and size an object including ClipArt | **Yes** | **322, 412** |
| PP2000.4.6 | Create tables within PowerPoint | **Yes** | **320** |
| PP2000.4.7 | Rotate and fill an object | No | **412** |

| Standardized Coding Number | Activity | ICV Performance based? | Lesson # |
|---|---|---|---|
| **PP2000.5** | **Customizing a presentation** | | |
| PP2000.5.1 | Add AutoNumber bullets | No | **313** |
| PP2000.5.2 | Add speaker notes | **Yes** | **532** |
| PP2000.5.3 | Add graphical bullets | No | **313** |
| PP2000.5.4 | Add slide transitions | **Yes** | **512** |
| PP2000.5.5 | Animate text and objects | **Yes** | **511** |
| **PP2000.6** | **Creating output** | | |
| PP2000.6.1 | Preview presentation in black and white | No | **141** |
| PP2000.6.2 | Print slides in a variety of formats | **Yes** | **142** |
| PP2000.6.3 | Print audience handouts | **Yes** | **533** |
| PP2000.6.4 | Print speaker notes in a specified format | **Yes** | **532** |
| **PP2000.7** | **Delivering a presentation** | | |
| PP2000.7.1 | Start a slide show on any slide | **Yes** | **241** |
| PP2000.7.2 | Use on-screen navigation tools | **Yes** | **241** |
| PP2000.7.3 | Print a slide as an overhead transparency | No | **534** |
| PP2000.7.4 | Use the pen during a presentation | **Yes** | **241** |
| **PP2000.8** | **Managing files** | | |
| PP2000.8.1 | Save changes to a presentation | **Yes** | **131** |
| PP2000.8.2 | Save as a new presentation | **Yes** | **131** |
| PP2000.8.3 | Publish a presentation to the Web | **Yes** | **522** |
| PP2000.8.4 | Use Office Assistant | No | **535** |
| PP2000.8.5 | Insert hyperlink | No | **521** |

**Microsoft PowerPoint 2000 Expert**
**Total Objectives: 44**

| Standardized Coding Number | Activity | ICV Performance based? | Lesson # |
|---|---|---|---|
| **PP2000E.1** | **Creating a presentation** | | |
| PP2000E.1.1 | Automatically create a summary slide | **Yes** | 6.4.3 |
| PP2000E.1.2 | Automatically create slides from a summary slide | No | 6.4.3 |
| PP2000E.1.3 | Design a template | **Yes** | 6.1.3 |
| PP2000E.1.4 | Format presentations for the Web | **Yes** | 7.2.1 |
| **PP2000E.2** | **Modifying a presentation** | | |
| PP2000E.2.1 | Change tab formatting | No | 6.1.3 |
| PP2000E.2.2 | Use the Wrap text in AutoShape feature | No | 4.2.1 |
| PP2000E.2.3 | Apply a template from another presentation | **Yes** | 2.2.3 |
| PP2000E.2.4 | Customize a color scheme | **Yes** | 6.1.1 |
| PP2000E.2.5 | Apply animation effects | **Yes** | 5.1.1 |
| PP2000E.2.6 | Create a custom background | **Yes** | 6.1.2 |
| PP2000E.2.7 | Add animated GIFs | **Yes** | 6.2.3 |
| PP2000E.2.8 | Add links to slides within the Presentation | **Yes** | 6.2.1 |
| PP2000E.2.9 | Customize clip art and other objects (resize, scale, etc.) | **Yes** | 4.1.2 |
| PP2000E.2.10 | Add a presentation within a presentation | **Yes** | 6.4.1 |
| PP2000E.2.11 | Add an action button | **Yes** | 6.2.2 |
| PP2000E.2.12 | Hide Slides | **Yes** | 6.4.4 |
| PP2000E.2.13 | Set automatic slide timings | No | 7.1.4 |
| **PP2000E.3** | **Working with visual elements** | | |
| PP2000E.3.1 | Add textured backgrounds | **Yes** | 6.1.2 |
| PP2000E.3.2 | Apply diagonal borders | No | 6.1.2 |
| **PP2000E.4** | **Using data from other sources** | | |
| PP2000E.4.1 | Export an outline to Word | **Yes** | 6.3.5 |
| PP2000E.4.2 | Add a table (from Word) | **Yes** | 6.3.2 |
| PP2000E.4.3 | Insert an Excel Chart | **Yes** | 6.3.3 |
| PP2000E.4.4 | Add sound | **Yes** | 6.2.4 |
| PP2000E.4.5 | Add video | No | 6.2.3 |
| **PP2000E.5** | **Creating output** | | |
| PP2000E.5.1 | Save slide as a graphic | No | 6.3.5 |
| PP2000E.5.2 | Generate meeting notes | **Yes** | 7.1.3 |
| PP2000E.5.3 | Change output format (Page setup) | No | 7.1.1 |
| PP2000E.5.4 | Export to 35mm slides | No | 7.1.1 |
| **PP2000E.6** | **Delivering a presentation** | | |
| PP2000E.6.1 | Save presentation for use on another computer (Pack and Go) | **Yes** | 7.1.2 |
| PP2000E.6.2 | Electronically incorporate meeting feedback | **Yes** | 7.1.3 |
| PP2000E.6.3 | Use Presentations on demand | No | 6.4.2 |
| **PP2000E.7** | **Managing files** | | |
| PP2000E.7.1 | Save embedded fonts in presentation | **Yes** | 7.2.1 |
| PP2000E.7.2 | Save HTML to a specific target browser | No | 7.2.1 |

| Standardized Coding Number | Activity | ICV Performance based? | Lesson # |
|---|---|---|---|
| **PP2000E.8** | **Working with PowerPoint** | | |
| PP2000E.8.1 | Customize the toolbar | **Yes** | 8.3.3 |
| PP2000E.8.2 | Create a toolbar | **Yes** | 8.3.4 |
| **PP2000E.9** | **Collaborating with workgroups** | | |
| PP2000E.9.1 | Subscribe to a presentation | **Yes** | 7.2.3 |
| PP2000E.9.2 | View a presentation on the Web | No | 7.2.2 |
| PP2000E.9.3 | Use Net Meeting to schedule a broadcast | No | 7.3.1 |
| PP2000E.9.4 | Use NetShow to deliver a broadcast | No | 7.3.2 |
| **PP2000E.10** | **Working with charts & Tables (Objectives moved from Proficient level)** | | |
| PP2000E.10.1 | Build a chart or graph | **Yes** | 2.3.3 |
| PP2000E.10.2 | Modify charts or graphs | **Yes** | 2.3.3 |
| PP2000E.10.3 | Build an organization chart | **Yes** | 2.3.4 |
| PP2000E.10.4 | Modify an organization chart | **Yes** | 2.3.4 |
| PP2000E.10.5 | Modify PowerPoint tables | No | 3.2.0 |